Given in memory of
Mrs Hilda Hall
&
Miss Mary King

1991

All your anxiety, all your care,
Bring to the Mercy-seat, leave it there.
Never a burden He cannot bear,
Never a friend like Jesus.

GOLDEN BELLS

GOLDEN
BELLS

CHRISTIAN YEAR PUBLICATIONS

THE GLEBE HOUSE, STANTON DREW, BRISTOL, BS18 4EH

© Christian Year Publications 1989
Reprinted 1990

ISBN 1 872734 01 4

Printed in Great Britain by
Richard Clay (The Chaucer Press) Ltd,
Bungay, Suffolk

Contents

Golden Bells

Praise and Worship

See also Hymns 704–717

1   6.6.6.6.6.6.

1 WHEN morning gilds the skies,
My heart awaking cries,
   May Jesus Christ be praised!
Alike at work and prayer
To Jesus I repair:
   May Jesus Christ be praised!

2 To Thee, my God above,
I cry with glowing love,
   May Jesus Christ be praised!
The fairest graces spring
In hearts that ever sing,
   May Jesus Christ be praised!

3 Does sadness fill my mind?
A solace here I find,
   May Jesus Christ be praised!
Or fades my earthly bliss?
My comfort still is this,
   May Jesus Christ be praised!

4 When evil thoughts molest,
With this I shield my breast,
   May Jesus Christ be praised!
The powers of darkness fear
When this sweet chant they hear,
   May Jesus Christ be praised!

5 When sleep her balm denies,
My silent spirit sighs,
   May Jesus Christ be praised!
The night becomes as day
When from the heart we say,
   May Jesus Christ be praised!

6 Be this, while life is mine,
My canticle divine,
   May Jesus Christ be praised!
Be this the eternal song
Through all the ages on,
   May Jesus Christ be praised!

2   S.M.D.

1   CROWN Him with many crowns,
  The Lamb upon His throne;
Hark! how the heavenly anthem drowns
  All music but its own:
  Awake, my soul, and sing
  Of Him who died for thee,
And hail Him as thy matchless King
  Through all eternity.

2   Crown Him the Lord of life,
  Who triumphed o'er the grave,
And rose victorious in the strife
  For those He came to save:
  His glories now we sing
  Who died, and rose on high;
Who died eternal life to bring,
  And lives that death may die.

3   Crown Him the Lord of love;
  Behold His hands and side,
Those wounds yet visible above
  In beauty glorified:
  No angel in the sky
  Can fully bear that sight,
But downward bends his burning eye
  At mysteries so bright.

4   Crown Him the Lord of peace,
     Whose power a sceptre sways
From pole to pole, that wars may cease,
     And all be prayer and praise:
     His reign shall know no end,
     And round His piercèd feet
Fair flowers of Paradise extend
     Their fragrance ever sweet.

5   Crown Him the Lord of years,
     The Potentate of time,
Creator of the rolling spheres,
     Ineffably sublime!
     All hail, Redeemer, hail!
     For Thou hast died for me;
Thy praise shall never, never fail
     Throughout eternity.

3   7.6.7.6.D.

1 WHEN, His salvation bringing,
     To Zion Jesus came,
The children all stood singing
     Hosanna to His Name;
Nor did their zeal offend Him,
     But as He rode along
He bade them still attend Him,
     And smiled to hear their song.

2 Then since the Lord retaineth
     His love for children still,
Though now as King He reigneth
     On Zion's heavenly hill,
We'll flock around His banner
     Who sits upon the throne,
And sing aloud, Hosanna!
     To David's royal Son!

3 For should we fail proclaiming
     Our great Redeemer's praise,
The stones, our silence shaming,
     Would their hosannas raise.
But should we only render
     The tribute of our words?
No; while our hearts are tender,
     They too shall be the Lord's.

4   C.M.

1 ALL hail the power of Jesus' Name,
     Let angels prostrate fall;
Bring forth the royal diadem,
     And crown Him Lord of all.

2 Crown Him, ye martyrs of our God
     Who from the altar call,
Extol the stem of Jesse's rod
     And crown Him Lord of all.

3 Ye saints redeemed of Adam's race,
     Ye ransomed from the fall,
Hail Him who saves you by His grace,
     And crown Him Lord of all.

4 Sinners, whose love can ne'er forget
     The wormwood and the gall,
Go, spread your trophies at His feet
     And crown Him Lord of all.

5 Let every kindred, every tribe
     On this terrestrial ball,
To Him all majesty ascribe,
     And crown Him Lord of all.

6 Oh, that with yonder sacred throng
     We at His feet may fall,
Join in the everlasting song,
     And crown Him Lord of all!

5   C.M.

1 COME, let us join our cheerful songs
     With angels round the throne;
Ten thousand thousand are their
     tongues,
     But all their joys are one.

2 "Worthy the Lamb that died!" they
     cry,
     "To be exalted thus!"
"Worthy the Lamb!" our lips reply,
     "For He was slain for us."

3 Jesus is worthy to receive
     Honour and power divine:
And blessings, more than we can give,
     Be, Lord, for ever Thine.

4 Let all that dwell above the sky,
     And air, and earth. and seas,
Conspire to lift Thy glories high,
     And speak Thine endless praise.

5 The whole creation join in one
     To bless the sacred Name
Of Him that sits upon the throne,
     And to adore the Lamb.

6   6.5.6.5.

1 JESUS, stand among us,
    In Thy risen power;
Let this time of worship
    Be a hallowed hour.

2 Breathe Thy Holy Spirit
    Into every heart;
Bid the fears and sorrows
    From each soul depart.

3 Thus with quickened footsteps
    We'll pursue our way,
Watching for the dawning
    Of eternal day.

7   7.6.7.6.D.

1 MY song shall be of Jesus;
    His mercy crowns my days,
He fills my cup with blessings,
    And tunes my heart to praise:
My song shall be of Jesus,
    The precious Lamb of God,
Who gave Himself my ransom,
    And bought me with His blood.

2 My song shall be of Jesus;
    When, sitting at His feet,
I call to mind His goodness,
    In meditation sweet:
My song shall be of Jesus,
    Whatever ill betide;
I'll sing the grace that saves me,
    And keeps me at His side.

3 My song shall be of Jesus,
    While pressing on my way
To reach the blissful region
    Of pure and perfect day:
And when my soul shall enter
    The gate of Eden fair,
A song of praise to Jesus
    I'll sing for ever there.

8   8.7.8.7.

1 I WILL sing of my Redeemer,
    And His wondrous love to me;
On the cruel cross He suffered,
    From the curse to set me free.

    Sing, oh sing, of my Redeemer!
        With His blood He purchased
        me!
    On the cross He sealed my pardon,
        Paid the debt, and made me free.

2 I will tell the wondrous story,
    How, my lost estate to save,
In His boundless love and mercy
    He the ransom freely gave.

3 I will praise my dear Redeemer,
    His triumphant power I'll tell;
How the victory He giveth
    Over sin, and death, and hell.

4 I will sing of my Redeemer,
    And His heavenly love to me;
He from death to life hath brought
    me,
    Son of God, with Him to be.

9   7.7.7.7.

1 CONQUERING kings their titles take
From the foes they captive make;
Jesus, by a nobler deed,
From the thousands He hath freed.

2 Yes, none other Name is given
Unto mortals under heaven,
Which can make the dead arise
And exalt them to the skies.

3 That which Christ so hardly wrought,
That which He so dearly bought,
That salvation, mortals, say,
Will ye madly cast away?

4 Rather gladly for that Name
Bear the cross, endure the shame;
Joyfully for Him to die
Is not death, but victory.

5 Jesus, who dost condescend
To be called the sinner's Friend,
Hear us, as to Thee we pray,
Glorying in Thy Name today.

6 Glory to the Father be,
Glory, risen Lord, to Thee,
Glory to the Holy Ghost,
From the saints and heavenly host.

10   L.M.

1 ALL people that on earth do dwell
   Sing to the Lord with cheerful voice;
Him serve with fear, His praise forth
   tell;
   Come ye before Him and rejoice.

2 Know that the Lord is God indeed,
   Without our aid He did us make:
We are His flock, He doth us feed,
   And, for His sheep, He doth us take.

3 Oh, enter then His gates with praise,
   Approach with joy His courts unto:
Praise, laud, and bless His Name
   always,
   For it is seemly so to do.

4 For why? the Lord our God is good:
   His mercy is for ever sure;
His truth at all times firmly stood,
   And shall from age to age endure.

11   L.M.

1 FATHER of Heaven, whose love pro-
   found
A ransom for our souls hath found,
Before Thy throne we sinners bend;
To us Thy pardoning love extend.

2 Almighty Son, Incarnate Word,
Our Prophet, Priest, Redeemer, Lord,
Before Thy throne we sinners bend;
To us Thy saving grace extend.

3 Eternal Spirit, by whose breath
The soul is raised from sin and death,
Before Thy throne we sinners bend;
To us Thy quickening power extend.

4 Almighty Father, Spirit, Son,
Mysterious Godhead, Three in One,
Before Thy throne we sinners bend;
Grace, pardon, life to us extend.

12   L.M.D.

1 SING to the Lord a joyful song:
   Lift up your hearts, your voices
   raise:
To us His gracious gifts belong,
   To Him our songs of love and praise.

For life and love, for rest and food,
   For daily help and nightly care,
Sing to the Lord, for He is good,
   And praise His Name, for it is fair.

2 For strength to those who on Him
   wait,
   His truth to prove, His will to do,
Praise ye our God, for He is great:
   Trust in His Name, for it is true.
For joys untold, that from above
   Cheer those who love His sweet
   employ,
Sing to our God, for He is love:
   Exalt His Name, for it is joy.

3 For life below, with all its bliss,
   And for that life, more pure and
   high—
That inner life, which over this
   Shall ever shine, and never die—
Sing to the Lord of heaven and earth,
   Whom angels serve and saints adore,
The Father, Son, and Holy Ghost,
   To whom be praise for evermore.

13   6.5.6.5.D.

1 IN the Name of Jesus
   Every knee shall bow,
   Every tongue confess Him
   King of glory now;
'Tis the Father's pleasure
   We should call Him Lord,
Who from the beginning
   Was the mighty Word.

2 At His voice creation
   Sprang at once to sight:
All the angel-faces,
   All the hosts of light,
Thrones and dominations,
   Stars upon their way,
All the heavenly orders,
   In their great array.

3 Humbled for a season
   To receive a Name
From the lips of sinners,
   Unto whom He came;
Faithfully He bore it,
   Spotless to the last;
Brought it back victorious
   When from death He passed.

4 Name Him, brothers, name Him
    With love strong as death,
But with awe and wonder,
    And with bated breath;
He is God the Saviour,
    He is Christ the Lord,
Ever to be worshipped,
    Trusted, and adored.

5 In your hearts enthrone Him,
    There let Him subdue
All that is not holy,
    All that is not true;
Crown Him as your Captain
    In temptation's hour;
Let His will enfold you
    In its light and power.

6 Brothers, this Lord Jesus
    Shall return again
With His Father's glory,
    With His angel train;
For all wreaths of empire
    Meet upon His brow,
And our hearts confess Him
    King of glory now.

14   8.7.8.7.D.

1 HAIL, Thou once despisèd Jesus,
    Hail, Thou Galilean King!
Thou didst suffer to release us,
    Thou didst free salvation bring.
Hail, Thou agonising Saviour,
    Bearer of our sin and shame;
By Thy merits we find favour,
    Life is given through Thy Name.

2 Paschal Lamb, by God appointed,
    All our sins were on Thee laid:
By Almighty love anointed,
    Thou hast full atonement made.
All Thy people are forgiven,
    Through the virtue of Thy blood;
Opened is the gate of heaven,
    Peace is made 'twixt man and God.

3 Jesus, hail! enthroned in glory,
    There for ever to abide;
All the heavenly hosts adore Thee,
    Seated at Thy Father's side:
There for sinners Thou art pleading,
    There Thou dost our place prepare,
Ever for us interceding,
    Till in glory we appear.

4 Worship, honour, power, and blessing
    Thou art worthy to receive;
Loudest praises, without ceasing,
    Meet it is for us to give:
Help, ye bright angelic spirits,
    Bring your sweetest, noblest lays;
Help to sing our Saviour's merits,
    Help to chant Immanuel's praise.

15   7.6.7.6.D.

1 O SAVIOUR, precious Saviour,
    Whom yet unseen we love,
O Name of might and favour,
    All other names above!
      We worship Thee, we bless Thee,
        To Thee alone we sing;
      We praise Thee, and confess Thee
        Our holy Lord and King.

2 O Bringer of salvation,
    Who wondrously hast wrought,
Thyself the revelation
    Of love beyond our thought;
      We worship Thee, we bless Thee,
        To Thee alone we sing;
      We praise Thee, and confess Thee
        Our gracious Lord and King.

3 In Thee all fulness dwelleth,
    All grace and power divine;
The glory that excelleth,
    O Son of God, is Thine;
      We worship Thee, we bless Thee,
        To Thee alone we sing;
      We praise Thee, and confess Thee
        Our glorious Lord and King.

4 Oh, grant the consummation
    Of this our song above,
In endless adoration
    And everlasting love!
      Then shall we praise and bless
        Thee
      Where perfect praises ring,
      And evermore confess Thee
        Our Saviour and our King.

16   C.M.

1 OH, for a thousand tongues to sing
    My great Redeemer's praise!
The glories of my God and King,
    The triumphs of His grace.

2 My gracious Master and my God,
    Assist me to proclaim,
And spread through all the earth
        abroad,
    The honours of Thy Name.

3 Jesus, the Name that charms our fears,
    That bids our sorrows cease;
'Tis music in the sinner's ears,
    'Tis life and health and peace.

4 He breaks the power of cancelled sin,
    He sets the prisoner free;
His blood can make the foulest clean,
    His blood availed for me.

5 He speaks, and, listening to His voice,
    New life the dead receive,
The mournful, broken hearts rejoice,
    The humble poor believe.

6 Hear Him, ye deaf: His praise, ye
        dumb,
    Your loosened tongues employ;
Ye blind, behold your Saviour come;
    And leap, ye lame, for joy!

17   C.M.
1 PRAISE to the Holiest in the height,
    And in the depth be praise:
In all His words most wonderful,
    Most sure in all His ways!

2 Oh, loving wisdom of our God!
    When all was sin and shame,
A second Adam to the fight
    And to the rescue came.

3 Oh, wisest love! that flesh and blood
    Which did in Adam fail
Should strive afresh against the foe,
    Should strive and should prevail;

4 And that a higher gift than grace
    Should flesh and blood refine,
God's presence and His very Self,
    And Essence all-Divine.

5 Oh, generous love! that He who smote
    In Man for man the foe,
The double agony in Man
    For man should undergo;

6 And in the garden secretly,
    And on the cross on high,
Should teach His brethren and inspire
    To suffer and to die.

7 Praise to the Holiest in the height,
    And in the depth be praise;
In all His words most wonderful,
    Most sure in all His ways!

18   5.5.5.5.6.5.6.5.
1 OH, worship the King,
    All-glorious above;
Oh, gratefully sing
    His power and His love:
Our Shield and Defender,
    The Ancient of Days,
Pavilioned in splendour,
    And girded with praise.

2 Oh, tell of His might,
    Oh, sing of His grace,
Whose robe is the light,
    Whose canopy space;
His chariots of wrath
    The deep thunder-clouds form,
And dark is His path
    On the wings of the storm.

3 The earth, with its store
    Of wonders untold,
Almighty! Thy power
    Hath founded of old;
Hath 'stablished it fast,
    By a changeless decree,
And round it hath cast,
    Like a mantle, the sea.

4 Thy bountiful care
    What tongue can recite?
It breathes in the air,
    It shines in the light;
It streams from the hills,
    It descends to the plain,
And sweetly distils
    In the dew and the rain.

5 Frail children of dust,
    And feeble as frail,
In Thee do we trust,
    Nor find Thee to fail;
Thy mercies, how tender!
    How firm to the end!
Our Maker, Defender,
    Redeemer, and Friend!

19 5.5.5.5.6.5.6.5.

1 YE servants of God,
   Your Master proclaim,
And publish abroad
   His wonderful Name;
The Name all-victorious
   Of Jesus extol;
His kingdom is glorious,
   And rules over all.

2 God ruleth on high,
   Almighty to save;
And still He is nigh,
   His presence we have!
The great congregation
   His triumph shall sing,
Ascribing salvation
   To Jesus our King.

3 Let children acclaim
   Their Saviour and Friend,
In songs to His Name
   Their praises ascend:
In such a salvation
   How great is their joy;
In true adoration
   How blest their employ!

4 Salvation to God,
   Who sits on the throne;
Let all cry aloud,
   And honour the Son;
The praises of Jesus
   All angels proclaim,
Fall down on their faces,
   And worship the Lamb.

5 Then let us adore
   And give Him His right;
All glory and power,
   All wisdom and might,
All honour and blessing,
   With angels above,
And thanks never-ceasing,
   And infinite love.

20 7.6.7.6.D.

1 HOSANNA! loud hosanna!
   The little children sang:
Through pillared court and temple
   The glorious anthem rang:

To Jesus who had blessed them,
   Close folded to His breast,
The children sang their praises,
   The simplest and the best.

2 From Olivet they followed,
   'Midst an exultant crowd,
Waving the victor palm-branch,
   And shouting clear and loud;
Bright angels joined the chorus
   Beyond the cloudless sky—
"Hosanna! in the highest:
   Glory to God on high!"

3 Fair leaves of silvery olive
   They strewed upon the ground,
Whilst Salem's circling mountains
   Echoed the joyful sound:
The Lord of men and angels
   Rode on in lowly state,
Nor scorned that little children
   Should on His bidding wait.

4 "Hosanna in the highest!"
   That ancient song we sing;
For Christ is our Redeemer,
   The Lord of heaven, our King.
Oh, may we ever praise Him
   With heart and life and voice,
And in His blissful presence
   Eternaily rejoice!

21 7.6.7.6.D.

1 HAIL to the Lord's anointed,
   Great David's greater Son!
Hail, in the time appointed,
   His reign on earth begun!
He comes to break oppression,
   To set the captive free;
To take away transgression,
   And rule in equity.

2 He shall come down like showers
   Upon the fruitful earth,
And love, joy, hope, like flowers,
   Spring in His path to birth;
Before Him, on the mountains,
   Shall peace, the herald, go,
And righteousness in fountains
   From hill to valley flow.

3 Kings shall fall down before Him,
   And gold and incense bring;
All nations shall adore Him,
   His praise all people sing.
For He shall have dominion
   O'er river, sea, and shore:
Far as the eagle's pinion
   Or dove's light wing can soar.

4 O'er every foe victorious,
He on His throne shall rest,
From age to age more glorious,
   All-blessing and all-blest;
The tide of time shall never
   His covenant remove;
His Name shall stand for ever;
   That Name to us is Love.

22   6.6.8.4.D.

1 THE God of Abraham praise,
   Who reigns enthroned above,
Ancient of everlasting days,
   And God of love!
Jehovah! great I AM!
   By earth and heaven confessed,
I bow, and bless the sacred Name,
   For ever blest.

2 The God of Abraham praise,
   At whose supreme command
From earth I rise, and seek the joys
   At His right hand.
I all on earth forsake,
   Its wisdom, fame, and power;
And Him my only portion make,
   My Shield and Tower.

3 He by Himself hath sworn;
   I on His oath depend:
I shall, on eagles' wings upborne,
   To heaven ascend.
I shall behold His face,
   I shall His power adore,
And sing the wonders of His grace
   For evermore.

4 There dwells the Lord our King,
   The Lord our righteousness,
Triumphant o'er the world and sin:
   The Prince of Peace.
On Zion's sacred height
   His kingdom still maintains,
And glorious with His saints in light
   For ever reigns.

5 The whole triumphant host
   Give thanks to God on high;
"Hail, Father, Son, and Holy Ghost!"
   They ever cry.
Hail, Abraham's God and mine!
   I join the heavenly lays;
All might and majesty are Thine,
   And endless praise.

23   L.M.

1 Now in a song of grateful praise,
To my dear Lord my voice I'll raise;
With all His saints I'll join to tell,
My Jesus hath done all things well.

   Above the rest this note shall swell:
   My Jesus hath done all things well.

2 All worlds His glorious power confess;
His wisdom all His works express;
But oh! His love what tongue can tell?
My Jesus hath done all things well!

3 And since my soul has known His love
What mercies has He made me prove!
Mercies which do all praise excel:
My Jesus hath done all things well.

4 And when to that bright world I rise,
And join the anthems of the skies,
Above the rest this note shall swell—
My Jesus hath done all things well.

24   7.7.7.7.

1 LET us with a gladsome mind
Praise the Lord, for He is kind;
For His mercies shall endure,
Ever faithful, ever sure.

2 He, with all-commanding might,
Filled the new-made world with light:
For His mercies shall endure,
Ever faithful, ever sure.

3 All things living He doth feed,
His full hand supplies their need:
For His mercies shall endure,
Ever faithful, ever sure.

4 He His chosen race did bless
In the wasteful wilderness:
For His mercies shall endure,
Ever faithful, ever sure.

5 He hath with a piteous eye
Looked upon our misery:
For His mercies shall endure,
Ever faithful, ever sure.

6 Let us, then, with gladsome mind,
Praise the Lord, for He is kind;
For His mercies shall endure,
Ever faithful, ever sure.

25   6.5.6.5.D.

1 SAVIOUR, blessèd Saviour,
   Listen whilst we sing,
Hearts and voices raising
   Praises to our King;
All we have to offer,
   All we hope to be,
Body, soul, and spirit,
   All we yield to Thee.

2 Nearer, ever nearer,
   Christ, we draw to Thee,
Deep in adoration
   Bending low the knee:
Thou, for our redemption,
   Cam'st on earth to die;
Thou, that we might follow,
   Hast gone up on high.

3 Clearer still, and clearer,
   Dawns the light from heaven,
In our sadness bringing
   News of sin forgiven;
Life has lost its shadows,
   Pure the light within;
Thou hast shed Thy radiance
   On a world of sin.

4 Onward, ever onward,
   Journeying o'er the road
Worn by saints before us,
   Journeying on to God:
Leaving all behind us,
   May we hasten on,
Backward never looking
   Till the prize is won.

5 Higher, then, and higher
   Bear the ransomed soul,
Earthly toils forgotten,
   Saviour, to its goal;

Where, in joys unthought of,
   Saints with angels sing,
Never weary, raising
   Praises to their King.

26   8.7.8.7.D.

1 A GLADSOME hymn of praise we sing,
   And thankfully we gather
To bless the love of God above,
   Our everlasting Father.

      In Him rejoice with heart and
         voice,
      Whose glory fadeth never,
      Whose providence is our defence,
      Who lives and loves for ever!

2 From shades of night He calls the light,
   And from the sod the flower;
From every cloud His blessings break,
   In sunshine or in shower.

3 Full in His sight His children stand,
   By His strong arm defended,
And He, whose wisdom guides the
      world,
   Our footsteps hath attended.

4 For nothing falls unknown to Him—
   Or care, or joy, or sorrow;
And He whose mercy ruled the past
   Will be our stay tomorrow.

5 Then praise the Lord with one accord,
   To His great Name give glory,
And of His never-changing love
   Repeat the wondrous story!

27   8.7.8.7.D.

1 GLORIOUS things of thee are spoken,
   Zion, city of our God!
He, whose word cannot be broken,
   Formed thee for His own abode:
On the Rock of Ages founded,
   What can shake thy sure repose?
With salvation's walls surrounded,
   Thou may'st smile at all thy foes.

2 See, the streams of living waters,
   Springing from eternal love.
Well supply thy sons and daughters,
   And all fear of want remove:

13

Who can faint, while such a river
  Ever flows their thirst to assuage?—
Grace, which like the Lord, the Giver,
  Ever flows from age to age.

3 Round each habitation hovering,
    See the cloud and fire appear!
  For a glory and a covering,
    Showing that the Lord is near—
  He who gives them daily manna,
    He who listens when they cry:
  Let Him hear the loud hosanna
    Rising to His throne on high.

4 Saviour, if of Zion's city
    I through grace a member am,
  Let the world deride or pity,
    I will glory in Thy Name;
  Fading is the worldling's pleasure,
    All his boasted pomp and show;
  Solid joys and lasting treasure
    None but Zion's children know.

28 P.M.

1 As through this world to a happier
      shore
      I go singing,
  The prospect brightens more and more,
  And a thousand joys unknown before
  Seem flooding my heart till it's brim-
      ming o'er,
      And I go singing.

    Singing, singing, I go singing,
      Yes, I'm always singing;
    Christ holds my hand, by faith I
        stand,
      And as the hours are winging,
    I press along with a joyful song,
      Singing, singing, singing.

2 In spite of the way so rough and long
      I go singing,
  Though hard the fight 'gainst sin and
      wrong,
  Though friends are few and foes are
      strong,
  The joy of the Lord, my strength and
      song,
      Still keeps me singing.

3 When things go wrong and I seem
      alone,
      I go singing,
  For His arm of power is round me
      thrown,
  Bright with the joy He gives His own,
  Along the way with blessings strewn,
      I go singing.

4 So onward, upward, homeward bound,
      I go singing,
  Singing the Gospel to all around,
  Sounding it forth till hearts resound;
  In heaven at last with the ransomed
      crowned,
      For ever singing.

29 11.11.

1 REJOICE and be glad! the Redeemer
      has come;
  Go, look on His cradle, His cross, and
      His tomb!

    Sound His praises, tell the story of
      Him who was slain;
    Sound His praises, tell with gladness
      He liveth again.

2 Rejoice and be glad! it is sunshine at
      last;
  The clouds have departed, the shadows
      are past.

3 Rejoice and be glad! for the blood hath
      been shed;
  Redemption is finished, the price hath
      been paid.

4 Rejoice and be glad! now the pardon is
      free;
  The Just for the unjust has died on the
      tree.

5 Rejoice and be glad! for the Lamb that
      was slain
  O'er death is triumphant, and liveth
      again.

6 Rejoice and be glad! for our King is on
      high;
  He pleadeth for us on His throne in the
      sky.

7 Rejoice and be glad! for He cometh
  again:
He cometh in glory, the Lamb that was
  slain.

Sound His praises, tell the story of
  Him who was slain;
Sound His praises, tell with gladness
He cometh again.

30   8.7.8.7.D.
1 HALLELUJAH! sing to Jesus!
  His the sceptre, His the throne;
Hallelujah! His the triumph,
  His the victory alone.
Hark, the songs of holy Zion
  Thunder like a mighty flood:
"Jesus out of every nation
  Hath redeemed us by His blood."

2 Hallelujah! Not as orphans
  Are we left in sorrow now;
Hallelujah! He is near us,
  Faith believes, nor questions how.
Though the clouds from sight received
  Him
When the forty days were o'er,
Shall our hearts forget His promise,
  "I am with you evermore"?

3 Hallelujah! Bread of heaven,
  Thou on earth our food, our stay;
Hallelujah! here the sinful
  Flee to Thee from day to day.
Intercessor, Friend of sinners,
  Earth's Redeemer, plead for me,
Where the songs of all the sinless
  Sweep across the crystal sea.

4 Hallelujah! sing to Jesus!
  His the sceptre, His the throne;
Hallelujah! His the triumph,
  His the victory alone.
Hark, the songs of holy Zion
  Thunder like a mighty flood:
"Jesus out of every nation
  Hath redeemed us by His blood."

31   S.M.
1   COME, ye that love the Lord,
    And let your joys be known,
Join in a song with sweet accord,
    And thus surround the throne.

We're marching to Zion,
Beautiful, beautiful Zion;
We're marching upward to Zion,
The beautiful city of God.

2   Let those refuse to sing
    Who never knew our God;
But children of the heavenly King
    Must speak their joys abroad.

3   The hill of Zion yields
    A thousand sacred sweets,
Before we reach the heavenly fields,
    Or walk the golden streets.

4   Then let our songs abound,
    And every tear be dry;
We're marching through Immanuel's
    ground,
To fairer worlds on high.

32   8.7.8.7.4.7.
1 PRAISE, my soul, the King of heaven;
    To His feet thy tribute bring;
Ransomed, healed, restored, forgiven,
    Who like thee His praise should sing
      Praise Him, praise Him!
Praise the everlasting King.

2 Praise Him for His grace and favour
    To our fathers in distress;
Praise Him, still the same for ever,
    Slow to chide, and swift to bless:
      Praise Him, praise Him!
Glorious in His faithfulness.

3 Father-like, He tends and spares us;
    Well our feeble frame He knows;
In His hands He gently bears us,
    Rescues us from all our foes:
      Praise Him, praise Him!
Widely yet His mercy flows.

4 Angels, help us to adore Him;
    Ye behold Him face to face;
Sun and moon, bow down before Him;
    Dwellers all in time and space:
      Praise Him, praise Him!
Praise with us the God of grace.

33   S.M.
1   OH, bless the Lord, my soul!
    His grace to thee proclaim,
And all that is within me join
    To bless His holy Name.

15

2   Oh, bless the Lord, my soul,
    His mercies bear in mind,
Forget not all His benefits:
    The Lord to thee is kind.

3   He will not always chide;
    He will with patience wait;
His wrath is ever slow to rise
    And ready to abate.

4   He pardons all thy sins,
    Prolongs thy feeble breath;
He healeth thine infirmities,
    And ransoms thee from death.

5   He clothes thee with His love,
    Upholds thee with His truth,
And, like the eagle, He renews
    The vigour of thy youth.

6   Then bless His holy Name,
    Whose grace hath made thee whole,
Whose loving-kindness crowns thy
    days;
    Oh, bless the Lord, my soul!

34   C.M.
1 THERE is sunshine in my soul today,
    More glorious and bright
Than glows in any earthly sky,
    For Jesus is my Light.

    Oh, there's sun- . . . shine, blessed
        sun- . . . shine,
    When the peaceful, happy moments
        roll; . . .
    When Jesus shows His smiling
        face,
    There is sunshine in my soul.

2 There is music in my soul today,
    A carol to my King;
And Jesus, listening, can hear
    The songs I cannot sing.

3 There is spring-time in my soul today,
    For, when the Lord is near,
The dove of peace sings in my heart,
    The flowers of grace appear.

4 There is gladness in my soul today,
    And hope, and praise, and love;
For blessings which He gives me now,
    For joys laid up above.

35   P.M.
1 PRAISE, praise ye the Name of Jehovah,
    our God,
Declare, oh, declare ye His glories
    abroad!
Proclaim ye His mercy from nation to
    nation,
Till the uttermost islands have heard
    His salvation.

    For His love floweth on, free and full
      as a river,
    And His mercy endureth for ever and
      ever.

2 Praise, praise ye the Lamb, who for
    sinners was slain,
Who went down to the grave and
    ascended again;
And who soon shall return when these
    dark days are o'er
To set up His kingdom in glory and
    power.

3 Her bridal attire and her festal array
    All nature shall wear on that glorious
      day;
For her King cometh down with His
    people to reign,
And His presence shall bless her with
    Eden again.

36   11.11.11.11.
1 To God be the glory! great things He
    hath done!
So loved He the world that He gave us
    His Son,
Who yielded His life an atonement for
    sin,
And opened the life-gate that all may
    go in.

    Praise the Lord! praise the Lord!
      Let the earth hear His voice!
    Praise the Lord! praise the Lord!
      Let the people rejoice!
    Oh, come to the Father, through
      Jesus the Son:
    And give Him the glory! great things
      He hath done!

2 Oh, perfect redemption, the purchase of
   blood!
   To every believer the promise of God;
   The vilest offender who truly believes,
   That moment from Jesus a pardon
   receives.

3 Great things He hath taught us, great
   things He hath done,
   And great our rejoicing through Jesus
   the Son:
   But purer and higher and greater will
   be
   Our wonder, our transport, when Jesus
   we see!

37   12.10.12.10.

1 OH, worship the Lord in the beauty of
   holiness!
   Bow down before Him, His glory
   proclaim;
   With gold of obedience, and incense of
   lowliness;
   Kneel and adore Him; the Lord is
   His Name.

2 Low at His feet lay thy burden of care-
   fulness;
   High on His heart He will bear it for
   thee,
   Comfort thy sorrows, and answer thy
   prayerfulness,
   Guiding thy steps as may best for
   thee be.

3 Fear not to enter His courts in the
   slenderness
   Of the poor wealth thou wouldst
   reckon as thine;
   Truth in its beauty, and love in its
   tenderness,
   These are the offerings to lay on His
   shrine.

4 These, though we bring them in
   trembling and fearfulness,
   He will accept for the Name that is
   dear;
   Mornings of joy give for evenings of
   tearfulness,
   Trust for our trembling, and hope
   for our fear.

5 Oh, worship the Lord in the beauty of
   holiness,
   Bow down before Him, His glory
   proclaim;
   With gold of obedience, and incense of
   lowliness,
   Kneel and adore Him; the Lord is
   His Name.

38   7.7.7.7.

1. CHILDREN of Jerusalem
   Sang the praise of Jesus' Name;
   Children too of later days
   Join to sing the Saviour's praise.

   Hark! hark! hark! while youthful
       voices sing,
   Hark! hark! hark! while youthful
       voices sing
   Loud hosannas,
   Loud hosannas,
   Loud hosannas to our King.

2 We are taught to love the Lord;
   We are taught to read His Word;
   We are taught the way to heaven:
   Praise for all to God be given.

3 Parents, teachers, old and young,
   All unite to swell the song;
   Higher and yet higher rise,
   Till hosannas reach the skies.

39   7.6.7.6.D.

1 ALL glory, laud, and honour,
       To Thee, Redeemer, King,
   To whom the lips of children
       Made sweet hosannas ring!

2 Thou art the King of Israel,
       Thou David's royal Son,
   Who in the Lord's Name comest,
       The King and blessèd One.
           All glory, etc.

3 The company of angels
       Are praising Thee on high;
   And mortal men, and all things
       Created, make reply.
           All glory, etc.

4 The people of the Hebrews
  With palms before Thee went:
Our praise and prayer and anthems
  Before Thee we present.
      All glory, etc.

5 To Thee, before Thy Passion,
  They sang their hymns of praise:
To Thee, now high exalted,
  Our melody we raise.
      All glory, etc.

6 Thou didst accept their praises;
  Accept the prayers we bring,
Who in all good delightest,
  Thou good and gracious King.
      All glory, etc.

40   P.M.

1   Now thank we all our God,
  With hearts, and hands, and voices,
  Who wondrous things hath done,
In whom His world rejoices;
  Who, from our mother's arms
  Hath blessed us on our way
  With countless gifts of love,
  And still is ours today.

2 ' Oh, may this bounteous God
Through all our life be near us,
  With ever-joyful hearts
And blessèd peace to cheer us;
  And keep us in His grace,
  And guide us when perplexed,
  And free us from all ills
  In this world and the next.

3   All praise and thanks to God
The Father now be given,
  The Son, and Him who reigns
With them in highest heaven;
  The one eternal God,
  Whom heaven and earth adore:
  For thus it was, is now,
  And shall be evermore.

41   S.M.

1   AWAKE, and sing the song
  Of Moses and the Lamb!
Wake every heart, and every tongue,
  To praise the Saviour's Name!

2   Sing of His dying love,
  Sing of His rising power;
Sing how He intercedes above
  For us whose sins He bore.

3   Sing on your heavenly way,
  Ye ransomed sinners, sing;
Sing on, rejoicing every day
  In Christ, the eternal King.

4   Soon shall we hear Him say,
  "Ye blessèd children, come!"
Soon will He call us hence away,
  And take His wanderers home.

5   There shall our raptured tongue
  His endless praise proclaim;
And sweeter voices swell the song
  Of Moses and the Lamb!

42   L.M.

1 WE sing the praise of Him who died,
  Of Him who died upon the cross;
The sinner's hope let men deride,
  For this we count the world but loss.

2 Inscribed upon the cross we see
  In shining letters, "God is Love";
He bears our sins upon the tree;
  He brings us mercy from above.

3 The cross! it takes our guilt away;
  It holds the fainting spirit up;
It cheers with hope the gloomy day,
  And sweetens every bitter cup.

4 It makes the coward spirit brave,
  And nerves the feeble arm for fight;
It takes its terror from the grave,
  And gilds the bed of death with
    light;

5 The balm of life, the cure of woe,
  The measure and the pledge of love,
The sinner's refuge here below,
  The angels' theme in heaven above.

6 To Christ, who won for sinners grace
  By bitter grief and anguish sore,
Be praise from all the ransomed race
  For ever and for evermore.

43   P.M.

1 COME, let us all unite to sing—
    God is love! God is love!
While heaven and earth their praises
        bring—
    God is love! God is love!
Let every soul from sin awake,
Each in his heart sweet music make,
And sweetly sing for Jesus' sake—
    God is love! God is love!

2 Oh, tell to earth's remotest bound—
    God is love! God is love!
In Christ is full redemption found—
    God is love! God is love!
His blood can cleanse our sins away;
His Spirit turns our night to day,
And leads our souls with joy to say—
    God is love! God is love!

3 How happy is our portion here—
    God is love! God is love!
His promises our spirits cheer—
    God is love! God is love!
He is our Sun and Shield by day,
By night He near our tents will stay,
He will be with us all the way—
    God is love! God is love!

4 What though my heart and flesh shall
        fail—
    God is love! God is love!
Through Christ I shall o'er death pre-
        vail—
    God is love! God is love!
E'en Jordan's swell I will not fear,
For Jesus will be with me there,
My soul above the waves to bear—
    God is love! God is love!

44   6.6.4.6.6.6.4.

1 PRAISE God, ye seraphs bright;
Praise Him, ye sons of light,
    Jesus adore!
What earthly choirs can swell,
What mortal tongues can tell
Thy love, Immanuel,
    God evermore?

2 Come, saints, in God rejoice!
Lift up a mighty voice;
    Sing to the Lamb!
For us His blood was shed,
For us He left the dead,
His foes discomfited!
    Praise the I AM!

3 Soon shall we see His face,
Wearing no mournful trace—
    Oh, what a sight!
Soon shall we hear Him say,
"Come, waiting child, away!
Lo, now has dawned the day
    That knows not night!"

45   P.M.

1 PRAISE Him! praise Him! Jesus, our
        blessèd Redeemer:
    Sing, O earth! His wonderful love
        proclaim!
Hail Him! hail Him! highest archangels
        in glory,
    Strength and honour give to His holy
        Name.
Like a shepherd, Jesus will guard His
        children;
    In His arms He carries them all day
        long.
O ye saints that dwell in the mountains
        of Zion!
    Praise Him! praise Him! ever in
        joyful song.

2 Praise Him! praise Him! Jesus, our
        blessèd Redeemer,
    For our sins He suffered and bled and
        died!
He, our Rock, our hope of eternal
        salvation,
    Hail Him! hail Him! Jesus the Cruci-
        fied;—
Loving Saviour, meekly enduring
        sorrow,
    Crowned with thorns that cruelly
        pierced His brow;
Once for us rejected, despised, and for-
        saken,
    Prince of glory, ever triumphant
        now.

3 Praise Him! praise Him! Jesus, our
　　blessèd Redeemer,
　　Heavenly portals loud with hosannas
　　　ring!
Jesus, Saviour, reigneth for ever and
　　ever,
　　Crown Him! crown Him! Prophet
　　　and Priest and King!
Death is vanquished! Tell it with joy,
　　ye faithful;
　　Where is now thy victory, boasting
　　　grave?
Jesus lives! no longer thy portals are
　　cheerless
　　Jesus lives, the mighty and strong to
　　　save.

46　　　　　　　　11.11.11.11.

1 WE praise Thee, we bless Thee, our
　　Saviour Divine;
　All power and dominion for ever be
　　Thine!
　We sing of Thy mercy with joyful
　　acclaim,
　For Thou hast redeemed us: all praise
　　to Thy Name!

2 All honour and praise to Thine excel-
　　lent Name;
　Thy love is unchanging—for ever the
　　same!
　We bless and adore Thee, O Saviour
　　and King;
　With joy and thanksgiving Thy praises
　　we sing!

3 The strength of the hills and the depths
　　of the sea,
　The earth and its fulness, belong unto
　　Thee;
　And yet to the lowly Thou bendest
　　Thine ear,
　So ready their humble petitions to hear.

4 Thine infinite goodness our tongues
　　shall employ·
　Thou givest us richly all things to
　　enjoy;
　We'll follow Thy footsteps, we'll rest in
　　Thy love,
　**And soon we shall praise Thee in
　　mansions above!**

47　　　　　　　　7.6.7.6.D.

1 COME, sing with holy gladness,
　　High Hallelujahs sing,
　Uplift your loud hosannas
　　To Jesus, Lord and King;
　Sing, boys, in joyful chorus
　　Your hymn of praise today,
　And sing, ye gentle maidens,
　　Your sweet responsive lay.

2 'Tis good for boys and maidens
　　Sweet hymns to Christ to sing,
　'Tis meet that children's voices
　　Should praise the children's King;
　For Jesus is salvation,
　　And glory, grace and rest;
　To babe, and boy and maiden
　　The one Redeemer blest.

3 Oh, boys! be strong in Jesus;
　　To toil for Him is gain;
　And Jesus wrought with Joseph
　　With chisel, saw and plane;
　Oh, maidens! live for Jesus,
　　Who was a maiden's Son;
　Be patient, pure and gentle,
　　And perfect grace begun.

4 Soon in the golden city
　　The boys and girls shall play;
　And in the dazzling mansions
　　Rejoice in endless day;
　O Christ, prepare Thy children
　　With that triumphant throng
　To pass the burnished portals,
　　And sing the eternal song.

48　　　　　　　　7.6.7.6.D.

1 COME, let us sing of Jesus,
　　While hearts and accents blend;
　Come, let us sing of Jesus,
　　The sinner's only Friend.
　His holy soul rejoices,
　　Amid the choirs above,
　To hear our youthful voices
　　Exulting in His love.

2 We love to sing of Jesus,
　　Who died our souls to save;
　We love to sing of Jesus,
　　Triumphant o'er the grave;

And in our hour of danger
  We'll trust His love alone,
Who once slept in a manger,
  And now sits on the throne.

3 Then let us sing of Jesus
  While yet on earth we stay,
And hope to sing of Jesus
  Throughout the eternal day.
For those who here confess Him
  He will in heaven confess;
And faithful hearts that bless Him
  He will for ever bless.

49   6.6.6.6.8.8

1 CHRIST is our corner-stone,
  On Him alone we build;
With His true saints alone
  The courts of heaven are filled;
On His great love our hopes we place
Of present grace and joys above.

2 Oh, then with hymns of praise
  These hallowed courts shall ring;
Our voices we will raise
  The Three in One to sing;
And thus proclaim in joyful song,
Both loud and long, that glorious
  Name.

3 Here may we gain from heaven
  The grace which we implore;
And may that grace, once given,
  Be with us evermore;
Until that day when all the blest
To endless rest are called away.

50   10.10.10.4.

1 FOR all the glories of the earth and sky,
For night's soft voice, and morning's
  silent haze,
For trees that whisper, and for winds
  that sigh,
    We give Thee praise.

2 For summer sunshine and for cooling
  showers,
For stars that light the heavens' darkening maze,
For dewdrops sparkling on the new-
  born flowers,
    Our hearts would praise.

3 For lightning's flash, and thunder's
  echoing roar,
For seas that beat upon their endless
  ways,
For wild waves' anthem on a rock-
  bound shore,
    We offer praise.

4 For mighty mountains and eternal
  snows,
Enduring changeless through the
  changing days,
For moon-lit valleys and for sunset
  glows,
    Accept our praise.

5 But for that great redeeming work of
  Thine,
Our souls their loftiest hymn of thanks
  would raise;
For free salvation through a love
  divine,
    We render praise.

6 For all the matchless wonders of Thy
  grace
Seen in that cross on which we humbly
  gaze,
For peace and pardon to a fallen race,
  Thy Name we praise.

51   11.12.12.10.

1 HOLY, Holy, Holy, Lord God Almighty !
  Early in the morning our song shall
    rise to Thee:
Holy, Holy, Holy ! merciful and
  mighty,
God in Three Persons, blessèd
  Trinity !

2 Holy, Holy, Holy ! all the saints adore
  Thee,
    Casting down their golden crowns
    around the glassy sea;
Cherubim and seraphim falling down
  before Thee,
    Who wert, and art, and evermore
    shalt be.

3 Holy, Holy, Holy! though the darkness
    hide Thee,
  Though the eye of sinful man Thy
    glory may not see;
Only Thou art holy, there is none beside
    Thee
  Perfect in power, in love, and purity.

4 Holy, Holy, Holy, Lord God Almighty!
  All Thy works shall praise Thy
    Name, in earth, and sky, and sea;
Holy, Holy, Holy, merciful and mighty,
  God in Three Persons, blessed
    Trinity!

52   8.7.8.7.8.7.

1 COME, ye children, praise the Saviour;
  He regards you from above;
Praise Him for His great salvation!
  Praise Him for His precious love!
Sweet hosannas, sweet hosannas
  To the Name of Jesus sing!

2 When He left His throne in glory,
  When He lived with mortals here,
Little children sang His praises,
  And it pleased His gracious ear.
Sweet hosannas, sweet hosannas
  To the Name of Jesus sing!

3 When the anxious mothers round Him
  With their tender infants pressed,
He with open arms received them,
  And the little ones He blessed.
Sweet hosannas, sweet hosannas
  To the Name of Jesus sing!

4 Up in yonder heavenly regions,
  Angels sound the chorus high;
Twice ten thousand times ten thousand
  Sound His praises through the sky.
Sweet hosannas, sweet hosannas
  To the Name of Jesus sing!

5 Come, ye children, praise the Saviour!
  Praise Him, your undying Friend;
Praise Him, till in heaven you meet
  Him,
  There to praise Him without end.
Sweet hosannas, sweet hosannas
  To the Name of Jesus sing!

53   L.M.

1 SWEET is the work, my God, my King,
To praise Thy Name, give thanks, and
  sing,
To show Thy love by morning light,
And talk of all Thy truth at night.

2 Sweet is the day of sacred rest;
No mortal cares shall seize my breast:
Oh, may my heart in tune be found,
Like David's harp of solemn sound!

3 My heart shall triumph in my Lord,
  And bless His works, and bless His
    Word;
Thy works of grace, how bright they
    shine!
How deep Thy counsels, how divine!

4 And I shall share a glorious part,
  When grace hath well refined my
    heart;
And fresh supplies of joy are shed.
Like holy oil, to cheer my head.

5 Then shall I see, and hear, and know
All I desired or wished below;
And every power find sweet employ
In that eternal world of joy.

54   C.M.

1 I FEEL like singing all the time;
  My tears are wiped away;
For Jesus is a Friend of mine;
  I'll serve Him every day.

    I'll praise Him! praise Him!
      Praise Him all the time.
    Praise Him! praise Him!
      I'll praise Him all the time.

2 When on the cross my Lord I saw,
  Nailed there by sins of mine,
Fast fell the burning tears; but now
  I'm singing all the time.

3 When fierce temptations try my heart
  I'll sing, "Jesus is mine":
And so, though tears at times may
  start,
  I'm singing all the time.

4 The wondrous story of the Lamb
   Tell with that voice of thine,
Till others with the glad new song
   Go singing all the time.

5 The angels sing a glorious song,
   But not a song like mine,
For I am washed in Jesus' blood,
   And singing all the time.

55   6.6.6.6.8.8.

1 SHALL hymns of grateful love
      Through heaven's high arches
         ring,
   And all the hosts above
      Their songs of triumph sing;
   And shall not we take up the strain,
   And send the echo back again?

2 Shall every ransomed tribe
      Of Adam's scattered race,
   To Christ all power ascribe,
      Who saved them by His grace;
   And shall not we take up the strain,
   And send the echo back again?

3 Shall they adore the Lord,
      Who bought them with His blood,
   And all the love record
      That led them home to God;
   And shall not we take up the strain,
   And send the echo back again?

4 Oh! spread the joyful sound,
      The Saviour's love proclaim,
   And publish all around
      Salvation through His Name;
   Till all the world take up the strain,
   And send the echo back again!

56   6.6.6.6.8.8.

1 COME, every youthful heart
      That loves the Saviour's Name:
   Your noblest powers exert
      To celebrate His fame:
   Tell all above and all below
   The debt of love to Him you owe.

2 He left His starry crown,
      And laid His robes aside,
   On wings of love came down,
      And wept, and bled, and died:
   What He endured, oh! who can tell,
   To save our souls from death and hell?

3 From the dark grave He rose,
      The mansion of the dead;
   And thence His mighty foes
      In glorious triumph led:
   Up through the sky the Conqueror
         rode,
   And reigns on high, the Saviour God.

4 From thence He'll quickly come,
      His chariot will not stay,
   And bear our spirits home
      To realms of endless day;
   Then shall we see His lovely face,
   And ever be in His embrace.

5 Jesus, we ne'er can pay
      The debt we owe Thy love;
   Yet tell us how we may '
      Our gratitude approve:
   Our hearts, our all to Thee we give;
   The gift, though small, do Thou
         receive.

57   10.10.10.10.

1 FATHER, again in Jesus' Name we
      meet,
   And bow in penitence beneath Thy
      feet:
   Again to Thee our feeble voices raise,
   To sue for mercy, and to sing Thy
      praise.

2 Lord, we would bless Thee for Thy
      ceaseless care,
   And all Thy love from day to day
      declare:
   Is not our life with hourly mercies
      crowned?
   Does not Thine arm encircle us around?

3 Alas! unworthy of Thy boundless love,
   Too oft with careless feet from Thee we
      rove,
   But now, encouraged by Thy voice, we
      come,
   Returning sinners to a Father's home.

23

4 Oh, by that Name, in whom all fulness
    dwells,
Oh, by that love, which every love
    excels,
Oh, by that blood, so freely shed for
    sin,
Open sweet mercy's gate, and let us in!

58   6.5.6.5.

1 GLORY be to Jesus,
    Who in bitter pains
Poured for me the life-blood
    From His sacred veins.

2 Grace and life eternal
    In that blood I find;
Blest be His compassion,
    Infinitely kind!

3 Blest through endless ages
    Be the precious stream,
Which from endless torments
    Did the world redeem.

4 Abel's blood for vengeance
    Pleaded to the skies;
But the blood of Jesus
    For our pardon cries.

5 Oft as earth exulting
    Wafts its praise on high,
Angel-hosts rejoicing
    Make their glad reply.

6 Lift ye then your voices;
    Swell the mighty flood;
Louder still and louder
    Praise the precious blood.

59   8.4.8.4.8.4.

1 MY God, I thank Thee who hast made
    The earth so bright,
So full of splendour and of joy,
    Beauty and light;
So many glorious things are here,
    Noble and right.

2 I thank Thee, too, that Thou hast
    made
    Joy to abound;
So many gentle thoughts and deeds
    Circling us round
That, in the darkest spot of earth,
    Some love is found.

3 I thank Thee more, that all our joy
    Is touched with pain,
That shadows fall on brightest hours,
    That thorns remain;
So that earth's bliss may be our guide,
    And not our chain.

4 For Thou, who knowest, Lord, how
    soon
    Our weak heart clings,
Hast given us joys, tender and true,
    Yet all with wings,
So that we see, gleaming on high,
    Diviner things.

5 I thank Thee, Lord, that Thou hast
    kept
    The best in store:
We have enough, yet not too much
    To long for more—
A yearning for a deeper peace
    Not known before.

6 I thank Thee, Lord, that here our souls,
    Though amply blest,
Can never find, although they seek,
    A perfect rest,
Nor ever shall, until they lean
    On Jesus' breast.

60   L.M.

1 AWAKE, my soul, in joyful lays,
And sing thy great Redeemer's praise;
He justly claims a song from thee:
His loving-kindness, oh, how free!

2 He saw me ruined in the Fall,
Yet loved me, notwithstanding all:
He saved me from my lost estate:
His loving-kindness, oh, how great!

3 Though numerous hosts of mighty foes,
Though earth and hell my way oppose,
He safely leads my soul along:
His loving-kindness, oh, how strong!

4 When trouble, like a gloomy cloud,
Has gathered thick and thundered
    loud,
He near my soul has always stood:
His loving-kindness, oh, how good!

5 Often I feel my sinful heart
  Prone from my Saviour to depart:
  But though I have Him oft forgot,
  His loving-kindness changes not.

61
11.12.

1 WITH harps and with vials there stand
    a great throng
  In the presence of Jesus, and sing this
    new song:

    Unto Him who hath loved us and
      washed us from sin,
    Unto Him be the glory for ever!
      Amen.

2 All these once were sinners, defiled in
    His sight;
  Now arrayed in pure garments in praise
    they unite:

3 He maketh the rebel a priest and a
    king;
  He hath bought us, and taught us this
    new song to sing:

4 How helpless and hopeless we sinners
    had been
  If He never had loved us till cleansed
    from our sin!

5 Aloud in His praises our voices shall
    ring,
  So that others, believing, this new song
    shall sing:

62
C.M.

1 MY God, how wonderful Thou art,
    Thy majesty how bright!
  How beautiful Thy mercy-seat
    In depths of burning light!

2 How dread are Thine eternal years,
    O everlasting Lord,
  By prostrate spirits day and night
    Incessantly adored!

3 How wonderful, how beautiful,
    The sight of Thee must be;
  Thine endless wisdom, boundless power,
    And awful purity!

4 Oh, how I fear Thee, Living God,
    With deepest, tenderest fears,
  And worship Thee with trembling hope
    And penitential tears!

5 Yet I may love Thee, too, O Lord,
    Almighty as Thou art,
  For Thou hast stooped to ask of me
    The love of my poor heart.

6 No earthly father loves like Thee;
    No mother, e'er so mild,
  Bears and forbears as Thou hast done
    With me, Thy sinful child.

7 Father of Jesus, love's reward,
    What rapture will it be,
  Prostrate before Thy throne to lie,
    And gaze and gaze on Thee!

63
6.6.6.6.8.8.

1   REJOICE, the Lord is King,
      Your Lord and King adore;
    Mortals, give thanks and sing,
      And triumph evermore:
  Lift up your heart, lift up your voice;
  Rejoice, again I say, rejoice!

2   Jesus, the Saviour, reigns,
      The God of truth and love:
    When He had purged our stains,
      He took His seat above:
  Lift up your heart, lift up your voice;
  Rejoice, again I say, rejoice!

3   His kingdom cannot fail;
      He rules o'er earth and heaven;
    The keys of death and hell
      Are to our Jesus given:
  Lift up your heart, lift up your voice;
  Rejoice, again I say, rejoice!

4   He sits at God's right hand
      Till all His foes submit,
    And bow to His command,
      And fall beneath His feet:
  Lift up your heart, lift up your voice;
  Rejoice, again I say, rejoice!

Prayer

64 8.7.8.7.D.

1 WHAT a Friend we have in Jesus,
  All our sins and griefs to bear!
What a privilege to carry
  Everything to God in prayer!
Oh, what peace we often forfeit!
  Oh, what needless pain we bear!
All because we do not carry
  Everything to God in prayer.

2 Have we trials and temptations?
  Is there trouble anywhere?
We should never be discouraged;
  Take it to the Lord in prayer.
Can we find a friend so faithful
  Who will all our sorrows share?
Jesus knows our every weakness;
  Take it to the Lord in prayer.

3 Are we weak and heavy-laden,
  Cumbered with a load of care?
Precious Saviour, still our refuge—
  Take it to the Lord in prayer.
Do thy friends despise, forsake thee?
  Take it to the Lord in prayer;
In His arms He'll take and shield thee,
  Thou wilt find a solace there.

65 6.4.6.4.6.6.6.4.

1 HERE from the world we turn,
    Jesus to seek;
Here may His loving voice
    Tenderly speak.
Jesus, our dearest Friend,
While at Thy feet we bend,
Oh, let Thy smile descend!
    'Tis Thee we seek.

2 Come, Holy Comforter,
    Presence Divine,
Now in our longing hearts
    Graciously shine;
Oh, for Thy mighty power,
Oh, for a blessèd shower,
Filling this hallowed hour
    With joy divine!

3 Saviour, Thy work revive,
    Here may we see
Those who are dead in sin
    Quickened by Thee;
Come to our hearts' delight,
Make every burden light,
Cheer Thou our waiting sight;
    We long for Thee.

66 L.M.

1 COMMAND Thy blessing from above,
  O God! on all assembled here:
Behold us with a Father's love,
  While we look up with filial fear.

2 Command Thy blessing, Jesus, Lord!
  May we Thy true disciples be;
Speak to each heart the mighty word,
  Say to the weakest, "Follow Me."

3 Command Thy blessing in this hour,
  Spirit of truth! and fill the place
With wounding and with healing power,
  With quickening and confirming grace.

4 With Thee and Thine for ever found,
  May all the souls who here unite,
With harps and songs Thy throne surround,
  Rest in Thy love, and reign in light.

67 7.7.7.7.

1 COME, my soul, thy suit prepare;
Jesus loves to answer prayer;
He Himself has bid thee pray,
Therefore will not say thee nay.

2 Thou art coming to a King;
Large petitions with thee bring;
For His grace and power are such,
None can ever ask too much.

3 With my burden I begin,
Lord, remove this load of sin!
Let Thy blood for sinners spilt
Set my conscience free from guilt.

4 Lord, I come to Thee for rest;
Take possession of my breast:
There Thy blood-bought right main-
tain,
And without a rival reign.

5 While I am a pilgrim here,
Let Thy love my spirit cheer:
As my Guide, my Guard, my Friend,
Lead me to my journey's end.

68 L.M.

1 FROM every stormy wind that blows,
From every swelling tide of woes,
There is a calm, a safe retreat:
'Tis found beneath the mercy-seat.

2 There is a place where Jesus sheds
The oil of gladness on our heads,
A place than all beside more sweet;
It is the blood-stained mercy-seat.

3 There is a spot where spirits blend,
And friend holds fellowship with
friend;
Though sundered far, by faith they
meet
Around one common mercy-seat.

4 There, there on eagle-wing we soar,
And time and sense seem all no more;
And heaven comes down our souls to
greet,
And glory crowns the mercy-seat.

69 C.M.

1 THERE is an eye that never sleeps
Beneath the wing of night;
There is an ear that never shuts
When sink the beams of light.

2 There is an arm that never tires
When human strength gives way;
There is a love which never fails
When earthly loves decay.

3 That eye is fixed on seraph throngs;
That arm upholds the sky;
That ear is filled with angel songs;
That love is throned on high.

4 But there's a power which man can
wield
When mortal aid is vain,
That eye, that arm, that love to reach,
That listening ear to gain.

5 That power is prayer, which soars on
high
Through Jesus to the throne,
And moves the hand which moves the
world,
To bring salvation down.

70 P.M.

1 "THERE shall be showers of blessing":
This is the promise of love:
There shall be seasons refreshing,
Sent from the Saviour above.

Show- . . . ers of blessing,
Showers of blessing we need;
Mercy drops round us are falling,
But for the showers we plead.

2 "There shall be showers of blessing"—
Precious reviving again;
Over the hills and the valleys,
Sound of abundance of rain.

3 "There shall be showers of blessing":]
Send them upon us, O Lord!
Grant to us now a refreshing;
Come, and now honour Thy word.

4 "There shall be showers of blessing":
Oh, that today they might fall,
Now as to God we're confessing,
Now as on Jesus we call!

71 L.M.

1 LORD Jesus Christ, we seek Thy face;
Within the veil we bow the knee,
Oh, let Thy glory fill the place,
And bless us while we wait on Thee.

We thank Thee for the precious blood
That purged our sins and brought us
nigh,
All cleansed and sanctified to God,
Thy holy Name to magnify.

27

3 Shut in with Thee far, far above
   The restless world that wars below,
We seek to learn and prove Thy love,
   Thy wisdom and Thy grace to know.

4 The brow that once with thorns was
      bound,
   Thy hands, Thy side, we fain would
      see,
Draw near, Lord Jesus, glory-crowned,
   And bless us while we wait on Thee.

72   L.M.

1 JESUS, where'er Thy people meet,
   There they behold Thy mercy-seat:
Where'er they seek Thee, Thou art
      found,
   And every place is hallowed ground.

2 For Thou, within no walls confined,
   Inhabitest the humble mind:
Such ever bring Thee where they come,
   And going take Thee to their home.

3 Great Shepherd of Thy chosen few,
   Thy former mercies here renew;
Here to our waiting hearts proclaim
   The sweetness of Thy saving Name.

4 Here may we prove the power of
      prayer,
   To strengthen faith, and sweeten care;
To teach our faint desires to rise,
   And bring all heaven before our eyes.

5 Lord, we are few, but Thou art near,
   Nor short Thine arm, nor deaf Thine
      ear;
Oh, rend the heavens, come quickly
      down,
And make a thousand hearts Thine
      own!

73   8.5.8.3.

1 HOLY Father, in Thy mercy
   Hear our anxious prayer,
Keep our loved ones, now far distant,
     'Neath Thy care.

2 Jesus, Saviour, let Thy presence
   Be their light and guide;
Keep, oh, keep them, in their weakness,
     At Thy side.

3 When in sorrow, when in danger,
   When in loneliness,
In Thy love look down and comfort
     Their distress.

4 May the joy of Thy salvation
   Be their strength and stay;
May they love and may they praise
     Thee
     Day by day.

5 Holy Spirit, let Thy teaching
   Sanctify their life;
Send Thy grace, that they may conquer
     In the strife.

6 Father, Son, and Holy Spirit,
   God the One in Three,
Bless them, guide them, save them,
     keep them
     Near to Thee.

74   P.M.

1 IN the secret of His presence how my
     soul delights to hide!
Oh, how precious are the lessons which
     I learn at Jesus' side!
Earthly cares can never vex me,
     neither trials lay me low;
For when Satan comes to tempt me, to
     the secret place I go.

2 When my soul is faint and thirsty,
     'neath the shadow of His wing
There is cool and pleasant shelter, and
     a fresh and crystal spring;
And my Saviour rests beside me, as we
     hold communion sweet;
If I tried, I could not utter what He
     says when thus we meet.

3 Only this I know: I tell Him all my
     doubts and griefs and fears;
Oh, how patiently He listens! and my
     drooping soul He cheers:
Do you think He ne'er reproves me?
     what a false friend He would be
If He never, never told me of the sins
     which He must see!

4 Would you like to know the sweetness
     of the secret of the Lord?
Go and hide beneath His shadow; this
     shall then be your reward;

And whene'er you leave the silence of
    that happy meeting-place,
You will bear the shining image of the
    Master in your face.

75   C.M.

1 APPROACH, my soul, the mercy-seat,
    Where Jesus answers prayer;
There humbly fall before His feet,
    For none can perish there.

2 Thy promise is my only plea;
    With this I venture nigh;
Thou callest burdened souls to Thee,
    And such, O Lord, am I.

3 Bowed down beneath a load of sin,
    By Satan sorely pressed,
By war without, and fears within,
    I come to Thee for rest.

4 Be Thou my Shield and Hiding-place,
    That, sheltered near Thy side,
I may my fierce accuser face,
    And tell him Thou hast died.

5 Oh, wondrous love! to bleed and die,
    To bear the cross and shame,
That guilty sinners, such as I,
    Might plead Thy gracious Name!

76   C.M.

1 LORD, when we bend before Thy
    throne,
    And our confessions pour,
Teach us to feel the sins we own,
    And hate what we deplore.

2 Our broken spirits pitying see,
    True penitence impart;
Then let a kindling glance from Thee
    Beam hope upon the heart.

3 When we disclose our wants in prayer,
    May we our wills resign;
And not a thought our bosoms share,
    Which is not wholly Thine.

4 May faith each weak petition fill,
    And waft it to the skies,
And teach our hearts 'tis goodness still
    That grants it or denies.

77   S.M.

1 BLEST be the tie that binds
    Our hearts in Christian love:
The fellowship of kindred minds
    Is like to that above.

2 Before our Father's throne
    We pour our ardent prayers:
Our fears, our hopes, our aims are one,
    Our comfort and our cares.

3 We share our mutual woes,
    Our mutual burdens bear,
And often for each other flows
    The sympathizing tear.

4 When we asunder part,
    It gives us inward pain;
But we shall still be joined in heart,
    And hope to meet again.

5 This glorious hope revives
    Our courage by the way,
While each in expectation lives,
    And longs to see the day.

6 From sorrow, toil and pain,
    And sin we shall be free;
And perfect love and friendship reign
    Through all eternity.

78   7.7.7.7.

1 JESUS, we Thy promise claim,
We are gathered in Thy Name,
In the midst do Thou appear;
Manifest Thy presence here.

2 Sanctify us, Lord, and bless:
Breathe Thy Spirit, give Thy peace:
Come and dwell within each heart,
Light and life and joy impart.

3 Make us all in Thee complete,
Make us all for glory meet—
Meet to appear before Thy sight,
Partners with the saints in light.

79   7.6.7.6.D.

1 Go, when the morning shineth;
    Go, when the noon is bright;
Go, when the eve declineth;
    Go, in the hush of night;

Go, with pure mind and feeling,
   Fling earthly cares away,
And, in thy chamber kneeling,
   Do thou in secret pray.

2 Remember all who love thee,
   All who are loved by thee;
Pray, too, for those who hate thee,
   If any such there be:
Then, for thyself, in meekness,
   A blessing humbly claim,
And link with each petition
   Thy great Redeemer's Name.

3 Or, if 'tis here denied thee
   In solitude to pray,
Should holy thoughts come o'er thee
   When friends are round thy way,
E'en then in silent pleading
   The spirit raised above
Will reach the throne of glory,
   Of mercy, truth, and love.

4 Oh, not a joy or blessing
   With this can we compare,
The power that He has given
   To pour our souls in prayer!
Whene'er thou art in sadness,
   Before His footstool fall;
Remember, in thy gladness,
   His grace who gives thee all.

80   6.6.6.6.

1 WE love Thy house, O God,
   Wherein Thy children meet:
For Thou, O Lord, art here
   Thy little flock to greet.

2 We love the hour of prayer,
   No hour on earth so sweet;
For then we cast our care
   At our Redeemer's feet.

3 We love the Word of life,
   The Word that tells of peace,
Of comfort in the strife,
   And joys that never cease.

4 We love to sing below
   Of mercies freely given;
But oh! we long to know
   The triumph-song of heaven.

5 Lord Jesus, give us grace
   On earth to love Thee more,
In heaven to see Thy face,
   And with Thy saints adore.

81   C.M.

1 PRAYER is the soul's sincere desire,
   Uttered or unexpressed,
The motion of a hidden fire
   That trembles in the breast.

2 Prayer is the burden of a sigh,
   The falling of a tear,
The upward glancing of an eye
   When none but God is near.

3 Prayer is the simplest form of speech
   That infant lips can try;
Prayer, the sublimest strains that reach
   The Majesty on high.

4 Prayer is the Christian's vital breath,
   The Christian's native air,
His watchword at the gate of death;
   He enters heaven with prayer.

5 Prayer is the contrite sinner's voice,
   Returning from his ways;
While angels in their songs rejoice,
   And cry, "Behold, he prays!"

6 O Thou by whom we come to God,
   The Life, the Truth, the Way!
The path of prayer Thyself hast trod;
   Lord, teach us how to pray!

82   6.6.6.6.8.8.

1   FATHER, to seek Thy face
   Thy children now draw near;
Before the throne of grace
   With boldness we appear:
We plead His Name, His precious
   blood,
Who loved, and made us priests to God.

2   No more we shun the light,
   No more Thy presence fear;
In robes of spotless white
   Before Thee we appear:
Our great High Priest for us is there,
And He presents our praise and prayer.

3   No power have we to praise
        Thy Name, O God of Love,
    Unless Thy Spirit raise
        Our thoughts and hearts above;
    His grace avails in all our need—
    May He our priestly worship lead.

4   Lord, give us faith to plead
        Thy true and faithful Word;
    Grace for each time of need,
        And help to us afford:
    Thy promises in Christ are yea,
    In Him Amen! to endless day.

83   8.7.8.7.

1 GOD is here, and that to bless us
        With the Spirit's quickening power!
    See, the cloud, already bending,
        Waits to drop the grateful shower.

            Let it come, . . . O Lord, we pray
                Thee,
            Let the shower . . . of blessing
                fall;
            We are wait- . . . ing, we are
                waiting—
            Oh, revive . . . the hearts of all!

2 God is here! we feel His presence
        In this consecrated place;
    But we need the soul-refreshing
        Of His free, unbounded grace.

3 God is here! oh, then, believing,
        Bring to Him our one desire,
    That His love may now be kindled,
        Till its flame each heart inspire.

4 Saviour, grant the prayer we offer,
        While in simple faith we bow;
    From the windows of Thy mercy
        Pour us out a blessing now.

84   8.8.8.4.

1 MY God, is any hour so sweet,
        From blush of morn to evening star,
    As that which calls me to Thy feet—
        The hour of prayer?

2 Then is my strength by Thee renewed;
        Then are my sins by Thee forgiven;
    Then dost Thou cheer my solitude
        With hopes of heaven.

3 No words can tell what sweet relief
        Here for my every want I find:
    What strength for warfare, balm for
        grief,
            What peace of mind!

4 Hushed is each doubt, gone every fear;
        My spirit seems in heaven to stay;
    And e'en the penitential tear
        Is wiped away.

5 Lord, till I reach yon blissful shore
        No privilege so dear shall be
    As thus my inmost soul to pour
        In prayer to Thee.

85   S.M.

1   JESUS, in Thy blest Name,
        With joyful hearts we meet,
    In fellowship with saints above,
        Around the mercy-seat.

2   Lord, animate our hearts
        With fervent love to Thee,
    And nerve each fainting warrior here
        With holy energy.

3   With joyfulness we wait
        To see our Master's face;
    Come, Jesus, to Thy waiting ones,
        And fill this lowly place!

4   Fill it with light and love,
        Fill it with power divine,
    And may Thy children hence depart
        Fresh sealed and signed as Thine!

31

God in Creation, Providence and Grace

86 S.M.D.

1 LORD God, from whom all life
And all true gladness springs,
Whose love and care shine everywhere
Among earth's common things;
Be present while we lift
Our song to Thee, and pay
Heart-gratitude for all things good
About our path today.

2 We praise Thee for the light
That floats on sea and hill,
The unstinted wealth of joy and health
With which our pulses thrill;
Oh, may the light of heaven
In us enkindled be,
Heaven's glory "roll from soul to soul,"
And make us strong for Thee!

3 We thank Thee for the grace
In friend and brother found;
For human love that points above
To where all love is crowned;
Oh, may such friendship here
To us Thy sons be given
As shall endure, deep, fair, and pure,
Till all be one in heaven!

4 But most we bless Thee, Lord,
That here Thy Spirit's breath
Blows clear and strong to baffle wrong
And win our lives from death;
Oh, may each heart accept
The entrance of Thy power,
And take Thee hence for sure defence
And help in evil hour!

5 So, when the lives, today
Within our circle brought,
Are sundered wide along the tide
Of human work and thought,
One song shall yet be ours,
One life, one family,
One pathway still, by vale or hill,
Shall lead us home to Thee.

87 7.6.7.6.

1 ALL things bright and beautiful,
All creatures great and small,
All things wise and wonderful,
The Lord God made them all.

2 Each little flower that opens,
Each little bird that sings,
He made their glowing colours,
He made their tiny wings.
All things bright, etc.

3 The purple-headed mountain,
The river running by,
The sunset, and the morning
That brightens up the sky.
All things bright, etc.

4 The cold wind in the winter,
The pleasant summer sun,
The ripe fruits in the garden,
He made them every one.
All things bright, etc.

5 He gave us eyes to see them,
And lips that we might tell
How great is God Almighty,
Who hath done all things well.
All things bright, etc.

88 7.7.5.7.7.5.

1 LORD, who by Thy word of power
Didst, in nature's earliest hour,
Fashion sun and star:
Dear are these great worlds to Thee;
Yet more dear than they can be
Souls of children are.

2 Earth has treasures strange and rare,
Skies are set with jewels fair,
Clear they shine and far.
Thou didst make those worlds of light;
Yet more precious in Thy sight
Hearts of children are.

3 Ever near Thy great white throne
Dwell our angels with Thine own,
There no sin can mar:
'Tis Thy will that we should stand,
Sinless in the deathless land,
Where Thy children are.

4 Thou who still dost guard and save,
Keep us faithful, make us brave
In Thy holy war;
Till Thy fuller life we find,
And in lowly heart and mind
Thy true children are.

89 8.8.8.4.

1 O LORD of Heaven, and earth, and sea,
To Thee all praise and glory be;
How shall we show our love to Thee,
Who givest all?

2 The golden sunshine, vernal air,
Sweet flowers and fruits, Thy love
declare;
Where harvests ripen, Thou art there,
Who givest all.

3 For peaceful homes and healthful days,
For all the blessings earth displays,
We owe Thee thankfulness and praise,
Who givest all.

4 Thou didst not spare Thine only Son,
But gav'st Him for a world undone:
And freely with the blessèd One
Thou givest all.

5 Thou giv'st the Spirit's blessèd dower,
Spirit of life and love and power,
And dost His sevenfold graces shower
Upon us all.

6 For souls redeemed, for sins forgiven,
For means of grace and hopes of
heaven,
Father, what can to Thee be given,
Who givest all?

7 We lose what on ourselves we spend,
We have as treasure without end
Whatever, Lord, to Thee we lend,
Who givest all.

8 To Thee, from whom we all derive
Our life, our gifts, our power to give!
Oh, may we ever with Thee live,
Who givest all!

90 C.M.

1 BEHOLD, what love, what boundless
love,
The Father hath bestowed
On sinners lost, that we should be
Now called "the sons of God."

"Behold . . . what manner of love . . .
what manner of love the Father hath
bestowed upon us, that we . . . that we
should be called . . . should be called the
sons of God!"

2 No longer far from Him, but now
By "precious blood" made nigh!
Accepted in the Well-beloved,
Near to God's heart we lie.

3 What we in glory soon shall be
"It doth not yet appear";
But when our precious Lord we see
We shall His image bear.

4 With such a blessèd hope in view,
We would more holy be,
More like our risen, glorious Lord,
Whose face we soon shall see.

91 7.6.7.6.D.

1 O GOD, the Rock of Ages,
Who evermore hast been,
What time the tempest rages,
Our dwelling-place serene:
Before Thy first creations,
O Lord, the same as now,
To endless generations
The Everlasting Thou!

2 Our years are like the shadows
On sunny hills that lie,
Or grasses in the meadows
That blossom but to die:
A sleep, a dream, a story
By strangers quickly told,
An unremaining glory
Of things that soon are old.

3 O Thou, who canst not slumber,
  Whose light grows never pale,
Teach us aright to number
  Our years before they fail.
On us Thy mercy lighten,
  On us Thy goodness rest,
And let Thy Spirit brighten
  The hearts Thyself hast blest.

4 Lord, crown our faith's endeavour
  With beauty and with grace,
Till, clothed in light for ever,
  We see Thee face to face:
A joy no language measures;
  A fountain brimming o'er;
An endless flow of pleasures;
  An ocean without shore.

92   P.M.

1 How fair are the lilies, what fragrance
    they yield,
  Unwatched and untended by man!
For the Lord gives them beauty to
    brighten the field,
  And the flowers are a part of His plan.
      Let me never despair
      Of His love and His care,
If He thinks of the flowers, if on fields
    He has smiled,
He will care so much more for a
    child.

2 There is not a sparrow that cleaves the
    blue air
  Unnoticed by God in its fall;
For He made them, He knows them,
    they all have His care,
  And He loves them, although they're
    so small.
        Let us bless His dear Name
        For the lesson so plain;
For He wants us to know that we're
    thought of above,
And that each little child has His love.

3 The moss grows unseen in the niche of
    the wall,
  But could not be there without God;
And the dewdrops, that find it where
    rain cannot fall,
  He has purposely scattered abroad.
      So in my lowly place,
      I may still feel His grace,

For the dew of His love can e'en fall on
    me there,
And His blessing in answer to prayer.

4 As we in His beautiful image were
    made,
  He loves us beyond all beside;
But it grieved Him when sin caused
    that image to fade;
  And then to redeem us He died.
            And He now from His throne
            In His beautiful home
Still is saying with love that is bound-
    less and free,
"Let the little ones come unto Me."

93   L.M.

1 Yes, God is good; in earth and sky,
    From ocean depths and spreading
      wood,
  Ten thousand voices seem to cry—
    God made us all, and God is good.

2 The sun that keeps his trackless way,
    And downward pours his golden
      flood,
  Night's sparkling host, all seem to say,
    In accents clear, that God is good.

3 The merry birds prolong the strain,
    Their song with every spring re-
      newed;
  And balmy air, and falling rain
    Each softly whisper—God is good.

4 I hear it in the rushing breeze;
    The hills that have for ages stood,
  The echoing sky and roaring seas
    All swell the chorus—God is good.

5 Yes, God is good, all nature says,
    By God's own hand with speech
      endued;
  And man, in louder notes of praise,
    Should sing for joy that God is good.

6 For all Thy gifts we bless Thee, Lord;
    But most for Thy redeeming blood,
  Thy pardoning grace, Thy quickening
      word,
    These prompt our song that God is
      good.

94   8.7.8.7.

1 SOULS of men, why will ye scatter
    Like a crowd of frightened sheep?
Foolish hearts, why will ye wander
    From a love so true and deep?

2 Was there ever kindest shepherd
    Half so gentle, half so sweet,
As the Saviour who would have us
    Come and gather round His feet?

3 There's a wideness in God's mercy
    Like the wideness of the sea;
There's a kindness in His justice
    Which is more than liberty.

4 There is plentiful redemption
    In the blood that has been shed;
There is joy for all the members
    In the sorrows of the Head.

5 For the love of God is broader
    Than the measures of man's mind;
And the heart of the Eternal
    Is most wonderfully kind.

6 If our love were but more simple
    We should take Him at His word,
And our lives would be all sunshine
    In the sweetness of our Lord.

95   C.M.

1 LORD, I would own Thy tender care,
    And all Thy love to me;
The food I eat, the clothes I wear
    Are all bestowed by Thee.

2 'Tis Thou preservest me from death
    And dangers every hour;
I cannot draw another breath
    Unless Thou give me power.

3 My health, and friends, and parents
    dear,
    To me by God are given;
I have not any blessing here
    But what is sent from heaven.

4 Such goodness, Lord, and constant care
    A child can ne'er repay;
But may it be my daily prayer
    To love Thee and obey.

96   7.6.7.6.D.

1 'TWAS God that made the ocean,
    And laid its sandy bed;
He gave the stars their motion,
    And built the mountain's head;
He made the rolling thunder,
    The lightning's flashing flame;
His works are full of wonder,
    All-glorious is His Name.

2 And must it not surprise us
    That One so high and great
Should see and not despise us,
    Poor sinners, at His feet?
Yet day by day He gives us
    Our raiment and our food;
In sickness He relieves us,
    And is in all things good.

3 But things that are far greater
    His mighty hand hath done,
And sent us blessings sweeter
    Through Christ, His only Son;
Who, when He saw us dying
    In sin and sorrow's night,
On wings of mercy flying,
    Came down with life and light.

4 He gives His Word to teach us
    Our danger and our wants,
And kindly doth beseech us
    To take the life He grants.
His Holy Spirit frees us
    From Satan's deadly powers,
Leads us by faith to Jesus,
    And makes His glory ours.

97   6.5.6.5.D.

1 PANSIES, lilies, roses,
    Flowers of every hue,
Take each one as coming
    Straight from God to you;
Telling wondrous secrets
    Of His power and•love,
Wearing still the brightness
    Of the home above.

    Oh! these flowers of summer,
      Angel-like are they;
    Listen to the message
      Which they bring today.

2 Just as earth's creation
   Showed the might of God,
So does every floweret
   Springing from the sod.
He who guides the star-worlds,
   Curbs the ocean's power,
With the same hand painteth
   Every leaf and flower.

3 Touch these sweet flowers gently,
   So divinely dressed;
They are, in earth's language,
   Thoughts of God expressed.
Thoughts of heavenly glory—
   Sweetness, purity:
Must not He who framed them
   Wholly lovely be?

4 Praise Him then with singing,
   Tell His love abroad;
Be the whole earth ringing
   With the Name of God.
Lakes and hills be telling,
   Sunset skies, and flowers,
Something of the beauty
   Of this God of ours.

Caroline Griffiths.
*Copyright. By permission of the National Sunday
School Union.*

98   6.5.6.5.D.

1 SUMMER suns are glowing
   Over land and sea;
Happy light is flowing,
   Bountiful and free.
Every thing rejoices
   In the mellow rays;
All earth's thousand voices
   Swell the psalm of praise.

2 God's free mercy streameth
   Over all the world,
And His banner gleameth,
   Everywhere unfurled.
Broad and deep and glorious
   As the heaven above,
Shines in might victorious
   His eternal love.

3 Lord, upon our blindness
   Thy pure radiance pour;
For Thy loving-kindness
   Make us love Thee more;
And, when clouds are drifting
   Dark across our sky,
Then, the veil uplifting,
   Father, be Thou nigh.

4 We will never doubt Thee,
   Though Thou veil Thy light;
Life is dark without Thee;
   Death with Thee is bright.
Light of Light! shine o'er us
   On our pilgrim way;
Go Thou still before us
   To the endless day.

99   7.7.7.7.7.7.

1 FOR the beauty of the earth,
   For the beauty of the skies,
For the love which from our birth
   Over and around us lies,
Christ, our God, to Thee we raise
This our sacrifice of praise.

2 For the beauty of each hour
   Of the day and of the night,
Hill and vale, and tree and flower,
   Sun and moon and stars of light,
Christ, our God, to Thee we raise
This our sacrifice of praise.

3 For the joy of ear and eye,
   For the heart and mind's delight,
For the mystic harmony
   Linking sense to sound and sight,
Christ, our God, to Thee we raise
This our sacrifice of praise.

4 For the joy of human love,
   Brother, sister, parent, child,
Friends on earth and friends above,
   For all gentle thoughts and mild,
Christ, our God, to Thee we raise
This our sacrifice of praise.

5 For each perfect gift of Thine
   To our race so freely given,
Graces human and divine,
   Flowers of earth and buds of heaven,
Christ, our God, to Thee we raise
This our sacrifice of praise.

100   5.6.6.4.

1   GOD, who made the earth,
    The air, the sky, the sea,
    Who gave the light its birth,
      Careth for me.

2   God, who made the grass,
    The flower, the fruit, the tree,
    The day and night to pass,
      Careth for me.

3   God, who made the sun,
    The moon, the stars, is He
    Who when life's clouds come on
      Careth for me.

4   God, who sent His Son
    To die on Calvary,
    He, if I lean on Him,
      Will care for me.

5   When in heaven's bright land
    I all His loved ones see,
    I'll sing with that blest band,
      God cared for me.

101   7.6.7.6.D.

1 How dearly God must love us,
    And this poor world of ours,
  To spread blue skies above us,
    And deck the earth with flowers!
  There's not a weed so lowly,
    Nor bird that cleaves the air,
  But tells, in accents holy,
    His kindness and His care.

2 He bids the sun to warm us,
    And light the path we tread:
  At night, lest aught should harm us,
    He guards our welcome bed;
  He gives us needful clothing,
    And sends our daily food;
  His love denies us nothing
    His wisdom deemeth good.

3 The Bible too He sends us,
    That tells how Jesus came,
  Whose blood can cleanse and save us
    From guilt and sin and shame.
  Oh, may God's mercies move us
    To serve Him with our powers;
  For, oh, how He must love us,
    And this poor world of ours!

102   C.M.

1 GOD moves in a mysterious way
    His wonders to perform;
  He plants His footsteps in the sea,
    And rides upon the storm.

2 Deep in unfathomable mines
    Of never-failing skill
  He treasures up His bright designs,
    And works His sovereign will.

3 Ye fearful saints, fresh courage take!
    The clouds ye so much dread
  Are big with mercy, and shall break
    In blessings on your head.

4 Judge not the Lord by feeble sense,
    But trust Him for His grace;
  Behind a frowning providence
    He hides a smiling face.

5 His purposes will ripen fast,
    Unfolding every hour;
  The bud may have a bitter taste,
    But sweet will be the flower.

6 Blind unbelief is sure to err,
    And scan His work in vain;
  God is His own interpreter,
    And He will make it plain.

103   7.6.7.6.D.

1 I KNOW who makes the daisies,
    And paints them starry bright;
  I know who clothes the lilies,
    So sweet and soft and white:
  And surely needful raiment
    He will for me provide,
  Who know Him as my Jesus,
    And in His love confide.

2 I know who feeds the sparrow,
    And robin, red and gay;
  I know who makes the skylark
    Soar up to greet the day:
  And me much more He cares for,
    And feeds with daily bread,
  Whom He has taught to love Him,
    And trust what He has said.

3 The daisy and the lily
  Obey Him all they can;
The robin and the skylark
  Fulfil His perfect plan:
And I, to whom are given
  A heart and mind and will,
Must try to serve Him better,
  And all His laws fulfil.

4 The daisies, they must perish,
  The lark and robin die;
But I shall live for ever
  Above the bright blue sky:
Dear Saviour, Thou wilt help me
  To love Thee more and more,
Until in heaven I see Thee,
  Am like Thee, and adore.

104   L.M.

1 OH, timely happy, timely wise,
Hearts that with rising morn arise,
Eyes that the beam celestial view
Which evermore makes all things new!

2 New every morning is the love
Our wakening and uprising prove;
Through sleep and darkness safely
  brought,
Restored to life, and power, and
  thought.

3 New mercies, each returning day,
Hover around us while we pray;
New perils past, new sins forgiven,
New thoughts of God, new hopes of
  heaven.

4 If, on our daily course, our mind
Be set to hallow all we find,
New treasures still of countless price
God will provide for sacrifice.

5 Old friends, old scenes will lovelier be,
As more of heaven in each we see;
Some softening gleam of love and
  prayer
Shall dawn on every cross and care.

6 The trivial round, the common task
Will furnish all we ought to ask:
Room to deny ourselves; a road
To bring us daily nearer God.

7 Only, O Lord, in Thy dear love
Fit us for perfect rest above,
And help us, this and every day,
To live more nearly as we pray.

105   S.M.

1   GRACE! 'tis a charming sound,
    Harmonious to the ear:
Heaven with the echo shall resound,
    And all the earth shall hear.

2   'Twas grace that wrote my name
    In life's eternal book:
'Twas grace that gave me to the Lamb,
    Who all my sorrows took.

3   Grace taught my wandering feet
    To tread the heavenly road;
And new supplies each hour I meet
    While pressing on to God.

4   Grace taught my soul to pray,
    And made my eyes o'erflow;
'Tis grace has kept me to this day,
    And will not let me go.

5   Grace all the work shall crown
    Through everlasting days;
It lays in heaven the topmost stone,
    And well deserves the praise.

6   Oh, let that grace inspire
    My soul with strength divine!
May all my powers to Thee aspire,
    And all my days be Thine!

106   P.M.

1 FOR the sunshine of the summer
    That makes all nature bright;
For the gladness which it brings us,
    With its joyous warmth and light:

  We will praise Thee, O our Father,
    We will praise Thee in our song:
  While the grateful thoughts of our
    loving hearts
  True praises shall prolong.

2 For the beauteous flowers and blossoms,
    Which speak Thy skill and love;
For the music of the song-birds
    All around us and above.

3 For the golden fruits of harvest,
  Which ripen o'er the plain,
Giving bread to all Thy children,
  And the seed to sow again.

4 For the message of the Gospel,
  For the Saviour's life and death,
For the blessings which He gives us,
  We will praise Thee with each breath.

107   S.M.

1 FAIR waved the golden corn
  In Canaan's pleasant land,
When full of joy, some shining morn,
  Went forth the reaper-band.

2 To God so good and great
  Their cheerful thanks they pour,
Then carry to His temple gate
  The choicest of their store.

3 For thus the holy word,
  Spoken by Moses, ran—
"The first ripe ears are for the Lord,
  The rest He gives to man."

4 Like Israel, Lord, we give
  Our earliest fruits to Thee,
And pray that, long as we shall live,
  We may Thy children be.

5 Thine is our youthful prime,
  And life and all its powers;
Be with us in our morning time,
  And bless our evening hours.

6 In wisdom let us grow,
  As years and strength are given,
That we may serve Thy church below
  And join Thy saints in heaven.

108   7.6.7.6.D.

1 GOD who hath made the daisies
  And every lovely thing,
He will accept our praises,
  And hearken while we sing.
He says (though we be simple,
  Though ignorant we be)—
"Suffer the little children,
  And let them come to Me!"

2 Though we are young and simple,
  In praise we may be bold;
The children in the Temple
  He heard in days of old.
And if our hearts are humble,
  He says to you and me—
"Suffer the little children,
  And let them come to Me!"

3 He sees the bird that wingeth
  Its way o'er earth and sky,
He hears the lark that singeth
  Up in the heaven so high;
He sees the heart's low breathing,
  And says (well pleased to see)—
"Suffer the little children,
  And let them come to Me!"

4 Therefore we will come near Him,
  And joyfully we'll sing;
No cause to shrink or fear Him,
  We'll make our voices ring;
For in our temple speaking,
  He says to you and me—
"Suffer the little children,
  And let them come to Me!"

The Lord Jesus Christ: (1) His Birth and Childhood

109   P.M.

1 THERE came a little Child to earth
      Long ago;
And the angels of God proclaimed His
      birth,
      High and low.

2 Out on the night, so calm and still,
      Their song was heard;
For they knew that the Child on
      Bethlehem's hill
   Was Christ the Lord.

3 Far away in a goodly land,
      Fair and bright,
Children with crowns of glory stand
      Robed in white;

4 In white more pure than the spotless
      snow;
   And their tongues unite
In the psalm which the angels sang
      long ago,
      On Christmas night.

5 They sing how the Lord of that world
    so fair
      A Child was born;
And that they might a crown of glory
    wear,
      Wore a crown of thorn.

6 And in mortal weakness, in want and
    pain,
      Came forth to die;
That the children of earth might for
    ever reign
      With Him on high.

7 And for evermore, in their robes most
    fair
      And undefiled,
Those ransomed children His praise
    declare,
      Who was once a Child.

110
8.7.8.7.4.7.

1 ANGELS from the realms of glory,
    Wing your flight o'er all the earth;
Ye who sang creation's story,
    Now proclaim Messiah's birth:
      Come and worship!
Worship Christ, the new-born King!

2 Shepherds in the fields abiding,
    Watching o'er their flocks by night;
God with man is now residing,
    Yonder shines the Infant light:
      Come and worship!
Worship Christ, the new-born King!

3 Sages, leave your contemplations;
    Brighter visions beam afar!
Seek the great "Desire of nations,"
    Ye have seen His natal star:
      Come and worship!
Worship Christ, the new-born King!

4 Saints before the altar bending,
    Watching long in hope and fear,
Suddenly the Lord, descending,
    In His temple shall appear:
      Come and worship!
Worship Christ, the new-born King!

111
C.M.

1 HARK, the glad sound! the Saviour
    comes,
    The Saviour promised long;
Let every heart prepare a throne,
    And every voice a song.

2 He comes, the prisoners to release
    In Satan's bondage held;
The gates of brass before Him burst,
    The iron fetters yield.

3 He comes from thickest films of vice
    To clear the mental ray,
And on the eye-balls of the blind
    To pour celestial day.

4 He comes the broken heart to bind,
    The bleeding soul to cure:
And with the treasures of His grace
    To enrich the humble poor.

5 Our glad hosannas, Prince of Peace,
    Thy welcome shall proclaim;
And heaven's eternal arches ring
    With Thy belovèd Name.

112
11.10.11.10.

1 WE praise Thee, Lord, for this Thy
    great provision
    For our great need—Thy Strong
      Deliverer sent.
Lo, unto us this day is born a Saviour,
    And on His shoulder is the govern-
      ment.

2 Thy ways, O Lord, are past our under-
    standing,
    Yet now, our Father, are we well
      content,
Since Thou hast told us in Thy word of
    promise
    That on His shoulder is the govern-
      ment.

3 Great are my needs and many my
    temptations,
    Thy loving wisdom knows their full
      extent:
I feel their burden, yet, my God, Thou
    bidd'st me
    Lay on His shoulder all the govern-
      ment.

4 So, then, O Father, I would claim Thy
promise,
 Resting on Jesus, for my strength is
  spent;
And thus will I, on Thy blest word
relying,
 Leave on His shoulder all the govern-
  ment.

113   P.M.

1 THOU didst leave Thy throne and Thy
kingly crown,
 When Thou camest to earth for me;
But in Bethlehem's home there was
found no room
 For Thy holy nativity.
Oh, come to my heart, Lord Jesus!
 There is room in my heart for Thee.

2 Heaven's arches rang when the angels
sang,
 Proclaiming Thy royal degree;
But of lowly birth cam'st Thou, Lord,
on earth,
 And in great humility.
Oh, come to my heart, Lord Jesus!
 There is room in my heart for Thee.

3 The foxes found rest, and the birds had
their nest,
 In the shade of the cedar tree;
But Thy couch was the sod, O Thou
Son of God,
 In the deserts of Galilee.
Oh, come to my heart, Lord Jesus!
 There is room in my heart for Thee.

4 Thou camest, O Lord, with the living
word
 That should set Thy children free;
But with mocking scorn, and with
crown of thorn,
 They bore Thee to Calvary.
Oh, come to my heart, Lord Jesus!
 Thy cross is my only plea.

5 When heaven's arches shall ring, and
her choirs shall sing,
 At Thy coming to victory,
Let Thy voice call me home, saying,
"Yet there is room,
 There is room at My side for thee."
And my heart shall rejoice, Lord Jesus,
 When Thou comest and callest for me.

114   C.M.

1 WHILE shepherds watched their flocks
by night,
 All seated on the ground,
The angel of the Lord came down,
 And glory shone around.

2 "Fear not," said he, for mighty dread
 Had seized their troubled mind;
"Glad tidings of great joy I bring
 To you and all mankind.

3 "To you, in David's town, this day,
 Is born, of David's line,
A Saviour, who is Christ the Lord;
 And this shall be the sign:

4 "The heavenly Babe you there shall
find
 To human view displayed,
All meanly wrapped in swathing bands,
 And in a manger laid."

5 Thus spake the seraph; and forthwith
 Appeared a shining throng
Of angels, praising God, who thus
 Addressed their joyful song:

6 "All glory be to God on high,
 And on the earth be peace;
Good-will henceforth from heaven to
men
 Begin and never cease."

115   10.10.10.10.10.10.

1 CHRISTIANS, awake, salute the happy
morn
 Whereon the Saviour of mankind was
born;
Rise to adore the mystery of love,
 Which hosts of angels chanted from
above;
With them the joyful tidings first
begun
 Of God Incarnate and the Virgin's Son.

2 Then to the watchful shepherds it was
told,
 Who heard the angelic herald's voice:
"Behold,

The Lord Jesus Christ

I bring good tidings of a Saviour's
   birth
To you and all the nations upon
   earth:
This day hath God fulfilled His pro-
   mised word,
This day is born a Saviour, Christ the
   Lord."

3 He spake: and straightway the celestial
      choir
   In hymns of joy, unknown before, con-
      spire:
   The praises of redeeming love they
      sang,
   And heaven's whole orb with halle-
      lujahs rang;
   God's highest glory was their anthem
      still,
   Peace upon earth, and unto men good
      will.

4 To Bethlehem straight the enlightened
      shepherds ran,
   To see the wonder God had wrought for
      man;
   And found, with Joseph and the blessèd
      Maid,
   Her Son, the Saviour, in a manger
      laid;
   Then to their flocks, still praising God,
      return,
   And their glad hearts with holy rapture
      burn.

5 Oh! may we keep and ponder in our
      mind,
   God's wondrous love in saving lost
      mankind;
   Trace we the Babe who hath retrieved
      our loss,
   From His poor manger to His bitter
      cross;
   Tread in His steps, assisted by His
      grace,
   Till man's first heavenly state again
      takes place.

6 Then may we hope, the angelic hosts
      among,
   To sing, redeemed, a glad triumphal
      song;

He that was born upon this joyful day
Around us all His glory shall display;
Saved by His love, incessant we shall
   sing
Eternal praise to heaven's Almighty
   King.

116   7.7.7.7.7.7.

1 As with gladness men of old
   Did the guiding star behold,
   As with joy they hailed its light,
   Leading onward, beaming bright,
   So, most gracious Lord, may we
   Evermore be led to Thee.

2 As with joyful steps they sped,
   Saviour, to Thy lowly bed,
   There to bend the knee before
   Thee whom heaven and earth adore:
   So may we with willing feet
   Ever seek the mercy-seat.

3 As they offered gifts most rare
   At Thy cradle rude and bare;
   So may we with holy joy,
   Pure, and free from sin's alloy,
   All our costliest treasures bring,
   Christ, to Thee, our heavenly King.

4 Holy Jesus, every day
   Keep us in the narrow way;
   And, when earthly things are past,
   Bring our ransomed souls at last
   Where they need no star to guide,
   Where no clouds Thy glory hide.

117   P.M.

1   Oh, come, all ye faithful,
      Joyful and triumphant;
   Oh, come ye! oh, come ye to Bethle-
      hem;
      Come and behold Him,
      Born the King of angels;
   Oh, come, let us adore Him,
      Christ the Lord!

2   God of God,
      Light of light,
   Lo! He abhors not the Virgin's womb;
      Very God,
      Begotten, not created;
   Oh, come, let us adore Him,
      Christ the Lord!

42

3   Sing, choirs of Angels,
    Sing in exultation,
  Sing, all ye powers of heaven above:
    "Glory to God
    In the highest:"
  Oh, come, let us adore Him,
    Christ the Lord!

4   Yea, Lord, we greet Thee,
    Born this happy morning;
  Jesus, to Thee be glory given,
    Word of the Father,
    In our flesh appearing:
  Oh, come, let us adore Him,
    Christ the Lord!

118   C.M.D.

1 IT came upon the midnight clear,
     That glorious song of old,
   From angels bending near the earth
     To touch their harps of gold:
   Peace on the earth, goodwill to men
     From heaven's all-gracious King—
   The world in solemn stillness lay
     To hear the angels sing.

2 Still through the cloven skies they
       come
     With peaceful wings unfurled;
   And still their heavenly music floats
     O'er all the weary world:
   Above its sad and lowly plains
     They bend on hovering wing,
   And ever, o'er its Babel-sounds,
     The blessèd angels sing.

3 O ye, beneath life's crushing load
     Whose forms are bending low,
   Who toil along the climbing way
     With painful steps and slow;
   Look up! for glad and golden hours
     Come swiftly on the wing;
   Oh, rest beside the weary road,
     And hear the angels sing!

4 For lo! the days are hastening on,
     By prophet-bards foretold,
   When, with the ever-circling years,
     Comes round the age of gold;
   When peace shall over all the earth
     Its ancient splendours fling,
   And the whole world send back the
       song
     Which now the angels sing!

119   7.7.7.7.D.

1 HARK! the herald angels sing,
     "Glory to the new-born King!
   Peace on earth and mercy mild,
   God and sinners reconciled."
   Joyful, all ye nations, rise,
   Join the triumph of the skies;
   With the angelic host proclaim,
   "Christ is born in Bethlehem!"
     Hark! the herald angels sing,
     "Glory to the new-born King!"

2 Hail, the heaven-born Prince of Peace!
   Hail, the Sun of Righteousness!
   Light and life to all He brings,
   Risen with healing in His wings.
   Mild He lays His glory by,
   Born that man no more may die;
   Born to raise the sons of earth,
   Born to give them second birth.

3 Come, Desire of nations, come,
   Fix in us Thy humble home:
   Rise, the woman's conquering Seed,
   Bruise in us the serpent's head:
   Sing we then, with angels sing,
   "Glory to the new-born King!
   Glory in the highest heaven,
   Peace on earth, and sins forgiven."

120   8.7.8.7.7.7.

1 ONCE, in royal David's city,
     Stood a lowly cattle-shed,
   Where a mother laid her Baby,
     In a manger for His bed.
   Mary was that mother mild,
   Jesus Christ her little child.

2 He came down to earth from heaven,
     Who is God and Lord of all,
   And His shelter was a stable,
     And His cradle was a stall:
   With the poor and mean and lowly
   Lived on earth our Saviour holy.

3 And through all His wondrous child-
       hood
     He would honour and obey,
   Love and watch the lowly mother,
     In whose gentle arms He lay.
   Christian children all must be
   Mild, obedient, good as He.

43

4 For He is our childhood's pattern,
  Day by day like us He grew;
He was little, weak and helpless;
  Tears and smiles like us He knew:
And He feeleth for our sadness,
And He shareth in our gladness.

5 And our eyes at last shall see Him,
  Through His own redeeming love;
For that Child, so dear and gentle,
  Is our Lord in heaven above;
And He leads His children on
To the place where He is gone.

6 Not in that poor, lowly stable,
  With the oxen standing by,
We shall see Him; but in heaven,
  Set at God's right hand on high;
When like stars His children crowned,
All in white shall wait around.

121   11.10.11.10.

1 BRIGHTEST and best of the sons of the
    morning,
  Dawn on our darkness, and lend us
    thine aid!
Star of the east, the horizon adorning,
  Guide where our infant Redeemer is
    laid!

2 Cold on His cradle the dewdrops are
    shining,
  Low lies His head with the beasts of
    the stall;
Angels adore Him in slumber reclin-
    ing—
  Maker, and Monarch, and Saviour of
    all!

3 Say, shall we yield Him, in costly
    devotion,
  Odours of Edom and offerings divine;
Gems of the mountain, and pearls of the
    ocean,
  Myrrh from the forest, and gold from
    the mine?

4 Vainly we offer each ample oblation,
  Vainly with gifts would His favour
    secure:
Richer by far is the heart's adoration;
  Dearer to God are the prayers of the
    poor.

5 Brightest and best of the sons of the
    morning,
  Dawn on our darkness, and lend us
    thine aid!
Star of the east, the horizon adorning,
  Guide where our infant Redeemer is
    laid!

The Lord Jesus Christ: (2) His Life and Work

122   8.7.8.7.D.

1 WHO is this so weak and helpless,
  Child of lowly Hebrew maid,
Rudely in a stable sheltered,
  Coldly in a manger laid?
'Tis the Lord of all creation,
  Who this wondrous path hath trod;
He is God from everlasting,
  And to everlasting God.

2 Who is this—a Man of Sorrows,
  Walking sadly life's hard way,
Homeless, weary, sighing, weeping
  Over sin and Satan's sway?
'Tis our God, our glorious Saviour,
  Who above the starry sky
Now for us a place prepareth,
  Where no tear can dim the eye.

3 Who is this—behold Him shedding
  Drops of blood upon the ground?
Who is this—despised, rejected,
  Mocked, insulted, beaten, bound?
'Tis our God, who gifts and graces
  On His Church now poureth down;
Who shall smite in righteous judgment
  All His foes beneath His throne.

4 Who is this that hangeth dying,
  While the rude world scoffs and
    scorns?
Numbered with the malefactors,
  Torn with nails, and crowned with
    thorns?
'Tis the God who ever liveth
  'Mid the shining ones on high,
In the glorious golden city
  Reigning everlastingly.

123

8.7.8.7.D.

1 TELL me the story of Jesus,
Write on my heart every word!
Tell me the story most precious,
Sweetest that ever was heard.
Tell how the angels in chorus
Sang, as they welcomed His birth,
"Glory to God in the highest,
Peace and good tidings to earth."

Tell me the story of Jesus,
Write on my heart every word,
Tell me the story most precious,
Sweetest that ever was heard.

2 Fasting alone in the desert,
Tell of the days that He passed;
How He was tried and was tempted,
Yet was triumphant at last.
Tell of the years of His labours,
Tell of the sorrows He bore;
He was despised and afflicted,
Homeless, rejected, and poor.

3 Tell of the cross where they nailed
Him,
Hanging in anguish and pain;
Tell of the grave where they laid Him;
Tell how He liveth again.
Love, in that story so tender,
Clearer than ever I see;
Stay, let me weep while you whisper—
Love paid the ransom for me.

124

8.8.8.8.8.8.

1 WE saw Thee not when Thou didst
come
To this poor world of sin and death,
Nor e'er beheld Thy cottage-home
In that despisèd Nazareth;
But we believe Thy footsteps trod
Its streets and plains, Thou Son of
God.

2 We did not see Thee lifted high
Amid that wild and savage crew,
Nor heard Thy meek imploring cry,
"Forgive; they know not what they
do":
Yet we believe the deed was done,
Which shook the earth and veiled the
sun.

3 We stood not by the empty tomb
Where late Thy sacred body lay,
Nor sat within that upper room,
Nor met Thee in the open way;
But we believe that angels said,
"Why seek the living with the
dead?"

4 We did not mark the chosen few,
When Thou didst through the clouds
ascend,
First lift to heaven their wondering
view,
Then to the earth all prostrate
bend;
Yet we believe that mortal eyes
Beheld that journey to the skies.

5 And now that Thou dost reign on high,
And thence Thy waiting people bless,
No ray of glory from the sky
Doth shine upon our wilderness;
But we believe Thy faithful Word,
And trust in our redeeming Lord.

125

P.M.

1 JESUS, my Saviour, to Bethlehem
came,
Born in a manger to sorrow and
shame;
Oh, it was wonderful—blest be His
Name!
Seeking for me, for me!

Seeking for me, for me!
Seeking for me, for me!
Oh, it was wonderful—blest be His
Name!
Seeking for me, for me!

2 Jesus, my Saviour, on Calvary's tree,
Paid the great debt, and my soul He set
free;
Oh, it was wonderful—how could it be?
Dying for me, for me!

Dying for me, for me!
Dying for me, for me!
Oh, it was wonderful—how could it
be?
Dying for me, for me!

45

3 Jesus, my Saviour, the same as of old,
While I was wandering afar from the
   fold,
Gently and long did He plead with my
   soul,
   Calling for me, for me!

   Calling for me, for me!
   Calling for me, for me!
   Gently and long did He plead with
      my soul,
   Calling for me, for me!

4 Jesus, my Saviour, shall come from on
   high—
Sweet is the promise as passing years
   fly;
Oh, I shall see Him descending the sky,
   Coming for me, for me!

   Coming for me, for me!
   Coming for me, for me!
   Oh, I shall see Him descending the
      sky,
   Coming for me, for me!

126   7.6.7.6.D.

1 THE Saviour loves all children,
   For He was once a child—
So joyous and so happy,
   So gentle, meek, and mild.
He loves the young in heaven,
   He loves the young on earth;
For every child that liveth
   Reminds Him of His birth.

2 Oh, happy were those children—
   We wish we had been there—
Who gained the Saviour's blessing,
   And heard His loving prayer.
We wish His hands had rested
   Upon our heads as well,
And we had heard the lessons
   Which from the Master fell.

3 And yet we know that Jesus
   Is with us every day;
He stands within our chamber,
   When we kneel down to pray.
He speaks when we are reading,
   Although no voice is heard;
And whispers many blessings
   To children in His Word.

4 And if we seek Him early
   He'll lead us by the hand,
Until some day in glory
   We at His side shall stand:
And then with those same children,
   Our harps of gold we'll bring,
And sit down at His footstool,
   And endless praises sing.

127   P.M

1 LITTLE thought Samaria's daughter,
   On that ne'er-forgotten day,
That the tender Shepherd sought her,
   As a sheep astray;
That from sin He longed to win her—
   Knowing more than she could tell
Of the wretchedness within her,
   Waiting at the well.

   Hear, oh hear, the wondrous story!
      Let the winds and waters tell—
   'Tis the Christ, the King of glory,
      Waiting at the well.

2 'Neath the stately palm-tree swaying,
   Listened she to words of truth:
While each thought was backward
      straying
   O'er her wasted youth.
Hastening homeward, with desire
   All His wondrous speech to tell,
Asked she, "Is not this Messiah
   Waiting at the well?"

3 Living waters still are flowing,
   Full and free for all mankind,
Blessings sweet on all bestowing;
   All a welcome find.
All the world may come and prove
      Him;
   Every doubt will Christ dispel,
When each heart shall truly love Him
   Waiting at the well.

128   P.M

1 WHO is He in yonder stall,
   At whose feet the shepherds fall?

   'Tis the Lord! oh, wondrous story!
   'Tis the Lord, the King of glory!
   At His feet we humbly fall—
   Crown Him! crown Him, Lord o
      all!

2 Who is He in deep distress
  Fasting in the wilderness?

3 Who is He the people bless
  For His words of gentleness?

4 Who is He to whom they bring
  All the sick and sorrowing?

5 Who is He that stands and weeps
  At the grave where Lazarus sleeps?

6 Who is He the gathering throng
  Greet with loud triumphant song?

7 Lo! at midnight, who is He
  Prays in dark Gethsemane?

8 Who is He on yonder tree
  Dies in grief and agony?

9 Who is He who from the grave
  Comes to succour, help, and save?

10 Who is He who from His throne
  Rules through all the worlds alone?

129   P.M.

1 ONE day when heaven was filled with
    His praises,
  One day when sin was as black as
    could be,
Jesus came forth to be born of a vir-
    gin—
  Dwelt amongst men, my example is
    He!

    Living, He loved me; dying, He
      saved me;
      Buried, He carried my sins far
        away;
    Rising, He justified freely for ever:
      One day He's coming—oh,
       glorious day!

2 One day they led Him up Calvary's
    mountain,
  One day they nailed Him to die on
    the tree;
Suffering anguish, despised, and re-
    jected;
  Bearing our sins, my Redeemer is
    He!

3 One day they left Him alone in the
    garden,
  One day He rested, from suffering
    free;
Angels came down o'er His tomb to
    keep vigil;
  Hope of the hopeless, my Saviour is
    He!

4 One day the grave could conceal Him
    no longer,
  One day the stone rolled away from
    the door;
Then He arose, over death He had
    conquered;
  Now is ascended, my Lord ever-
    more!

5 One day the trumpet will sound for
    His coming,
  One day the skies with His glory will
    shine;
Wonderful day, my beloved ones
    bringing;
  Glorious Saviour, this Jesus is mine!

130   S.M.

1 O PERFECT life of love!
  All, all is finished now;
All that He left His throne above
  To do for us below.

2 No work is left undone
  Of all the Father willed;
His toil, His sorrows, one by one
  The Scriptures have fulfilled.

3 No pain that we can share
  But He has felt its smart;
All forms of human grief and care
  Have pierced that tender heart.

4 And on His thorn-crowned head,
  And on His sinless soul,
Our sins in all their guilt were laid,
  That He might make us whole.

5 In perfect love He dies—
  For me He dies, for me;
O all-atoning Sacrifice,
  I cling by faith to Thee.

6 In every time of need,
   Before the judgment-throne,
Thy work, O Lamb of God, I'll plead,
   Thy merits, not my own.

7 Yet work, O Lord, in me
   As Thou for me hast wrought;
And let my love the answer be
   To grace Thy love has brought.

131   9.8.9.8.D.

1 A CROWD fills the court of the temple,
   A sound as of praise fills the air,
Jerusalem thrills with emotion,
   The Lord of the temple is there!
In vain is the priestly displeasure,
   To silence the anthems that ring.
Hosanna! Hosanna! Hosanna!
   The children all joyfully sing.

2 And if in this temple of worship,
   Where now we are met in His Name,
The Lord should appear in His beauty,
   Himself His own Gospel proclaim,
What anthems of grateful devotion
   Around Him would echo and ring!
Hosanna! Hosanna! Hosanna!
   The children would joyfully sing.

3 Lord, make each young heart Thine
   own temple,
   Reveal Thy sweet presence within,
Illumine our minds by Thy coming,
   Expel every longing for sin;
For when in our souls we adore Thee,
   How pure the glad praise we shall
   bring!
Hosanna! Hosanna! Hosanna!
   The children will joyfully sing.

4 And when in that temple of glory,
   Where falls never shadow of night,
Where sorrow and sin never sadden,
   And Thou shalt Thyself be the
   Light!
When round Thee the ransomed are
   thronging,
   High heaven with their praises will
   ring.
Hosanna! Hosanna! Hosanna!
   Thy children for ever will sing.

132   C.M

1 A LITTLE ship was on the sea,
   It was a pretty sight;
It sailed along so pleasantly,
   And all was calm and bright.

2 When, lo! a storm began to rise,
   The wind grew loud and strong;
It blew the clouds across the skies,
   It blew the waves along.

3 And all but One were sore afraid
   Of sinking in the deep;
His head was on a pillow laid,
   And He was fast asleep.

4 "Master, we perish: Master, save!"
   They cried. Their Master heard;
He rose, rebuked the wind and wave,
   And stilled them with a word.

5 He to the storm says, "Peace, be still!"
   The raging billows cease;
The mighty winds obey His will,
   And all are hushed to peace.

6 Oh! well we know it was the Lord,
   Our Saviour and our Friend,
Whose care of those who trust His
   word
   Will never, never end.

133   7.6.7.6.D

1 WE sing a loving Jesus,
   Who left His throne above,
And came on earth to ransom
   The children of His love;
It is an oft-told story,
   And yet we love to tell
How Christ, the King of glory,
   Once deigned with man to dwell.

2 We sing a holy Jesus:
   No taint of sin defiled
The Babe of David's city,
   The pure and stainless Child.
Oh, teach us, blessèd Saviour,
   Thy heavenly grace to seek;
And let our whole behaviour,
   Like Thine, be mild and meek.

We sing a lowly Jesus:
  No kingly crown He had;
His heart was bowed with anguish,
  His face was marred and sad;
In deep humiliation
  He came, His work to do:
O Lord of our salvation,
  Let us be humble too.

We sing a mighty Jesus,
  Whose voice could raise the dead;
The sightless eyes He opened,
  The famished souls He fed.
Thou camest to deliver
  Mankind from sin and shame;
Redeemer and Life-giver,
  We praise Thy holy Name!

We sing a coming Jesus:
  The time is drawing near
When Christ with all His angels
  In glory shall appear.
Lord, save us, we entreat Thee,
  In this Thy day of grace,
That we may gladly meet Thee,
  And see Thee face to face.

134 C.M.

JESUS, the very thought of Thee
  With sweetness fills my breast;
But sweeter far Thy face to see,
  And in Thy presence rest.

Nor voice can sing, nor heart can frame,
  Nor can the memory find
A sweeter sound than Thy blest Name,
  O Saviour of mankind!

Oh, hope of every contrite heart,
  Oh, joy of all the meek;
To those who fall, how kind Thou art,
  How good to those who seek!

But what to those who find? Ah! this
  Nor tongue nor pen can show;
The love of Jesus, what it is
  None but His loved ones know.

Jesus, our only joy be Thou,
  As Thou our prize wilt be;
Jesus, be Thou our glory now,
  And through eternity.

135 C.M.

1 SEE Israel's gentle Shepherd stands,
    With all-engaging charms:
  Hark! how He calls the tender lambs
    And folds them in His arms.

2 "Permit them to approach," He cries,
    "Nor scorn their humble name";
  For 'twas to bless such souls as these
    The Lord of angels came.

3 The feeblest lamb amidst the flock
    Shall be its Shepherd's care;
  While folded in the Saviour's arms,
    We're safe from every snare.

4 Ye little flock, with pleasure hear;
    Ye children, seek His face:
  And fly with transport to receive
    The blessings of His grace.

136 7.7.7.7.

1 CHRIST is merciful and mild;
  He was once a little child;
  He whom heavenly hosts adore
  Lived on earth among the poor.

2 Thus He laid His glory by
  When for us He stooped to die;
  How I wonder when I see
  His unbounded love to me!

3 He the sick to health restored,
  To the poor He preached the word;
  Even children had a share
  Of His love and tender care.

4 Every bird can build its nest,
  Foxes have their place of rest;
  He by whom the world was made
  Had not where to lay His head.

5 He who is the Lord most high
  Then was poorer far than I,
  That I might hereafter be
  Rich to all eternity.

137 L.M.

1 RIDE on! ride on in majesty!
  Hark! all the tribes "Hosanna!" cry;
  O Saviour meek, pursue Thy road,
  With palms and scattered garments
    strowed.

2 Ride on! ride on in majesty!
In lowly pomp ride on to die:
O Christ, Thy triumphs now begin
O'er captive death and conquered sin.

3 Ride on! ride on in majesty!
The angel armies of the sky
Look down with sad and wondering
    eyes
To see the approaching sacrifice.

4 Ride on! ride on in majesty!
Thy last and fiercest strife is nigh:
The Father on His sapphire throne
Awaits His own anointed Son.

5 Ride on! ride on in majesty!
In lowly pomp ride on to die:
Bow Thy meek head to mortal pain,
Then take, O God, Thy power, and
    reign.

The Lord Jesus Christ: (3) His Redeeming Love

138 8.7.8.7.D.

1 OH, the deep, deep love of Jesus!
    Vast, unmeasured, boundless, free;
Rolling as a mighty ocean
    In its fulness over me.
Underneath me, all around me,
    Is the current of Thy love;
Leading onward, leading homeward,
    To my glorious rest above.

2 Oh, the deep, deep love of Jesus!
    Spread His praise from shore to
        shore;
How He loveth, ever loveth,
    Changeth never, nevermore;
How He watcheth o'er His loved ones,
    Died to call them all His own;
How for them He intercedeth,
    Watcheth o'er them from the throne.

3 Oh, the deep, deep love of Jesus!
    Love of every love the best;
'Tis an ocean vast of blessing,
    'Tis a haven sweet of rest.
Oh, the deep, deep love of Jesus!
    'Tis a heaven of heavens to me;
And it lifts me up to glory,
    For it lifts me up to Thee.

139 P.M.

1 THERE is a word I fain would speak—
        Jesus died.
Eyes that weep and hearts that break;
        Jesus died.
No music from the quivering string
Could such sweet sounds of rapture
    bring;
Oh! may I always love to sing—
        Jesus died.

2 Satan seeks my soul to have:
        Jesus died.
Jesus died my soul to save:
        Jesus died.
The holy Lord, the bleeding Lamb,
The Crucified, the great I AM;
There's life in every lovely Name:
        Jesus died.

3 And now I need not fear to pray:
        Jesus died.
He washes all my sins away:
        Jesus died.
He washes all my sins away,
He is the Life, the Truth, the Way,
And now to all men I can say—
        Jesus died.

4 'Twill soothe my heart with death in
        view:
        Jesus died.
And bear me that cold river through:
        Jesus died.
That word will heaven's bright gates
    unclose,
Release me from my mortal woes,
And bear me where His glory glows;
        Jesus died.

*After verse 4 repeat verse 1 with refrain—Jesus
lives.*

140 5.5.6.5.

1 GOD commends His love—
        Greater could not be:
While I was a sinner,
        Jesus died for me.

2 Justified by faith,
　　I have peace with God;
　In my heart the Spirit
　　Sheds His love abroad.

3 Thus, where sin abounded,
　　Grace did more abound:
　And where death was reigning,
　　Life in Christ I found.

4 Jesus, Son of God,
　　Now Thy grace I see:
　Thou who lov'dst the sinner
　　Gav'st Thyself for me.

141
8.6.8.6.8.6.

O CHRIST, what burdens bowed Thy
　　head!
　Our load was laid on Thee;
Thou stoodest in the sinner's stead,
　　Didst bear all ill for me.
A Victim led, Thy blood was shed!
　Now there's no load for me.

2 Death and the curse were in our cup:
　　O Christ, 'twas full for Thee!
But Thou hast drained the last dark
　　drop,
　　'Tis empty now for me:
That bitter cup, love drank it up,
　Now blessing's draught for me.

3 Jehovah lifted up His rod:
　　O Christ, it fell on Thee!
Thou wast sore stricken of Thy God;
　　There's not one stroke for me.
Thy tears, Thy blood, beneath it
　　flowed;
　Thy bruising healeth me.

4 The tempest's awful voice was heard;
　　O Christ, it broke on Thee!
Thy open bosom was my ward,
　　It braved the storm for me.
Thy form was scarred, Thy visage
　　marred;
　Now cloudless peace for me.

5 Jehovah bade His sword awake:
　　O Christ, it woke 'gainst Thee;
Thy blood the flaming blade must
　　slake,
　Thy heart its sheath must be.
All for my sake, my peace to make:
　Now sleeps that sword for me.

6 For me, Lord Jesus, Thou hast died,
　　And I have died in Thee:
Thou'rt risen—my bands are all un-
　　tied;
　And now Thou liv'st in me;
When purified, made white, and tried,
　Thy glory then for me.

142
P.M.

1 CAN it be true that Thou didst leave,
　　For this cold, barren wild,
　Thy heaven, that I might become
　　God's own belovèd child?

　　Forgive me, Lord, for it is true,
　　　On Thee my guilt was laid;
　　My punishment Thy body bore,
　　　By Thee my debt was paid.

2 Can it be true that Thou didst bear
　　Upon the accursèd tree
　My load of sin, its curse, its sting,
　　Its stripes, instead of me?

3 Can it be true that I have scorned
　　The offer mercy made,
　And vainly hoped myself to pay
　　The debt Thy death has paid?

4 Can it be true that I still cling
　　To earth and all my sin;
　That I have closely barred the door,
　　Lest Thou should'st enter in?

5 Lord, enter now, possession take,
　　And cleanse me from my sin;
　Thy kingdom come, Thy will be done;
　　Lord, reign Thyself within.

6 Oh, make me Thine, and give me grace
　　To live for Thee alone.
　Shine in my heart, till it becomes
　　A mirror of Thine own.

143
L.M.

1 IT is a thing most wonderful,
　　Almost too wonderful to be,
　That God's own Son should come from
　　heaven
　　And die to save a child like me.

51

2 And yet I know that it is true:
    He came to this poor world below,
And wept and toiled and mourned and
      died,
    Only because He loved us so.

3 I cannot tell how He could love
    A child so weak and full of sin;
His love must be most wonderful,
    If He could die my love to win.

4 I sometimes think about His cross,
    And shut my eyes, and try to see
The cruel nails, and crown of thorns,
    And Jesus crucified for me.

5 But even could I see Him die,
    I could but see a little part
Of that great love which, like a fire,
    Is always burning in His heart.

6 It is most wonderful to know
    His love for me so free and sure;
But 'tis more wonderful to see
    My love for Him so faint and poor.

7 And yet I want to love Thee, Lord:
    Oh, light the flame within my heart,
And I will love Thee more and more
    Until I see Thee as Thou art!

144 P.M.

1 "MAN of Sorrows!" what a name
For the Son of God, who came
Ruined sinners to reclaim!
    Hallelujah! what a Saviour!

2 Bearing shame and scoffing rude,
In my place condemned He stood;
Sealed my pardon with His blood:
    Hallelujah! what a Saviour!

3 Guilty, vile, and helpless, we:
Spotless Lamb of God was He:
"Full atonement"—can it be?
    Hallelujah! what a Saviour!

4 "Lifted up" was He to die,
"It is finished!" was His cry:
Now in heaven exalted high:
    Hallelujah! what a Saviour!

5 When He comes, our glorious King,
All His ransomed home to bring,
Then anew this song we'll sing:
    "Hallelujah! what a Saviour!"

145 9.8.9.8

1 OH, sweet is the story of Jesus,
    The wonderful Saviour of men,
Who suffered and died for the sinner—
    I'll tell it again and again!

    Oh, wonderful, wonderful story,
    The dearest that ever was told;
      I'll repeat it in glory,
      The wonderful story,
    Where I shall His beauty behold.

2 He came from the mansions of glory;
    His blood as a ransom He gave,
To purchase eternal redemption,
    And oh, He is mighty to save!

3 His mercy flows on like a river,
    His love is unmeasured and free;
His grace is for ever sufficient,
    It reaches and purifies me.

146 P.M

1 WHAT can wash away my stain?
    Nothing but the blood of Jesus!
What can make me whole again?
    Nothing but the blood of Jesus!

    Oh, precious is the flow
    That makes me white as snow!
    No other fount I know,
      Nothing but the blood of Jesus!

2 For my cleansing this I see—
    Nothing but the blood of Jesus!
For my pardon this my plea—
    Nothing but the blood of Jesus!

3 Nothing can for sin atone—
    Nothing but the blood of Jesus!
Naught of good that I have done—
    Nothing but the blood of Jesus!

4 This is all my hope and peace—
    Nothing but the blood of Jesus!
This is all my righteousness—
    Nothing but the blood of Jesus!

147 8.5.8.3.

1 PRECIOUS, precious blood of Jesus,
 Shed on Calvary;
Shed for rebels, shed for sinners,
 Shed for thee!

  Precious, precious blood of
   Jesus,
  Shed on Calvary:
  Oh, believe it; oh, receive it,
   'Tis for thee.

2 Precious, precious blood of Jesus,
 Let it make thee whole;
Let it flow in mighty cleansing
 O'er thy soul.

3 Though thy sins are red like crimson,
 Deep in scarlet glow,
Jesus' precious blood shall wash thee
 White as snow.

4 Precious blood that hath redeemed us!
 All the price is paid!
Perfect pardon now is offered,
 Peace is made.

5 Now the holiest with boldness
 We may enter in;
For the open fountain cleanseth
 From all sin.

6 Precious blood, by this we conquer
 In the fiercest fight,
Sin and Satan overcoming
 By its might.

7 Precious blood whose full atonement
 Makes us nigh to God!
Precious blood, our way of glory,
 Praise and laud.

148 C.M.

1 THERE is a fountain filled with blood
 Drawn from Immanuel's veins;
And sinners plunged beneath that flood,
 Lose all their guilty stains.

  I do believe, I will believe,
   That Jesus died for me,
  That on the cross He shed His
   blood,
  From sin to set me free.

2 The dying thief rejoiced to see
 That fountain in his day;
And there may I, though vile as he,
 Wash all my sins away.

3 Dear dying Lamb, Thy precious blood
 Shall never lose its power,
Till all the ransomed church of God
 Be saved, to sin no more.

4 E'er since, by faith, I saw the stream
 Thy flowing wounds supply,
Redeeming love has been my theme,
 And shall be till I die.

5 Then in a nobler, sweeter song
 I'll sing Thy power to save,
When this poor lisping, stammering
  tongue
 Lies silent in the grave.

149 C.M.

1 ALAS! and did my Saviour bleed?
 And did my Sovereign die?
Would He devote that sacred head
 For such a worm as I?

  Help me, dear Saviour, Thee to
   own,
  And ever faithful be;
  And when Thou sittest on Thy
   throne,
  O Lord, remember me!

2 Was it for sins that I had done
 He groaned upon the tree?
Amazing pity! grace unknown!
 And love beyond degree!

3 Well might the sun in darkness hide,
 And shut his glories in,
When Christ, the mighty Maker, died
 For man the creature's sin.

4 Thus might I hide my blushing face
 While His dear cross appears,
Dissolve my heart in thankfulness,
 And melt mine eyes to tears.

5 But drops of grief can ne'er repay
 The debt of love I owe:
Here, Lord, I give myself away:
 'Tis all that I can do.

The Lord Jesus Christ

150
6.6.8.6.10.12.

1 No blood, no altar now:
  The sacrifice is o'er;
No flame, no smoke ascends on high,
  The lamb is slain no more:
But richer blood has flowed from
  nobler veins
To purge the soul from guilt, and
  cleanse the reddest stains.

2 We thank Thee for the blood,
  The blood of Christ, Thy Son:
The blood by which our peace is
  made,
  Our victory is won;
Great victory o'er hell, and sin, and
  woe,
That needs no second fight, and leaves
  no second foe.

3 We thank Thee for the grace,
  Descending from above,
That overflows our widest guilt—
  The Eternal Father's love:
Love of the Father's everlasting Son,
Love of the Holy Ghost—Jehovah,
  Three in One.

4 We thank Thee for the hope,
  So glad, and sure, and clear;
It holds the drooping spirit up
  Till the long dawn appear:
Fair hope! with what a sunshine does it
  cheer
Our roughest path on earth, our
  dreariest desert here.

151
S.M.

1 JESUS, the sinner's Friend!
  We hide ourselves in Thee:
God looks upon Thy sprinkled blood—
  It is our only plea.

2 He hears Thy precious Name,
  We claim it as our own:
The Father must accept and bless
  His well-belovèd Son.

3 He sees Thy spotless robe,
  It covers all our sin;
The golden gates have welcomed Thee,
  And we may enter in.

4 Thou hast fulfilled the law,
  And we are justified:
Ours is the blessing, Thine the curse;
  We live, for Thou hast died!

5 Jesus, the sinner's Friend!
  We cannot speak Thy praise!
No mortal voice can sing the song
  That ransomed hearts would raise.

6 But when before the throne,
  Upon the glassy sea,
Clothed in our blood-bought robes of
  white,
  We stand complete in Thee:

7 Jesus, we'll give Thee then
  Such praises as are meet,
And cast ten thousand golden crowns,
  Adoring, at Thy feet!

152
P.M.

1 I STAND all amazed at the love Jesus
  offers me,
Confused at the grace that so fully He
  proffers me;
I tremble to know that for me He was
  crucified—
That for me, a sinner, He suffered, He
  bled, He died.

  Oh, it is wonderful that He should
    care for me
    Enough to die for me!
  Oh, it is wonderful, wonderful to
    me!

2 I marvel that He should descend from
  His throne divine
To rescue a soul so rebellious and proud
  as mine;
That He should extend His great love
  unto such as I;
Sufficient to own, to redeem, and to
  justify.

3 I think of His hands pierced and bleed-
  ing to pay the debt!
Such mercy, such love and devotion
  can I forget?
No, no! I will praise and adore at the
  mercy-seat,
Until at the glorified throne I kneel at
  His feet.

54

153
8.8.8.6.

1 THE love that Jesus had for me,
To suffer on the cruel tree,
That I a ransomed soul might be,
Is more than tongue can tell!

His love is more than tongue can
tell! . . .
His love is more than tongue can
tell! . . .
The love that Jesus had for me
Is more than tongue can tell!

2 The bitter sorrow that He bore,
And, oh, the crown of thorns He wore,
That I might live for evermore,
Is more than tongue can tell!

3 The peace I have in Him, my Lord,
Who pleads before the throne of God
The merit of His precious blood,
Is more than tongue can tell!

4 The joy that comes when He is near,
The rest He gives, so free from fear,
The hope in Him, so bright and clear,
Is more than tongue can tell!

154
7.6.7.6.D.

1 OH, teach me what it meaneth—
That cross uplifted high,
With One—the Man of Sorrows—
Condemned to bleed and die!
Oh, teach me what it cost Thee
To make a sinner whole;
And teach me, Saviour, teach me
The value of a soul!

2 Oh, teach me what it meaneth—
That sacred, crimson tide—
The blood and water flowing
From Thine own wounded side.
Teach me that if none other
Had sinned, but I alone,
Yet still, Thy blood, Lord Jesus,
Thine only, must atone.

3 Oh, teach me what it meaneth—
Thy love beyond compare,
The love that reacheth deeper
Than depths of self-despair!

Yea, teach me, till there gloweth
In this cold heart of mine
Some feeble, pale reflection
Of that pure love of Thine.

4 Oh, teach me what it meaneth,
For I am full of sin;
And grace alone can reach me,
And love alone can win.
Oh, teach me, for I need Thee,
I have no hope beside—
The chief of all the sinners
For whom the Saviour died!

5 O infinite Redeemer!
I bring no other plea,
Because Thou dost invite me
I cast myself on Thee.
Because Thou dost accept me
I love and I adore;
Because Thy love constraineth,
I'll praise Thee evermore!

155
C.M.

1 THERE is a story sweet to hear,
I love to tell it too:
It fills my heart with hope and cheer,
'Tis old, yet ever new.

'Tis old, . . . yet ever new!
'Tis old, . . . yet ever new!
I know, . . . I feel it's true;
'Tis old, yet ever new!

2 They tell me God the Son came down
From His bright throne to die,
That I might wear a starry crown,
And dwell with Him on high.

3 They say He bore the cross for me,
And suffered in my place,
That I might always happy be,
And ransomed by His grace.

4 Oh, wondrous love, so great, so vast,
So boundless, and so free!
Low at Thy feet my all I cast;
I covet only Thee.

156
C.M.

1 THERE is a green hill far away,
Without a city wall,
Where the dear Lord was crucified,
Who died to save us all.

55

The Lord Jesus Christ

2 We may not know, we cannot tell,
   What pains He had to bear;
   But we believe it was for us
   He hung and suffered there.

3 He died that we might be forgiven,
   He died to make us good,
   That we might go at last to heaven,
   Saved by His precious blood.

4 There was no other good enough
   To pay the price of sin,
   He only could unlock the gate
   Of heaven, and let us in.

5 Oh, dearly, dearly has He loved!
   And we must love Him too,
   And trust in His redeeming blood,
   And try His works to do.

Note.—When the second tune (C.M.D.) is used, verse 5 forms second half of first double verse.

157 S.M.

1 BEHOLD the amazing sight!
   The Saviour lifted high;
   The Son of God, His soul's delight,
   Expires in agony.

2 For whom, for whom, my heart,
   Were all those sorrows borne?
   Why did He feel that piercing smart,
   And wear that crown of thorn?

3 For us in love He bled,
   For us in anguish died;
   'Twas love that bowed His sacred head,
   And pierced His precious side.

4 We see, and we adore,
   We trust that dying love;
   We feel its strong attractive power
   To lift our souls above.

5 Behold the amazing sight!
   Nor trace His griefs alone,
   But from the cross pursue our flight
   To His triumphant throne.

158 8.7.8.7.

1 I WILL sing the wondrous story
   Of the Christ who died for me;
   How He left His home in glory
   For the cross on Calvary.

   Yes, I'll sing the wondrous story
   Of the Christ who died for me;
   Sing it with the saints in glory,
   Gathered by the crystal sea.

2 I was lost: but Jesus found me—
   Found the sheep that went astray;
   Threw His loving arms around me,
   Drew me back into His way.

3 I was bruised: but Jesus healed me—
   Faint was I from many a fall;
   Sight was gone, and fears possessed me:
   But He freed me from them all.

4 Days of darkness still come o'er me;
   Sorrow's paths I often tread:
   But the Saviour still is with me,
   By His hand I'm safely led.

5 He will keep me till the river
   Rolls its waters at my feet:
   Then He'll bear me safely over,
   Where the loved ones I shall meet.

159 C.M.

1 WHEN God of old the way of life
   Would teach to all His own,
   He placed them safe beyond the reach
   Of death, by blood alone.

   It is His word, God's precious word,
   It stands for ever true:
   "When I the Lord shall see the blood,
   I will pass over you."

2 By Christ, the sinless Lamb of God,
   The precious blood was shed,
   When He fulfilled God's holy word,
   And suffered in our stead.

3 O soul, for thee salvation thus
   By God is freely given;
   The blood of Christ atones for sin,
   And makes us meet for heaven.

56

4 The wrath of God that was our due
   Upon the Lamb was laid;
  And by the shedding of His blood
   The debt for us was paid.

5 How calm the judgment hour shall pass
   To all who do obey
  The word of God, and trust the blood,
   And make that word their stay!

160   6.5.6.5.D.

1 SHEEP without a shepherd,
   We have gone astray,
  Turning in our blindness
   Each to his own way;
  But upon His Servant
   God in grace has laid
  All our guilt and trespass,
   Who the debt has paid.

2 Yet when we beheld Him
   Beauty was there none,
  That we should desire Him
   Or His title own;
  We esteemed Him stricken,
   Smitten of His God,
  Man of grief and sorrows,
   Bruised beneath the rod.

3 'Twas for our transgressions
   He was wounded sore,
  And for our iniquities
   He the bruising bore;
  By the bitter scourging
   He secured our peace,
  By His stripes so many
   Brought us sweet release.

4 Of the generation
   Living in His day
  Who could tell the mystery,
   Or believing say:
  "For His people's trespass
   He has suffered thus,
  And His bitter portion
   Was to ransom us."

5 As a lamb He suffered,
   To the slaughter brought,
  "Sheep before her shearers,"
   Dumb, He answered not;
  Of His soul's deep travail
   He the fruit shall see,
  And in many thousands
   Satisfied shall be.

161   P.M.

1 GIVE me a sight, O Saviour,
  Of Thy wondrous love to me,
  Of the love that brought Thee down to
   earth,
   To die on Calvary.

    Oh, make me understand it,
     Help me to take it in,
    What it meant to Thee, the Holy
     One,
    To bear away my sin.

2 Was it the nails, O Saviour,
   That bound Thee to the tree?
  Nay, 'twas Thine everlasting love,
   Thy love for me, for me.

3 Oh, wonder of all wonders,
   That through Thy death for me,
  My open sins, my secret sins,
   Can all forgiven be!

4 Then melt my heart, O Saviour,
   Bend me, yes, break me down,
  Until I own Thee Conqueror,
   And Lord and Sovereign crown.

162   P.M.

1 DEAR to the heart of the Shepherd,
   Dear are the sheep of His fold;
  Dear is the love that He gives them;
   Dearer than silver or gold.
  Dear to the heart of the Shepherd,
   Dear are His "other" lost sheep;
  Over the mountains He follows,
   Over the waters so deep.

    Out in the desert they wander,
     Hungry and helpless and cold;
    Oft to the rescue He hastens,
     Bringing them back to the fold.

2 Dear to the heart of the Shepherd,
   Dear are the lambs of His fold;
  Some from the pastures are straying,
   Hungry and helpless and cold.
  See, the Good Shepherd is seeking,
   Seeking the lambs that are lost;
  Bringing them in with rejoicing,
   Saved at such infinite cost.

    Out in the desert, etc.

57

3 Dear to the heart of the Shepherd,
  Dear are the "ninety and nine,"
Dear are the sheep that have wandered
  Out in the desert to pine.
Hark! He is earnestly calling,
  Tenderly pleading today;
"Will you not seek for My lost ones,
  Far from My shelter astray?"

    Out in the desert, etc.

4 Green are the pastures inviting,
  Sweet are the waters and still;
Lord, we will answer Thee gladly,
  "Yes, blessed Master, we will!
Make us Thy true under-shepherds,
  Give us a love that is deep,
Send us out into the desert,
  Seeking Thy wandering sheep."

    Out in the desert they wander,
      Hungry and helpless and cold;
    Oft to the rescue we'll hasten,
      Bringing them back to the fold.

163   C.M.

1 GOD loved the world of sinners lost
  And ruined by the Fall;
Salvation full, at highest cost,
  He offers free to all.

    Oh, 'twas love, 'twas wondrous
        love!
      The love of God to me;
    It brought my Saviour from above
      To die on Calvary.

2 E'en now by faith I claim Him mine,
  The risen Son of God;
Redemption by His death I find,
  And cleansing through the blood.

3 Believing ones, rejoicing go;
  There shall to you be given
A glorious foretaste, here below,
  Of endless life in heaven.

4 Of victory now o'er Satan's power
  Let all the ransomed sing,
And triumph, in the dying hour,
  Through Christ the Lord, our King.

164   8.7.8.7.4.7.

1 HARK! the voice of love and mercy
  Sounds aloud from Calvary;
See! it rends the rocks asunder,
  Shakes the earth, and veils the sky:
      "It is finished!"
  Hear the dying Saviour cry.

2 "It is finished!" Oh, what pleasure
  Do the wondrous words afford!
Heavenly blessings without measure
  Flow to us through Christ the Lord:
      "It is finished!"
  Saints the dying words record!

3 Finished all the types and shadows
  Of the ceremonial law,
Finished what our God had promised;
  Death and hell no more shall awe.
      "It is finished!"
  Saints, from hence your comfort
    draw.

4 Saints and angels shout His praises!
  Children, join to sing the same!
All on earth and all in heaven
  Join to praise Immanuel's Name!
      Hallelujah!
  Endless glory to the Lamb!

The Lord Jesus Christ: (4) His Resurrection and Ascension

165   8.8.8.4.

1 HALLELUJAH! Hallelujah! Hallelujah!
  The strife is o'er, the battle done;
  The victory of life is won;
  The song of triumph has begun.
      Hallelujah!

2 The powers of death have done their
      worst,
  But Christ their legions hath dispersed;
  Let shouts of holy joy outburst.
      Hallelujah!

The three sad days have quickly sped:
He rises glorious from the dead;
All glory to our risen Head!
Hallelujah!

He brake the bonds of death and hell;
The bars from heaven's high portals
fell;
Let hymns of praise His triumph tell.
Hallelujah!

Lord, by the stripes which wounded
Thee,
From death's dread sting Thy servants
free,
That we may live, and sing to Thee—
Hallelujah!

166 P.M.

1 Low in the grave He lay—
Jesus, my Saviour!
Waiting the coming day—
Jesus, my Lord!

Up from the grave He arose,
With a mighty triumph o'er His
foes;
He arose a Victor from the dark
domain,
And He lives for ever with His
saints to reign!
He arose! He arose!
Hallelujah! Christ arose!

2 Vainly they watch His bed—
Jesus, my Saviour!
Vainly they seal the dead—
Jesus, my Lord!

3 Death cannot keep his prey—
Jesus, my Saviour!
He tore the bars away—
Jesus, my Lord!

167 7.8.7.8.4.

1 JESUS lives! Thy terrors now
Can, O Death, no more appal us;
Jesus lives! by this we know
Thou, O Grave, canst not enthral us.
Hallelujah!

2 Jesus lives! henceforth is death
But the gate of life immortal;
This shall calm our trembling breath
When we pass its gloomy portal.
Hallelujah!

3 Jesus lives! for us He died;
Then, alone to Jesus living,
Pure in heart may we abide,
Glory to our Saviour giving.
Hallelujah!

4 Jesus lives! our hearts know well
Naught from us His love shall sever;
Life, nor death, nor powers of hell
Tear us from His keeping ever.
Hallelujah!

5 Jesus lives! to Him the throne
Over all the world is given;
May we go where He is gone,
Rest and reign with Him in heaven.
Hallelujah!

168 L.M.

1 I KNOW that my Redeemer lives:
What comfort this sweet sentence
gives!
He lives, He lives, who once was dead;
He lives, my everlasting Head.

2 He lives, triumphant from the grave;
He lives, eternally to save;
He lives, all-glorious in the sky;
He lives, exalted there on high.

3 He lives to bless me with His love,
And still He pleads for me above;
He lives to raise me from the grave
And me eternally to save.

4 He lives, my kind, wise, constant
Friend;
Who still will keep me to the end;
He lives, and while He lives I'll sing,
Jesus, my Prophet, Priest, and King.

5 He lives my mansion to prepare;
And He will bring me safely there;
He lives, all glory to His Name!
Jesus, unchangeably the same!

169   7.7.7.7.

1 CHRIST, the Lord, is risen today:
    Hallelujah!
Sons of men and angels say,
    Hallelujah!
Raise your joys and triumphs high;
    Hallelujah!
Sing, ye heavens; thou earth, reply,
    Hallelujah!

2 Love's redeeming work is done;
Fought the fight, the battle won:
Lo! our Sun's eclipse is o'er;
Lo! He sets in blood no more.

3 Vain the stone, the watch, the seal,
Christ hath burst the gates of hell:
Death in vain forbids Him rise!
Christ hath opened paradise.

4 Lives again our glorious King!
Where, O death, is now thy sting?
Once He died our souls to save;
Where thy victory, O grave?

5 Soar we now where Christ hath led,
Following our exalted Head:
Made like Him, like Him we rise,
Ours the cross, the grave, the skies.

6 Hail the Lord of earth and heaven,
Praise to Thee by both be given;
Thee we greet triumphant now,
Hail, the Resurrection Thou!

170   7.7.7.7.

1 JESUS CHRIST is risen today,
    Hallelujah!
Our triumphant holy day,
    Hallelujah!
Who did once, upon the cross,
    Hallelujah!
Suffer to redeem our loss.
    Hallelujah!

2 Hymns of praise then let us sing
Unto Christ, our heavenly King,
Who endured the cross and grave,
Sinners to redeem and save.

3 But the pains which He endured
Our salvation have procured;
Now above the sky He's King,
Where the angels ever sing.

171   7.7.7.7.7.4.

1 CHRIST the Lord is risen again;
Christ hath broken every chain;
Hark! angelic voices cry,
Singing evermore on high,
    Hallelujah!

2 He who gave for us His life,
Who for us endured the strife,
Is our Paschal Lamb today;
We too sing for joy, and say
    Hallelujah!

3 He who bore all pain and loss
Comfortless upon the cross,
Lives in glory now on high,
Pleads for us, and hears our cry.
    Hallelujah!

4 He who slumbered in the grave,
Is exalted now to save:
Now through Christendom it rings
That the Lamb is King of kings.
    Hallelujah!

5 Now He bids us tell abroad
How the lost may be restored,
How the penitent forgiven,
How we too may enter heaven.
    Hallelujah!

6 Thou, our Paschal Lamb indeed,
Christ, Thy ransomed people feed:
Take our sins and guilt away,
That we all may sing for aye
    Hallelujah!

172   11s, with refrain.

1 "WELCOME, happy morning!" age to
    age shall say;
Hell today is vanquished; Heaven is
    won today!
Lo! the Dead is living, God for ever-
    more!
Him, their true Creator, all His works
    adore.
  "Welcome, happy morning!" age to
    age shall say.

2 Earth with joy confesses, clothing her
    for spring,
All good gifts returned with her return-
    ing King:
Bloom in every meadow, leaves on
    every bough
Speak His sorrows ended, hail His
    triumph now.
        Hell today is vanquished; heaven is
        won today!

3 Months in due succession, days of
    lengthening light,
Hours and passing moments praise
    Thee in their flight;
Brightness of the morning, sky and
    fields and sea,
Vanquisher of darkness, bring their
    praise to Thee.
        "Welcome, happy morning!" age to
        age shall say.

4 Maker and Redeemer, Life and Health
    of all,
Thou from heaven beholding human
    nature's fall,
Of the Father's Godhead true and only
    Son,
Manhood to deliver, manhood didst put
    on.
        Hell today is vanquished; Heaven is
        won today!

5 Thou, of Life the Author, death didst
    undergo,
Tread the path of darkness, saving
    strength to show:
Come, then, True and Faithful, now
    fulfil Thy word;
'Tis Thine own third morning! Rise,
    O buried Lord!
        "Welcome, happy morning!" age to
        age shall say.

6 Loose the souls long prisoned, bound
    with Satan's chain;
All that now is fallen raise to life again;
Show Thy face in brightness, bid the
    nations see;
Bring again our daylight: day returns
    with Thee!
        Hell today is vanquished; Heaven is
        won today!

173   C.M.

1 THE head that once was crowned with
    thorns
    Is crowned with glory now;
A royal diadem adorns
    The mighty Victor's brow.

2 The highest place that heaven affords
    Is His by sovereign right,
The King of kings, the Lord of lords,
    And heaven's eternal Light.

3 The joy of all who dwell above,
    The joy of all below,
To whom He manifests His love,
    And grants His Name to know.

4 To them the cross, with all its shame,
    With all its grace, is given;
Their name an everlasting name,
    Their joy the joy of heaven.

5 They suffer with their Lord below,
    They reign with Him above;
Their profit and their joy to know
    The mystery of His love.

6 The cross He bore is life and health,
    Though shame and death to Him:
His people's hope, His people's wealth,
    Their everlasting theme.

174   6.5.6.5.D.

1 GOLDEN harps are sounding,
    Angel voices sing,
Pearly gates are opened,
    Opened for the King;
Christ, the King of glory,
    Jesus, King of love,
Is gone up in triumph
    To His throne above.

        All His work is ended;
            Joyfully we sing—
        Jesus has ascended!
            Glory to our King!

2 He, who came to save us,
    He, who bled and died,
Now is crowned with glory
    At His Father's side;

Never more to suffer,
Never more to die,
Jesus, King of Glory,
Has gone up on high!

3 Praying for His children,
In that blessèd place;
Calling them to glory,
Sending them His grace;
His bright home preparing,
Faithful ones, for you;
Jesus ever liveth,
Ever loveth too.

175　　　　8.7.8.7.4.7.

1 LOOK, ye saints, the sight is glorious,
See the "Man of Sorrows" now
From the fight return victorious:
Every knee to Him shall bow!
Crown Him! crown Him!
Crowns become the Victor's brow.

2 Crown the Saviour! angels, crown Him
Rich the trophies Jesus brings;
In the seat of power enthrone Him,
While the vault of heaven rings!
Crown Him! crown Him!
Crown the Saviour "King of kings."

3 Sinners in derision crown Him,
Mocking thus the Saviour's claim;
Saints and angels crowd around Him,
Own His title, praise His Name.
Crown Him! crown Him!
Spread abroad the Victor's fame.

4 Hark, the bursts of acclamation!
Hark, those loud triumphant chords!
Jesus takes the highest station—
Oh, what joy the sight affords!
Crown Him! crown Him!
"King of kings, and Lord of lords!"

The Lord Jesus Christ: (5) His Second Coming

176　　　　P.M.

1 THOU art coming, O my Saviour,
Thou art coming, O my King,
In Thy beauty all-resplendent,
In Thy glory all-transcendent;
Well may we rejoice and sing:
Coming! In the opening east
Herald brightness slowly swells;
Coming! O my glorious Priest,
Hear we not Thy golden bells?

2 Thou art coming, Thou art coming:
We shall meet Thee on Thy way,
We shall see Thee, we shall know Thee,
We shall bless Thee, we shall show Thee
All our hearts could never say:
What an anthem that will be,
Ringing out our love to Thee,
Pouring out our rapture sweet
At Thine own all-glorious feet!

3 Thou art coming; we are waiting
With a hope that cannot fail,
Asking not the day or hour,
Resting on Thy word of power,
Anchored safe within the veil.
Time appointed may be long,

But the vision must be sure;
Certainty shall make us strong,
Joyful patience can endure.

4 Oh, the joy to see Thee reigning,
Thee, my own belovèd Lord!
Every tongue Thy Name confessing,
Worship, honour, glory, blessing,
Brought to Thee with one accord;
Thee, my Master and my Friend,
Vindicated and enthroned,
Unto earth's remotest end
Glorified, adored, and owned!

177　　　　P.M.

1 IT may be at morn, when the day is
awaking,
When sunlight through darkness and
shadow is breaking,
That Jesus will come in the fulness of
glory,
To receive from the world "His own."

Oh, Lord Jesus, how long?
How long ere we shout the glad
song?—
Christ returneth, Hallelujah!
Hallelujah! Amen.
Hallelujah! Amen.

2 It may be at midday, it may be at twi-
      light,
   It may be, perchance, that the black-
      ness of midnight
   Will burst into light in the blaze of His
      glory,
   When Jesus receives "His own."

3 While hosts cry "Hosanna!" from
      heaven descending,
   With glorified saints and the angels
      attending,
   With grace on His brow, like a halo of
      glory,
   Will Jesus receive "His own."

4 Oh, joy! Oh, delight! should we go
      without dying;
   No sickness, no sadness, no dread, and
      no crying;
   Caught up through the clouds with our
      Lord into glory,
   When Jesus receives "His own."

178   P.M.
1 THEY come and go, the seasons fair,
      And bring their spoil to vale and
      hills;
   But oh, there is waiting in the air,
      And a passionate hope the spirit
      fills.
   Why doth He tarry, the absent Lord?
   When shall the Kingdom be restored,
   And earth and heaven with one accord
      Ring out the cry that the King
      comes?

            What will it be when the King
               comes!
            What will it be when the King
               comes!
               What will it be when He
                  comes! . . .
            What will it be when the King
               comes!

2 The floods have lifted up their voice:
      The King hath come to His own, His
      own!
   The little hills and vales rejoice;
      His right it is to take the crown.

Sleepers awake, and meet Him first!
Now let the marriage-hymn outburst!
And powers of darkness flee, dispersed:
   What will it be when the King
      comes!

3 A ransomed earth breaks forth in song,
      Her sin-stained ages overpast,
   Her yearning "Lord, how long, how
      long?"
   Exchanged for joy, at last, at last!
Angels carry the royal commands;
Peace beams forth throughout all the
   lands;
The trees of the field shall clap their
   hands:
   What will it be when the King
      comes!

4 O brothers, stand as men that wait:
      The dawn is purpling in the east,
   And banners wave from heaven's high
      gate;
      The conflict now, but soon the feast!
Mercy and truth shall meet again;
Worthy the Lamb that once was slain!
We can suffer now, He will know us
   then:
   What will it be when the King
      comes!

179   8.7.8.7.4.4.4.7.
1 Lo! He comes with clouds descending,
      Once for favoured sinners slain;
   Thousand thousand saints attending
      Swell the triumph of His train.
         Hallelujah!
      Christ appears on earth to reign.

2 Every eye shall now behold Him
      Robed in dreadful majesty;
   Those who set at naught and sold Him,
      Pierced and nailed Him to the tree,
         Deeply wailing,
      Shall the true Messiah see.

3 Now redemption, long expected,
      See in solemn pomp appear!
   All His saints, by man rejected,
      Now shall meet Him in the air.
         Hallelujah!
      See the day of God appear.

63

4 Yea, Amen, let all adore Thee,
  High on Thine eternal throne;
Saviour, take the power and glory,
  Claim the kingdoms for Thine own.
    Hallelujah!
Hallelujah! Come, Lord, come!

180   P.M.

1 OUR Lord is now rejected,
    And by the world disowned,
By the many still neglected,
    And by the few enthroned;
But soon He'll come in glory!
  The hour is drawing nigh,
For the crowning day is coming
    By-and-by.

    Oh, the crowning day is coming!
      Is coming by-and-by!
    When our Lord shall come in
      power
      And glory from on high!
    Oh, the glorious sight will gladden
      Each waiting, watchful eye,
    In the crowning day that's coming
        By-and-by!

2 The heavens shall glow with splendour;
    But brighter far than they,
The saints shall shine in glory,
    As Christ shall them array;
The beauty of the Saviour
  Shall dazzle every eye,
In the crowning day that's coming
    By-and-by.

3 Our pain shall then be over,
    We'll sin and sigh no more,
Behind us all of sorrow,
    And naught but joy before:
A joy in our Redeemer,
  As we to Him are nigh,
In the crowning day that's coming
    By-and-by.

4 Let all that look for hasten
    The coming joyful day,
By earnest consecration
    To walk the narrow way;
By gathering in the lost ones,
  For whom our Lord did die,
For the crowning day that's coming
    By-and-by.

181   7.7.7.7.7.7.

1 "TILL He come!" Oh, let the words
  Linger on the trembling chords;
Let the little while between
  In their golden light be seen;
Let us think how heaven and home
Lie beyond that "Till He come!"

2 When the weary ones we love
Enter on their rest above,
Seems the world so poor and vast?
All our life-joy overcast?
Hush! be every murmur dumb,
It is only till He come!

3 Clouds and darkness round us press!
Would we have one sorrow less?
All the sharpness of the cross,
All that tells the world is loss,
Death, and darkness, and the tomb,
Only whisper, "Till He come."

4 See, the feast of love is spread,
Drink the wine and break the bread:
Sweet memorials—till the Lord
Call us round His heavenly board;
Some from earth, from glory some,
Severed only till He come.

182   P.M.

1 JESUS is coming! sing the glad word!
  Coming for those He redeemed by His
    blood,
  Coming to reign as the glorified Lord!
    Jesus is coming again!

      Jesus is coming, is coming
        again!
      Jesus is coming again!
      Oh, shout the glad tidings o'er
        mountain and plain!
      Jesus is coming again!

2 Jesus is coming! the dead shall arise,
  Loved ones shall meet in a joyful sur-
    prise,
  Caught up together to Him in the skies:
    Jesus is coming again!

Jesus is coming! His saints to release;
Coming to give to the warring earth
        peace!
Sinning and sighing and sorrow shall
        cease:
    Jesus is coming again!

4 Jesus is coming! the promise is true:
Who are the chosen, the faithful, the
        few,
Waiting and watching, prepared for re-
        view?
    Jesus is coming again!

The Work of the Holy Spirit

183   C.M.

1 COME, Holy Ghost, our hearts inspire;
Let us Thine influence prove,
Source of the old prophetic fire,
Fountain of light and love.

2 Come, Holy Ghost, for moved by Thee
The prophets wrote and spoke;
Unlock the truth, Thyself the key,
Unseal the sacred Book.

3 Expand Thy wings, celestial Dove,
Brood o'er our nature's night;
On our disordered spirits move,
And let there now be light.

4 God, through Himself, we then shall
        know
If Thou within us shine,
And sound, with all Thy saints below,
The depths of love divine.

184   6.5.6.5.

1 HOLY Spirit, hear us;
    Help us while we sing;
Breathe into the music
    Of the praise we bring.

2 Holy Spirit, prompt us
    When we kneel to pray;
Nearer come and teach us
    What we ought to say.

3 Holy Spirit, shine Thou
    On the Book we read;
Gild its holy pages
    With the light we need.

4 Holy Spirit, give us
    Each a lowly mind:
Make us more like Jesus,
    Gentle, pure, and kind.

5 Holy Spirit, help us
    Daily by Thy might,
What is wrong to conquer,
    And to choose the right.

Copyright. By permission of the National Sunday School Union.

185   7.7.7.7.7.7.

1 GRACIOUS Spirit, dwell with me!
I myself would gracious be,
And with words that help and heal
Would Thy life in mine reveal;
And with actions bold and meek
Would for Christ, my Saviour, speak.

2 Truthful Spirit, dwell with me!
I myself would truthful be,
And with wisdom kind and clear
Let Thy life in mine appear;
And with actions brotherly
Speak my Lord's sincerity.

3 Tender Spirit, dwell with me!
I myself would tender be;
Shut my heart up like a flower
In temptation's darksome hour;
Open it when shines the sun,
And His love by fragrance own.

4 Mighty Spirit, dwell with me!
I myself would mighty be,
Mighty so as to prevail
Where unaided man must fail,
Ever by a mighty hope
Pressing on and bearing up.

5 Holy Spirit, dwell with me!
I myself would holy be;
Separate from sin, I would
Choose and cherish all things good;
And whatever I can be
Give to Him who gave me Thee.

186 S.M.

1 O HOLY Spirit, come,
And Jesus' love declare;
Oh, tell us of our heavenly home
And guide us safely there!

2 Our unbelief remove
By Thine almighty breath;
Oh, work the wondrous work of love,
The mighty work of faith!

3 Come, with resistless power;
Come, with almighty grace;
Come, with the long-expected shower,
And fall upon this place!

187 8.6.8.4.

1 OUR blest Redeemer, ere He breathed
His tender last farewell,
A Guide, a Comforter, bequeathed,
With us to dwell.

2 He came in semblance of a dove,
With sheltering wings outspread,
The holy balm of peace and love
On earth to shed.

3 He came in tongues of living flame
To teach, convince, subdue;
All-powerful as the wind He came—
As viewless too.

4 He comes sweet influence to impart,
A gracious, willing Guest,
Where He can find one humble heart
Wherein to rest.

5 And His that gentle voice we hear,
Soft as the breath of even,
That checks each fault, that calms each
fear,
And speaks of heaven.

6 For every virtue we possess,
And every victory won,
And every thought of holiness,
Are His alone.

7 Spirit of purity and grace,
Our weakness, pitying, see;
Oh make our hearts Thy dwelling-
place,
And worthier Thee.

188 S.M

1 BREATHE on me, Breath of God,
Fill me with life anew,
That I may love what Thou dost love
And do what Thou wouldst do.

2 Breathe on me, Breath of God,
Until my heart is pure;
Until my will is one with Thine
To do and to endure.

3 Breathe on me, Breath of God
Till I am wholly Thine;
Until this earthly part of me
Glows with Thy fire divine.

4 Breathe on me, Breath of God,
So shall I never die,
But live with Thee the perfect life
Of Thine eternity.

189 L.M

1 COME, gracious Spirit, heavenly Dove,
With light and comfort from above;
Be Thou our Guardian, Thou our Guide,
O'er every thought and step preside.

2 Conduct us safe, conduct us far
From every sin and hurtful snare;
Lead to Thy Word, which rules must
give,
And teach us lessons how to live.

3 The light of truth to us display,
And make us know and choose Thy
way;
Plant holy fear in every heart,
That we from God may ne'er depart.

4 Lead us to holiness, the road
That we must take to dwell with God;
Lead us to Christ, the living Way,
Nor let us from His pastures stray.

5 Lead us to God, our final rest,
To be with Him for ever blest;
Lead us to heaven, that we may share
Fulness of joy for ever there.

190 L.M.

1 O HOLY Dove, on wings divine,
In all Thy tender might descend:
In these dark hearts irradiant shine,
With saving light our path attend.

2 Into all truth and wisdom's ways
 Guide Thou, and every fear dispel:
Spirit Divine, throughout the days
 Direct our steps, and with us dwell.

3 From all the weight of sin's alloy
 Now set us free, blest Paraclete:
Fill every heart with purest joy,
 For Christ's employ may we be meet.

4 In trouble's hour as sorrows come,
 Blest Comforter, Thy voice be heard,
And when in sorest grief we're dumb,
 Breathe Thou within the healing
  word.

5 Oh, take our faulty lives so frail,
 And 'neath the glow of Thy pure
  sway
May we in faith's stern fight prevail,
 And to the world Thy power display.

191   C.M.

1 SPIRIT Divine, attend our prayers
 And make this house Thy home;
Descend with all Thy gracious powers,
 Oh, come, Great Spirit, come!

2 Come as the Light: to us reveal
 Our emptiness and woe;
And lead us in those paths of life
 Where all the righteous go.

3 Come as the Fire, and purge our hearts
 Like sacrificial flame;
Let our whole soul an offering be
 To our Redeemer's Name.

4 Come as the Dew, and sweetly bless
 This consecrated hour;
May barrenness rejoice to own
 Thy fertilizing power.

5 Come as the Dove, and spread Thy
  wings,
 The wings of perfect love;
And let Thy church on earth become
 Blest as the church above.

6 Spirit Divine, attend our prayers;
 Make a lost world Thy home;
Descend with all Thy gracious powers,
 Oh, come, Great Spirit, come!

Gospel Hymns

192   7.7.7.7.

SINNERS Jesus will receive;
 Sound this word of grace to all
Who the heavenly pathway leave,
 All who linger, all who fall!

    Sing it o'er ... and o'er again; ...
     Christ receiveth sinful men; ...
    Make the mess- ... age clear
     and plain: ...
    Christ receiveth sinful men.

2 Come: and He will give you rest;
 Trust Him: for His word is plain;
He will take the sinfulest:
 Christ receiveth sinful men.

3 Now my heart condemns me not,
 Pure before the law I stand;
He who cleansed me from all spot,
 Satisfied its last demand.

4 Christ receiveth sinful men,
 Even me with all my sin;
Purged from every spot and stain,
 Heaven with Him I enter in.

193   P.M.

1 DOWN from the splendour of His everlasting throne
Came the Lord of glory, for our guilt to
  atone;
Son of God eternal, He the sinner's
  surety stood,
Paid the sinner's ransom in His
  precious blood.

    Glory, glory, glory unto Jesus!
     Anyone, everyone He can
      fully save.
    Glory, glory, glory unto Jesus!
     Hallelujah! All who trust
      Him He will save.

67

2 Over death triumphant He is risen
   from the grave;
  Back to heaven ascended, Jesus now
   lives to save.
  Nothing else remaineth but salvation
   to receive,
  When with true repentance you on Him
   believe.

3 Come today to Jesus, do not longer stay
   away;
  Come and take salvation, come to
   Christ, while you may;
  Heavenly voices call you, and the
   Saviour waits to bless:
  Come to Him believing, and His Name
   confess.

194   7.6.7.6.D.

1 "COME unto Me, ye weary,
   And I will give you rest:"
  Oh, blessed voice of Jesus,
   Which comes to hearts oppressed!
  It tells of benediction,
   Of pardon, grace, and peace,
  Of joy that hath no ending,
   Of love which cannot cease.

2 "Come unto Me, ye wanderers,
   And I will give you light:"
  Oh, loving voice of Jesus,
   Which comes to cheer the night!
  Our hearts were filled with sadness,
   And we had lost our way;
  But morning brings us gladness,
   And songs the break of day.

3 "And whosoever cometh,
   I will not cast him out:"
  Oh, welcome voice of Jesus,
   Which drives away our doubt,
  Which calls us very sinners,
   Unworthy though we be
  Of love so free and boundless,
   To come, dear Lord, to Thee!

195   P.M.

1 GOD is now willing, in Christ reconciled,
  Willing to pardon and cleanse the
   defiled,

Willing to take you and make you His
   child;
  God is now willing: are you?

    God is now willing: are you? are
     you?
     Will you not trust Him, so
      faithful, so true?
     If you refuse Him, oh, what will
      you do?
     God is now willing: are you?

2 God is now willing to give you His
   peace,
  Willing from bondage of sin to release,
  Willing the conflict within you should
   cease;
  God is now willing: are you?

3 God is now willing to answer your
   prayer,
  Perfectly willing your burden to bear,
  Ready and waiting to take all your
   care;
  God is now willing: are you?

4 God is now willing within you to dwell,
  Willing with blessing your spirit to fill;
  Yield to His pleading and give up your
   will;
  God is now willing: are you?

196   6.5.6.5.D.

1 JESUS, I *will* trust Thee,
   Trust Thee with my soul;
  Guilty, lost, and helpless,
   Thou canst make me whole.
  There is none in heaven
   Or on earth like Thee:
  Thou hast died for sinners—
   Therefore, Lord, for me.

    Jesus, I will trust Thee,
     Trust Thee with my soul;
    Guilty, lost, and helpless,
     Thou canst make me whole.

2 Jesus, I *must* trust Thee,
   Pondering Thy ways,
  Full of love and mercy
   All Thine earthly days;
  Sinners gathered round Thee
   Lepers sought Thy face:
  None too vile or loathsome
   For a Saviour's grace.

3 Jesus, I *can* trust Thee,
   Trust Thy written Word,
Though Thy voice of pity
   I have never heard;
When Thy Spirit teacheth,
   To my taste how sweet!
Only may I hearken,
   Sitting at Thy feet.

4 Jesus, I *do* trust Thee,
   Trust without a doubt;
Whosoever cometh
   Thou wilt not cast out.
Faithful is Thy promise,
   Precious is Thy blood:
These my soul's salvation,
   Thou my Saviour God!

197 C.M.

1 COME, every soul by sin oppressed,
   There's mercy with the Lord;
And He will surely give you rest
   By trusting in His Word.

      Only trust Him, only trust Him,
         Only trust Him now!
      He will save you, He will save you,
         He will save you now!

2 For Jesus shed His precious blood,
   Rich blessings to bestow;
Plunge now into the crimson flood
   That washes white as snow.

3 Yes, Jesus is the Truth, the Way
   That leads you into rest;
Believe in Him without delay,
   And you are fully blest.

4 Come then and join this holy band,
   And on to glory go,
To dwell in that celestial land
   Where joys immortal flow.

198 P.M.

1 BLESSÈD be the fountain of blood,
   To a world of sinners revealed;
Blessèd be the dear Son of God:
   Only by His stripes we are healed.

Though I've wandered far from His
   fold,
   Bringing to my heart pain and woe,
Wash me in the blood of the Lamb,
   And I shall be whiter than snow;

      Whiter than the snow!
      Whiter than the snow!
      Wash me in the blood of the
         Lamb!
      And I shall be whiter than snow!

2 Thorny was the crown that He wore
   On the cross, with scoffing and
      shame;
Grievous were the sorrows He bore,
   My eternal salvation to gain.
May I to that fountain be led,
   Opened for my sins here below;
Wash me in the blood that He shed,
   And I shall be whiter than snow!

3 Father, I have wandered from Thee,
   Often has my heart gone astray;
Crimson do my sins seem to me—
   Water cannot wash them away.
Jesus, to that fountain of Thine,
   Leaning on Thy promise, I go!
Cleanse me by Thy washing divine,
   And I shall be whiter than snow!

199 7.7.7.7.

1 DEPTH of mercy! can there be
Mercy still reserved for me?
Can my God His wrath forbear?
Me, the chief of sinners, spare?

2 I have long withstood His grace,
Long provoked Him to His face;
Would not hearken to His calls,
Grieved Him by a thousand falls.

3 Whence to me this waste of love?
Ask my Advocate above!
See the cause in Jesus' face,
Now before the throne of grace.

4 There for me the Saviour stands,
Shows His wounds, and spreads His
   hands;
God is love, I know, I feel;
Jesus weeps, and loves me still.

5 Jesus, answer from above;
  Is not all Thy nature love?
  Wilt Thou not the wrong forget?
  Suffer me to kiss Thy feet?

6 If I rightly read Thy heart,
  If Thou all compassion art,
  Bow Thine ear, in mercy bow,
  Pardon and accept me now!

200 P.M.

1 THE Gospel bells are ringing,
  Over land, from sea to sea;
  Blessèd news of free salvation
  Do they offer you and me.
  "For God so loved the world,
  That His only Son He gave!
  Whosoe'er believeth in Him
  Everlasting life shall have."

  Gospel bells! . . . how they ring, . . .
  Over land, from sea to sea;
  Gospel bells . . . freely bring . . .
  Blessèd news to you and me.

2 The Gospel bells invite us
  To a feast prepared for all:
  Do not slight the invitation,
  Nor reject the gracious call.
  "I am the Bread of life;
  Eat of Me, thou hungry soul;
  Though your sins be red as crimson,
  They shall be as white as wool."

3 The Gospel bells give warning,
  As they sound from day to day,
  Of the fate which doth await them
  Who for ever will delay.
  "Escape thou for thy life!
  Tarry not in all the plain;
  Nor behind thee look, oh, never,
  Lest thou be consumed in pain."

4 The Gospel bells are joyful
  As they echo far and wide,
  Bearing notes of perfect pardon
  Through a Saviour crucified:
  "Good tidings of great joy
  To all people do I bring;
  Unto you is born a Saviour,
  Which is Christ, the Lord and King."

201 P.M.

1 NOTHING either great or small—
  Nothing, sinner, no;
  Jesus did it, did it all,
  Long, long ago.

  "It is finished!" yes, indeed,
  Finished, every jot:
  Sinner, this is all you need—
  Tell me, is it not?

2 When He, from His lofty throne,
  Stooped to do and die,
  Everything was fully done:
  Hearken to His cry.

3 Weary, working, burdened one,
  Wherefore toil you so?
  Cease your doing: all was done
  Long, long ago.

4 Till to Jesus' work you cling
  By a simple faith,
  "Doing" is a deadly thing—
  "Doing" ends in death.

5 Cast your deadly "doing" down—
  Down at Jesus' feet;
  Stand in Him, in Him alone,
  Gloriously complete.

202 P.M.

1 THROW out the Life-line across the
    dark wave,
  There is a brother whom someone
    should save;
  Somebody's brother! oh, who then will
    dare
  To throw out the Life-line, his peril to
    share?

  Throw out the Life-line!
  Throw out the Life-line!
  Someone is drifting away.
  Throw out the Life-line!
  Throw out the Life-line!
  Someone is sinking today.

2 Throw out the Life-line with hand
    quick and strong:
  Why do you tarry, my brother, so
    long?
  See—he is sinking; oh, hasten today—
  And out with the Life-boat! away,
    then, away!

3 Throw out the Life-line to danger-
    fraught men,
Sinking in anguish where you've never
    been:
Winds of temptation and billows of
    woe
Will soon hurl them out where the dark
    waters flow.

4 Soon will the season of rescue be o'er,
Soon will they drift to eternity's shore;
Haste, then, my brother! no time for
    delay,
But throw out the Life-line, and save
    them today.

203   7.6.7.6.D.

1 I LAY my sins on Jesus,
    The spotless Lamb of God;
He bears them all, and frees us
    From the accursèd load.
I bring my guilt to Jesus,
    To wash my crimson stains
White in His blood most precious
    Till not a spot remains.

2 I bring my wants to Jesus,
    All fulness dwells in Him;
He heals all my diseases,
    He doth my soul redeem.
I lay my griefs on Jesus,
    My burdens and my cares;
He from them all releases,
    He all my sorrows shares.

3 I long to be like Jesus,
    Meek, loving, lowly, mild;
I long to be like Jesus,
    The Father's holy Child.
I long to be with Jesus,
    Amid the heavenly throng;
To sing with saints His praises,
    To learn the angels' song.

204   7.6.7.6.D.

1 TELL me the old, old story
    Of unseen things above,
Of Jesus and His glory,
    Of Jesus and His love:

Tell me the story simply,
    As to a little child,
For I am weak and weary,
    And helpless and defiled.

    Tell me the old, old story,
    Tell me the old, old story,
    Tell me the old, old story
      Of Jesus and His love.

2 Tell me the story slowly,
    That I may take it in—
That wonderful redemption,
    God's remedy for sin.
Tell me the story often,
    For I forget so soon;
The early dew of morning
    Has passed away at noon.

3 Tell me the story softly,
    With earnest tones and grave;
Remember! I'm the sinner
    Whom Jesus came to save.
Tell me that story always,
    If you would really be,
In any time of trouble,
    A comforter to me.

4 Tell me the same old story
    When you have cause to fear
That this world's empty glory
    Is costing me too dear.
Yes, and when *that* world's glory
    Is dawning on my soul,
Tell me the old, old story—
    "Christ Jesus makes thee whole."

205   P.M.

1 THE whole world was lost in the dark-
    ness of sin:
The Light of the world is Jesus;
Like sunshine at noonday His glory
    shone in:
The Light of the world is Jesus.

    Come to the Light, 'tis shining
      for thee;
    Sweetly the Light has dawned
      upon me;
    Once I was blind, but now I can
      see:
      The Light of the world is
      Jesus.

2 No darkness have we who in Jesus
    abide:
  The Light of the world is Jesus;
We walk in the light when we follow
    our Guide:
  The Light of the world is Jesus.

3 Ye dwellers in darkness, with sin-
    blinded eyes,
  The Light of the world is Jesus;
Go, wash at His bidding, and light will
    arise:
  The Light of the world is Jesus.

4 No need of the sunlight in heaven, we're
    told:
  The Light of that world is Jesus;
The Lamb is the Light in the City of
    Gold;
  The Light of that world is Jesus.

206   P.M.

1 I COULD not do without Him,
    Jesus is more to me
Than all the richest, fairest gifts
    Of earth could ever be.
But the more I find Him precious—
    And the more I find Him true—
The more I long for you to find
    What He can be to you.

2 You need not do without Him?
    For He is passing by,
He is waiting to be gracious,
    Only waiting for your cry;
He is waiting to receive you—
    To make you all His own:
Why will you do without Him,
    And wander on alone?

3 Why will you do without Him
    Is He not kind indeed?
Did He not die to save you?
    Is He not all you need?
Do you not want a Saviour?
    Do you not want a Friend,
One who will love you faithfully,
    And love you to the end?

4 You cannot do without Him,
    There is no other name
By which you ever can be saved,
    No way, no hope, no claim,

But with Him—all the empty hearts
    Filled with His perfect love;
With Jesus—perfect peace below,
    And perfect bliss above.

5 He would not do without you,
    He calls and calls again—
"Come unto Me! Come unto Me!"
    Oh, shall He call in vain?
He wants to have you with Him;
    Do you not want Him too?
You cannot do without Him,
    And He wants—even you.

207   P.M.

1 HAVE you been to Jesus for the clean-
    sing power?
  Are you washed in the blood of the
    Lamb?
Are you fully trusting in His grace this
    hour?
  Are you washed in the blood of the
    Lamb?

    Are you washed . . . in the blood,
    In the soul-cleansing blood of the
      Lamb?
    Are your garments spotless? Are
      they white as snow?
    Are you washed in the blood of the
      Lamb?

2 Are you walking daily by the Saviour's
    side?
  Are you washed in the blood of the
    Lamb?
Do you rest each moment in the Cruci-
    fied?
  Are you washed in the blood of the
    Lamb?

3 When the Bridegroom cometh, will
    your robes be white—
  Pure and white in the blood of the
    Lamb?
Will your soul be ready for the man-
    sions bright,
  And be washed in the blood of the
    Lamb?

4 Lay aside the garments that are stained
    with sin,
  And be washed in the blood of the
    Lamb!

There's a fountain flowing for the soul unclean—
Oh, be washed in the blood of the Lamb!

208 P.M.

1 A RULER once came to Jesus by night,
To ask Him the way of salvation and light:
The Master made answer in words true and plain,
"Ye must be born again!"

"Ye must be born again!"
"Ye must be born again!"
I verily, verily say unto thee,
"Ye must be born again!"

2 Ye children of men, attend to the word,
So solemnly uttered by Jesus the Lord;
And let not this message to you be in vain:
"Ye must be born again!"

3 O ye who would enter this glorious rest,
And sing with the ransomed the song of the blest;
The life everlasting if ye would obtain,
"Ye must be born again!"

4 A dear one in heaven thy heart yearns to see
At the beautiful gate may be watching for thee;
Then list to the note of this solemn refrain:
"Ye must be born again!"

209 P.M.

1 OH, what will you do with Jesus?
The call comes low and sweet,
And tenderly He bids you
Your burdens lay at His feet;
O soul, so sad and weary,
That sweet voice speaks to thee:
Then what will you do with Jesus?
Oh, what shall the answer be?

What shall the answer be?
What shall the answer be?
What will you do with Jesus?
Oh, what shall the answer be?

2 Oh, what will you do with Jesus?
The call comes loud and clear;
The solemn words are sounding
In every listening ear;
Eternal life's in the question,
And joy through eternity;
Then what will you do with Jesus?
Oh, what shall the answer be?

3 Oh, think of the King of glory,
From heaven to earth come down;
His life so pure and holy,
His death, His cross, His crown;
Of His divine compassion,
His sacrifice for thee;
Then what will you do with Jesus?
Oh, what shall the answer be?

210 P.M.

1 JESUS lingers still; 'tis for you He waits,
And He's waited for you long;
He waits that Heaven, with its fadeless joys,
May yet to you belong.

Come and wel- . . . come, who-soever will,
'Tis the Saviour's gracious call;
He is able, willing, waiting now to save,
Simply trust Him, that is all.

2 Though your wayward feet may have wandered far,
And you're deeply sunk in sin;
Yet the Saviour waits, with His patient grace,
Your stony heart to win.

3 Though His gracious call you have oft refused,
And He's sought your trust in vain;
Yet, with love unchanged by your cold neglect,
He is seeking you again.

4 Oh, surrender now! yield to love divine;
Jesus lingers for you still:
While in grace He says, "Oh, come to Me,"
Let your answer be, "I will."

211　　　　　　　　7.6.7.6.D.

1 O WORD, of words the sweetest,
　　O word, in which there lie
All promise, all fulfilment,
　　And end of mystery!
Lamenting or rejoicing,
　　With doubt or terror nigh,
I hear the "Come!" of Jesus,
　　And to His cross I fly.

　　　　"Come! oh, come to Me! . . .
　　　　Come! oh, come to Me! . . .
　　　　　　Weary, heavy-laden,
　　　　Come! oh, come to Me! . . ."

2 O soul! why should'st thou wander
　　From such a loving Friend?
Cling closer, closer to Him,
　　Stay with Him to the end:
Alas! I am so helpless,
　　So very full of sin,
For I am ever wandering,
　　And coming back again.

3 Oh, each time draw me nearer,
　　That soon the "Come" may be
Naught but a gentle whisper
　　To one so close to Thee;
Then, over sea and mountain,
　　Far from or near my home,
I'll take Thy hand and follow
　　At that sweet whisper, "Come!"

212　　　　　　　　11.11.11.11.

1 So near to the Kingdom! yet what dost
　　thou lack?
So near to the Kingdom! what keepeth
　　thee back?
Renounce every idol, though dear it
　　may be,
And come to the Saviour, now pleading
　　with thee!

　　　　Plead- . . . ing with thee! . . .
　　　　The Saviour is pleading!
　　　　Is pleading with thee!

2 So near, that thou hearest the strains
　　that resound
From those who, believing, a pardon
　　have found!

So near, yet unwilling to give up thy
　　sin,
When Jesus is waiting to welcome thee
　　in!

3 To die with no hope! hast thou counted
　　the cost—
To die out of Christ, and thy soul to be
　　lost?
So near to the Kingdom! oh, come, we
　　implore!
While Jesus is pleading, come, enter the
　　door!

213　　　　　　　　7.6.7.6.D.

1 TODAY Thy mercy calls us
　　To wash away our sin,
However great our trespass,
　　Whatever we have been:
However long from mercy
　　Our hearts have turned away,
Thy precious blood can cleanse us
　　And make us white today.

2 Today Thy gate is open,
　　And all who enter in
Shall find a Father's welcome,
　　And pardon for their sin.
The past shall be forgotten,
　　A present joy be given,
A future grace be promised,
　　A glorious crown in heaven.

3 Today our Father calls us;
　　His Holy Spirit waits;
The blessèd angels gather
　　Around the heavenly gates:
No question will be asked us
　　How often we have come;
Although we oft have wandered,
　　It is our Father's home!

4 Oh, all-embracing mercy!
　　Oh, ever-open door!
What should we do without thee
　　When heart and eye run o'er?
When all things seem against us,
　　To drive us to despair,
We know one gate is open,
　　One ear will hear our prayer!

214
6.4.6.4.6.6.4.

1 No; not despairingly
   Come I to Thee:
No; not distrustingly
   Bend I the knee.
Sin hath gone over me,
Yet is this still my plea,
   Jesus hath died.

2 Lord, I confess to Thee
   Sadly my sin;
All I am tell I Thee,
   All I have been.
Purge Thou my sin away,
Wash Thou my soul this day,
   Lord, make me clean.

3 Faithful and just art Thou,
   Forgiving all;
Low at Thy piercèd feet,
   Saviour, I fall:
Oh, let the cleansing blood,
Blood of the Lamb of God,
   Pass o'er my soul!

4 Then all is peace and light
   This soul within:
Thus shall I walk with Thee
   The Loved unseen,
Leaning on Thee, my God,
Guided along the road,
   Nothing between.

215
P.M.

1 KNOCKING, knocking, who is there?
Waiting, waiting, oh, how fair!
'Tis a Pilgrim, strange and kingly,
Never such was seen before;
Ah! my soul, for such a wonder
   Wilt thou not undo the door?

2 Knocking, knocking, still He's there;
Waiting, waiting, wondrous fair;
But the door is hard to open,
   For the weeds and ivy-vine,
With their dark and clinging tendrils,
   Ever round the hinges twine.

3 Knocking, knocking—what, still there!
Waiting, waiting, grand and fair:
Yes, the piercèd hand still knocketh,
   And beneath the crownèd hair
Beam the patient eyes, so tender,
   Of thy Saviour, waiting there.

4 Enter, enter, heavenly Guest,
Welcome, welcome to my breast.
I have long withstood Thy knocking,
   For my heart was full of sin;
But Thy love has overcome me:
   Blessèd Jesus, oh, come in!

216
8.7.8.7.

1 HAVE you any room for Jesus—
   He who bore your load of sin?
As He knocks and asks admission,
   Sinner, will you let Him in?

      Room for Jesus, King of glory!
      Hasten now, His word obey!
      Swing the heart's door widely
         open!
      Bid Him enter while you may!

2 Room for pleasure, room for business;
   But for Christ, the crucified,
Not a place that He can enter,
   In the heart for which He died!

3 Have you any time for Jesus,
   As in grace He calls again?
Oh, "TODAY" is "time accepted,"
   Tomorrow you may call in vain.

4 Room and time now give to Jesus;
   Soon will pass God's day of grace:
Soon thy heart be cold and silent,
   And thy Saviour's pleadings cease.

217
C.M.

1 THOU art the Way—to Thee alone
   From sin and death we flee;
And he who would the Father seek
   Must seek Him, Lord, by Thee.

2 Thou art the Truth—Thy Word alone
   True wisdom can impart;
Thou only canst inform the mind
   And purify the heart.

3 Thou art the Life—the rending tomb
   Proclaims Thy conquering arm;
And those who put their trust in Thee
   Nor death nor hell shall harm.

4 Thou art the Way, the Truth, the Life:
   Grant us that Way to know,
That Truth to keep, that Life to win
   Whose joys eternal flow.

218 P.M.

1 HARK! there comes a whisper
    Stealing on thine ear;
'Tis the Saviour calling,
    Soft, soft and clear:

    "Give thy heart to Me!
    Once I died for thee."
Hark! hark! thy Saviour calls,
Come, sinner, come!

2 With that voice so gentle,
    Dost thou hear Him say?—
"Tell Me all thy sorrows;
    Come, come away!"

3 Would'st thou find a refuge
    For thy soul oppressed?
Jesus kindly answers,
    "I am thy rest."

4 At the cross of Jesus
    Let thy burden fall,
While He gently whispers,
    "I'll bear it all."

219 L.M.

1 BEHOLD One standing at the door,
And hear Him pleading evermore
With gentle voice, O heart of sin,
"Let Me come in, let Me come in!"

    'Tis Jesus standing at the door,
    Oh, hear Him pleading evermore;
    Come, weary heart, oppressed with sin,
    Say, "Enter in, Lord, enter in!"

2 He bore the cruel thorns for thee,
Has waited long and patiently;
Say, weary heart, oppressed with sin,
Say, "Enter in, Lord, enter in!"

3 He brings thee joy from heaven above,
He brings thee pardon, peace, and love;
Say, weary heart, oppressed with sin,
Say, "Enter in, Lord, enter in!"

220 S.M.

1 How solemn are the words,
    And yet to faith how plain,
Which Jesus uttered while on earth—
    "Ye must be born again!"

2 "Ye must be born again,"
    And life in Christ must have;
In vain the soul may elsewhere go—
    'Tis He alone can save.

3 "Ye must be born again,"
    Or never enter heaven:
'Tis only blood-washed ones go there,
    The ransomed and forgiven.

4 "Ye must be born again!"
    Then look to Christ, and live;
He is "the Life," and waits in heaven
    Eternal life to give.

221 P.M.

1 COME to the Saviour, make no delay;
Here in His Word He has shown us the
    way;
Here in our midst He's standing today,
    Tenderly saying, "Come!"

    Joyful, joyful will the meeting be,
    When from sin our hearts are pure
        and free;
    And we shall gather, Saviour, with
        Thee,
    In our eternal home.

2 "Suffer the children"—oh! hear His
        voice,
Let every heart leap forth and rejoice,
And let us freely make Him our choice;
    Do not delay, but come.

3 Think once again, He's with us today;
Heed now His blest command and
        obey;
Hear now His accents tenderly say,
    "Will you, My children, come?"

222 P.M.

1 THERE were ninety and nine that safely
        lay
    In the shelter of the fold;
But one was out on the hills away,
    Far off from the gates of gold—
Away on the mountains wild and bare,
Away from the tender Shepherd's care.

"Lord, Thou hast here Thy ninety and
   nine,
   Are they not enough for Thee?"
But the Shepherd made answer, "This
   of Mine
   Has wandered away from Me;
And although the road be rough and
   steep,
I go to the desert to find My sheep."

But none of the ransomed ever knew
   How deep were the waters crossed,
Nor how dark was the night that the
   Lord passed through
   Ere He found His sheep that was lost.
Out in the desert He heard its cry,
Sick and helpless, and ready to die.

"Lord, whence are those blood-drops
   all the way,
   That mark out the mountain's
   track?"
"They were shed for one who had gone
   astray
   Ere the Shepherd could bring him
   back."
"Lord, whence are Thy hands so rent
   and torn?"
"They are pierced tonight by many a
   thorn."

But all through the mountains,
   thunder-riven,
   And up from the rocky steep
There arose a cry to the gate of heaven,
   "Rejoice! I have found My sheep!"
And the angels echoed around the
   throne,
"Rejoice, for the Lord brings back His
   own!"

223
6.5.6.5.D.

1 ONWARD, children, onward!
   Leave the paths of sin;
Hasten to the strait gate,
   Strive to enter in;
None can knock unheeded,
   None can strive in vain,
For the Saviour's welcome
   All that seek obtain.

2 Onward, children, onward!
   In the narrow way,
Christ your Lord shall lead you
   Safely day by day;
And with such a Leader
   What have you to fear?
Satan may oppose you,
   But your King is near.

3 Onward, ever onward!
   Till you join the throng
Who in dazzling raiment
   Sing the triumph-song,
And to heavenly music
   Cry with one accord,
"Holy! holy! holy!
   Is our sovereign Lord."

224
10.10.10.

1 "YET there is room!" the Lamb's
   bright hall of song,
With its fair glory, beckons thee along.

   Room, room, still room! Oh,
   enter, enter now!

2 It fills, it fills, that hall of jubilee!
Make haste, make haste; 'tis not too
   full for thee.

3 Yet there is room! still open stands the
   gate,
The gate of love; it is not yet too late.

4 Pass in, pass in! that banquet is for
   thee;
That cup of everlasting love is free.

5 Louder and sweeter sounds the loving
   call;
Come, lingerer, come; enter that festal
   hall.

6 Ere night that gate may close, and seal
   thy doom:
Then the last low, long cry: "No room,
   no room!"

   No room, no room! O woeful
   cry—"No room!"

225　　　　　　　12.11.12.11.

1 OH, come to the merciful Saviour who
　　calls you,
　　Oh, come to the Lord who forgives
　　　and forgets;
　Though dark be the fortune on earth
　　that befalls you,
　　There's a bright home above, where
　　　the sun never sets.

2 Oh, come then to Jesus, whose arms are
　　extended
　　To fold His dear children in closest
　　　embrace.
　Oh, come, for your exile will shortly be
　　ended,
　　And Jesus will show you His beauti-
　　　ful face.

3 Then come to His feet and lay open
　　your story
　　Of suffering and sorrow, of guilt and
　　　of shame;
　For the pardon of sin is the crown of
　　His glory,
　　And the joy of our Lord to be true to
　　　His Name.

226　　　　　　　8.8.8.6.

1 JESUS, my Lord, to Thee I cry:
　Unless Thou help me, I must die:
　Oh, bring Thy free salvation nigh,
　　And take me as I am!

2 Helpless I am, and full of guilt;
　But yet for me Thy blood was spilt,
　And Thou canst make me what Thou
　　wilt,
　　And take me as I am!

3 No preparation can I make,
　My best resolves I only break,
　Yet save me for Thine own Name's
　　sake,
　　And take me as I am!

4 Behold me, Saviour, at Thy feet;
　Deal with me as Thou seest meet;
　Thy work begin, Thy work complete,
　　But take me as I am!

227　　　　　　　8.8.8.6.

1 JUST as I am—without one plea,
　But that Thy blood was shed for me,
　And that Thou bidd'st me come to
　　Thee,
　　O Lamb of God, I come!

2 Just as I am—and waiting not
　To rid my soul of one dark blot,
　To Thee whose blood can cleanse each
　　spot,
　　O Lamb of God, I come!

3 Just as I am, though tossed about
　With many a conflict, many a doubt,
　Fightings and fears, within, without,
　　O Lamb of God, I come!

4 Just as I am—poor, wretched, blind—
　Sight, riches, healing of the mind,
　Yea, all I need, in Thee to find,
　　O Lamb of God, I come!

5 Just as I am—Thou wilt receive,
　Wilt welcome, pardon, cleanse, relieve:
　Because Thy promise I believe,
　　O Lamb of God, I come!

6 Just as I am—Thy love unknown
　Has broken every barrier down;
　Now to be Thine, yea, Thine alone,
　　O Lamb of God, I come!

228　　　　　　　P.M.

1 "WHOSOEVER heareth!" shout, shout
　　the sound!
　Send the blessèd tidings all the world
　　around!
　Spread the joyful news wherever man is
　　found:
　　"Whosoever will may come."

　　"Whosoever will! whosoever will!"
　Send the proclamation over vale and
　　hill;
　　'Tis a loving Father calls the
　　　wanderer home:
　　　"Whosoever will may come!"

2 "Whosoever cometh!" need not delay;
　Now the door is open, enter while you
　　may;
　Jesus is the true, the only Living Way:
　　"Whosoever will may come."

"Whosoever will"—the promise is
    secure;
"Whosoever will"—for ever shall en-
    dure;
"Whosoever will"—'tis life for ever-
    more;
    "Whosoever will may come."

229   P.M.

Out of my bondage, sorrow, and night,
    Jesus, I come! Jesus, I come!
Into Thy freedom, gladness, and light,
    Jesus, I come to Thee!
Out of my sickness into Thy health,
Out of my want and into Thy wealth,
Out of my sin and into Thyself,
    Jesus, I come to Thee!

2 Out of my shameful failure and loss,
    Jesus, I come! Jesus, I come!
Into the glorious gain of Thy cross,
    Jesus, I come to Thee!
Out of earth's sorrows into Thy balm,
Out of life's storm and into Thy calm,
Out of distress to jubilant psalm,
    Jesus, I come to Thee!

3 Out of unrest and arrogant pride,
    Jesus, I come! Jesus, I come!
Into Thy blessèd will to abide,
    Jesus, I come to Thee!
Out of myself to dwell in Thy love,
Out of despair into raptures above,
Upward for aye on wings like a dove,
    Jesus, I come to Thee!

4 Out of the fear and dread of the tomb,
    Jesus, I come! Jesus, I come!
Into the joy and light of Thy home,
    Jesus, I come to Thee!
Out of the depths of ruin untold,
Into the peace of Thy sheltering fold,
Ever Thy glorious face to behold,
    Jesus, I come to Thee!

230   7.7.7.7.

1 Jesus Christ is passing by;
Sinner, lift to Him thine eye;
As the precious moments flee,
Cry, "Be merciful to me!"

2 Jesus Christ is passing by;
Will He always be so nigh?
Now is the accepted day,
Seek for healing while you may.

3 Lo! He stands and calls to thee,
"What wilt thou then have of Me?"
Rise, and tell Him all thy need;
Rise—He calleth thee indeed.

4 "Lord, I would Thy mercy see;
Lord, reveal Thy love to me;
Let it penetrate my soul,
All my heart and life control."

5 Oh, how sweet! the touch of power
Comes—it is salvation's hour;
Jesus gives from guilt release:
"Faith hath saved thee, go in peace!"

231   C.M.

1 Here, Lord, relying on Thy Word,
    I claim Thy promise true,
That whosoe'er receiveth Thee
    At once is born anew.

2 I have no gift to offer Thee,
    Nor dost Thou aught require;
'Tis Thine to give, and mine to take
    The gift I most desire.

3 As Saviour from the guilt of sin,
    And from its awful power,
As Lord of all, to reign within,
    I take Thee from this hour.

4 The words I sing are nothing worth,
    If words alone they be;
But Thou canst read my heart and
    know
    The love none else can see.

5 My Saviour, I have taken Thee,
    God's gift through perfect grace,
And now among the sons of God
    By birth I have a place.

6 Help me to serve Thee faithfully,
    And daily conquer sin,
Then let me hear the glad "Well done!"
    The crown of glory win.

232   6.6.6.6.D.

1 COME to the Saviour now!
　　He gently calleth thee;
　In true repentance bow,
　　Before Him bend the knee.
　He waiteth to bestow
　　Salvation, peace, and love,
　True joy on earth below,
　　A home in heaven above.
　　　　Come, come, come!

2 Come to the Saviour now!
　　Gaze on that crimson tide—
　Water and blood—that flow
　　Forth from His wounded side.
　Hark to that suffering One!—
　　" 'Tis finished!'' now He cries:
　Redemption's work is done;
　　Then bows His head, and dies.

3 Come to the Saviour now!
　　He suffered all for thee,
　And in His merits thou
　　Hast an unfailing plea.
　No vain excuses frame,
　　For feelings do not stay;
　None who to Jesus came
　　Were ever sent away.

4 Come to the Saviour now!
　　Ye who have wandered far;
　Renew your solemn vow,
　　For His by right you are.
　Come, like poor wandering sheep
　　Returning to His fold;
　His arm will safely keep,
　　His love will ne'er grow cold.

5 Come to the Saviour, all!
　　Whate'er your burdens be;
　Hear now His loving call—
　　"Cast all your care on Me."
　Come, and for every grief
　　In Jesus you will find
　A sure and safe relief,
　　A loving Friend, and kind.

233   8.5.8.3.

1 ART thou longing? Jesus calls thee
　　To His wounded side;
　"Come to Me," saith He, "and ever
　　Safe abide."

2 Seeking Jesus? Jesus seeks thee—
　　Wants thee as thou art;
　He is knocking, ever knocking
　　At thy heart.

3 If thou let Him, He will save thee—
　　Make thee all His own;
　Guide thee, keep thee, take thee
　　dying,
　　　　To His throne.

4 Wilt thou still refuse His offer?
　　Wilt thou say Him nay?
　Wilt thou let Him, grieved, rejected,
　　Go away?

234   8.5.8.3

1 Lo, a loving Friend is waiting,
　　He is calling thee;
　Listen to His voice so tender,
　　"Come to Me."

2 "On the cross for thee I suffered,
　　Death I bore for thee,
　Canst thou still refuse My mercy?
　　Trust to Me.

3 "Long hast thou been Satan's captive;
　　I will set thee free;
　Then, rejoicing in thy freedom,
　　Follow Me."

4 Many times has Jesus spoken,
　　Now He speaks again:
　Shall thy Saviour's invitation
　　Be in vain?

5 Soon that voice will cease its calling;
　　Wilt thou still delay?
　Wait no longer, sins grows stronger,
　　Yield today.

6 Saviour, I will wait no longer,
　　Now to Thee I come;
　And when life's short voyage is over
　　Take me home.

235   8.5.8.3.

1 ART thou weary? art thou languid?
　　Art thou sore distrest?
　"Come to Me," saith One; "and
　　coming,
　　　　Be at rest!"

Hath He marks to lead me to Him,
If He be my Guide?
"In His feet and hands are wound-prints,
    And His side."

3 Is there diadem as Monarch
That His brow adorns?
"Yea, a crown in very surety,
    But of thorns."

4 If I find Him, if I follow,
What His guerdon here?
"Many a sorrow, many a labour,
    Many a tear."

5 If I still hold closely to Him,
What hath He at last?
"Sorrow vanquished, labour ended,
    Jordan passed."

6 If I ask Him to receive me,
Will He say me nay?
"Not till earth and not till heaven,
    Pass away."

7 Finding, following, keeping, struggling,
Is He sure to bless?
"Saints, apostles, prophets, martyrs
    Answer—Yes!"

236 S.M.

1 "Now is the accepted time!"
Now is the day of grace;
Now, children, come without delay
And seek the Saviour's face.

2 "Now is the accepted time,"
The Saviour calls today;
Tomorrow it may be too late—
Then why should you delay?

3 "Now is the accepted time,"
And Jesus bids you come;
And every promise in His Word
Declares there yet is room.

4 Lord, draw our youthful hearts
To seek a Saviour's love;
Then shall rejoicing angels sing
The joyful news above.

237 P.M.

1 SOFTLY and tenderly Jesus is calling—
Calling for you and for me;
Patiently Jesus is waiting and watching—
Watching for you and for me.

"Come home! . . . come home! . . .
Ye who are weary, come home!"
Earnestly, tenderly Jesus is calling,
Calling, "O sinner, come home!"

2 Why should we tarry when Jesus is pleading—
Pleading for you and for me?
Why should we linger and heed not His mercies—
Mercies for you and for me?

3 Time is now fleeting, the moments are passing—
Passing from you and from me;
Shadows are gathering, death may be coming—
Coming for you and for me!

4 Oh, for the wonderful love He has promised—
Promised for you and for me!
Though we have sinned, He has mercy and pardon—
Pardon for you and for me!

238 P.M.

1 JESUS is tenderly calling thee home—
Calling today, calling today!
Why from the sunshine of love wilt thou roam,
Farther and farther away?

Call- . . . ing today! call- . . . ing today!
Je- . . . sus is call- . . . ing, is tenderly calling today!

2 Jesus is calling the weary to rest—
Calling today, calling today!
Bring Him thy burden, and thou shalt be blest:
He will not turn thee away.

3 Jesus is waiting, oh, come to Him
  now—
   Waiting today, waiting today!
Come with thy sins, at His feet lowly
  bow;
   Come, and no longer delay!

4 Jesus is pleading: oh, list to His voice—
   Hear Him today, hear Him today!
They who believe on His Name shall
  rejoice;
   Quickly arise and away!

239   6.5.6.4.

1 TENDERLY the shepherd,
   O'er the mountains cold,
Goes to bring his lost one
   Back to the fold.

   Seeking to save, seeking to save;
   Lost one, 'tis Jesus seeking to
    save!

2 Patiently the owner
   Seeks, with earnest care,
In the dust and darkness,
   Her treasures rare.

3 Lovingly the father
   Sends the news around,
"He, once dead, now liveth—
   Once lost, is found."

240   S.M.

1 I HEAR Thy welcome voice,
   That calls me, Lord, to Thee,
For cleansing in Thy precious blood
   That flowed on Calvary.

   I am coming, Lord,
   Coming now to Thee;
Wash me, cleanse me, in the blood
   That flowed on Calvary.

2 'Tis Jesus calls me on
   To perfect faith and love,
To perfect hope, and peace, and trust,
   For earth and heaven above.

3 'Tis Jesus who confirms
   The blessed work within,
By adding grace to welcomed grace,
   Where reigned the power of sin.

4   And He the witness gives
   To loyal hearts and free,
That every promise is fulfilled,
   If faith but brings the plea.

5   All hail, atoning blood!
   All hail, redeeming grace!
All hail, the gift of Christ, our Lord,
   Our Strength and Righteousness!

241   7.7.7.7

1 TIME is earnest, passing by;
   Death is earnest, drawing nigh:
Sinner, wilt thou trifling be?
   Time and death appeal to thee.

2 Life is earnest; when 'tis o'er,
   Thou returnest nevermore;
Soon to meet eternity,
   Wilt thou never serious be?

3 God is earnest: kneel and pray,
   Ere the season pass away;
Ere He set His judgment throne;
   Ere the day of grace be gone.

4 Christ is earnest, bids thee come,
   Paid thy spirit's priceless sum;
Wilt thou spurn thy Saviour's love,
   Pleading with thee from above?

5 Oh, be earnest, do not stay!
   Thou may'st perish, e'en today:
Rise, thou lost one, rise and flee:
   Lo! thy Saviour waits for thee.

242   8.7.8.7.D.

1 LOVING Saviour, Thou art calling
   Sinners to Thyself today;
They have wandered from the shelter
   Of Thy fold and gone astray.
Bring them back to peace and safety;
   May they hear Thy loving call;
Thou art waiting to receive them,
   Draw each one, receive them all.

2 Loving Saviour, I am coming,
   Bringing all my sins to Thee;
As I am, in shame and sorrow,
   Lord, receive and rescue me.
At the cross I lay my burden,
   Lowly at Thy feet I bow;
I no longer doubt and grieve Thee,
   Cleanse my heart: Lord, save me
   now!

Loving Saviour, Thou art pleading
For my heart, my life, my all;
Long without I've kept Thee waiting,
Now I open at Thy call.
Come Thou in, take full possession,
Consecrated it shall be;
Take my life, direct and use it,
I will live it all for Thee!

243 P.M.

1 PASS me not, O gracious Saviour,
Hear my humble cry;
While on others Thou art calling,
Do not pass me by.

Saviour, Saviour,
Hear my humble cry;
While on others Thou art calling,
Do not pass me by.

2 Let me at a throne of mercy
Find a sweet relief;
Kneeling there in deep contrition,
Help my unbelief.

3 Trusting only in Thy merit,
Would I seek Thy face;
Heal my wounded, broken spirit,
Save me by Thy grace.

4 Thou, the spring of all my comfort,
More than life to me;
Whom have I on earth beside Thee?
Whom in heaven but Thee?

244 12.10.12.10.

1 JESUS is calling in accents of tenderness,
Jesus is calling, O sinner, to thee,
Just as of old, by the waters of Galilee,
Fell from His lips the command,
"Follow Me."

2 Take to the Saviour thy sorrow and selfishness,
Break from the fetters of sin, and be free;
Jesus has promised thee strength as thou needest it,
If thou obey the command, "Follow Me."

3 O Thou who knowest our wants and infirmities,
Thou who hast promised our Helper to be,
Grant us Thy grace, that with heartsearching earnestness
We may respond to the call, "Follow Me."

245 10.10.10.6.

1 OH, what a Saviour—that He died for me!
From condemnation He hath made me free;
"He that believeth on the Son," saith He,
"Hath everlasting life."

"Verily, verily, I say unto you;
Verily, verily,"—message ever new!—
"He that believeth on the Son"
—'tis true!—
"Hath everlasting life!"

2 All my iniquities on Him were laid,
All my indebtedness by Him was paid;
All who believe on Him, the Lord hath said,
"Have everlasting life."

3 Though poor and needy, I can trust my Lord;
Though weak and sinful, I believe His word;
Oh, glad message; every child of God
"Hath everlasting life."

4 Though all unworthy, yet I will not doubt;
For him that cometh He will not cast out;
"He that believeth"—oh, the good news shout!—
"HATH everlasting life."

246 P.M.

1 NOTHING to pay! ah, nothing to pay!
Never a word of excuse to say!
Year after year thou hast filled the score,
Owing thy Lord still more and more.

Hear the voice of Jesus say,
"Verily thou hast nothing to pay!
Ruined, lost art thou, and yet
I forgave thee all that debt!"

2 Nothing to pay! the debt is so great;
What will you do with the awful
weight?
How shall the way of escape be made?
Nothing to pay! yet it must be paid!
Hear the voice of Jesus say,
"Verily, thou hast nothing to pay!
All has been put to My account,
I have paid the full amount."

3 Nothing to pay! yes, nothing to pay!
Jesus has cleared all the debt away,
Blotted it out with His bleeding hand.
Free and forgiven, and loved, you
stand.
Hear the voice of Jesus say,
"Verily thou hast nothing to pay!
Paid is the debt and the debtor free!
Now I ask thee, Lovest thou Me?"

247   C.M.

1 Oh, precious words that Jesus said!—
"The soul that comes to Me,
I will in no wise cast him out,
Whoever he may be."
"Whoever he may be,
Whoever he may be;
I will in no wise cast him out,
Whoever he may be."

2 Oh, precious words that Jesus said!—
"Behold, I am the Door;
And all who enter in by Me
Have life for evermore."
"Have life for evermore,
Have life for evermore;
And all who enter in by Me
Have life for evermore."

3 Oh, precious words that Jesus said!—
"Come, weary souls oppressed,
Come, take My yoke and learn of Me,
And I will give you rest."
"And I will give you rest,
And I will give you rest;
Come, take My yoke and learn of
Me,
And I will give you rest."

4 Oh, precious words that Jesus said!—
"The world I overcame;
And they who follow where I lead
Shall conquer in My Name."
"Shall conquer in My Name,
Shall conquer in My Name;
And they who follow where I lead
Shall conquer in My Name."

248   7.6.7.6.D

1 Go thou in life's fair morning,
Go in the bloom of youth,
And buy, for thine adorning,
The precious pearl of truth.
Secure this heavenly treasure,
And bind it on thy heart,
And let not earthly pleasure
E'er cause it to depart.

2 Go, while the day-star shineth,
Go, while thy heart is light,
Go, ere thy strength declineth,
While every sense is bright.
Sell all thou hast, and buy it;
'Tis worth all earthly things,
Rubies and gold and diamonds,
Sceptres and crowns of kings.

3 Go, ere the clouds of sorrow,
Steal o'er the bloom of youth;
Defer not till tomorrow,
Go now, and buy the truth.
Go, seek thy great Creator,
Learn early to be wise;
Go, place upon His altar
A morning sacrifice.

249   P.M.

1 Oh, tender and sweet was the Master's
voice,
As He lovingly called to me:
"Come over the line! it is only a step;
I am waiting, My child, for thee!"

"Over the line!" Hear the sweet
refrain!
Angels are chanting the heavenly
strain!
"Over the line!" Why should I
remain
With a step between me and
Jesus?

2 "But my sins are many, my faith is
    small;"
  Lo! the answer came quick and clear;
"Thou needest not trust in thyself at
    all;
  Step over the line; I am here!"

3 "But my flesh is weak," I tearfully
    said,
  "And the way I cannot see;
I fear if I try I may sadly fail,
  And thus may dishonour Thee."

4 Ah! the world is cold, and I cannot go
    back:
  Press forward I surely must:
I will place my hand in His wounded
    palm,
  Step over the line and *trust.*

        "Over the line!" Hear the sweet
          refrain!
        Angels are chanting the heavenly
          strain!
        "Over the line" I *will not* remain;
          I'll cross it, and go to Jesus.

250   P.M.

1 THERE is life for a look at the crucified
    One,
  There is life at this moment for
    thee;
Then look, sinner, look unto Him, and
    be saved,
  Unto Him who was nailed to the
    tree.

        Look! look! look and live!
        There is life for a look at the
          crucified One;
        There is life at this moment for
          thee.

2 Oh, why was He there as the Bearer of
    sin,
  If on Jesus thy sins were not laid?
Oh, why from His side flowed the sin-
    cleansing blood,
  If His dying thy debt has not paid?

3 It is not thy tears of repentance, nor
    prayers,
  But the *blood,* that atones for the
    soul;

On Him then who shed it thou mayest
    at once
  Thy weight of iniquities roll.

4 We are "healed by His stripes":
    would'st thou add to the word?
  And He is our Righteousness made;
The best robe of heaven He bids thee
    put on:
  Oh, could'st thou be better arrayed?

5 Then take with rejoicing from Jesus at
    once
  The life everlasting He gives;
And know with assurance thou never
    canst die,
  Since Jesus, thy Righteousness, lives.

6 There is life for a look at the crucified
    One,
  There is life at this moment for
    thee:
Then look, sinner, look unto Him, and
    be saved,
  And know thyself spotless as He.

251   8.8.8.8.8.8.

1 A KINGLY summons now I hear;
It is the Saviour drawing near:
His knock is clear above earth's din;
Oh, shall I, shall I let Him in?

2 His brow no longer crowned with
    thorn,
His hands with nails no longer torn:
"My child," saith He, "give up thy
    sin;"
Oh, shall I, shall I let Him in?

3 Glory and honour crown Him now;
Shall my proud will refuse to bow?
Conscience to chide doth now begin;
Oh, shall I, shall I let Him in?

4 Again His knock is loud and clear;
His wondrous love casts out all fear:
Thy mighty arm my fight shall win;
Jesus, my Saviour, enter in.
    Repeat last two lines when using first tune.

252 7.7.7.7.7.7.

1 ROCK of Ages, cleft for me,
Let me hide myself in Thee;
Let the water and the blood,
From Thy riven side which flowed,
Be of sin the double cure—
Cleanse me from its guilt and power.

2 Not the labour of my hands
Can fulfil Thy law's demands:
Could my zeal no respite know,
Could my tears for ever flow,
All for sin could not atone;
Thou must save, and Thou alone.

3 Nothing in my hand I bring,
Simply to Thy cross I cling:
Naked, come to Thee for dress;
Helpless, look to Thee for grace;
Foul, I to the fountain fly,
Wash me, Saviour, or I die!

4 While I draw this fleeting breath,
When mine eyelids close in death,
When I soar to worlds unknown,
See Thee on Thy judgment throne:
Rock of Ages, cleft for me,
Let me hide myself in Thee!

253 8.7.8.7.4.7.

1 COME, ye sinners, poor and needy,
Weak and wounded, sick and sore;
Jesus ready stands to save you,
Full of pity, love, and power:
He is able,
He is willing; doubt no more.

2 Now, ye needy, come and welcome;
God's free bounty glorify;
True belief and true repentance—
Every grace that brings you nigh—
Without money,
Come to Jesus Christ and buy.

3 Let not conscience make you linger,
Nor of fitness fondly dream;
All the fitness He requireth
Is to feel your need of Him:
This He gives you—
'Tis the Spirit's rising beam.

4 Come, ye weary, heavy-laden,
Bruised and ruined by the Fall;
If you tarry till you're better,
You will never come at all:
Not the righteous—
Sinners Jesus came to call.

5 View Him prostrate in the garden,
On the ground your Maker lies!
On the awful tree behold Him,
Hear Him cry before He dies,
"It is finished!"
Sinner, will not this suffice?

6 Lo, the incarnate God, ascended,
Pleads the merit of His blood;
Venture on Him, venture wholly,
Let no other trust intrude:
None but Jesus
Can do helpless sinners good.

254 P.M.

1 I HEAR the Saviour say,
"Thy strength indeed is small;
Child of weakness, watch and pray,
Find in Me thine all in all."

Jesus paid it all—
All to Him I owe;
Sin had left a crimson stain;
He washed it white as snow.

2 Lord, now indeed I find
Thy power, and Thine alone,
Can change the leper's spots,
And melt the heart of stone.

3 For nothing good have I
Whereby Thy grace to claim—
I'll wash my garments white
In the blood of Calvary's Lamb.

4 And when before the throne
I stand in Him complete,
I'll lay my trophies down,
All down at Jesus' feet.

255 8.5.8.3.

1 PROVE Him! An almighty Saviour
Is the Saviour still;
Prove that He can save you fully—
Can and will.

2 Prove Him! He is God eternal,
  An unchanging Friend,
  With a love that never knoweth
    Bound or end.

3 Boundless is His love as ocean,
  Wide as heaven's own roof,
  Put the riches of His mercy
    To the proof.

4 Prove Him now—for now you need
    Him;
  Life is poor indeed
  Lacking His great love that filleth
    All our need.

5 Prove Him—now the time of mercy,
  'Tis the Saviour's day;
  Make it yours, nor let it sadly
    Die away.

6 Prove Him—with your sin and sorrow,
  Come; He longs to give
  Pardon, freedom, with all gladness,
    Joys that live!

7 Heaven within you, heaven above you,
  Then your heart will raise
  Glad thanksgiving for His mercies,
    Songs of praise!

256   10.10.10.10.

1 WEARY of earth, and laden with my
    sin,
  I look at heaven, and long to enter in;
  But there no evil thing may find a
    home,
  And yet I hear a voice that bids me
    "Come!"

2 So vile I am, how dare I hope to stand
  In the pure glory of that holy land?
  Before the whiteness of that throne
    appear?
  Yet there are hands stretched out to
    draw me near.

3 The while I fain would tread the
    heavenly way,
  Seems evil ever with me day by day;
  Yet on mine ears the gracious tidings
    fall:
  "Repent, confess, and thou art loosed
    from all."

4 It is the voice of Jesus that I hear,
  His are the hands outstretched to draw
    me near,
  And His the blood that can for all
    atone,
  And set me faultless there before the
    throne.

5 Yea, Thou wilt answer for me, righteous
    Lord;
  Thine all the merits, mine the great
    reward;
  Thine the sharp thorns, and mine the
    golden crown;
  Mine the life won, and Thine the life
    laid down.

6 Naught can I bring Thee, Lord, for all
    I owe,
  Yet let my full heart what it can
    bestow;
  Like Mary's gift, let my devotion
    prove,
  Forgiven greatly, how I greatly love.

257   P.M.

1 THERE is no love like the love of
    Jesus—
  Never to fade or fall,
  Till into the fold of the peace of God
  He has gathered us all.

    Jesus' love, precious love,
      Boundless and pure and free;
    Oh, turn to that love, weary
      wandering soul:
    Jesus pleadeth with thee!

2 There is no heart like the heart of
    Jesus,
  Filled with a tender love;
  No throb nor throe that our hearts can
    know,
  But He feels it above.

3 There is no eye like the eye of Jesus,
  Piercing so far away;
  Ne'er out of the sight of its tender light
  Can the wanderer stray.

4 There is no voice like the voice of
    Jesus—
  Tender and sweet its chime,
  Like musical ring of a flowing spring
  In the bright summer time.

87

5 Oh, let us hark to the voice of Jesus;
   Oh, may we never roam,
Till safe we rest on His loving breast,
   In the dear heavenly home.

258   6.5.6.5.D.

1 LOOK away to Jesus,
   Soul by sin oppressed;
'Twas for thee He suffered,
   Come to Him and rest:
All thy griefs He carried;
   All thy sins He bore;
Look away to Jesus;
   Trust Him evermore.

2 Look away to Jesus,
   Soldier in the fight;
When the battle thickens,
   Keep thine armour bright:
Though thy foes be many,
   Though thy strength be small,
Look away to Jesus:
   He will conquer all.

3 Look away to Jesus,
   When the skies are fair:
Calm seas have their dangers;
   Mariner, beware!
Earthly joys are fleeting,
   Going as they came:
Look away to Jesus,
   Evermore the same.

259   8.7.8.7.3.

1 LORD, I hear of showers of blessing
   Thou art scattering, full and free,
Showers the thirsty land refreshing:
   Let some drops now fall on me—
             Even me!

2 Pass me not, O gracious Father,
   Sinful though my heart may be;
Thou might'st leave me, but the rather
   Let Thy mercy light on me—
             Even me!

3 Pass me not, O tender Saviour,
   Let me love and cling to Thee;
I am longing for Thy favour,
   Whilst Thou'rt calling, oh, call me—
             Even me!

4 Pass me not, O mighty Spirit,
   Thou canst make the blind to see:
Witnesser of Jesus' merit,
   Speak the word of power to me—
             Even me!

5 Love of God, so pure and changeless;
   Blood of Christ, so rich and free;
Grace of God, so strong and boundless;
   Magnify them all in me—
             Even me!

6 Pass me not: Thy lost one bringing,
   Bind my heart, O Lord, to Thee;
Whilst the streams of life are springing,
   Blessing others, oh, bless me—
             Even me!

260   P.M.

1 CHILDREN, think on Jesus' love—
         All for you!
How He came from heaven above—
         All for you!
He whom angels did adore,
Full of wisdom, grace, and power,
How He all your sorrows bore.

    Yes, children, 'twas for you! yes, all
      for you!
    Yes, children, 'twas for you! yes, all
      for you!

2 Think how He contrived the plan—
         All for you!
And, to save, became a Man—
         All for you!
Left His glorious throne on high,
Came to suffer, bleed, and die,
You to raise above the sky.

3 See! He hangs upon the tree—
         All for you!
Crowned with thorns in agony—
         All for you!
Yes, for you all this He bore,
And for thousands, thousands more,
All to save from hell's dark door.

261   5.5.11.5.5.11.

1   ALL ye that pass by
       To Jesus draw nigh;
To you is it nothing that Jesus should
      die?

Your ransom and peace,
Your surety He is:
Come, see if there ever was sorrow like
  His.

2   For what you have done
His blood must atone:
The Father hath punished for you His
  dear Son:
The Lord, in the day
Of His anger, did lay
Your sins on the Lamb, and He bore
  them away.

3   He dies to atone
For sins not His own;
Your debt He hath paid, and your work
  He hath done.
Ye all may receive
The peace He did leave,
Who made intercession, "My Father,
  forgive!"

4   For you and for me
He prayed on the tree;
The prayer is accepted, the sinner is
  free.
That sinner am I,
Who on Jesus rely,
And come for the pardon God cannot
  deny.

5   My pardon I claim;
For a sinner I am,
A sinner believing in Jesus' dear Name;
He purchased the grace
Which now I embrace:
O Father, Thou know'st He hath died
  in my place.

262   P.M.

1 SING them over again to me,
  Wonderful words of life!
Let me more of their beauty see,
  Wonderful words of life!
    Words of life and beauty,
    Teach me faith and duty!

      Beautiful words! wonderful
        words!
      Wonderful words of life!

2 Christ, the blessed One, gives to all
  Wonderful words of life!
Sinner, list to the loving call,
  Wonderful words of life!
    All so freely given,
    Wooing us to heaven!

3 Sweetly echo the Gospel call,
  Wonderful words of life!
Offer pardon and peace to all,
  Wonderful words of life!
    Jesus, only Saviour,
    Sanctify for ever!

263   P.M.

1   WEEPING will not save me;
Though my face were bathed in tears,
That could not allay my fears,
Could not wash the sins of years:
  Weeping will not save me.

    Jesus wept and died for me;
    Jesus suffered on the tree;
    Jesus waits to make me free;
    He alone can save me.

2   Working will not save me;
Purest deeds that I can do,
Holiest thoughts and feelings, too,
Cannot form my soul anew:
  Working will not save me.

3   Waiting will not save me;
Helpless, guilty, lost I lie;
In my ear is mercy's cry;
If I wait I can but die:
  Waiting will not save me.

4   Praying will not save me;
All the prayers that I could say
Could not wash my sins away—
The debt I owe could never pay:
  Praying will not save me.

5   Faith in Christ *will* save me;
Let me trust Thy gracious Son,
Trust the work that He has done;
To His arms, Lord, help me run:
  Faith in Christ *will* save me.

264 P.M.

1 SHE only touched the hem of His garment,
　As to His side she stole
Amid the crowd that gathered around Him,
　And straightway she was whole.

　　Oh, touch the hem of His garment!
　　And thou too shalt be free;
　　His saving power this very hour
　　Shall give new life to thee!

2 She came in fear and trembling before Him,
　She knew her Lord had come;
She felt that from Him virtue had healed her;
　The mighty deed was done.

3 He turned with, "Daughter, be of good comfort;
　Thy faith hath made thee whole!"
And peace that passeth all understanding
　With gladness filled her soul.

265 P.M.

1 "ALMOST persuaded"—now to believe:
"Almost persuaded"—Christ to receive:
　　Seems now some soul to say—
　　"Go, Spirit, go Thy way;
　　Some more convenient day
　　　On Thee I'll call"?

2 "Almost persuaded," come, come today;
"Almost persuaded," turn not away:
　　Jesus invites you here,
　　Angels are lingering near,
　　Prayers rise from hearts so dear;
　　　Oh, wanderer, come!

3 "Almost persuaded"—harvest is past!
"Almost persuaded"—doom comes at last!
　　"Almost" cannot avail;
　　"Almost" is but to fail!
　　Sad, sad that bitter wail—
　　　"Almost"—*but lost.*

266 P.M.

1 LOOK to Jesus, weary one,
　Look and live! look and live!
Look at what the Lord has done,
　Look and live!
See Him lifted on the tree,
　Look and live! look and live!
Hear Him say, "Look unto Me!"
　Look and live!

　　Look! the Lord is lifted high,
　　Look to Him, He's ever nigh:
　　Look and live! why will ye die?
　　Look and live!

2 Though unworthy, vile, unclean,
　Look and live! look and live!
Look away from self and sin,
　Look and live!
Long by Satan's power enslaved,
　Look and live! look and live!
Look to Him, you shall be saved,
　Look and live!

3 Though you've wandered far away,
　Look and live! look and live!
Harden not your heart today,
　Look and live!
'Tis your Father calls you home,
　Look and live! look and live!
Whosoever will may come.
　Look and live!

267 P.M.

1 ONE there is who loves thee,
　Waiting still for thee:
Canst thou yet reject Him?
　None so kind as He!
Do not grieve Him longer,
　Come and trust Him now!
He has waited all thy days:
　Why waitest thou?

　　One there is who loves thee,
　　Oh, receive Him now!
　　He has waited all thy days;
　　Why waitest thou?

2 Tenderly He woos thee;
　Do not slight His call;
Though thy sins are many,
　He'll forgive them all.
Turn to Him, repenting,

He will cleanse thee now;
He is waiting at thy heart:
Why waitest thou?

3 Jesus still is waiting;
Sinner, why delay?
To His arms of mercy
Rise and haste away!
Only come believing,
He will save thee now;
He is waiting at the door:
Why waitest thou?

268   9.8.9.8.

1 REDEMPTION! oh, wonderful story—
Glad message for you and for me:
That Jesus has purchased our pardon,
And paid all the debt on the tree.

Believe it, O sinner, believe it;
Receive the glad message—
'tis true;
Trust now in the crucified
Saviour,
Salvation He offers to you.

2 From death unto life He has brought
us,
And made us by grace sons of God;
A fountain is opened for sinners:
Oh, wash and be cleansed in the
blood!

3 No longer shall sin have dominion,
Though present to tempt and annoy;
For Christ, in His blessèd redemption,
The power of sin shall destroy.

4 Accept now God's offer of mercy;
To Jesus, oh, hasten today;
For He will receive him that cometh,
And never will turn him away.

269   6.6.6.6.8.8.

1   THE Gospel of Thy grace
My stubborn heart has won;
For God so loved the world,
He gave His only Son,
That "Whosoever will believe
Shall everlasting life receive!"

2   The serpent "lifted up"
Could life and healing give,
So Jesus on the cross
Bids me to look and live;
For "Whosoever will believe
Shall everlasting life receive!"

3   "The soul that sinneth dies:"
My awful doom I heard;
I was for ever lost,
But for Thy gracious word
That "Whosoever will believe
Shall everlasting life receive!"

4   "Not to condemn the world"
The "Man of Sorrows" came;
But that the world might have
Salvation through His Name;
For "Whosoever will believe
Shall everlasting life receive!"

5   "Lord, help my unbelief!"
Give me the peace of faith,
To rest with childlike trust
On what Thy Gospel saith,
That "Whosoever will believe
Shall everlasting life receive!"

The Christian Life: (1) Assurance

270   C.M.D.

1 I HEARD the voice of Jesus say,
"Come unto Me and rest:
Lay down, thou weary one, lay down
Thy head upon My breast:"
I came to Jesus as I was,
Weary, and worn, and sad,
I found in Him a resting-place,
And He has made me glad.

2 I heard the voice of Jesus say,
"Behold, I freely give
The living water—thirsty one,
Stoop down, and drink, and live:"
I came to Jesus, and I drank
Of that life-giving stream;
My thirst was quenched, my soul re-
vived.
And now I live in Him.

3 I heard the voice of Jesus say,
"I am this dark world's Light;
Look unto Me: thy morn shall rise,
And all thy day be bright:"
I looked to Jesus, and I found
In Him my Star, my Sun;
And in that light of life I'll walk,
Till travelling days are done.

271   P.M.

1 CHRIST has for sin atonement made:
What a wonderful Saviour!
We are redeemed! the price is paid!
What a wonderful Saviour!

    What a wonderful Saviour is Jesus,
    my Jesus!
    What a wonderful Saviour is Jesus,
    my Lord!

2 I praise Him for the cleansing blood:
What a wonderful Saviour!
That reconciled my soul to God:
What a wonderful Saviour!

3 He dwells within me day by day:
What a wonderful Saviour!
And keeps me faithful all the way:
What a wonderful Saviour!

4 He gives me overcoming power:
What a wonderful Saviour!
And triumph in each conflict hour:
What a wonderful Saviour!

5 To Him I've given all my heart:
What a wonderful Saviour!
The world shall never share a part:
What a wonderful Saviour!

272   P.M.

1 STANDING on the promises of Christ my
King,
Through eternal ages let His praises
ring;
Glory in the highest, I will shout and
sing,
Standing on the promises of God.

        Stand- . . . ing, . . . stand- . . .
        ing, . . .
    Standing on the promises of God
        my Saviour;
        Stand- . . . ing, . . . stand- . . .
        ing, . . .
    I'm standing on the promises of
        God.

2 Standing on the promises that cannot
fail,
When the howling storms of doubt and
fear assail;
By the living Word of God I shall prevail,
Standing on the promises of God.

3 Standing on the promises I now can see
Perfect, present cleansing in the blood
for me;
Standing in the liberty where Christ
makes free,
Standing on the promises of God.

4 Standing on the promises of Christ the
Lord,
Bound to Him eternally by love's
strong cord,
Overcoming daily with the Spirit's
sword,
Standing on the promises of God.

5 Standing on the promises I cannot fall,
Listening every moment to the Spirit's
call,
Resting in my Saviour as my All-in-
all,
Standing on the promises of God.

273   8.7.8.7.

1 ONCE I thought I walked with Jesus,
Yet such changeful moods I had;
Sometimes trusting, sometimes doubt-
ing,
Sometimes joyful, sometimes sad.

    Oh, the peace my Saviour gives!
    Peace I never knew before!
    For my way has brighter grown
    Since I learned to trust Him
    more.

2 For He called me closer to Him,
Bade my doubting tremors cease:
And when I had fully trusted—
Filled my soul with perfect peace.

3 Now I'm trusting every moment,
Less than this is not enough;
And my Saviour bears me gently
O'er the places once so rough.

4 Blessèd Saviour, Thou dost keep me
    By Thy power from day to day,
And my heart is full of gladness;
    Thou wilt keep me all the way!

274   P.M.

1 WHEN peace, like a river, attendeth my
    way,
    When sorrows, like sea-billows, roll;
Whatever my lot, Thou hast taught me
    to know,
    It is well, it is well with my soul.

        It is well . . . with my soul, . . .
        It is well, it is well with my soul.

2 Though Satan should buffet, though
    trials should come,
    Let this blest assurance control,
That Christ hath regarded my helpless
    estate,
    And hath shed His own blood for my
    soul.

3 My sin—oh, the bliss of this glorious
    thought!
    My sin—not in part, but the whole,
Is nailed to His cross, and I bear it no
    more:
    Praise the Lord, praise the Lord, O
    my soul!

4 For me be it Christ, be it Christ hence
    to live!
    If Jordan above me shall roll,
No pang shall be mine, for in death as
    in life
    Thou wilt whisper Thy peace to my
    soul.

5 But, Lord, 'tis for Thee, for Thy
    coming, we wait;
    The sky, not the grave, is our goal;
Oh, trump of the angel! oh, voice of the
    Lord!
    Blessèd hope! blessèd rest of my soul!

275   S.M.

1   I HEAR the words of love,
    I gaze upon the blood,
I see the mighty Sacrifice,
    And I have peace with God.

2   'Tis everlasting peace!
    Sure as Jehovah's Name;
'Tis stable as His steadfast throne,
    For evermore the same.

3   The clouds may come and go,
    And storms may sweep my sky—
This blood-sealed friendship changes
    not:
    The cross is ever nigh.

4   My love is oft-times low,
    My joy still ebbs and flows;
But peace with Him remains the
    same—
    No change Jehovah knows.

5   I change, He changes not;
    The Christ can never die;
His love, not mine, the resting-place,
    His truth, not mine, the tie.

276   8.7.8.7.

1 ALL my doubts I give to Jesus!
    I've His gracious promise heard—
I "shall never be confounded"—
    I am trusting in that word.

2 All my sins are laid on Jesus!
    He doth wash me in His blood;
He will keep me pure and holy,
    And will bring me home to God.

3 All my fears I give to Jesus!
    Rests my weary soul on Him;
Though my way be hid in darkness,
    Never can His light grow dim.

4 All my joys I give to Jesus!
    He is all I want of bliss;
He of all the worlds is Master—
    He has all I need in this.

5 All I am I give to Jesus!
    All my body, all my soul;
All I have, and all I hope for,
    While eternal ages roll.

277 C.M.

1 O Son of God, my Saviour dear,
  If Thou dost meet my need,
And loose my bonds of guilt and fear,
  I shall be free indeed.

> Free indeed, free indeed,
> For, if the Son shall set me free,
>   I shall be free indeed.

2 Lord, I would know the daily power
  That keeps Thy children free,
The glorious liberty of sons,
  From all iniquity.

3 Then let me know the saving grace
  That conquers every foe,
That opens wide the prison door
  And bids the captive go.

4 Call me with Thy life-giving voice,
  That I may rise again;
And from the grave-clothes set me
  free,
In life by Thee to reign.

278 L.M.

1 Some day the silver cord will break,
  And I no more as now shall sing;
But, oh, the joy when I shall wake
  Within the palace of the King!

> And I shall see . . . Him face to
>   face, . . .
> And tell the story—Saved by
>   grace!

2 Some day my earthly house will fall,
  I cannot tell how soon 'twill be;
But this I know—my All-in-all
  Has now a place in heaven for me.

3 Some day, when fades the golden sun
  Beneath the rosy-tinted west,
My blessèd Lord will say, "Well
  done!"
And I shall enter into rest.

4 Some day; till then I'll watch and
  wait—
  My lamp all trimmed and burning
    bright—
That when my Saviour opes the gate
  My soul to Him may take its flight.

279 P.M.

1 Blessed assurance—Jesus is mine!
Oh, what a foretaste of glory divine!
Heir of salvation, purchase of God;
Born of His Spirit, washed in His blood.

> This is my story, this is my song,
>   Praising my Saviour all the day long.

2 Perfect submission, perfect delight,
Visions of rapture burst on my sight;
Angels, descending, bring from above
Echoes of mercy, whispers of love.

3 Perfect submission, all is at rest,
I in my Saviour am happy and blest;
Watching and waiting, looking above,
Filled with His goodness, lost in His
  love.

280 8.8.8.8.

1 A debtor to mercy alone,
  Of covenant mercy I sing;
Nor fear to draw near to Thy throne,
  My person and offerings to bring.

2 The wrath of a sin-hating God
  With me can have nothing to do;
My Saviour's obedience to blood
  Hides all my transgressions from
    view.

3 The work which His goodness began
  The arm of His strength will com-
    plete;
His promise is "Yea and Amen,"
  And never was forfeited yet.

4 Things future, nor things that are now,
  Not all things below or above
Can make Him His promise forgo,
  Or sever my soul from His love.

5 My name from the palms of His hands
  Eternity will not erase:
Impressed on His heart it remains,
  In marks of indelible grace;

6 And I to the end shall endure,
  As sure as the earnest is given;
More happy, but not more secure,
  When glorified with Him in Heaven.

281   8.8.8.8.

1 How good is the God we adore,
   Our faithful, unchangeable Friend!
His love is as great as His power,
   And knows neither measure nor end!

2 'Tis Jesus the First and the Last,
   Whose Spirit shall guide us safe
     home;
We'll praise Him for all that is past,
   And trust Him for all that's to come.

282   C.M.

1 I'm not ashamed to own my Lord,
   Or to defend His cause,
Maintain the honour of His Word,
   The glory of His cross.

     At the cross! at the cross! where
       I first saw the light,
     And the burden of my heart rolled
       away;
     It was there by faith I received my
       sight,
     And now I am happy all the day!

2 Jesus, my God! I know His Name—
   His Name is all my trust;
Nor will He put my soul to shame,
   Nor let my hope be lost.

3 Firm as His throne His promise stands,
   And He can well secure
What I've committed to His hands,
   Till the decisive hour.

4 Then will He own my worthless name
   Before His Father's face;
And, in the New Jerusalem,
   Appoint my soul a place.

283   L.M.

1 Before the throne of God above
   I have a strong, a perfect plea;
A great High Priest, whose Name is
     Love,
   Who ever lives and pleads for me.

2 My name is graven on His hands,
   My name is written on His heart;
I know that while in heaven He stands
   No tongue can bid me thence
     depart.

3 When Satan tempts me to despair,
   And tells me of the guilt within,
Upward I look, and see Him there
   Who made an end of all my sin.

4 Because the sinless Saviour died,
   My sinful soul is counted free;
For God, the Just, is satisfied
   To look on Him and pardon me.

5 Behold Him there! the risen Lamb!
   My perfect, spotless Righteousness,
The great unchangeable I AM,
   The King of glory and of grace!

6 One with Himself, I cannot die;
   My soul is purchased by His blood;
My life is hid with Christ on high,
   With Christ, my Saviour and my
     God.

284   C.M.

1 A mind at "perfect peace" with God:
   Oh, what a word is this!
A sinner reconciled through blood;
   This, this indeed is peace!

2 By nature and by practice far—
   How very far from God!
Yet now by grace brought nigh to Him
   Through faith in Jesus' blood.

3 So nigh, so very nigh to God,
   I cannot nearer be;
For in the person of His Son
   I am as near as He.

4 So dear, so very dear to God,
   More dear I cannot be;
The love wherewith He loves the Son—
   Such is His love to me!

5 Why should I ever anxious be,
   Since such a God is mine?
He watches o'er me night and day,
   And tells me "Mine is thine."

285   P.M.

1 Will your anchor hold in the storms of
     life?
When the clouds unfold their wings of
     strife;

When the strong tides lift and the
  cables strain,
Will your anchor drift or firm remain?

We have an anchor that keeps the
  soul
Steadfast and sure while the
  billows roll;
Fastened to the Rock which can-
  not move,
Grounded firm and deep in the
  Saviour's love.

2 Will your anchor hold in the straits of
  fear?
When the breakers roar and the reef is
  near:
While the surges rave and the wild
  winds blow,
Shall the angry waves then your bark
  o'erflow?

3 Will your anchor hold in the floods of
  death,
When the waters cold chill your latest
  breath?
On the rising tide you can never fail,
While your anchor holds within the
  veil.

4 Will your eyes behold through the
  morning light
The city of gold, and the harbour
  bright?
Will you anchor safe by the heavenly
  shore,
When life's storms are past for evermore?

286   7.7.7.7.

1 SIMPLY trusting every day,
Trusting through a stormy way;
Even when my faith is small,
Trusting Jesus, that is all.

  Trusting Him while life shall last,
  Trusting Him till earth is past,
  Till within the jasper wall—
  Trusting Jesus, that is all.

2 Brightly doth His Spirit shine
Into this poor heart of mine:
While He leads I cannot fall,
Trusting Jesus, that is all.

3 Singing if my way be clear:
Praying if the path be drear:
If in danger, for Him call;
Trusting Jesus, that is all.

4 Trusting as the moments fly,
Trusting as the days go by,
Trusting Him, whate'er befall;
Trusting Jesus, that is all.

287   S.M.

1 NOT all the blood of beasts
   On Jewish altars slain
Could give the guilty conscience peace
   Or wash away its stain.

2 But Christ, the heavenly Lamb,
   Takes all our sins away;
A sacrifice of nobler Name
   And richer blood than they.

3 My faith would lay her hand
   On that dear head of Thine,
While like a penitent I stand,
   And there confess my sin.

4 My soul looks back to see
   The burden Thou didst bear,
When hanging on the accursed tree,
   And knows her guilt was there.

5 Believing, we rejoice
   To see the curse remove;
We bless the Lamb with cheerful voice,
   And sing His wondrous love.

288   L.M.

1 JESUS, Thy blood and righteousness
My beauty are, my glorious dress;
'Midst flaming worlds, in these arrayed,
With joy shall I lift up my head.

2 Bold shall I stand in that great day,
For who aught to my charge shall lay?
Fully absolved through these I am,
From sin and fear, from guilt and
  shame.

3 When from the dust of death I rise
To claim my mansion in the skies,
E'en then shall this be all my plea,
"Jesus hath lived, and died, for me."

This spotless robe the same appears,
When ruined nature sinks in years;
No age can change its glorious hue,
The robe of Christ is ever new.

Oh, let the dead now hear Thy voice,
Bid, Lord, Thy banished ones rejoice;
Their beauty this, their glorious dress,
Jesus, the Lord our Righteousness!

289 P.M.

1 REJOICE in the Lord! oh, let His mercy
      cheer;
   He sunders the bands that enthrall;
Redeemed by His blood, why should
      we ever fear—
   Since Jesus is our "all in all"?

      "If God be for us, if God be for us,
         if God be for us,
      Who can be against us?
      Who? . . . who? . . . who? . . .
      Who can be against us, against
         us?"

2 Be strong in the Lord! rejoicing in His
      might,
   Be loyal and true day by day;
When evils assail, be valiant for the
      right,
   And He will be our strength and
      stay.

3 Confide in His Word—His promises so
      sure;
   In Christ they are "yea and amen";
Though earth pass away, they ever shall
      endure,
   'Tis written o'er and o'er again.

4 Abide in the Lord: secure in His con-
      trol,
   'Tis life everlasting begun;
To pluck from His hand the weakest,
      trembling soul—
   It never, never can be done!

290 8.8.8.8.8.8.

1 MY hope is built on nothing less
   Than Jesus' blood and righteousness;
I dare not trust the sweetest frame,
   But wholly lean on Jesus' Name.

      On Christ, the solid Rock, I stand;
      All other ground is sinking sand.

2 When darkness seems to veil His face
   I rest on His unchanging grace;
In every high and stormy gale
   My anchor holds within the veil.

3 His oath, His covenant, and blood
   Support me in the 'whelming flood:
When all around my soul gives way,
   He then is all my hope and stay.

291 C.M.

1 MY faith has found a resting-place,
      Not in a form or creed;
I trust the Ever-living One,
      His wounds for me shall plead.

      I need no other argument,
         I need no other plea;
      It is enough that Jesus died,
         And that He died for me.

2 Enough for me that Jesus saves,
      This ends my fear and doubt;
A sinful soul, I come to Him,
      He'll never cast me out.

3 My heart is leaning on the Word,
      The written Word of God;
Salvation by my Saviour's Name,
      Salvation through His blood.

4 My great Physician heals the sick,
      The lost He came to save;
For me His precious blood He shed,
      For me His life He gave.

292 7.7.7.7.7.7.

1 BLESSED are the sons of God;
   They are bought with Jesus' blood;
They are ransomed from the grave,
   Life eternal they shall have.

      With them numbered may I be
      Now and through eternity!

The Christian Life

2 God did love them in His Son,
Long before the world begun:
They the seal of this receive
When on Jesus they believe.

3 They are justified by grace;
They enjoy a solid peace;
All their sins are washed away,
They shall stand in God's great day.

4 They produce the fruits of grace
In the works of righteousness;
Born of God, they hate all sin,
God's pure Word remains within.

5 They have fellowship with God,
Through the Mediator's blood;
One with God, through Jesus one,
Glory is in them begun.

The Christian Life: (2) Guidance and Safety

293   8.7.8.7.D.

1 ALL the way my Saviour leads me:
  What have I to ask beside?
Can I doubt His tender mercy,
  Who through life has been my Guide?
Heavenly peace, divinest comfort,
  Here by faith in Him to dwell!
For I know whate'er befall me,
  Jesus doeth all things well.

2 All the way my Saviour leads me:
  Cheers each winding path I tread;
Gives me grace for every trial,
  Feeds me with the living bread.
Though my weary steps may falter,
  And my soul athirst may be,
Gushing from the rock before me,
  Lo! a spring of joy I see.

3 All the way my Saviour leads me;
  Oh, the fulness of His love!
Perfect rest to me is promised
  In my Father's house above.
When my spirit, clothed immortal,
  Wings its flight to realms of day,
This my song through endless ages—
  Jesus led me all the way.

294   S.M.D.

1 I WAS a wandering sheep,
  I did not love the fold,
I did not love my Shepherd's voice,
  I would not be controlled:
I was a wayward child,
  I did not love my home,
I did not love my Father's voice,
  I loved afar to roam.

2 The Shepherd sought His sheep,
  The Father sought His child;
They followed me o'er vale and hill,
  O'er deserts waste and wild:
They found me nigh to death,
  Famished, and faint, and lone;
They bound me with the bands of love,
  They saved the wandering one.

3 Jesus my Shepherd is;
  'Twas He that loved my soul,
'Twas He that washed me in His blood,
  'Twas He that made me whole:
'Twas He that sought the lost,
  That found the wandering sheep;
'Twas He that brought me to the fold,
  'Tis He that still doth keep.

4 I was a wandering sheep,
  I would not be controlled;
But now I love my Shepherd's voice,
  I love, I love the fold:
I was a wayward child,
  I once preferred to roam;
But now I love my Father's voice,
  I love, I love His home.

295   10.4.10.4.10.10.

1 LEAD, kindly Light, amid the encircling gloom,
  Lead Thou me on;
The night is dark, and I am far from home;
  Lead Thou me on.
Keep Thou my feet; I do not ask to see
The distant scene; one step enough for me.

98

2 I was not ever thus, nor prayed that Thou
  Should'st lead me on;
I loved to choose and see my path; but now
  Lead Thou me on.
I loved the garish day, and, spite of fears,
Pride ruled my will: remember not past years.

3 So long Thy power hath blest me, sure it still
  Will lead me on
O'er moor and fen, o'er crag and torrent, till
  The night is gone,
And with the morn those angel-faces smile,
Which I have loved long since and lost awhile.

296   8.4.8.4.

1 LORD, for tomorrow and its needs
  I do not pray;
Keep me, my God, from stain of sin—
  Just for today.

2 Let me do faithfully Thy work,
  And duly pray;
Let me be kind in word and deed—
  Just for today.

3 Let me no wrong or idle word
  Unthinking, say;
Set Thou a seal upon my lips—
  Just for today.

4 So for tomorrow and its needs
  I do not pray;
But keep me, guide me, hold me, Lord—
  Just for today.

297   S.M.D.

1 ALONG the shining road
  That leads to life so free
I tread with glad and glowing heart,
  For Jesus leadeth me;
  Though long ago He passed
  Beyond our mortal sight,
The very pathway that He went
  Still shines with heavenly light.

2 I know that but for Him
  The road would darkened be,
And shapes and shadows dark and dread
  Might gather threateningly;
  But He has trodden first
  The long, the changeful way,
And left His light upon it all
  To turn the night to day.

3 The shining road may seem
  To lose itself in night;
The valley mist, the winter cloud
  May hide it from my sight.
  I know full well it winds,
  Until, or soon or late,
It finds upon the hills of God
  His shining City gate.

298   10.4.10.4.

1 I DO not ask, O Lord, that life may be
  A pleasant road;
I do not ask that Thou would'st take from me
  Aught of its load.

2 I do not ask that flowers should always spring
  Beneath my feet;
I know too well the poison and the sting
  Of things too sweet.

3 For one thing only, Lord, dear Lord, I plead:
  Lead me aright,
Though strength should falter, and though heart should bleed,
  Through peace to light.

4 I do not ask, O Lord, that Thou should'st shed
  Full radiance here;
Give but a ray of peace, that I may tread
  Without a fear.

5 I do not ask my cross to understand,
  My way to see;
Better in darkness just to feel Thy hand,
  And follow Thee.

6 Joy is like restless day, but peace
    divine
      Like quiet night:
Lead me, O Lord, till perfect day shall
    shine
      Through peace to light.

299   8.8.8.3.

1 FIERCE raged the tempest o'er the
    deep,
Watch did Thine anxious servants
    keep;
But Thou wast wrapped in guileless
    sleep,
      Calm and still.

2 "Save, Lord, we perish," was their cry,
"Oh, save us in our agony!"
Thy word above the storm rose high,
      "Peace, be still."

3 The wild winds hushed; the angry deep
Sank, like a little child, to sleep;
The sullen billows ceased to leap,
      At Thy will.

4 So, when our life is clouded o'er,
And storm-winds drift us from the
    shore,
Say, lest we sink to rise no more,
      "Peace, be still."

300   6.5.6.5.D.

1 JESUS is our Pilot:
    No one else can guide
Our frail barque in safety
    O'er life's stormy tide:
When the waves of trouble
    Baffle human skill,
He can always calm them
    With His "Peace, be still."

    Jesus is our Pilot:
      Guided by His hand
    We shall reach the haven
      On the golden strand.

2 Jesus is our Pilot:
    Through His mighty arm
We are safe from danger—
    Safe from fear and harm:
In His strong protection
    We may ever rest;
Refuge from all sorrow
    Is His faithful breast.

3 Jesus is our Pilot:
    Well He knows the way
From this vale of shadows
    To the realm of day:
He can find the harbour
    Others seek in vain;
There, the Lord of glory,
    Evermore He'll reign.

301   P.M.

1 O PILGRIM bound for the heavenly land,
    Never lose sight of Jesus!
He'll lead you gently with loving hand:
    Never lose sight of Jesus!

    Never lose sight of Jesus!
    Never lose sight of Jesus!
    Day and night He will lead you
      right;
    Never lose sight of Jesus!

2 When you are tempted to go astray,
    Never lose sight of Jesus!
Press onward, upward, the narrow way;
    Never lose sight of Jesus!

3 Though dark the pathway may seem
    ahead,
    Never lose sight of Jesus!
"I will be with you," His Word hath
    said:
    Never lose sight of Jesus!

4 When death is knocking outside the
    door,
    Never lose sight of Jesus!
Till safe with Him on the golden shore:
    Never lose sight of Jesus!

302   P.M.

1 HE leadeth me! Oh, blessed thought!
Oh, words with heavenly comfort
    fraught!
Whate'er I do, where'er I be,
Still 'tis God's hand that leadeth me!

    He leadeth me! He leadeth me!
    By His own hand He leadeth me!
    His faithful follower I would be;
    For by His hand He leadeth me!

2 Sometimes 'mid scenes of deepest
    gloom,
Sometimes where Eden's bowers bloom,
By waters still, o'er troubled sea,
Still 'tis His hand that leadeth me!

3 Lord, I would place my hand in Thine,
Nor ever murmur nor repine;
Content, whatever lot I see,
Since 'tis my God that leadeth me.

4 And when my task on earth is done,
When, by Thy grace, the victory's won,
E'en death's cold wave I will not flee;
Since Thou through Jordan leadest me.

303   P.M.

1 WHEN I fear my faith will fail,
    Christ can hold me fast!
When the tempter would prevail,
    He can hold me fast!

    He will hold me fast,
    He will hold me fast,
    For my Saviour loves me so,
    He will hold me fast!

2 I could never keep my hold,
    He must hold me fast!
For my love is often cold,
    He must hold me fast!

3 I am precious in His sight,
    He will hold me fast!
Those He saves are His delight,
    He will hold me fast!

4 He'll not let my soul be lost,
    Christ will hold me fast;
Bought by Him at such a cost,
    He will hold me fast!

304   P.M.

1 LIGHT in the darkness, sailor, day is at
    hand!
See o'er the foaming billows fair
    haven's land;
Drear was the voyage, sailor, now
    almost o'er;
Safe within the life-boat, sailor, pull for
    the shore.

    Pull for the shore, sailor, pull for the
    shore;
    Heed not the rolling waves, but bend
    to the oar;
    Safe in the life-boat, sailor, cling to
    self no more!
    Leave the poor old stranded wreck
    and pull for the shore.

2 Trust in the life-boat, sailor, all else
    will fail;
Stronger the surges dash and fiercer the
    gale,
Heed not the stormy winds, though
    loudly they roar;
Watch the "Bright and Morning Star,"
    and pull for the shore.

3 Bright gleams the morning, sailor, up-
    lift the eye;
Clouds and darkness disappearing,
    glory is nigh:
Safe in the life-boat, sailor; sing ever-
    more,
"Glory in so great salvation!" Pull for
    the shore!

305   P.M.

1 JESUS the Saviour, dying on Calvary,
    Purchased my pardon, setting me
    free:
Love so abundant, should I not serve
    Him,
    When He so gladly suffered for me?

    Lord, I am Thine, Saviour divine!
    Oh, what a joy just to know Thou
    art mine!

2 Oh, what a Saviour, tender and loving,
    Guarding my footsteps lest I should
    stray:
Love so abundant, leading me ever
    Out of the darkness into the day.

3 Constant Companion, leaving me never,
    Bidding me follow close by His side:
He is my Refuge, safely I shelter,
    Knowing He loves me, whate'er
    betide.

306
P.M.

1 I KNOW not what awaits me,
  God kindly veils my eyes,
And o'er each step of my onward way
  He makes new scenes to rise;
And every joy He sends me comes
  A sweet and glad surprise.

    Where He may lead I'll follow,
      My trust in Him repose;
    And every hour in perfect peace
      I'll sing, "He knows, He knows."

2 One step I see before me,
  'Tis all I need to see,
The light of heaven more brightly
    shines
  When earth's illusions flee;
And sweetly through the silence comes
  His loving "Follow Me!"

3 Oh, blissful lack of wisdom!
  'Tis blessed not to know;
He holds me with His own right hand,
  And will not let me go,
And lulls my troubled soul to rest
  In Him who loves me so.

4 So on I go not knowing;
  I would not if I might;
I'd rather walk in the dark with God
  Than go alone in the light;
I'd rather walk by faith with Him
  Than go alone by sight.

307
5.5.5.5.6.5.6.5.

1 THOUGH troubles assail,
  And dangers affright,
Though friends should all fail,
  And foes all unite—
Yet one thing secures us,
  Whatever betide:
The Scripture assures us,
  "The Lord will provide."

2 The birds, without barn
  Or storehouse, are fed;
From them let us learn
  To trust for our bread:
His saints what is fitting
  Shall ne'er be denied,
So long as 'tis written,
  "The Lord will provide."

3 His call we obey,
  Like Abram of old,
Not knowing our way;
  But faith makes us bold:
For though we are strangers
  We have a good Guide;
And trust, in all dangers,
  "The Lord will provide."

4 No strength of our own,
  Or goodness we claim;
Yet, since we have known
  The Saviour's great Name,
In this our strong tower
  For safety we hide,
Almighty His power:
  "The Lord will provide."

308
5.5.5.5.6.5.6.5

1 BEGONE, unbelief!
  My Saviour is near,
And for my relief
  Will surely appear.
By prayer let me wrestle,
  And He will perform:
With Christ in the vessel,
  I smile at the storm.

2 If dark be my way,
  Since He is my Guide,
'Tis mine to obey,
  'Tis His to provide:
Though cisterns be broken,
  And creatures all fail,
The word He hath spoken
  Shall surely prevail.

3 His love in time past
  Forbids me to think
He'll leave me at last
  In trouble to sink:
Each sweet Ebenezer
  I have in review
Confirms His good pleasure
  To help me quite through.

4 Since all that I meet
  Shall work for my good,
The bitter is sweet,
  The medicine is food;
Though painful at present,
  'Twill cease before long;
And then, oh, how pleasant
  The conqueror's song!

309   7.6.7.6.D.

1 SOMETIMES a light surprises
    The Christian while he sings:
It is the Lord who rises
    With healing in His wings.
When comforts are declining,
    He grants the soul again
A season of clear shining,
    To cheer it, after rain.

2 In holy contemplation
    We sweetly then pursue
The theme of God's salvation,
    And find it ever new.
Set free from present sorrow,
    We cheerfully can say,
E'en let the unknown morrow
    Bring with it what it may.

3 It can bring with it nothing,
    But He will bear us through;
Who gives the lilies clothing,
    Will clothe His people too:
Beneath the spreading heavens,
    No creature but is fed;
And He who feeds the ravens
    Will give His children bread.

4 Though vine nor fig-tree neither
    Their wonted fruit should bear,
Though all the fields should wither,
    Nor flocks nor herds be there;
Yet God the same abiding,
    His praise shall tune my voice;
For, while in Him confiding,
    I cannot but rejoice!

310   P.M.

1 CHRIST shall lead us in the time of
    youth,
Christ shall lead us in the way of truth,
Christ shall lead us in the love of right,
    Homeward to the light.

        Though the way be long and
          dreary,
        Though in darkest night we
          roam,
        By His side, we never weary,
        Christ shall lead us home.

2 Christ shall lead us in the hour of
    gloom,
He hath known it, Victor o'er the
    tomb;
When from grief we vainly seek re-
    lease,
    He can give us peace.

3 Christ shall lead us in the hour of strife,
Fill our hearts with everlasting life,
Give us, even with our latest breath,
    Victory over death.

4 Christ shall lead us when the fight shall
    cease
To the fields of everlasting peace,
Where the soul that all the way hath
    trod,
    Resteth calm in God.

311   7.6.7.6.D.

1 IN heavenly love abiding,
    No change my heart shall fear;
And safe is such confiding,
    For nothing changes here.
The storm may roar without me,
    My heart may low be laid,
But God is round about me,
    And can I be dismayed?

2 Wherever He may guide me,
    No want shall turn me back;
My Shepherd is beside me,
    And nothing can I lack.
His wisdom ever waketh,
    His sight is never dim;
He knows the way He taketh,
    And I will walk with Him.

3 Green pastures are before me
    Which yet I have not seen;
Bright skies will soon be o'er me,
    Where the dark clouds have been.
My hope I cannot measure;
    My path to life is free;
My Saviour has my treasure,
    And He will walk with me.

312   8.7.8.7.4.7.

1 GUIDE me, O Thou great Jehovah,
    Pilgrim through this barren land;
I am weak, but Thou art mighty;
    Hold me with Thy powerful hand:
        Bread of heaven,
    Feed me till I want no more.

2 Open now the crystal fountain,
 Whence the healing waters flow;
Let the fiery cloudy pillar
 Lead me all my journey through:
 Strong Deliverer,
 Be Thou still my strength and
 shield.

3 When I tread the verge of Jordan,
 Bid my anxious fears subside;
Bear me through the swelling current,
 Land me safe on Canaan's side:
 Songs of praises
 I will ever give to Thee.

313   7.6.7.6.D.

1 OH, trust thyself to Jesus
 When conscious of thy sin—
 Its heavy weight upon thee,
 Its mighty power within:
 Then is the hour for pleading
 His finished work for thee;
 Then is the time for singing,
 "His blood was shed for me."

2 Oh, trust thyself to Jesus
 When tempted to transgress,
 By word or look of anger,
 Or thought of bitterness:
 Then is the hour for claiming
 Thy Lord to fight for thee;
 Then is the time for singing,
 "He doth deliver me."

3 Oh, trust thyself to Jesus
 When thou art wearied sore,
 When head or hand refuses
 To think or labour more:
 Then is the hour for leaning
 Upon the Master's breast;
 Then is the time for singing,
 "My Saviour gives me rest."

4 Oh, trust thyself to Jesus
 When thou art full of care,
 For loved ones still refusing
 Our blessed hope to share:
 Then is the hour for trusting
 Thy Lord to bring them nigh;
 Then is the time for singing,
 "He loves them more than I."

314   S.M.D.

1   "FOR ever with the Lord!"
 Amen, so let it be!
Life from the dead is in that word,
 'Tis immortality.
 Here in the body pent,
 Absent from Him I roam,
Yet nightly pitch my moving tent
 A day's march nearer home.

2   My Father's house on high,
 Home of my soul, how near
At times to faith's foreseeing eye
 Thy golden gates appear!
 Ah! then my spirit faints
 To reach the land I love,
The bright inheritance of saints,
 Jerusalem above.

3   "For ever with the Lord!"
 Father, if 'tis Thy will,
The promise of that faithful word
 E'en here to me fulfil.
 Be Thou at my right hand,
 Then can I never fail;
Uphold Thou me, and I shall stand;
 Fight, and I must prevail.

4   So when my latest breath
 Shall rend the veil in twain,
By death I shall escape from death,
 And life eternal gain.
 That resurrection-word,
 That shout of victory;
Once more, "For ever with the Lord!"
 Amen, so let it be!

315   10.10.10.10.

1 I TAKE Thy promise, Lord, in all its
 length,
 And breadth and fulness, as my daily
 strength,
Into life's future fearless I may gaze,
For, Jesus, Thou art with me all the
 days.

2 Days may be coming fraught with loss
 and change,
 New scenes surround my life and faces
 strange;

I thank Thee that no day can ever
break,
Saviour, when Thou wilt leave me or
forsake.

3 There may be days of darkness and
distress,
When sin has power to tempt, and care
to press—
Yet in the darkest day I will not fear,
For, 'mid the shadows, Thou wilt still
be near.

4 Days there may be of joy, and deep
delight,
When earth seems fairest, and her skies
most bright;
Then draw me closer to Thee, lest I
rest
Elsewhere, my Saviour, than upon Thy
breast.

5 And all the other days that make my
life,
Marked by no special joy or grief or
strife,
Days filled with quiet duties, trivial
care,
Burdens too small for other hearts to
share;

6 Spend Thou these days with me, all
shall be Thine—
So shall the darkest hour with glory
shine.
Then when these earthly years have
passed away,
Let me be with Thee in the perfect
day.

316   8.4.8.4.8.8.8.4.

1 THROUGH the love of God our Saviour,
All will be well;
Free and changeless is His favour,
All, all is well:
Precious is the blood that healed us,
Perfect is the grace that sealed us,
Strong the hand stretched out to shield
us,
All must be well.

2 Though we pass through tribulation,
All will be well;
Ours is such a full salvation,
All, all is well:
Happy, still in God confiding,
Fruitful, if in Christ abiding,
Holy, through the Spirit's guiding,
All must be well.

3 We expect a bright tomorrow,
All will be well;
Faith can sing, through days of sorrow,
All, all is well:
On our Father's love relying,
Jesus every need supplying,
Or in living or in dying,
All must be well.

317   7.7.7.7.

1 IN Thy book, where glory bright
Shines with never-fading light,
Where Thy saved Thou dost record,
Write my name, my name, O Lord.

Write my name in the book of life,
Lamb of God, write it there;
Where Thy saved Thou dost record,
Write my name, my name, O Lord.

2 In the book, whose pages tell
Who have tried to serve Thee well,
O'er my name let mercy trace,
"Child of God, redeemed by grace."

3 In the book, where Thou dost keep
Record still of years that sleep,
Let my name be written down,
"Heir to life's immortal crown."

4 O my Saviour, Thou canst show
What I long so much to know:
Let my faith behold and see
That my life is hid with Thee.

318   12.11.12.11.D.

1 THE Master hath come, and He calls us
to follow
The track of the footprints He leaves
on our way;
Far over the mountain, and through
the deep hollow,
The path leads us on to the mansions
of day.

The Master hath called us, the children who fear Him,
  Who march 'neath Christ's banner, His own little band:
We love Him, and seek Him, we long to be near Him,
  And rest in the light of His beautiful land.

2 The Master hath called us; the road may be dreary,
  And dangers and sorrows are strewn on the track;
But God's Holy Spirit shall comfort the weary—
  We follow the Saviour, and cannot turn back.
The Master hath called us: though doubt and temptation
  May compass our journey, we cheerfully sing,
"Press onward, look upward," through much tribulation
  The children of Zion must follow their King.

3 The Master hath called us: in life's early morning
  With spirits as fresh as the dew on the sod:
We turn from the world, with its smiles and its scorning,
  To cast in our lot with the people of God.
The Master hath called us, His sons and His daughters,
  We plead for His blessing, and trust in His love;
And through the green pastures, beside the still waters,
  He'll lead us at last to His kingdom above.

319 11.10.11.10.

1 HOLD Thou my hand! so weak I am, and helpless,
  I dare not take one step without Thy aid;
Hold Thou my hand! for then, O loving Saviour,
  No dread of ill shall make my soul afraid,

2 Hold Thou my hand! and closer, closer draw me
  To Thy dear self—my hope, my joy, my all:
Hold Thou my hand, lest haply I should wander;
  And, missing Thee, my trembling feet should fall.

3 Hold Thou my hand! the way is dark before me
  Without the sunlight of Thy face divine:
But when by faith I catch its radiant glory,
  What heights of joy, what rapturous songs are mine!

4 Hold Thou my hand! that when I reach the margin
  Of that lone river Thou didst cross for me,
A heavenly light may flash along its waters,
  And every wave, like crystal, bright shall be.

320 8.7.8.7.

1 WHEN the storms of life are raging,
  Tempests wild on sea and land,
I will seek a place of refuge
  In the shadow of God's hand.

  He will hide me! He will hide me!
  Where no harm can e'er betide me;
  He will hide me! safely hide me . . .
  In the shadow of His hand.

2 Though He may send some affliction,
  'Twill but make me long for home;
For in love, and not in anger,
  All His chastenings will come.

3 Enemies may strive to injure,
  Satan all his arts employ;
God will turn what seems to harm me
  Into everlasting joy.

4 So, while here the cross I'm bearing,
  Meeting storms and billows wild,
Jesus for my soul is caring,
  Naught can harm His Father's child.

321 C.M.

1 WHY should I charge my soul with care?
The wealth in every mine
Belongs to Christ, God's Son and Heir,
And He's a Friend of mine.

    Yes, He's a Friend of mine,
    And He with me doth all things share;
    Since all is Christ's and Christ is mine,
    Why should I have a care?
    For Jesus is a Friend of mine.

2 The silver moon, the golden sun,
And all the stars that shine,
Are His alone, yes, every one,
And He's a Friend of mine.

3 He daily spreads a glorious feast,
And at His table dine
The whole creation, man and beast,
And He's a Friend of mine.

4 And when He comes in bright array,
And leads the conquering line,
It will be glory then to say,
That He's a Friend of mine.

322 P.M.

1 A MIGHTY fortress is our God,
A bulwark never failing;
Our Helper He, amid the flood
Of mortal ills prevailing.
    For still our ancient foe
    Doth seek to work his woe;
    His craft and power are great,
    And armed with cruel hate—
    On earth is not his equal.

2 Did we in our own strength confide,
Our striving would be losing;
Were not the right Man on our side,
The Man of God's own choosing.
    Doth ask who that may be?
    Christ Jesus, it is He!
    Lord Sabaoth is His Name,
    From age to age the same;
    And He must win the battle.

3 And though this world, with devils filled,
Should threaten to undo us,
We will not fear, for God hath willed
His truth to triumph through us.
    Let goods and kindred go,
    This mortal life also;
    The body they may kill,
    God's truth abideth still,
    His kingdom is for ever.

323 P.M.

1 OPEN my eyes that I may see
Glimpses of truth Thou hast for me;
Place in my hands the wonderful key
That shall unclasp and set me free.
    Silently now I wait for Thee,
    Ready, my God, Thy will to see;
    Open my eyes, illumine me,
    Spirit Divine!

2 Open my ears that I may hear
Voices of truth Thou sendest clear;
And while the wave-notes fall on my ear,
Everything false will disappear.
    Silently now I wait for Thee,
    Ready, my God, Thy will to see;
    Open my ears, illumine me,
    Spirit Divine!

3 Open my mouth and let me bear
Tidings of mercy everywhere;
Open my heart and let me prepare
Love with Thy children thus to share.
    Silently now I wait for Thee,
    Ready, my God, Thy will to see;
    Open my heart, illumine me,
    Spirit Divine!

4 Open my mind, that I may read
More of Thy love in word and deed:
What shall I fear while yet Thou dost lead?
Only for light from Thee I plead.
    Silently now I wait for Thee,
    Ready, my God, Thy will to see;
    Open my mind, illumine me,
    Spirit Divine!

324
10.10.10.10.

1 CHRISTIAN, walk carefully, danger is
near!
On in thy journey with trembling and
fear;
Snares from without, and temptations
within,
Seek to entice thee once more into sin.
Christian, walk carefully,
Christian, walk carefully,
Christian, walk carefully, danger is
near!

2 Christian, walk cheerfully, through the
fierce storm,
Dark though the sky with its threats of
alarm;
Soon will the clouds and the tempest be
o'er,
Then with thy Saviour thou'lt rest
evermore.
Christian, walk cheerfully, through
the fierce storm.

3 Christian, walk prayerfully; oft wilt
thou fall,
If thou forget on thy Saviour to call;
Safe thou shalt walk through each trial
and care,
If thou art clad in the armour of prayer.
Christian, walk prayerfully—fear lest
thou fall.

4 Christian, walk hopefully; sorrow and
pain
Cease when the haven of rest thou shalt
gain;
Then from the lips of the Judge thy
reward:
"Enter thou into the joy of thy Lord."
Christian, walk hopefully, rest thou
shalt gain.

325
6.6.6.6.

1 THY way, not mine, O Lord,
However dark it be;
Lead me by Thine own hand,
Choose Thou the path for me.

2 Smooth let it be or rough,
It will be still the best;
Winding or straight, it leads
Right onward to Thy rest.

3 I dare not choose my lot;
I would not if I might;
Choose Thou for me, my God,
So shall I walk aright.

4 Take Thou my cup, and it
With joy or sorrow fill,
As best to Thee may seem;
Choose Thou my good or ill.

5 Choose Thou for me my friends,
My sickness or my health:
Choose Thou my cares for me,
My poverty or wealth.

6 Not mine, not mine the choice,
In things or great or small:
Be Thou my Guide, my Strength,
My Wisdom and my All.

326
12.8.12.8.

1 "MY grace is sufficient"—the Saviour
hath spoken—
I rest on the truth of His word;
I know that His promise hath never
been broken,
The faithful, unchangeable Lord.

2 "*My* grace is sufficient"—no word of a
stranger
Could give me this confidence deep;
But He is my succour in doubt or in
danger,
Almighty to save and to keep.

3 "My *grace* is sufficient"—unmerited
favour
To me, full of failure and sin;
Though I am but weakness, my glorious
Saviour
Will finish what He did begin.

4 "My grace *is* sufficient"—I tremble no
longer;
My best resolutions may fail;
Yet I trust Him with faith ever stronger
and stronger:
His promise must ever prevail.

5 "My grace is *sufficient*"—exhaustless in
measure,
Though millions appeal in their need;
My Saviour, I praise Thee, I take of the
treasure,
Thy grace is sufficient indeed.

327 8.4.8.4.8.8.8.4.

ONE there is above all others—
Oh, how He loves!
His is love beyond a brother's—
Oh, how He loves!
Earthly friends may fail or leave us,
One day soothe, the next day grieve
us,
But this Friend will ne'er deceive us:
Oh, how He loves!

'Tis eternal life to know Him—
Oh, how He loves!
Think, oh think, how much we owe
Him—
Oh, how He loves!
With His precious blood He bought us,
In the wilderness He sought us,
To His fold He safely brought us:
Oh, how He loves!

We have found a Friend in Jesus—
Oh, how He loves!
'Tis His great delight to bless us—
Oh, how He loves!
How our hearts delight to hear Him
Bid us dwell in safety near Him!
Why should we distrust or fear Him?
Oh, how He loves!

Through His Name we are forgiven—
Oh, how He loves!
Backward shall our foes be driven—
Oh, how He loves!
Best of blessings He'll provide us,
Naught but good shall e'er betide us,
Safe to glory He will guide us:
Oh, how He loves!

328 7.7.7.7.7.7.

QUIET, Lord, my froward heart;
Make me teachable and mild,
Upright, simple, free from art;
Make me as a little child—
From distrust and envy free,
Pleased with all that pleases Thee.

What Thou shalt today provide,
Let me as a child receive;
What tomorrow may betide,
Calmly to Thy wisdom leave:
'Tis enough that Thou wilt care—
Why should I the burden bear?

3 As a little child relies
On a care beyond his own,
Knows he's neither strong nor wise,
Fears to stir a step alone—
Let me thus with Thee abide,
As my Father, Guard, and Guide!

329 10.10.10.10.

1 GOD will take care of you: all through
the day
Jesus is near you to keep you from
ill;
Waking or resting, at work or at play,
Jesus is with you, and watching you
still.

2 He will take care of you: all through the
night
Jesus, the Shepherd, His little one
keeps;
Darkness to Him is the same as the
light;
He never slumbers, and He never
sleeps.

3 He will take care of you: all through
the year
Crowning each day with His kindness
and love,
Sending you blessings, and shielding
from fear,
Leading you on to the bright home
above.

4 He will take care of you: yes, to the
end:
Nothing can alter His love for His
own;
Children, be glad that you have such a
Friend;
He will not leave you one moment
alone.

330 P.M.

1 TENDERLY guide us, O Shepherd of
love,
To the green pastures and waters
above;

Guarding us ever by night and by day,
Never from Thee would we stray.

Never! ... Never! ...
Never! oh, never, for Thou art the
Way;
Never! ... Never! ...
Never from Thee would we stray!

2 What though the heavens with clouds
be o'ercast—
Fearful the tempest, and bitter the
blast?
Still with the light of Thy Word on the
way,
Never from Thee would we stray.

3 Over our weakness Thy strength has
been cast;
Keep us in meekness, Thine own till the
last:
Then, safely folded, with joy we shall
say,
Never from Thee would we stray.

331   7.7.7.7.

1 THINE for ever: God of love,
Hear us from Thy throne above;
Thine for ever may we be,
Here and in eternity.

2 Thine for ever: Lord of life,
Shield us through our earthly strife;
Thou the Life, the Truth, the Way,
Guide us to the realms of day.

3 Thine for ever: oh, how blest
They who find in Thee their rest;
Saviour, Guardian, heavenly Friend,
Oh, defend us to the end!

4 Thine for ever: Shepherd, keep
These Thy frail and trembling sheep;
Safe alone beneath Thy care,
Let us all Thy goodness share.

5 Thine for ever: Thou our Guide,
All our wants by Thee supplied,
All our sins by Thee forgiven,
Lead us, Lord, from earth to heaven.

332   C.M

1 THROUGH all the changing scenes o
life,
In trouble and in joy,
The praises of my God shall still
My heart and tongue employ.

2 Oh, magnify the Lord with me!
With me exalt His Name;
When in distress to Him I called,
He to my rescue came.

3 The hosts of God encamp around
The dwellings of the just;
Deliverance He affords to all
Who on His succour trust.

4 Oh, make but trial of His love!
Experience will decide
How blest they are, and only they,
Who in His truth confide.

5 Fear Him, ye saints; and you will then
Have nothing else to fear;
Make you His service your delight,
Your wants shall be His care.

333   6.5.6.5.D

1 LIKE a river glorious
Is God's perfect peace,
Over all victorious
In its bright increase;
Perfect, yet it floweth
Fuller every day;
Perfect, yet it groweth
Deeper all the way.

Stayed upon Jehovah,
Hearts are fully blest;
Finding, as He promised,
Perfect peace and rest.

2 Hidden in the hollow
Of His blessèd hand,
Never foe can follow,
Never traitor stand;
Not a surge of worry,
Not a shade of care,
Not a blast of hurry
Touch the spirit there.

3 Every joy or trial
　　Falleth from above,
Traced upon our dial
　　By the Sun of Love:
We may trust Him fully
　　All for us to do;
They who trust Him wholly
　　Find Him wholly true.

334　　　　6.4.6.4.6.6.6.4.

1 TEACH me Thy way, O Lord,
　　Teach me Thy way!
Thy gracious aid afford,
　　Teach me Thy way!
Help me to walk aright,
More by faith, less by sight;
Lead me with heavenly light:
　　Teach me Thy way!

2 When doubts and fears arise,
　　Teach me Thy way!
When storms o'erspread the skies,
　　Teach me Thy way!
Shine through the cloud and rain,
Through sorrow, toil, and pain;
Make Thou my pathway plain:
　　Teach me Thy way!

3 Long as my life shall last,
　　Teach me Thy way!
Where'er my lot be cast,
　　Teach me Thy way!
Until the race is run,
Until the journey's done,
Until the crown is won,
　　Teach me Thy way!

335　　　　8.7.8.7.4.7.

1 SAVIOUR, like a shepherd lead us,
　　Much we need Thy tender care;
In Thy pleasant pastures feed us,
　　For our use Thy fold prepare:
　　　　Blessèd Jesus,
Thou hast bought us, Thine we are.

2 We are Thine, do Thou befriend us;
　　Be the Guardian of our way:
Keep Thy flock, from sin defend us,
　　Seek us when we go astray:
　　　　Blessèd Jesus,
Hear Thy children when they pray.

3 Thou hast promised to receive us,
　　Poor and sinful though we be;
Thou hast mercy to relieve us,
　　Grace to cleanse, and power to free:
　　　　Blessèd Jesus,
Let us early turn to Thee.

4 Early let us seek Thy favour,
　　Early let us do Thy will;
Blessèd Lord and only Saviour,
　　With Thyself our bosoms fill:
　　　　Blessèd Jesus,
Thou hast loved us—love us still.

336　　　　C.M.

1 I KNOW not why God's wondrous grace
　　To me hath been made known;
Nor why—unworthy as I am—
　　He claimed me for His own.

　　　But "I know whom I have be-
　　lievèd; and am persuaded that He
　　is able to keep that which I've
　　committed unto Him against that
　　day."

2 I know not how this saving faith
　　To me He did impart;
Or how believing in His Word
　　Wrought peace within my heart.

3 I know not how the Spirit moves,
　　Convincing men of sin;
Revealing Jesus through the Word,
　　Creating faith in Him.

4 I know not what of good or ill
　　May be reserved for me—
Of weary ways or golden days
　　Before His face I see.

5 I know not when my Lord may come;
　　I know not how, nor where;
If I shall pass the vale of death,
　　Or "meet Him in the air."

337　　　　8.7.8.7.4.7.

1 FATHER, let Thy benediction,
　　Gently falling as the dew,
And Thy ever-gracious presence
　　Bless us all our journey through:
　　　May we ever,
In our lives keep Christ in view!

2 Young in years, we need the wisdom
　Which can only come from Thee;
In the morn of our existence
　Let us Thy salvation see:
　　Changed in spirit,
　We shall then Thy children be.

3 When temptations shall assail us,
　When we falter by the way,
Let Thine arm of strength defend us;
　Saviour, hear us when we pray:
　　Thou art mighty
　Be Thou then our rock and stay.

4 Praise and blessing, power and glory
　Will we render, Lord, to Thee;
For the news of Thy salvation
　Shall extend from sea to sea;
　　And the nations
　Joyfully shall worship Thee.

338   10.10.

1 PEACE, perfect peace, in this dark
　　world of sin?
　The blood of Jesus whispers peace
　　within.

2 Peace, perfect peace, by thronging
　　duties pressed?
　To do the will of Jesus, this is rest.

3 Peace, perfect peace, with sorrows
　　surging round?
　On Jesus' bosom naught but calm is
　　found.

4 Peace, perfect peace, with loved ones
　　far away?
　In Jesus' keeping we are safe, and they.

5 Peace, perfect peace, our future all un-
　　known?
　Jesus we know, and He is on the
　　throne.

6 Peace, perfect peace, death shadowing
　　us and ours?
　Jesus has vanquished death and all its
　　powers.

7 It is enough: earth's struggles soon shall
　　cease,
　And Jesus call us to heaven's perfect
　　peace.

339   8.7.8.7

1 LEAD me to the Rock that's higher
　　Than the rock poor self can show;
Lead me to its perfect "shelter,"
　　The "strong tower" from every foe.

　　In the higher Rock I'm trusting,
　　　Restful, peaceful, saved, and
　　　free;
　　'Tis the tested Rock of Ages,
　　　Its dear shadow shelters me.

2 Yes, the higher Rock, so towering,
　　Gives, amid life's rudest storms,
Perfect refuge, surest safety,
　　Sweetest rest amid alarms.

3 'Tis the higher Rock that gives me
　　Faith's glad strength for every hour;
Oh to measure all its gladness,
　　All its preciousness of power!

4 'Tis the higher Rock sustains me
　　Joyously from day to day;
Lifting heart and soul and spirit
　　To the purer, holier way.

5 'Tis the higher Rock that saves me,
　　'Tis the higher Rock I've found,
Where abide the crowning graces—
　　Faith and hope and love abound.

6 So will I sing praises to Thee
　　For Thy wondrous power to save;
Daily 'neath Thy shadow resting,
　　Till the victor's palm I wave.

340   7.7.7.7.7.7.

1 LIFE and light and joy are found
　　In the presence of the Lord;
Life, with richest blessings crowned,
　　Light, from many fountains poured:
Life and light and holy joy
None can darken or destroy.

2 Bring to Him life's brightest hours,
　　He will make them still more bright;
Give to Him your noblest powers,
　　He will hallow all your might;
Come to Him with eager quest,
You shall hear His high behest.

All your questions large and deep,
  All the open thoughts of youth,
Bring to Him, and you shall reap
  All the harvest of His truth;
You shall find in that great store
Largest love and wisest lore.

Then, when comes life's wider sphere
  And its busier enterprise,
You shall find Him ever near,
  Looking with approving eyes
On all honest work and true
His dear servants' hands can do.

And if care should dim your eye,
  And life's shadows come apace,
You shall find Him ever nigh
  In His all-abounding grace,
Changing sorrow's darkest night
Into morning clear and bright.

341   P.M.

WALKING with Jesus day by day,
  Taking Him for our Guide;
Holding His hand we can never stray
  Far from His wounded side.

Looking to Jesus day by day,
  Ever for fresh supply,
Never a blessing will He delay,
  Naught but in love deny.

Speaking for Jesus day by day,
  Telling what He has done;
Helping some wanderer to find the
    way,
  Guiding some erring one.

Singing for Jesus day by day,
  Praising His Name in song;
Telling His love in a happy lay
  Gladly the whole day long.

Living for Jesus day by day,
  Sharing His grace and love,
Bearing His cross, that by this we may
  Share in His joy above.

342   P.M.

SAFE in the arms of Jesus,
  Safe on His gentle breast,
There by His love o'ershaded,
  Sweetly my soul shall rest:

Hark! 'tis the voice of angels
  Borne in a song to me,
Over the fields of glory,
  Over the jasper sea.

      Safe in the arms of Jesus,
        Safe on His gentle breast,
      There by His love o'ershaded,
        Sweetly my soul shall rest.

2 Safe in the arms of Jesus,
    Safe from corroding care,
  Safe from the world's temptations,
    Sin cannot harm me there:
  Free from the blight of sorrow,
    Free from my doubts and fears;
  Only a few more trials,
    Only a few more tears.

3 Jesus, my heart's dear Refuge,
    Jesus has died for me;
  Firm on the Rock of Ages
    Ever my trust shall be:
  Here let me wait with patience,
    Wait till the night is o'er;
  Wait till I see the morning
    Break on the golden shore.

343   8.7.8.7.

1 I MUST have the Saviour with me,
    For I dare not walk alone;
  I must feel His presence near me,
    And His arm around me thrown.

        Then my soul shall fear no ill;
        Let Him lead me where He will,
          I will go without a murmur,
          And His footsteps follow still.

2 I must have the Saviour with me,
    For my faith, at best, is weak;
  He can whisper words of comfort
    That no other voice can speak.

3 I must have the Saviour with me,
    In the onward march of life,
  Through the tempest and the sunshine,
    Through the battle and the strife.

4 I must have the Saviour with me,
    And His eye the way must guide;
  Till I reach the vale of Jordan,
    Till I cross the rolling tide.

344 P.M.

1 THE Lord's our Rock, in Him we hide,
A shelter in the time of storm;
Secure, whatever ill betide:
A shelter in the time of storm.

Oh, Jesus is a Rock in a weary
land,
A weary land, a weary land;
Oh, Jesus is a Rock in a weary
land,
A shelter in the time of storm.

2 A shade by day, defence by night,
A shelter in the time of storm;
No fears alarm, no foes affright,
A shelter in the time of storm.

3 The raging storms may round us beat,
A shelter in the time of storm;
We'll never leave our safe retreat,
A shelter in the time of storm.

4 O Rock divine, O Refuge dear,
A shelter in the time of storm,
Be Thou our Helper, ever near,
A shelter in the time of storm.

345 P.M.

1 JESUS, Lord and Master,
Keep me now, I pray;
If I but resist him
Satan cannot stay.
When the storm-clouds gather,
When temptation's nigh,
Thou wilt then protect me,
And whisper, "It is I."

2 Though I fain would follow
Where my Lord once trod,
Drawing ever nearer
To the throne of God;
Yet I often stumble
On my upward way,
Come, then, loving Saviour,
Help me to watch and pray.

3 Though my faith is feeble,
Though my strength is small,
I will ever trust Thee,
Who art over all.
I am now persuaded
Thou wilt keep me true;
If looking unto Jesus
Then I can all things do.

4 On that last great morning
When all men shall meet,
Shall I dare to face Him
Kneeling at His feet?
Yes! for now I'll serve Him
Till my life is gone,
That I may lead men to Him,
And hear Him say, "Well done!"

346 C.M.

1 O GOD, our help in ages past,
Our hope for years to come;
Our shelter from the stormy blast,
And our eternal home.

2 Under the shadow of Thy throne
Thy saints have dwelt secure;
Sufficient is Thine arm alone,
And our defence is sure.

3 Before the hills in order stood,
Or earth received her frame,
From everlasting Thou art God,
To endless years the same.

4 A thousand ages in Thy sight
Are like an evening gone;
Short as the watch that ends the night
Before the rising sun.

5 Time, like an ever-rolling stream,
Bears all its sons away;
They fly, forgotten, as a dream
Dies at the opening day.

6 O God, our help in ages past,
Our hope for years to come;
Be Thou our guard while life shall last,
And our eternal home.

347 11.11.11.11

1 OH, safe to the Rock that is higher than
I
My soul in its conflicts and sorrows
would fly;
So sinful, so weary, Thine, Thine would
I be;
Thou blest "Rock of Ages," I'm hiding
in Thee.

Hiding in Thee,
Hiding in Thee,
Thou blest "Rock of Ages,"
I'm hiding in Thee.

In the calm of the noontide, in sorrow's
    lone hour,
In times when temptation casts o'er me
    its power;
In the tempests of life, on its wide,
    heaving sea,
Thou blest "Rock of Ages," I'm hiding
    in Thee.

How oft in the conflict, when pressed
    by the foe,
I have fled to my Refuge and breathed
    out my woe;
How often when trials like sea-billows
    roll,
Have I hidden in Thee, O Thou Rock of
    my soul.

348   7.7.7.7.

POOR and needy though I be,
God Almighty cares for me;
Gives me clothing, shelter, food,
Gives me all I have of good.

He will hear me when I pray—
He is with me night and day;
When I sleep and when I wake—
For the Lord my Saviour's sake.

He who reigns above the sky
Once became as poor as I;
He whose blood for me was shed
Had not where to lay His head.

Though I labour here awhile,
He will bless me with His smile,
And when this short life is past
I shall rest with Him at last.

Then to Him I'll tune my song,
Happy as the day is long:
This my joy for ever be—
God Almighty cares for me.

349   7.7.7.7.

CHILDREN of the heavenly King,
As ye journey gladly sing;
Sing your Saviour's worthy praise,
Glorious in His works and ways.

2 We are travelling home to God,
In the way the fathers trod:
They are happy now; and we
Soon their happiness shall see.

3 Shout, ye little flock and blest;
You on Jesus' throne shall rest;
There your seat is now prepared,
There your kingdom and reward

4 Lift your eyes, ye sons of light;
Zion's city is in sight;
There our endless home shall be,
There our Lord we soon shall see.

5 Fear not, brethren; joyful stand
On the borders of your land;
Christ, the everlasting Son,
Bids you undismayed go on.

6 Lord, obediently we go,
Gladly leaving all below;
Only Thou our Leader be,
And we still will follow Thee.

350   6.6.4.6.6.6.4.

1 My faith looks up to Thee,
Thou Lamb of Calvary,
    Saviour Divine:
Now hear me while I pray,
Take all my guilt away,
Oh, let me from this day
    Be wholly Thine!

2 May Thy rich grace impart
Strength to my fainting heart,
    My zeal inspire;
As Thou hast died for me,
Oh, may my love to Thee
Pure, warm, and changeless be,
    A living fire!

3 When life's dark maze I tread,
And griefs around me spread,
    Be Thou my Guide:
Bid darkness turn to day,
Wipe sorrow's tears away,
Nor let me ever stray
    From Thee aside.

4 When ends life's transient dream,
When death's cold, sullen stream
    Shall o'er me roll;
Blest Saviour, then in love
Fear and distrust remove;
Oh, bear me safe above,
    A ransomed soul.

351 8.4.8.8.4.

1 GOD holds the key of all unknown,
   And I am glad:
If other hands should hold the key,
Or if He trusted it to me,
   I might be sad.

2 What if tomorrow's cares were here
   Without its rest?
I'd rather He unlocked the day,
And, as the hours swing open, say,
   "My will is best."

3 The very dimness of my sight
   Makes me secure;
For, groping in my misty way,
I feel His hand; I hear Him say,
   "My help is sure."

4 I cannot read His future plans;
   But this I know:
I have the smiling of His face,
And all the refuge of His grace,
   While here below.

5 Enough: this covers all my wants;
   And so I rest!
For what I cannot, He can see,
And in His care I saved shall be,
   For ever blest.

352 7.7.7.7.7.7.

1 JESUS, Saviour, pilot me
Over life's tempestuous sea;
Unknown waves before me roll,
Hiding rock and treacherous shoal;
Chart and compass come from Thee:
Jesus, Saviour, pilot me!

2 As a mother stills her child,
Thou canst hush the ocean wild;
Boisterous waves obey Thy will
When Thou say'st to them, "Be still!"
Wondrous Sovereign of the sea—
Jesus, Saviour, pilot me!

3 When at last I near the shore,
And the fearful breakers roar
'Twixt me and the peaceful rest—
Then, while leaning on Thy breast,
May I hear Thee say to me—
"Fear not, I will pilot thee!"

353 P.M

1   DEAR Lord, I cannot see
     Where Thou art leading me!
I cannot tell if thorns or roses strew the
     way;
     My future is concealed;
     Thou hast not yet revealed
Thy will in me, nor do I for the know
     ledge pray.

          Thy will be done in me
          Lord!
          My all I yield to Thee, Lord!
          In life, in death,
          Be Thou my Guide,
          And I shall be satisfied!

2   What streams I have to cross,
     Of sorrow, pain, or loss,
Are not for me to fear—I shall not be
     dismayed;
     Content if Thou, my Guide,
     Art ever near my side,
That I may hear Thee whisper, "Child
     be not afraid!"

3   Rejoicing, on I go:
     I do not ask to know
The path I tread, or whither be the way
     I take.
     Thy will be done in me;
     This is my only plea:
Forgive, and love, and guide me, for
     Thy mercy's sake.

354 8.7.8.7.D.

1 COURAGE, brother! do not stumble,
   Though thy path be dark as night;
There's a star to guide the humble;
   "Trust in God, and do the right."
Let the road be rough and dreary,
   And its end far out of sight,
Foot it bravely! strong or weary,
   "Trust in God, and do the right."

2 Perish policy and cunning,
   Perish all that fears the light!
Whether losing, whether winning,
   "Trust in God, and do the right."
Simple rule, and safest guiding,
   Inward peace, and inward light,
Star upon our path abiding—
   "Trust in God, and do the right."

Guidance and Safety

Some will hate thee, some will love
thee,
Some will flatter, some will slight:
Cease from man, and look above thee:
"Trust in God, and do the right."
Courage, brother! do not stumble,
Though thy path be dark as night;
There's a star to guide the humble;
"Trust in God, and do the right."

355   8.7.8.7.8.7.

1 LEAD us, heavenly Father, lead us
O'er the world's tempestuous sea;
Guard us, guide us, keep us, feed us,
For we have no help but Thee;
Yet possessing every blessing,
If our God our Father be.

2 Saviour, breathe forgiveness o'er us;
All our weakness Thou dost know;
Thou didst tread this earth before us,
Thou didst feel its keenest woe;
Lone and dreary, faint and weary,
Through the desert Thou didst go.

3 Spirit of our God, descending,
Fill our hearts with heavenly joy;
Love with every passion blending,
Pleasure that can never cloy:
Thus provided, pardoned, guided,
Nothing can our peace destroy.

356   C.M.

1 WALK in the light, so shalt thou know
That fellowship of love
His Spirit only can bestow
Who reigns in light above.

2 Walk in the light, and thou shalt find
Thy heart made truly His
Who dwells in cloudless light en-
shrined,
In whom no darkness is.

3 Walk in the light—and sin abhorred
Shall not defile again;
The blood of Jesus Christ the Lord
Shall cleanse from every stain.

4 Walk in the light, and e'en the tomb
No fearful shade shall wear;
Glory shall chase away its gloom,
For Christ hath conquered there.

5 Walk in the light, and thou shalt own
Thy darkness passed away,
Because that light hath on thee shone,
In which is perfect day.

6 Walk in the light—thy path shall be
Peaceful, serene, and bright;
For God, by grace, shall dwell in thee,
And God Himself is Light.

357   11.11.11.11.

1 How firm a foundation, ye saints of the
Lord,
Is laid for your faith in His excellent
Word!
What more can He say than to you He
hath said,
You who unto Jesus for refuge have
fled?

2 "In every condition—in sickness, in
health,
In poverty's vale, or abounding in
wealth;
At home and abroad, on the land, on
the sea,
As thy days may demand, shall thy
strength ever be.

3 "Fear not, I am with thee, oh, be not
dismayed!
For I am thy God and will still give
thee aid:
I'll strengthen thee, help thee, and
cause thee to stand,
Upheld by My righteous, omnipotent
hand.

4 "When through fiery trials thy pathway shall lie,
My grace all-sufficient shall be thy
supply;
The flame shall not hurt thee; I only
design
Thy dross to consume, and thy gold to
refine.

5 "The soul that on Jesus hath leaned for
repose,
I will not, I will not, desert to its foes;
That soul, though all hell should endeavour to shake,
I'll never, no, never, no, never forsake!"

117

358 P.M.

1 THERE s not a friend like the lowly
    Jesus,
  No, not one! no, not one!
None else could heal all our souls'
    diseases,
  No, not one! no, not one!
        Jesus knows all about our
            struggles,
          He will guide till the day is
            done.
        There's not a friend like the
            lowly Jesus,
          No, not one! no, not one!

2 No friend like Him is so high and holy,
  No, not one! no, not one!
And yet no friend is so meek and lowly,
  No, not one! no, not one!

3 There's not an hour that He is not near
    us,
  No, not one! no, not one!
No night so dark but His love can cheer
    us,
  No, not one! no, not one!

4 Did ever saint find this Friend forsake
    him?
  No, not one! no, not one!
Or sinner find that He would not take
    him?
  No, not one! no, not one!

5 Was e'er a gift like the Saviour
    given?
  No, not one! no, not one!
Will He refuse us a home in heaven?
  No, not one! no, not one!

The Christian Life: (3) Fellowship with God and Union with Christ

359 P.M.

1 JESUS! I am resting, resting
    In the joy of what *Thou* art;
  I am finding out the greatness
    Of Thy loving heart.
  Thou hast bid me gaze upon Thee,
    And Thy beauty fills my soul,
  For, by Thy transforming power,
    Thou hast made me whole.

        Jesus! I am resting, resting
          In the joy of what *Thou* art;
        I am finding out the greatness
          Of Thy loving heart.

2 Oh, how great Thy loving-kindness,
    Vaster, broader than the sea!
  Oh, how marvellous Thy goodness,
    Lavished all on me!
  Yes, I rest in Thee, Beloved,
    Know what wealth of grace is Thine,
  Know Thy certainty of promise,
    And have made it mine.

3 Simply trusting Thee, Lord Jesus,
    I behold Thee as Thou art,
  And Thy love so pure, so changeless,
    Satisfies my heart;
  Satisfies its deepest longings,
    Meets, supplies its every need,
  Compasseth me round with blessings;
    Thine is love indeed!

4 Ever lift Thy face upon me,
    As I work and wait for Thee;
  Resting 'neath Thy smile, Lord Jesus,
    Earth's dark shadows flee.
  Brightness of my Father's glory,
    Sunshine of my Father's face,
  Keep me ever trusting, resting,
    Fill me with Thy grace.

360 P.M.

1 IN tenderness He sought me,
    Weary and sick with sin,
  And on His shoulders brought me
    Back to His fold again.

While angels in His presence sang,
Until the courts of heaven rang.

> Oh, the love that sought me!
> Oh, the blood that bought me!
> Oh, the grace that brought me to
> the fold,
> Wondrous grace that brought me
> to the fold!

2 He found me bruised and dying,
   And poured in oil and wine;
He whispered to assure me,
   "I've found thee—thou art Mine;"
I never heard a sweeter voice,
It made my aching heart rejoice.

3 He pointed to the nail-prints:
   For me His blood was shed,
A mocking crown so thorny
   Was placed upon His head:
I wondered what He saw in me
To suffer such deep agony.

4 I'm sitting in His presence,
   The sunshine of His face,
While with adoring wonder
   His blessings I retrace.
It seems as if eternal days
Are far too short to sound His praise.

5 So, while the hours are passing,
   All now is perfect rest;
I'm waiting for the morning,
   The brightest and the best,
When He will call us to His side
To be with Him, His spotless Bride.

361   7.7.7.7.D.

1 JESUS, Lover of my soul,
   Let me to Thy bosom fly,
While the nearer waters roll,
   While the tempest still is high:
Hide me, O my Saviour, hide,
   Till the storm of life be past!
Safe into the haven guide,
   Oh, receive my soul at last!

2 Other refuge have I none,
   Hangs my helpless soul on Thee:
Leave, ah, leave me not alone,
   Still support and comfort me.

All my trust on Thee is stayed,
   All my help from Thee I bring;
Cover my defenceless head
   With the shadow of Thy wing.

3 Thou, O Christ, art all I want;
   More than all in Thee I find:
Raise the fallen, cheer the faint,
   Heal the sick, and lead the blind;
Just and holy is Thy Name,
   I am all unrighteousness;
Vile, and full of sin I am,
   Thou art full of truth and grace.

4 Plenteous grace with Thee is found,
   Grace to pardon all my sin;
Let the healing streams abound,
   Make and keep me pure within.
Thou of life the fountain art,
   Freely let me take of Thee,
Spring Thou up within my heart,
   Rise to all eternity.

362   8.7.8.7.D.

1 LOVE divine, all loves excelling,
   Joy of heaven, to earth come down!
Fix in us Thy humble dwelling,
   All Thy faithful mercies crown.
Jesus, Thou art all compassion,
   Pure, unbounded love Thou art;
Visit us with Thy salvation,
   Enter every trembling heart.

2 Breathe, oh, breathe Thy loving Spirit
   Into every troubled breast!
Let us all in Thee inherit,
   Let us find Thy promised rest;
Take away the love of sinning;
   Alpha and Omega be;
End of faith, as its beginning,
   Set our hearts at liberty.

3 Come, almighty to deliver,
   Let us all Thy grace receive!
Suddenly return, and never,
   Never more Thy temples leave;
Thee we would be always blessing,
   Serve Thee as Thy hosts above,
Pray, and praise Thee without ceasing,
   Glory in Thy perfect love.

4 Finish then Thy new creation,
    Pure and spotless may we be;
Let us see our whole salvation
    Perfectly restored in Thee!
Changed from glory into glory,
    Till in heaven we take our place;
Till we cast our crowns before Thee,
    Lost in wonder, love, and praise.

363
7.6.7.6.D.

1 O JESUS, I have promised
    To serve Thee to the end;
Be Thou for ever near me,
    My Master and my Friend;
I shall not fear the battle
    If Thou art by my side,
Nor wander from the pathway
    If Thou wilt be my Guide.

2 Oh, let me feel Thee near me;
    The world is ever near;
I see the sights that dazzle,
    The tempting sounds I hear;
My foes are ever near me,
    Around me and within;
But, Jesus, draw Thou nearer,
    And shield my soul from sin.

3 Oh, let me hear Thee speaking,
    In accents clear and still,
Above the storms of passion,
    The murmurs of self-will;
Oh, speak to reassure me,
    To hasten, or control;
Oh, speak, and make me listen,
    Thou Guardian of my soul.

4 O Jesus, Thou hast promised
    To all who follow Thee
That where Thou art in glory
    There shall Thy servant be;
And, Jesus, I have promised
    To serve Thee to the end;
Oh, give me grace to follow
    My Master and my Friend.

5 Oh, let me see Thy footmarks,
    And in them plant mine own:
My hope to follow duly
    Is in Thy strength alone.
Oh, guide me, call me, draw me,
    Uphold me to the end;
And then in heaven receive me,
    My Saviour and my Friend.

364
L.M.

1 JESUS! and shall it ever be,
A sinful child ashamed of Thee?
Ashamed of Thee whom angels praise,
Whose glories shine through endless
    days?

2 Ashamed of Jesus! that dear Friend
On whom my hopes of heaven depend!
No; when I blush, be this my shame
That I no more revere His Name.

3 Ashamed of Jesus! yes, I may,
When I've no guilt to wash away,
No tears to wipe, no joys to crave,
No fears to quell, no soul to save.

4 Till then, nor is my boasting vain,
Till then I'll boast a Saviour slain!
And, oh, may this my glory be
That Christ is not ashamed of me!

365
6.4.6.4.6.6.4.

1 NEARER, my God, to Thee,
    Nearer to Thee;
E'en though it be a cross
    That raiseth me;
Still all my song shall be—
Nearer, my God, to Thee,
    Nearer to Thee.

2 Though, like the wanderer,
    The sun gone down,
Darkness comes over me,
    My rest a stone;
Yet in my dreams I'd be
Nearer, my God, to Thee,
    Nearer to Thee.

3 There let my way appear
    Steps unto heaven;
All that Thou sendest me
    In mercy given;
Angels to beckon me
Nearer, my God, to Thee,
    Nearer to Thee.

4 Then, with my waking thoughts
    Bright with Thy praise,
Out of my stony griefs
    Bethel I'll raise;
So by my woes to be
Nearer, my God, to Thee,
    Nearer to Thee.

5 Or if on joyful wing,
    Cleaving the sky,
Sun, moon, and stars forgot,
    Upward I fly;
Still all my song shall be,
Nearer, my God, to Thee,
    Nearer to Thee.

366   10.10.10.10.

COME in, oh, come! the door stands
    open now;
I knew Thy voice; Lord Jesus, it was
    Thou;
The sun has set long since; the storms
    begin;
'Tis time for Thee, my Saviour, oh,
    come in!

Alas, ill-ordered shows the dreary
    room;
The household-stuff lies heaped amidst
    the gloom;
The table empty stands, the couch un-
    dressed;
Ah, what a welcome for the Eternal
    Guest!

Yet welcome, and today; this doleful
    scene
Is e'en itself my cause to hail Thee in;
This dark confusion e'en at once
    demands
Thine own bright presence, Lord, and
    ordering hands.

I seek no more to alter things, or mend,
Before the coming of so great a Friend;
All were at best unseemly; and 'twere
    ill
Beyond all else to keep Thee waiting
    still.

Come, not to find, but make this
    troubled heart
A dwelling worthy of Thee as Thou art;
To chase the gloom, the terror, and the
    sin;
Come, all Thyself, yea, come, Lord
    Jesus, in!

367   8.7.8.7.7.7.

1 THOU whose Name is called Jesus,
    Risen Lord of life and power,
Oh, it is so sweet to trust Thee!
    Every day and every hour.
      Of Thy wondrous grace I sing,
      Saviour, Counsellor, and King.

2 Thou canst keep my feet from falling,
    Even my poor wayward feet—
Thou who dost present me faultless,
    In Thy righteousness complete:
      Jesus, Lord, in knowing Thee,
      Oh, what strength and victory!

3 All the sin in me, my Saviour,
    Thou canst conquer and subdue;
With Thy sanctifying power
    Permeate my spirit through;
      Let Thy government increase,
      Risen, crowned, Prince of Peace.

4 Thou canst keep me upward looking;
    Ever upward in Thy face;
Thou canst make me stand, upholden
    By the greatness of Thy grace;
      Every promise of Thy Word
      Now I claim from Thee, dear Lord.

5 Oh! what joy to trust Thee, Jesus,
    Mighty Victor o'er the grave,
And to learn amid earth's shadows
    Thine unceasing power to save!
      Only those who prove Thee know
      What the grace Thou dost bestow.

6 Make my life a bright outshining
    Of Thy life, that all may see
Thine own resurrection power
    Mightily put forth in me;
      Ever let my heart become
      Yet more consciously Thy home.

368   8.6.8.6.8.6.

1 FATHER, I know that all my life
    Is portioned out for me;
The changes that will surely come
    I do not fear to see;
I ask Thee for a present mind
    Intent on pleasing Thee.

2 I ask Thee for a thoughtful love,
    Through constant watching wise,
To meet the glad with joyful smiles,
    And wipe the weeping eyes;
A heart at leisure from itself
    To soothe and sympathize.

3 I would not have the restless will
    That hurries to and fro,
Seeking for some great thing to do,
    Or secret thing to know;
I would be treated as a child,
    And guided where I go.

4 Wherever in the world I am,
    In whatsoe'er estate,
I have a fellowship with hearts
    To keep and cultivate;
A work of lowly love to do
    For Him on whom I wait.

369   L.M.

1 O HAPPY day! that fixed my choice
On Thee, my Saviour and my God;
Well may this glowing heart rejoice,
And tell its raptures all abroad.

    Happy day, happy day,
When Jesus washed my sins away!
He teaches me to watch and pray;
And live rejoicing every day.
    Happy day, happy day,
When Jesus washed my sins away!

2 'Tis done! the great transaction's done!
    I am my Lord's, and He is mine;
He drew me, and I followed on,
    Charmed to confess the voice divine.

3 Now rest, my long-divided heart;
    Fixed on this blissful centre, rest;
Nor ever from thy Lord depart,
    With Him of every good possessed.

4 High heaven that heard the solemn vow,
    That vow renewed shall daily hear;
Till in life's latest hour I bow,
    And bless in death a bond so dear.

370   C.M.

1 OH, for a heart to praise my God,
    A heart from sin set free;
A heart that's sprinkled with the blood
    So freely shed for me:

2 A heart resigned, submissive, meek,
    My dear Redeemer's throne;
Where only Christ is heard to speak,
    Where Jesus reigns alone:

3 A humble, lowly, contrite heart,
    Believing, true, and clean;
Which neither death nor life can part
    From Him that dwells within:

4 A heart in every thought renewed
    And filled with love divine;
Perfect, and right, and pure, and good
    A copy, Lord, of Thine!

5 Thy nature, gracious Lord, impart!
    Come quickly from above;
Write Thy new Name upon my heart,
    Thy new, best Name of Love.

371   C.M.

1 JESUS, these eyes have never seen
    That radiant form of Thine;
The veil of sense hangs dark between
    Thy blessèd face and mine.

2 I see Thee not, I hear Thee not,
    Yet art Thou oft with me;
And earth hath ne'er so dear a spot
    As where I meet with Thee.

3 Like some bright dream that comes unsought
    When slumbers o'er me roll,
Thine image ever fills my thought
    And charms my ravished soul.

4 Yet, though I have not seen, and still
    Must rest in faith alone,
I love Thee, dearest Lord, and will,
    Unseen, but not unknown.

5 When death these mortal eyes shall seal,
    And still this throbbing heart,
The rending veil shall Thee reveal
    All-glorious as Thou art.

372 P.M.

1 FAITH looks to Jesus crucified and risen
from the dead.
Faith rests upon His promises, believing all He said.
Faith makes confession of His Name,
holds forth the faithful Word.
Faith takes her cross and follows Him,
her Saviour and her Lord.

2 Faith sees beyond this passing world,
with open vision keen.
Faith all endures as seeing Him,
beloved, but yet unseen.
Faith suffers with her Lord below to
reign with Him above.
Faith ever seeks to walk in light and
ever works by love.

3 Faith loves to be obedient, for she hears
her Master's voice.
Faith walks in separation, and a pilgrim
is by choice.
Faith hastens to His coming—oh, the
rapture and the bliss!
Faith knows she will be like Him when
she sees Him as He is.

4 Oh, grant us, Lord, like precious faith
with them that went before,
That we may keep our garments white
until the conflict's o'er;
Nor lose our crown, nor faint until the
race is fully run,
When we at last shall see Thy face and
hear Thee say, "Well done!"

373 8.7.8.7.

1 SWEET the moments, rich in blessing,
Which before the cross I spend,
Life, and health, and peace possessing
From the sinner's dying Friend!

2 Here I rest, in wonder viewing
All my sins on Jesus laid,
And a full redemption flowing
From the sacrifice He made.

3 Here I find my hope of heaven,
While upon the Lamb I gaze;
Loving much, and much forgiven,
Let my heart o'erflow in praise.

4 Love and grief my heart dividing,
With my tears His feet I'll bathe;
Constant still in faith abiding—
Life deriving from His death.

5 Lord, in ceaseless contemplation
Fix my thankful heart on Thee!
Till I taste Thy full salvation,
And Thine unveiled glory see.

374 7.6.7.6.D.

1 I NEED Thee, precious Jesus!
For I am full of sin:
My soul is dark and guilty,
My heart is dead within:
I need the cleansing fountain,
Where I can always flee,
The blood of Christ most precious,
The sinner's perfect plea.

2 I need Thee, precious Jesus!
For I am very poor;
A stranger and a pilgrim,
I have no earthly store:
I need the love of Jesus
To cheer me on my way,
To guide my doubting footsteps,
To be my strength and stay.

3 I need Thee, precious Jesus!
I need a friend like Thee;
A Friend to soothe and comfort—
A Friend to care for me:
I need the heart of Jesus
To feel each anxious care,
To tell my every trouble
And all my sorrows share.

4 I need Thee, precious Jesus!
And hope to see Thee soon,
Encircled with the rainbow,
And seated on Thy throne;
There with Thy blood-bought children
My joy shall ever be
To sing Thy praise, Lord Jesus—
To gaze, my Lord, on Thee.

375 9.6.9.6.

1 LET me come closer to Thee, Jesus,
Oh, closer day by day;
Let me lean harder on Thee, Jesus,
Yes, harder all the way.

2 Let me show forth Thy beauty, Jesus,
  Like sunshine on the hills;
Oh, let my lips pour forth Thy sweet-
    ness
  In joyous sparkling rills!

3 Yes, like a fountain, precious Jesus,
  Make me and let me be;
Keep me and use me daily, Jesus,
  For Thee, for only Thee.

4 In all my heart and will, O Jesus,
  Be altogether King;
Make me a loyal subject, Jesus,
  To Thee in everything.

5 Thirsting and hungering for Thee,
    Jesus,
  With blessèd hunger here,
Looking for home on Zion's mountain—
  No thirst, no hunger there.

The author permits the ascription "Lord Jesus",
when preferred, to the first line of verses (and line 3
in verses 1, 3, 4): but as the additional word alters
the rhythm, it cannot be printed thus.

376   7.6.7.6.D.
1 I COULD not do without Thee,
  O Saviour of the lost,
Whose precious blood redeemed me
  At such tremendous cost;
Thy righteousness, Thy pardon,
  Thy precious blood must be
My only hope and comfort,
  My glory and my plea.

2 I could not do without Thee,
  I cannot stand alone,
I have no strength or goodness,
  No wisdom of my own;
But Thou, belovèd Saviour,
  Art all in all to me,
And perfect strength in weakness
  Is theirs who lean on Thee.

3 I could not do without Thee,
  For, oh, the way is long!
And I am often weary,
  And sigh replaces song.
How could I do without Thee?
  I do not know the way;
Thou knowest, and Thou leadest,
  And wilt not let me stray.

4 I could not do without Thee,
  O Jesus, Saviour dear:
E'en when my eyes are holden,
  I know that Thou art near;
How dreary and how lonely
  This changeful life would be
Without the sweet communion,
  The secret rest with Thee!

5 I could not do without Thee,
  For years are fleeting fast,
And soon in solemn loneliness
  The river must be passed;
But Thou wilt never leave me,
  And though the waves roll high,
I know Thou wilt be near me,
  And whisper, "It is I."

377   P.M.
1 NOTHING between, Lord, nothing be-
    tween;
  Let me Thy glory see,
  Draw my soul close to Thee;
Then speak in love to me—
  Nothing between.

2 Nothing between, Lord, nothing be-
    tween;
  Let not earth's din and noise
  Stifle Thy still small voice;
In it let me rejoice—
  Nothing between.

3 Nothing between, Lord, nothing be-
    tween;
  Unbelief disappear,
  Vanish each doubt and fear,
Fading when Thou art near—
  Nothing between.

4 Nothing between, Lord, nothing be-
    tween;
  Till Thine eternal light,
  Rising on earth's dark night,
Bursts on my open sight—
  Nothing between.

378   L.M.
1 JESUS, Thou joy of loving hearts,
  Thou Fount of Life, Thou Light of
    men,
From the best bliss that earth imparts
  We turn unfilled to Thee again.

124

2 Thy truth unchanged hath ever stood;
　　Thou savest those that on Thee call;
　To them that seek Thee, Thou art
　　　good;
　　To them that find Thee, All in all.

3 We taste Thee, O Thou living Bread,
　　And long to feast upon Thee still;
　We drink of Thee, the Fountain-head,
　　And thirst our souls from Thee to
　　　fill.

4 Our restless spirits yearn for Thee,
　　Where'er our changeful lot is cast:
　Glad, when Thy gracious smile we see;
　　Blest, when our faith can hold Thee
　　　fast.

5 O Jesus, ever with us stay;
　　Make all our moments calm and
　　　bright;
　Chase the dark night of sin away;
　　Shed o'er the world Thy holy light.

379　　　　　　　　　　　7.7.7.7.D.

1 SAVIOUR, teach me, day by day,
　Love's sweet lesson to obey:
　Sweeter lesson cannot be—
　Loving Him who first loved me.
　Teach me, I am not my own,
　I am Thine, and Thine alone;
　May I serve and copy Thee,
　Loving Him who first loved me.

2 With a child's glad heart of love,
　At Thy bidding may I move,
　Prompt to serve and follow Thee,
　Loving Him who first loved me.
　Teach me thus Thy steps to trace,
　Strong to follow in Thy grace,
　Learning how to love from Thee,
　Loving Him who first loved me.

3 Love, in loving, finds employ,
　In obedience all her joy;
　Ever new that joy will be,
　Loving Him who first loved me.
　Thus may I rejoice to show
　That I feel the love I owe;
　Singing, till Thy face I see,
　Of His love who first loved me.

380　　　　　　　　　　8.8.8.8.8.8.

1 O LOVE, who formedst me to wear
　　The image of Thy Godhead here;
　Who soughtest me with tender care
　　Through all my wanderings wild and
　　　drear;
　O Love, I give myself to Thee,
　Thine ever, only Thine to be.

2 O Love, who once in time wast slain,
　　Pierced through and through with
　　　bitter woe;
　O Love, who wrestling thus didst gain,
　　That we eternal joy might know;
　O Love, I give myself to Thee,
　Thine ever, only Thine to be.

3 O Love, who lovest me for aye,
　　Who for my soul dost ever plead;
　O Love, who didst my ransom pay,
　　Whose power sufficeth in my stead;
　O Love, I give myself to Thee,
　Thine ever, only Thine to be.

4 O Love, whose voice shall bid me rise
　　From out this dying life of ours;
　O Love, whose hand o'er yonder skies
　　Shall set me in the fadeless bowers;
　O Love, I give myself to Thee,
　Thine ever, only Thine to be.

381　　　　　　　　　　　　P.M.

1 "FEAR not, I am with thee";
　　Blessèd golden ray,
　　　Like a star of glory,
　　　　Lighting up my way!
　Through the clouds of midnight
　　This bright promise shone,
　"I will never leave thee,
　　Never will leave thee alone."

　　　No, never alone;
　　　No, never alone;
　　He promised never to leave me,
　　　Never to leave me alone.

2 Roses fade around me,
　　Lilies bloom and die,
　Earthly sunbeams vanish—
　　Radiant still the sky!
　Jesus, Rose of Sharon,
　　Blooming for His own,
　Jesus, heaven's sunshine,
　　Never will leave me alone.

3 Steps unseen before me,
    Hidden dangers near;
Nearer still my Saviour,
    Whispering, "Be of cheer."
Joys, like birds of spring-time,
    To my heart have flown,
Singing all so sweetly,
    "He will not leave me alone."

382   P.M.

1 I NEED Thee every hour,
    Most gracious Lord;
No tender voice like Thine
    Can peace afford.

    I need Thee, oh, I need Thee!
    Every hour I need Thee:
    Oh, bless me now, my Saviour!
    I come to Thee.

2 I need Thee every hour:
    Stay Thou near by;
Temptations lose their power
    When Thou art nigh.

3 I need Thee every hour,
    In joy or pain;
Come quickly and abide,
    Or life is vain.

4 I need Thee every hour;
    Teach me Thy will;
And Thy rich promises
    In me fulfil.

5 I need Thee every hour,
    Most Holy One;
Oh, make me Thine indeed,
    Thou blessèd Son!

383   C.M.

1 O CHRIST, in Thee my soul hath found,
    And found in Thee alone,
The peace, the joy I sought so long,
    The bliss till now unknown.

    Now none but Christ can satisfy,
    None other name for me;
    There's love and life and lasting joy,
    Lord Jesus, found in Thee.

2 I sighed for rest and happiness,
    I yearned for them, not Thee;
But, while I passed my Saviour by,
    His love laid hold on me.

3 I tried the broken cisterns, Lord,
    But, ah, the waters failed!
E'en as I stooped to drink they fled,
    And mocked me as I wailed.

4 The pleasures lost I sadly mourned,
    But never wept for Thee,
Till grace the sightless eyes received,
    Thy loveliness to see.

384   11.10.11.10.

1 WE would see Jesus—for the shadows lengthen
    Across this little landscape of our life;
We would see Jesus, our weak faith to strengthen,
    For the last weariness—the final strife.

2 We would see Jesus—the great Rock-foundation,
    Whereon our feet were set with sovereign grace;
Not life, nor death, with all their agitation,
    Can thence remove us if we see His face.

3 We would see Jesus; sense is all too blinding,
    And heaven appears too dim, too far away;
We would see Thee Thyself, our hearts reminding
    What Thou hast suffered our great debt to pay.

4 We would see Jesus—this is all we're needing,
    Strength, joy, and willingness come with the sight;
We would see Jesus, dying, risen, pleading:
    Then welcome, day, and farewell, mortal night!

385 L.M.

MORE about Jesus would I know,
More of His grace to others show;
More of His saving fulness see,
More of His love who died for me.

More, more about Jesus,
More, more about Jesus;
More of His saving fulness see,
More of His love who died for me.

2 More about Jesus let me learn,
More of His holy will discern;
Spirit of God, my Teacher be,
Showing the things of Christ to me.

3 More about Jesus in His Word,
Holding communion with my Lord;
Hearing His voice in every line,
Making each faithful saying mine.

4 More about Jesus, on His throne,
Riches in glory all His own;
More of His kingdom's sure increase;
More of His coming, Prince of Peace.

386 7.7.7.7.D.

1 LOVED with everlasting love,
Led by grace that love to know,
Spirit, breathing from above,
Thou hast taught me it is so.
Oh, this full and perfect peace!
Oh, this transport all divine!
In a love which cannot cease,
I am His, and He is mine.

2 Heaven above is softer blue,
Earth around is sweeter green;
Something lives in every hue
Christless eyes have never seen:
Birds with gladder songs o'erflow,
Flowers with deeper beauties shine
Since I know, as now I know,
I am His, and He is mine.

3 Things that once were wild alarms
Cannot now disturb my rest;
Closed in everlasting arms,
Pillowed on the loving breast:
Oh, to lie for ever here!
Doubt and care and self resign,
While He whispers in my ear—
I am His, and He is mine.

4 His for ever, only His;
Who the Lord and me shall part?
Ah, with what a rest of bliss
Christ can fill the loving heart!
Heaven and earth may fade and flee;
Firstborn light in gloom decline;
But, while God and I shall be,
I am His, and He is mine.

387 P.M.

1 IT passeth knowledge, that dear love of Thine,
My Jesus, Saviour; yet this soul of mine
Would of Thy love, in all its breadth and length,
Its height and depth, its everlasting strength,
Know more and more.

2 It passeth telling, that dear love of Thine,
My Jesus, Saviour; yet these lips of mine
Would fain proclaim to sinners, far and near,
A love which can remove all guilty fear,
And love beget.

3 It passeth praises, that dear love of Thine,
My Jesus, Saviour; yet this heart of mine
Would sing that love, so full, so rich, so free,
Which brings a rebel sinner, such as me,
Nigh unto God.

4 But though I cannot sing, or tell, or know
The fulness of Thy love, while here below,
My empty vessel I may freely bring:
O Thou, who art of love the living spring,
My vessel fill.

5 I am an empty vessel—not one thought,
Or look of love, I ever to Thee brought;
Yet I may come, and come again to
   Thee,
With this, the empty sinner's only
   plea—
     Thou lovest me.

6 Oh, fill me, Jesus, Saviour, with Thy
   love!
Lead, lead me to the living fount
   above;
Thither may I, in simple faith, draw
   nigh,
And never to another fountain fly,
     But unto Thee.

388   P.M.

1 I LEFT it all with Jesus long ago;
All my sin I brought Him, and my
   woe:
When by faith I saw Him on the tree,
Heard His still, small whisper, " 'Tis for
   thee,"
From my heart the burden rolled
   away—
     Happy day!

2 I leave it all with Jesus; for He knows
How to steal the bitter from life's
   woes,
How to gild the tear-drop with His
   smile,
Make the desert garden bloom awhile:
When my weakness leaneth on His
   might,
     All seems light.

3 I leave it all with Jesus day by day:
Faith can firmly trust Him, come what
   may:
Hope has dropped her anchor, found
   her rest
In the calm, sure haven of His breast:
Love esteems it heaven to abide
     At His side.

4 Oh, leave it all with Jesus, drooping
   soul!
Tell not half thy story, but the whole:

Worlds on worlds are hanging on Hi
   hand,
Life and death are waiting His com
   mand;
Yet His tender bosom makes *thee* room
     Oh, come home!

389   C.M.D

1 MY heart is resting, O my God,
I will give thanks and sing:
My heart is at the secret source
Of every precious thing.
Now the frail vessel Thou hast made,
No hand but Thine shall fill;
The waters of the earth have failed,
And I am thirsty still.

2 I thirst for springs of heavenly life,
And here all day they rise;
I seek the treasure of Thy love,
And close at hand it lies.
And a "new song" is in my mouth,
To long-loved music set;
Glory to Thee for all the grace
I have not tasted yet!

3 I have a heritage of joy
That yet I must not see;
The hand that bled to make it mine
Is keeping it for me.
My heart is resting on Thy truth,
Who hath made all things mine;
That draws my captive will to Thee,
And makes it one with Thine.

4 My heart is resting, O my God,
My heart is in Thy care;
I hear the voice of joy and health
Resounding everywhere.
"Thou art my portion, saith my soul,"
Ten thousand voices say:
The music of their glad Amen
Will never die away.

390   8.7.8.7.

1 THE King of love my Shepherd is,
Whose goodness faileth never;
I nothing lack if I am His,
And He is mine for ever.

2 Where streams of living water flow
My ransomed soul He leadeth,
And, where the verdant pastures grow,
With food celestial feedeth.

3 Perverse and foolish oft I strayed,
    But yet in love He sought me,
And on His shoulder gently laid,
    And home rejoicing brought me.

4 In death's dark vale I fear no ill
    With Thee, dear Lord, beside me;
Thy rod and staff my comfort still,
    Thy cross before to guide me.

5 Thou spread'st a table in my sight;
    Thy unction grace bestoweth:
And oh, what transport of delight
    From Thy pure chalice floweth!

6 And so through all the length of days
    Thy goodness faileth never;
Good Shepherd, may I sing Thy praise
    Within Thy house for ever!

391   L.M.

1 OH, walk with Jesus, would'st thou know
    How deep, how wide His love can flow!
They only fail His love to prove
Who in the ways of sinners rove.

2 Walk thou with Him; that way is light,
All other pathways end in night:
Walk thou with Him; that way is rest,
All other pathways are unblest.

3 Oh, walk with Jesus! to thy view
He will make all things sweet and new;
Will bring new fragrance from each flower,
And hallow every passing hour.

4 Jesus, a great desire have we
To walk life's troubled path with Thee.
Come to us now, in converse stay;
And oh! walk with us day by day.

392   10.10.10.10.

1 DYING with Jesus, by death reckoned mine;
Living with Jesus a new life divine;
Looking to Jesus till glory doth shine;
Moment by moment, O Lord, I am Thine.

    Moment by moment I'm kept in His love,
    Moment by moment I've life from above;
    Looking to Jesus till glory doth shine;
    Moment by moment, O Lord, I am Thine.

2 Never a battle with wrong for the right,
Never a contest that He doth not fight;
Lifting above us His banner so white—
Moment by moment I'm kept in His sight.

3 Never a trial that He is not there,
Never a burden that He doth not bear,
Never a sorrow that He doth not share—
Moment by moment I'm under His care.

4 Never a heart-ache, and never a groan,
Never a tear-drop, and never a moan;
Never a danger but there on the throne
Moment by moment He thinks of His own.

5 Never a weakness that He doth not feel,
Never a sickness that He cannot heal;
Moment by moment, in woe or in weal,
Jesus, my Saviour, abides with me still.

393   C.M.

1 How sweet the Name of Jesus sounds
    In a believer's ear!
It soothes his sorrows, heals his wounds,
    And drives away his fear.

2 It makes the wounded spirit whole,
    And calms the troubled breast;
'Tis manna to the hungry soul,
    And to the weary rest.

3 Dear Name, the rock on which I build,
   My shield and hiding-place,
My never-failing treasury, filled
   With boundless stores of grace!

4 Jesus! my Shepherd, Saviour, Friend;
   My Prophet, Priest, and King;
My Lord, my Life, my Way, my End;
   Accept the praise I bring.

5 Weak is the effort of my heart,
   And cold my warmest thought;
But when I see Thee as Thou art,
   I'll praise Thee as I ought.

6 Till then, I would Thy love proclaim
   With every fleeting breath;
And may the music of Thy Name
   Refresh my soul in death.

394   S.M.

1 HELP me, my God, to speak
   True words to Thee each day;
Real let my voice be when I praise,
   And trustful when I pray.

2   Thy words are true to me—
   Let mine to Thee be true—
The speech of my whole heart and soul,
   However low and few.

3   True words of grief for sin,
   Of longing to be free,
Of yearning for deliverance,
   And likeness, Lord, to Thee.

4   True words of faith, and hope,
   Of godly joy and grief;
Lord, I believe!—oh, hear my cry—
   Help Thou my unbelief!

395   C.M.

1 IMMORTAL Love, for ever full,
   For ever flowing free,
For ever shared, for ever whole,
   A never-ebbing sea!

2 Our outward lips confess the Name
   All other names above;
Love only knoweth whence it came,
   And comprehendeth love.

3 We may not climb the heavenly steeps
   To bring the Lord Christ down:
In vain we search the lowest deeps,
   For Him no depths can drown.

4 But warm, sweet, tender, even yet
   A present help is He:
And faith has still its Olivet,
   And love its Galilee.

5 The healing of His seamless dress
   Is by our beds of pain;
We touch Him in life's throng and press
   And we are whole again.

6 Through Him the first fond prayers are
     said
   Our lips of childhood frame,
The last low whispers of our dead
   Are burdened with His Name.

7 O Lord and Master of us all!
   Whate'er our name or sign,
We own Thy sway, we hear Thy call,
   We test our lives by Thine.

8 We faintly hear, we dimly see,
   In differing phrase we pray;
But, dim or clear, we own in Thee
   The Life, the Truth, the Way!

396   6.6.6.6.

1 DEAR Saviour, Thou art mine,
   How sweet the thought to me!
Let me repeat Thy Name,
   And lift my heart to Thee.

    Mine! mine! mine! I know Thou art
     mine;
    Saviour, dear Saviour, I know Thou
     art mine.

2 Thou art the sinner's Friend,
   So I Thy friendship claim;
A sinner saved by grace,
   When Thy sweet message came.

3 My hardened heart was touched:
   Thy pardoning voice I heard;
And joy and peace came in
   While listening to Thy Word.

4 So, let me sing Thy praise,
   So, let me call Thee mine.
I cannot doubt Thy word,
   I know that I am Thine.

397   C.M.

1 SEARCH me, O God! my actions try,
   And let my life appear
As seen by Thine all-searching eye—
   To mine my ways make clear.

2 Search all my sense, and know my
      heart,
   Who only canst make known,
And let the deep, the hidden part
   To me be fully shown.

3 Throw light into the darkened cells
   Where passion reigns within;
Quicken my conscience till it feels
   The loathsomeness of sin.

4 Search all my thoughts, the secret
      springs,
   The motives that control;
The chambers where polluted things
   Hold empire o'er the soul.

5 Search, till Thy fiery glance has cast
   Its holy light through all,
And I by grace am brought at last
   Before Thy face to fall.

6 Thus prostrate I shall learn of Thee,
   What now I feebly prove,
That God alone in Christ can be
   Unutterable love!

398   8.8.8.8.6.

1 O LOVE, that wilt not let me go,
   I rest my weary soul in Thee;
I give Thee back the life I owe,
That in Thine ocean depths its flow
   May richer, fuller be.

2 O Light, that followest all my way,
   I yield my flickering torch to Thee;
My heart restores its borrowed ray,
That in Thy sunshine's blaze its day
   May brighter, fairer be.

3 O Joy, that seekest me through pain,
   I cannot close my heart to Thee;
I trace the rainbow through the rain,
And feel the promise is not vain
   That morn shall tearless be.

4 O Cross, that liftest up my head,
   I dare not ask to fly from thee;
I lay in dust life's glory dead,
And from the ground there blossoms
      red
   Life that shall endless be.

399   8.8.8.4.

1 LOVED! then the way will not be drear;
For One we know is ever near,
Proving it to our hearts so clear
   That we are loved.

2 Loved with an everlasting love
By Him who left His home above,
To bring us life, and light, and love
   Because He loved.

3 Loved, when our sky is clouded o'er,
And days of sorrow press us sore;
Still will we trust Him evermore,
   For we are loved.

4 Loved, when we leave our native soil,
In heathen lands to live and toil;
Under His shadow naught can foil—
   Still we are loved.

5 Time, that affects all things below,
Can never change the love He'll show;
The heart of Christ with love will flow,
   And we are loved.

6 Loved in the past of yesterday,
And all along our future way,
And in the present of today—
   For ever loved.

7 Loved when we sing the glad new song
To Christ, for whom we've waited long;
With all the happy, ransomed throng—
   For ever loved.

400   6.6.6.6.8.8.

1 HUSHED was the evening hymn,
   The temple courts were dark,
The lamp was burning dim
   Before the sacred ark:
When suddenly a voice divine
Rang through the silence of the shrine.

2 The old man, meek and mild,
  The priest of Israel, slept;
His watch the temple-child,
  The little Levite, kept;
And what from Eli's sense was sealed
The Lord to Hannah's son revealed.

3 Oh, give me Samuel's ear!
  The open ear, O Lord,
Alive and quick to hear
  Each whisper of Thy word;
Like him to answer at Thy call,
And to obey Thee first of all.

4 Oh, give me Samuel's heart!
  A lowly heart that waits
Where in Thy house Thou art,
  Or watches at Thy gates,
By day and night, a heart that still
Moves at the breathing of Thy will.

5 Oh, give me Samuel's mind!
  A sweet, unmurmuring faith,
Obedient and resigned
  To Thee in life and death;
That I may read with child-like eyes
Truths that are hidden from the wise.

401 P.M.

1 ONCE I heard a sound at my heart's
  dark door,
  And was roused from the slumber of
  sin:
It was Jesus knocked, He had knocked
  before;
  Now I said, "Blessed Master, come
  in!"

  Then o- . . . pen! o- . . . pen! open,
   let the Master in!
  For the heart will be bright with a
   heavenly light
  When you let the Master in.

2 Then He spread a feast of redeeming
  love,
  And He made me His own happy
  guest;
In my joy I thought that the saints
  above
  Could be hardly more favoured or
  blest.

3 In the holy war with the foes of truth
  He's my shield; He my table pre-
  pares,
He restores my soul, He renews my
  youth,
  And gives triumph in answer to
  prayers.

4 He will feast me still with His presence
  dear,
  And the love He so freely hath
  given;
While His promise tells, as I serve Him
  here,
  Of the banquet of glory in heaven.

402 8.6.8.8.6

1 DEAR Lord and Father of mankind,
  Forgive our foolish ways!
Re-clothe us in our rightful mind;
In purer lives Thy service find,
  In deeper reverence, praise.

2 In simple trust like theirs who heard
  Beside the Syrian sea
The gracious calling of the Lord,
Let us, like them, without a word
  Rise up and follow Thee.

3 Oh, Sabbath rest by Galilee!
  Oh, calm of hills above,
Where Jesus knelt to share with Thee
The silence of eternity,
  Interpreted by love.

4 With that deep hush subduing all
  Our words and works that drown
The tender whisper of Thy call,
As noiseless let Thy blessing fall
  As fell Thy manna down.

5 Drop Thy still dews of quietness,
  Till all our strivings cease:
Take from our souls the strain and
  stress:
And let our ordered lives confess
  The beauty of Thy peace.

6 Breathe through the heats of our desire
  Thy coolness and Thy balm;
Let sense be dumb—let flesh retire;
Speak through the earthquake, wind,
  and fire,
  O still small voice of calm!

403   7.7.7.7.

HARK, my soul! it is the Lord;
'Tis thy Saviour, hear His word;
Jesus speaks, and speaks to thee,
"Say, poor sinner, lov'st thou Me?

2 "I delivered thee when bound,
And, when bleeding, healed thy wound;
Sought thee wandering, set thee right,
Turned thy darkness into light.

3 "Mine is an unchanging love,
Higher than the heights above;
Deeper than the depths beneath:
Free and faithful, strong as death.

4 "Thou shalt see My glory soon,
When the work of grace is done;
Partner of My throne shalt be;
Say, poor sinner, lov'st thou Me?"

5 Lord! it is my chief complaint
That my love is weak and faint;
Yet I love Thee, and adore:
Oh, for grace to love Thee more!

404   C.M.

1 OH, for a closer walk with God,
A calm and heavenly frame,
A light to shine upon the road
That leads me to the Lamb!

2 Where is the blessedness I knew
When first I saw the Lord?
Where is the soul-refreshing view
Of Jesus and His Word?

3 What peaceful hours I once enjoyed!
How sweet their memory still!
But they have left an aching void
The world can never fill.

4 The dearest idol I have known,
Whate'er that idol be,
Help me to tear it from Thy throne,
And worship only Thee.

5 So shall my walk be close with God,
Calm and serene my frame:
So purer light shall mark the road
That leads me to the Lamb.

405   8.8.8.6.

1 O SAVIOUR, I have naught to plead,
On earth beneath, or heaven above.
But just my own exceeding need,
And Thy exceeding love.

2 The need will soon be past and gone,
Exceeding great, but quickly o'er;
Thy love unbought is all Thine own,
And lasts for evermore.

406   7.6.7.6.

1 O LAMB of God, still keep me
Close to Thy wounded side;
'Tis only there in safety
And peace I can abide.

2 What foes and snares surround me,
What lusts and fears within!
The grace that sought and found me
Alone can keep me clean.

3 'Tis only in Thee hiding
I feel myself secure;
Only in Thee abiding
The conflict can endure;

4 Thine arm the victory gaineth
O'er every hateful foe;
Thy love my heart sustaineth
In all its care and woe.

5 Soon shall my eyes behold Thee,
With rapture face to face;
One half hath not been told me
Of all Thy power and grace;

6 Thy beauty, Lord, and glory,
The wonders of Thy love
Shall be the endless story
Of all Thy saints above.

407   10.10.10.10.

1 HERE, O my Lord, I see Thee face to
face;
Here faith can touch and handle
things unseen;
Here would I grasp with firmer hand
Thy grace,
And all my weariness upon Thee
lean.

2 Here would I feed upon the bread of
God;
    Here drink with Thee the royal wine
    of heaven;
  Here would I lay aside each earthly
  load;
    Here taste afresh the calm of sin for-
    given.

3 This is the hour of banquet and of
song;
    This is the heavenly table spread for
    me;
  Here let me feast, and, feasting, still
  prolong
    The brief, bright hour of fellowship
    with Thee.

4 Too soon we rise; the symbols disappear;
    The feast, though not the love, is past
    and gone;
  The bread and wine remove, but Thou
  art here,
    Nearer than ever, still our Shield and
    Sun.

5 Feast after feast thus comes and passes
by,
    Yet passing points to the glad feast
    above;
  Giving sweet foretastes of the festal
  joy,
    The Lamb's great bridal-feast of bliss
    and love.

408   10.10.10.10.

1 NOT what I am, O Lord, but what
Thou art!
    That, that alone, can be my soul's
    true rest;
  Thy love, not mine, bids fear and
  doubt depart,
    And stills the tempest of my tossing
    breast.

2 It is Thy perfect love that casts out
fear;
    I know the voice that speaks the
    "It is I,"
  And in these well-known words of
  heavenly cheer
    I hear the joy that bids each sorrow
    fly.

3 Thy Name is Love! I hear it from yon
cross;
    Thy Name is Love! I read it in yon
    tomb;
  All meaner love is perishable dross,
    But this shall light me through
    time's thickest gloom.

4 It blesses now, and shall for ever bless.
    It saves me now, and shall for ever
    save;
  It holds me up in days of helplessness,
    It bears me safely o'er each swelling
    wave.

5 'Tis what I know of Thee, my Lord and
God,
    That fills my soul with peace, my lips
    with song;
  Thou art my health, my joy, my staff
  my rod;
    Leaning on Thee, in weakness I am
    strong.

6 More of Thyself, oh, show me, hour by
hour;
    More of Thy glory, O my God and
    Lord;
  More of Thyself, in all Thy grace and
  power;
    More of Thy love and truth, In-
    carnate Word.

409   6.5.6.5.

1 SPEAK, Lord, in the stillness,
    While I wait on Thee;
  Hushed my heart to listen
    In expectancy.

2 Speak, O blessèd Master,
    In this quiet hour;
  Let me see Thy face, Lord,
    Feel Thy touch of power.

3 For the words Thou speakest,
    "They are life" indeed;
  Living Bread from heaven
    Now my spirit feed!

4 All to Thee is yielded,
    I am not my own;
  Blissful, glad surrender—
    I am Thine alone.

5 Speak, Thy servant heareth!
　Be not silent, Lord;
Waits my soul upon Thee
　For the quickening word!

6 Fill me with the knowledge
　Of Thy glorious will;
All Thine own good pleasure
　In Thy child fulfil.

7 Like "a watered garden,"
　Full of fragrance rare,
Lingering in Thy presence,
　Let my life appear.

410　　　　　　　　　　7.6.7.6.D.

ON Thee my heart is resting!
　Ah, this is rest indeed!
What else, almighty Saviour,
　Can a poor sinner need?
Thy light is all my wisdom,
　Thy love is all my stay;
Our Father's home in glory
　Draws nearer every day.

My guilt is great, but greater
　The mercy Thou dost give;
Thyself, a spotless Offering,
　Hast died that I should live.
With Thee my soul unfettered
　Has risen from the dust;
Thy blood is all my treasure,
　Thy Word is all my trust.

Through me, Thou gentle Master,
　Thy purposes fulfil!
I yield myself for ever
　To Thy most holy will.
What though I be but weakness?
　My strength is not in me;
The poorest of Thy people
　Has all things, having Thee.

411　　　　　　　　　　8.8.8.6.

O HOLY Saviour, Friend unseen,
The faint, the weak, on Thee may lean;
Help me throughout life's varying
　scene
　By faith to cling to Thee!

2 Blest with communion so divine,
Take what Thou wilt, shall I repine
When, as the branches to the vine,
　My soul may cling to Thee?

3 What though the world deceitful prove,
And earthly friends and joys remove?
With patient, uncomplaining love
　Still would I cling to Thee!

4 Though faith and hope awhile be tried,
I ask not, need not, aught beside:
How safe, how calm, how satisfied
　The soul that clings to Thee!

5 Blest is my lot, whate'er befall!
What can disturb me, who appal,
While as my Strength, my Rock, my
　All,
　Saviour, I cling to Thee?

412　　　　　　　　　　8.7.8.7.

1 SOMETHING every heart is loving;
　If not Jesus, none can rest:
Lord, my heart to Thee is given;
　Take it, for it loves Thee best.

2 Thus I cast the world behind me;
　Jesus most beloved shall be;
Beauteous　more　than　all　things
　　beauteous,
　He alone is joy to me.

3 Bright with all eternal radiance
　Is the glory of Thy face;
Thou art loving, sweet, and tender,
　Full of pity, full of grace.

4 When I hated, Thou didst love me,
　Shedd'st for me Thy precious blood;
Still Thou lovest, lovest ever,
　Shall I not love Thee, my God?

5 Keep my heart still faithful to Thee,
　That my earthly life may be
But a shadow to that glory
　Of my hidden life in Thee.

413 P.M.

1 HE will never disappoint you! Jesus is
    far more to me
Than in all my glowing day-dreams I
    had fancied He could be;
And the more I get to know Him, so
    the more I find Him true,
And the more I long that others should
    be led to know Him too.

2 He will never disappoint you! He has
    saved my soul from sin;
All the guilt, and all the anguish, which
    oppressed my heart within,
He has banished by His presence, and
    His blessèd kiss of peace
Has assured my heart for ever that His
    love will never cease.

3 He will never disappoint you! He is
    coming by-and-by,
In my heart I have the witness that His
    coming draweth nigh.
All the scoffers may despise me, and no
    change around may see,
But He tells me He is coming, and
    that's quite enough for me.

4 He will never disappoint you! He is All
    in all to me—
Blessèd Saviour, Sanctifier; the un-
    changing Christ is He!
He has won my heart's affections, and
    He meets my every need;
He will never disappoint you, for He
    satisfies indeed!

414 C.M.

1 THE Lord's my Shepherd, I'll not want:
    He makes me down to lie
In pastures green; He leadeth me
    The quiet waters by.

2 My soul He doth restore again;
    And me to walk doth make
Within the paths of righteousness,
    E'en for His own Name's sake.

3 Yea, though I walk in death's dark
    vale,
    Yet will I fear none ill:
For Thou art with me; and Thy rod
    And staff me comfort still.

4 My table Thou hast furnishèd
    In presence of my foes;
My head Thou dost with oil anoint,
    And my cup overflows.

5 Goodness and mercy all my life
    Shall surely follow me;
And in God's house for evermore
    My dwelling-place shall be.

415 C.M.

1 THERE is a Name I love to hear,
    I love to speak its worth;
It sounds like music in my ear,
    The sweetest Name on earth.

2 It tells me of a Saviour's love,
    Who died to set me free;
It tells me of His precious blood,
    The sinner's perfect plea.

3 It tells of One whose loving heart
    Can feel my deepest woe,
Who in my sorrow bears a part
    That none can bear below.

4 It bids my trembling heart rejoice,
    It dries each rising tear;
It tells me in a "still, small voice"
    To trust and never fear.

5 Jesus, the Name I love so well,
    The Name I love to hear!
No saint on earth its worth can tell,
    No heart conceive how dear!

416 P.M.

1 NOT I, but Christ, be honoured, loved,
    exalted;
Not I, but Christ, be seen, be known,
    be heard;
Not I, but Christ, in every look and
    action;
Not I, but Christ, in every thought
    and word.

    Oh, to be saved from myself, dear
      Lord,
      Oh, to be lost in Thee;
    Oh, that it may be no more I,
      But Christ that lives in me.

Not I, but Christ, to gently soothe in
  sorrow;
  Not I, but Christ, to wipe the falling
    tear;
Not I, but Christ, to lift the weary
  burden;
  Not I, but Christ, to hush away all
    fear.

Not I, but Christ, in lowly, silent
  labour;
  Not I, but Christ, in humble, earnest
    toil;
Christ, only Christ! no show, no ostentation;
  Christ, none but Christ, the gatherer
    of the spoil.

Christ, only Christ, ere long will fill my
  vision;
  Glory excelling, soon, full soon, I'll
    see—
Christ, only Christ, my every wish fulfilling—
  Christ, only Christ, my All in all to
    be.

417   8.5.8.3.

1 I AM trusting Thee, Lord Jesus,
  Trusting only Thee!
Trusting Thee for full salvation,
  Great and free.

2 I am trusting Thee for pardon,
  At Thy feet I bow;
For Thy grace and tender mercy,
  Trusting now.

3 I am trusting Thee for cleansing
  In the crimson flood;
Trusting Thee to make me holy
  By Thy blood.

4 I am trusting Thee to guide me,
  Thou alone shalt lead;
Every day and hour supplying
  All my need.

5 I am trusting Thee, Lord Jesus;
  Never let me fall;
I am trusting Thee for ever
  And for all.

418   S.M.

1   BLEST are the pure in heart,
    For they shall see their God,
The secret of the Lord is theirs,
    Their soul is Christ's abode.

2   The Lord, who left the heavens
    Our life and peace to bring,
To dwell in lowliness with men,
    Their Pattern and their King;

3   Still to the lowly soul
    He doth Himself impart,
And for His dwelling and His throne
    Chooseth the pure in heart.

4   Lord, we Thy presence seek:
    May ours this blessing be;
Give us a pure and lowly heart,
    A temple meet for Thee.

419   7.6.7.6.D.

1 O SAVIOUR, we adore Thee!
  We bless Thy precious Name,
That Thou abidest faithful,
  That Thou art still the same
As when Thy children saw Thee,
  And heard Thy loving voice,
"Behold My hands, and touch Me,
  Oh, fear not, but rejoice!"

2 We cried to Thee for succour,
  We looked for light to Thee;
Thy smile our souls has gladdened
  With holy radiancy!
And now with quickened footsteps
  We'll run our heavenly way,
Until the shadows vanish,
  Until the break of day!

3 We've sat beside the river,
  And tasted of Thy grace;
We long to drink the fountain,
  And see Thee face to face!
Sweet, sweet have been the moments
  That we have spent in prayer;
But, oh, the holy worship
  Wherewith we'll praise Thee there!

4 Come, let us blend our voices
    With yonder choirs above;
Swell, swell, the mighty anthem
    Which tells that "God is love";
Soon shall the fainting warrior,
    Soon shall the pilgrim band,
Have fought the last great battle,
    Have reached the promised land.

5 Almighty Lord, we bless Thee!
    Eternal Father, Son,
And Holy, Holy Spirit—
    Mysterious Three in One!
Thou hast done mighty marvels
    Before our wondering gaze:
We've learnt that Thou art faithful,
    In all Thy words and ways.

The Christian Life: (4) Service

420   P.M.

1 THERE'S a work for Jesus
    Ready at your hand,
'Tis a task the Master
    Just for you has planned.
Haste to do His bidding,
    Yield Him service true;
There's a work for Jesus
    None but you can do.

    Work for Jesus, day by day,
    Serve Him ever, falter never,
        Christ obey.
    Yield Him service, loyal, true:
    There's a work for Jesus none but
        you can do.

2 There's a work for Jesus,
    Humble though it be,
'Tis the very service
    He would ask of thee.
Go where fields are whitened
    And the labourers few;
There's a work for Jesus
    None but you can do.

3 There's a work for Jesus,
    Precious souls to bring;
Tell them of His mercies,
    Tell them of your King.
Faint not, grow not weary,
    He will strength renew;
There's a work for Jesus
    None but you can do.

421   8.7.8.7

1 How I praise Thee, precious Saviour,
    That Thy love laid hold of me;
Thou hast saved and cleansed and
        filled me,
    That I might Thy channel be.

    Channels only, blessèd Master,
        But with all Thy wondrous
        power
    Flowing through us, Thou canst
        use us
    Every day and every hour.

2 Just a channel, full of blessing,
    To the thirsty hearts around;
To tell out Thy full salvation,
    All Thy loving message sound.

3 Emptied that Thou shouldest fill me,
    A clean vessel in Thine hand;
With no power but as Thou givest
    Graciously with each command.

4 Witnessing Thy power to save me,
    Setting free from self and sin;
Thou hast bought me to possess me:
    In Thy fulness, Lord, come in.

5 Jesus, fill now with Thy Spirit
    Hearts that full surrender know;
That the streams of living water
    From our inner man may flow.

422 7.6.7.6.D.

How many sheep are straying,
    Lost from the Saviour's fold!
Upon the lonely mountain
    They shiver with the cold;
Within the tangled thickets,
    Where poison-vines do creep,
And over rocky ledges
    Wander the poor, lost sheep.

    Oh, come! let us go and find them:
        In the paths of death they roam;
    At the close of the day, 'twill be
        sweet to say,
        "I have brought some lost one
        home."

Oh, who will go to find them?
    Who, for the Saviour's sake,
Will search with tireless patience
    Through brier and through brake?
Unheeding thirst or hunger,
    Who still, from day to day,
Will seek, as for a treasure,
    The sheep that go astray?

Say, will you seek to find them?
    From pleasant bowers of ease,
Will you go forth determined
    To find the "least of these"?
For still the Saviour calls them,
    And looks across the wold,
And still He holds wide open
    The door into His fold.

How sweet 'twould be at evening,
    If you and I could say,
"Good Shepherd, we've been seeking
    The sheep that went astray!
Heart-sore and faint with hunger,
    We heard them making moan.
And, lo! we come at nightfall,
    And bear them safely home."

423 7.6.7.6.D.

Lord of the living harvest
    That whitens o'er the plain,
Where angels soon shall gather
    Their sheaves of golden grain;
Accept these hands to labour,
    These hearts to trust and love,
And deign with them to hasten
    Thy kingdom from above.

2 As labourers in Thy vineyard,
    Still faithful may we be,
Content to bear the burden
    Of weary days for Thee;
We ask no other wages,
    When Thou shalt call us home,
But to have shared the travail
    Which makes Thy kingdom come.

3 Come down, Thou Holy Spirit,
    And fill our souls with light,
Clothe us in spotless raiment,
    In vesture clean and white;
Within Thy sacred temple
    Be with us, where we stand,
And sanctify Thy people,
    Throughout this happy land.

4 Be with us, God the Father!
    Be with us, God the Son!
And God the Holy Spirit!
    O Blessèd Three in One!
Make us a royal priesthood,
    Thee rightly to adore,
And fill us with Thy fulness,
    Both now and evermore.

424 S.M.

1   We give Thee but Thine own,
        Whate'er the gift may be,
    For all we have is Thine alone,
        A trust, O Lord, from Thee.

2   And hearts are bruised and dead,
        And homes are bare and cold;
    And lambs, for whom the Shepherd
        bled,
        Are straying from the fold.

3   To comfort and to bless,
        To find a balm for woe,
    To tend the lone and fatherless
        Is angels' work below.

4   The captive to release,
        To God the lost to bring,
    To teach the way of life and peace
        Is a most Christ-like thing.

5   And we believe Thy word,
        Though dim our faith may be;
    Whate'er for Thine we do, O Lord,
        We do it unto Thee.

425
S.M.

1 Sow in the morn thy seed,
    At eve hold not thine hand;
To doubt and fear give thou no heed,
    Broadcast it o'er the land.

2 Thou know'st not which may thrive,
    The late or early sown;
Grace keeps the chosen germ alive,
    When and wherever strown.

3 And duly shall appear
    In verdure, beauty, strength,
The tender blade, the stalk, the ear,
    And the full corn at length.

4 Thou canst not toil in vain;
    Cold, heat, and moist, and dry
Shall foster and mature the grain
    For garners in the sky.

5 Thence, when the glorious end,
    The day of God, is come,
The angel-reapers shall descend,
    And heaven cry, Harvest-home!

426
7.6.7.6.D.

1 O MASTER! when Thou callest,
    No voice may say Thee nay,
For blest are they that follow
    Where Thou dost lead the way;
In freshest prime of morning,
    Or fullest glow of noon,
The note of heavenly warning
    Can never come too soon.

2 O Master! where Thou callest,
    No foot may shrink in fear,
For they who trust Thee wholly
    Shall find Thee ever near;
And quiet room and lonely,
    Or busy harvest field,
Where Thou, Lord, rulest only
    Shall precious produce yield.

3 O Master! whom Thou callest
    No heart may dare refuse;
'Tis honour, highest honour,
    When Thou dost deign to use
Our brightest and our fairest,
    Our dearest—all are Thine;
Thou who for each one carest,
    We hail Thy love's design.

4 They who go forth to serve Thee,
    We, too, who serve at home,
May watch and pray together
    Until Thy kingdom come;
In Thee for aye united,
    Our song of hope we raise,
Till that blest shore is sighted,
    Where all shall turn to praise!

427
P.M

1 OH, where are the reapers that garner
    in
The sheaves of the good from the fields
    of sin?
With sickles of truth must the work be
    done,
And no one may rest till the "harvest
    home."

    Where are the reapers? Oh, who
        will come
    And share in the glory of the
        "harvest home"?
    Oh, who will help us to garner in
    The sheaves of good from the fields
        of sin?

2 Go out in the bye-ways and search
    them all:
The wheat may be there, though the
    weeds are tall;
Then search in the highway, and pass
    none by,
But gather from all for the home on
    high.

3 The fields are all ripening, and far and
    wide
The world now is waiting the harvest
    tide;
But reapers are few, and the work is
    great,
And much will be lost should the
    harvest wait.

4 So come with your sickles, ye sons of
    men,
And gather together the golden grain;
Toil on till the Lord of the harvest
    come,
Then share in the joy of the "harvest
    home."

428
7.7.7.7.7.7.

1 HEARTILY thy life should be
Spent for Him who died for thee,
All thy being's ransomed powers,
His each day throughout its hours,
"Till He come," when thou wilt be
All for Him eternally.

2 Heartily thy tongue should tell
Of His grace, that saved from hell,
Singing forth in joyous lays
Thy Redeemer's worthy praise,
"Till He come," when thou wilt be
Praising Him eternally.

3 Heartily thy hands should move
In the service of His love,
With unceasing labour true,
Both to saint and sinner too,
"Till He come," when thou wilt be
Serving Him eternally.

4 Heartily thy feet should run,
Heartily His will be done,
Heartily thy zeal be shown,
Heartily His smile be won,
"Till He come," when thou wilt be
Pleasing Him eternally.

429
P.M.

1 OUT in the darkness, shadowed by sin,
Souls are in bondage, souls we would win;
How can we win them? How show the way?
"Love never faileth", love is the way.

2 Think how the Master came from above,
Suffered on Calvary, breathing out love;
Think how He loves us, e'en when we stray:
We must love others, love is His way.

3 See, they are waiting, looking at you,
Silently watching all that you do;
Seeming so careless, hardened and lost:
"Love never faileth"—count not the cost.

4 "Love never faileth", love is pure gold;
Love is what Jesus came to unfold;
Make us more loving, Master, we pray,
Help us remember, love is Thy way.

430
8.7.8.7.4.7.

1 SPEED Thy servants, Saviour, speed them;
Thou art Lord of winds and waves;
They were bound, but Thou hast freed them;
Now they go to free the slaves;
Be Thou with them,
'Tis Thine arm alone that saves.

2 Friends and home and all forsaking,
Lord, they go at Thy command;
As their stay Thy promise taking,
While they traverse sea and land:
Oh, be with them:
Lead them safely by the hand.

3 When no fruit appears to cheer them,
And they seem to toil in vain,
Then in mercy, Lord, draw near them,
Then their sinking hopes sustain:
Thus supported,
Let their zeal revive again.

4 In the midst of opposition
Let them trust, O Lord, in Thee:
When success attends their mission,
Let Thy servants humble be:
Never leave them,
Till Thy face in heaven they see;

5 There to reap in joy for ever
Fruit that grows from seed here sown;
There to be with Him, who never
Ceases to preserve His own,
And with triumph
Sing a Saviour's grace alone.

431
6.4.6.4.6.6.6.4.

1 "LET not thy hands be slack,"
Live not in vain;
Out on life's lonely track
Men toil in pain.
Play thou a brother's part,
Strength, love, and hope impart,
Bid thou the fainting heart
Look up again!

141

2 "Let not thy hands be slack,"
  Grip thou thy sword!
  Why should'st thou courage lack?
  Think of thy Lord.
  Did He not fight for thee?
  Stronger than all is He,
  And He thy strength will be,
  Rest on His word.

3 "Let not thy hands be slack,"
  Haste to the fray!
  Dream not of turning back:
  Life is not play!
  Gird thou thy armour on,
  Fight till the battle's won,
  Then shall thy Lord's "Well done!"
  More than repay!

4 "Let not thy hands be slack!
  Fear not! Be strong!"
  Cease not to make attack
  On every wrong.
  Press on for truth and right,
  Hold high the Gospel light,
  Expel the dirge of night
  With heaven's song!

5 "Let not thy hands be slack,"
  The days fly fast.
  Lost moments come not back
  From the dark past.
  Then be not slack of hand!
  Help thou the weak to stand!
  To God and Fatherland
  Give all thou hast!

432   P.M.
1 To the work! to the work! we are
    servants of God,
  Let us follow the path that our Master
    has trod;
  With the balm of His counsel our
    strength to renew,
  Let us do with our might what our
    hands find to do.

      Toiling on, ... Toiling on, ...
      Toiling on, ... Toiling on, ...
      Let us hope,... Let us watch,...
        And labour till the Master
        comes.

2 To the work! to the work! let the
    hungry be fed,
  To the fountain of life let the weary be
    led!

In the cross and its banner our glory
    shall be,
  While we herald the tidings, "Salvation
    is free!"

3 To the work! to the work! there is
    labour for all,
  For the kingdom of darkness and error
    shall fall:
  And the name of Jehovah exalted shall
    be
  In the loud-swelling chorus, "Salvation
    is free!"

4 To the work! to the work! in the
    strength of the Lord,
  And a robe and a crown shall our
    labour reward,
  When the home of the faithful our
    dwelling shall be,
  And we shout with the ransomed,
    "Salvation is free!"

433   P.M.
1 RESCUE the perishing, care for the
    dying,
  Snatch them in pity from sin and the
    grave;
  Weep o'er the erring one, lift up the
    fallen,
  Tell them of Jesus, the Mighty to
    save.

      Rescue the perishing,
      Care for the dying;
      Jesus is merciful,
      Jesus will save.

2 Though they are slighting Him, still
    He is waiting,
  Waiting the penitent child to re-
    ceive:
  Plead with them earnestly, plead with
    them gently;
  He will forgive if they only believe.

3 Down in the human heart, crushed by
    the tempter,
  Feelings lie buried that grace can
    restore;
  Touched by a loving hand, wakened by
    kindness,
  Chords that were broken will vibrate
    once more.

4 Rescue the perishing, duty demands it;
   Strength for thy labour the Lord will
      provide:
Back to the narrow way patiently win
   them;
   Tell the poor wanderers a Saviour has
     died.

434   8.7.8.7.

1 LIFE is real, life is earnest,
   And the grave is not its goal;
"Dust thou art, to dust returnest,"
   Was not spoken of the soul.

2 Not enjoyment, and not sorrow,
   Is our destined end or way;
But to act that each tomorrow
   Finds us farther than today.

3 Lives of good men all remind us
   We can make our lives sublime;
And departing leave behind us
   Footprints on the sands of time;

4 Footprints that perhaps another,
   Sailing o'er life's solemn main,
Some forlorn and shipwrecked brother,
   Seeing, shall take heart again.

5 Let us then be up and doing,
   Nor our onward course abate;
Still achieving, still pursuing,
   Learn to labour and to wait.

435   8.5.8.3.

1 HE expecteth, He expecteth!
   Down the stream of time
Still the words come softly ringing
   Like a chime.

2 Oft-times faint, now waxing louder
   As the hour draws near,
When the King, in all His glory,
   Shall appear.

3 He is waiting with long patience
   For His crowning day,
For that kingdom which shall never
   Pass away.

4 And till every tribe and nation
   Bow before His throne,
He expecteth loyal service
   From His own.

5 He expecteth—but He heareth
   Still the bitter cry
From earth's millions, "Come and help
   us,
     For we die."

6 He expecteth—doth He see us
   Busy here and there,
Heedless of those pleading accents
   Of despair?

7 Shall we—dare we—disappoint Him?
   Brethren, let us rise!
He who died for us is watching
   From the skies—

8 Watching till His royal banner
   Floateth far and wide,
Till He seeth of His travail—
   Satisfied!

436   P.M.

1 IF any little word of mine
   May make a life the brighter,
If any little song of mine
   May make a heart the lighter,
God help me speak the little word,
   And take my bit of singing,
And drop it in some lonely vale,
   To set the echoes ringing.

2 If any little love of mine
   May make a life the sweeter,
If any little care of mine
   May make a friend's the fleeter,
If any lift of mine may ease
   The burden of another,
God give me love, and care, and
   strength
   To help my toiling brother.

3 If any little word of mine
   Can make the pathway clearer,
If any little thought of mine
   Can bring a soul the nearer,
If any little deed of mine
   Can clear away a sorrow,
God help me speak, and think, and do,
   And wait not for the morrow.

4 Then many a burden shall be eased,
    Because I help to bear it,
And many a care be lighter made,
    Because I try to share it;
And many a grief shall fly away
    When my bright song shall bid it;
And Christ, the Lord of love, will say,
    " 'Twas unto Me ye did it.''

437   P.M.

1 THE sower went forth sowing;
    The seed in secret slept
Through weeks of faith and patience,
    Till out the green blade crept;
And warmed by golden sunshine
    And fed by silver rain,
At last the fields were whitened
    To harvest once again.
Oh, praise the heavenly Sower
    Who gave the fruitful seed,
And watched and watered duly,
    And ripened for our need.

2 Behold, the heavenly Sower
    Goes forth with better seed,
The word of sure salvation,
    With feet and hands that bleed;
Here in His church 'tis scattered,
    Our spirits are the soil;
Then let an ample fruitage
    Repay His pain and toil.
Oh, beauteous is the harvest
    Wherein all goodness thrives,
And this the true thanksgiving,
    The first-fruits of our lives.

3 Within a hallowed acre
    He sows yet other grain,
When peaceful earth receiveth
    The dead He died to gain;
For though the growth be hidden,
    We know that they shall rise;
Yea, even now they ripen
    In sunny Paradise.
Oh, summer land of harvest,
    Oh, fields for ever white
With souls that wear Christ's raiment,
    With crowns of golden light!

4 One day the heavenly Sower
    Shall reap where He hath sown,
And come again rejoicing,
    And with Him bring His own;

And then the fan of judgment
    Shall winnow from His floor
The chaff into the furnace
    That flameth evermore.
O holy, awful Reaper,
    Have mercy in the day
Thou puttest in Thy sickle,
    And cast us not away.

438   P.M.

1 SOWING in the morning, sowing seeds of
        kindness,
    Sowing in the noontide and the dewy
        eves:
Waiting for the harvest, and the time
        of reaping:
    We shall come rejoicing, bringing in
        the sheaves!

        Bringing in the sheaves!
        Bringing in the sheaves!
        We shall come rejoicing,
        Bringing in the sheaves!

2 Sowing in the sunshine, sowing in the
        shadows,
    Fearing neither clouds nor winter's
        chilling breeze;
By and by the harvest, and the labour
        ended,
    We shall come rejoicing, bringing in
        the sheaves!

439   8.6.8.6.8.6.

1 DISMISS me not Thy service, Lord,
    But train me for Thy will;
For even I, in fields so broad,
    Some duties may fulfil;
And I will ask for no reward,
    Except to serve Thee still.

2 How many serve, how many more
    May to the service come;
To tend the vines, the grapes to store,
    Thou dost appoint for some;
Thou hast Thy young men at the war,
    Thy little ones at home.

3 All works are good, and each is best
    As most it pleases Thee.
Each worker pleases when the rest
    He serves in charity;
And neither man nor work unblest
    Wilt Thou permit to be.

4 Our Master all the work has done
  He asks of us today;
Sharing His service, every one
  Share too His Sonship may:
Lord, I would serve and be a son;
  Dismiss me not, I pray.

440 P.M.

1 WORK, for the night is coming,
  Work through the morning hours,
Work, while the dew is sparkling,
  Work 'mid springing flowers:
Work, when the day grows brighter,
  Work in the glowing sun;
Work, for the night is coming,
  When man's work is done.

2 Work, for the night is coming,
  Work through the sunny noon;
Fill brightest hours with labour,
  Rest comes sure and soon.
Give every flying minute
  Something to keep in store:
Work, for the night is coming,
  When man works no more.

3 Work, for the night is coming,
  Under the sunset skies;
While their bright tints are glowing,
  Work, for daylight flies.
Work, till the last beam fadeth,
  Fadeth to shine no more:
Work, while the night is darkening,
  When man's work is o'er.

441 S.M.

1 REVIVE Thy work, O Lord!
  Thy mighty arm make bare;
Speak with the voice that wakes the
    dead,
  And make Thy people hear!

    Revive Thy work, O Lord!
    While here to Thee we bow;
    Descend, O gracious Lord, descend!
    Oh, come, and bless us now!

2 Revive Thy work, O Lord!
  Exalt Thy precious Name!
And may Thy love in every heart
  Be kindled to a flame!

3 Revive Thy work, O Lord!
  And bless to all Thy Word!
And may its pure and sacred truth
  In living faith be heard!

4 Revive Thy work, O Lord!
  Give Pentecostal showers!
Be Thine the glory, Thine alone!
  The blessing, Lord, be ours!

442 8.8.8.4.

1 DEAR Master, what can children do?
The angels came from heaven above
To comfort Thee; may children too
    Give Thee their love?

2 No more, as on that night of shame,
Art Thou in dark Gethsemane,
Where, worshipping, an angel came
    To strengthen Thee.

3 But Thou hast taught us that Thou art
Still present in the crowded street,
In every lonely, suffering heart
    That there we meet.

4 And not one simple, loving deed
That lessens gloom, or lightens pain,
Or answers some unspoken need,
    Is done in vain—

5 Since every passing joy we make
For men and women that we see,
If it is offered for Thy sake,
    Is given to Thee.

6 O God, our Master, help us then
To bless the weary and the sad,
And, comforting the hearts of men,
    To make Thee glad.

Annie Matheson.
Copyright. By permission of the National Sunday School Union.

443 L.M.

1 LORD, speak to me, that I may speak
  In living echoes of Thy tone;
As Thou hast sought, so let me seek
  Thy erring children, lost and lone.

2 Oh, lead me, Lord, that I may lead
    The wandering and the wavering
      feet;
Oh, feed me, Lord, that I may feed
    Thy hungering ones with manna
      sweet.

3 Oh, strengthen me, that while I stand
    Firm on the rock, and strong in
      Thee,
I may stretch out a loving hand
    To wrestlers with the troubled sea!

4 Oh, teach me, Lord, that I may teach
    The precious things Thou dost im-
      part;
And wing my words, that they may
      reach
    The hidden depths of many a heart!

5 Oh, give Thine own sweet rest to me,
    That I may speak, with soothing
      power,
A word in season, as from Thee,
    To weary ones in needful hour.

6 Oh, fill me with Thy fulness, Lord,
Until my very heart o'erflow
In kindling thought and glowing word,
    Thy love to tell, Thy praise to show.

7 Oh, use me, Lord, use even me,
    Just as Thou wilt, and when, and
      where,
Until Thy blessèd face I see,
    Thy rest, Thy joy, Thy glory share.

444   7.6.7.6.D.

1 I LOVE to tell the Story
    Of unseen things above,
Of Jesus and His glory,
    Of Jesus and His love:
I love to tell the Story,
    Because I know it's true;
It satisfies my longings
    As nothing else would do.

      I love to tell the Story,
        'Twill be my theme in glory,
      To tell the old, old Story
        Of Jesus and His love.

2 I love to tell the Story:
    More wonderful it seems
Than all the golden fancies
    Of all our golden dreams:
I love to tell the Story;
    It did so much for me;
And that is just the reason
    I tell it now to thee.

3 I love to tell the Story:
    'Tis pleasant to repeat
What seems, each time I tell it,
    More wonderfully sweet:
I love to tell the Story:
    For some have never heard
The message of salvation
    From God's own holy Word.

4 I love to tell the Story:
    For those who know it best
Seem hungering and thirsting
    To hear it like the rest:
And when in scenes of glory
    I sing the new, new song,
'Twill be the old, old Story
    That I have loved so long.

445   L.M.

1 Go, labour on; spend, and be spent,
    Thy joy to do the Father's will;
It is the way the Master went;
    Should not the servant tread it still?

2 Go, labour on; 'tis not for naught;
    Thy earthly loss is heavenly gain:
Men heed thee, love thee, praise thee
      not;
    The Master praises—what are men?

3 Go, labour on; your hands are weak,
    Your knees are faint, your soul cast
      down;
Yet falter not; the prize you seek
    Is near—a kingdom and a crown.

4 Go, labour on while it is day:
    The world's dark night is hastening
      on;
Speed, speed thy work; cast sloth
      away:
    It is not thus that souls are won.

Toil on, faint not, keep watch, and
  pray;
  Be wise, the erring soul to win;
Go forth into the world's highway,
  Compel the wanderer to come in.

Toil on, and in thy toil rejoice;
  For toil comes rest, for exile home;
Soon shalt thou hear the Bridegroom's
  voice,
  The midnight cry, "Behold, I come!"

446   S.M.

  YE servants of the Lord,
    Each in his office wait,
  Observant of His heavenly word,
    And watchful at His gate.

2 Let all your lamps be bright,
     And trim the golden flame;
   Gird up your loins, as in His sight,
     For holy is His Name.

3 Watch: 'tis your Lord's command,
     And while we speak He's near;
   Mark the first signal of His hand,
     And ready all appear.

4 Oh, happy servant he
     In such a posture found!
   He shall his Lord with rapture see,
     And be with honour crowned.

5 Christ shall the banquet spread
     With His own royal hand,
   And raise that favoured servant's head
     Amidst the angelic band.

The Christian Life: (5) Consecration and Love to Christ

447   7.6.7.6.D.

1 O JESUS, Thou art standing
     Outside the fast-closed door,
   In lowly patience waiting
     To pass the threshold o'er:
   Shame on us, Christian brethren,
     His Name and sign who bear;
   Oh, shame, thrice shame upon us,
     To keep Him standing there!

2 O Jesus, Thou art knocking,
     And lo! that hand is scarred,
   And thorns Thy brow encircle,
     And tears Thy face have marred:
   Oh, love that passeth knowledge
     So patiently to wait!
   Oh, sin that hath no equal,
     So fast to bar the gate!

3 O Jesus, Thou art pleading
     In accents meek and low;
   "I died for you, My children,
     And will ye treat Me so?"
   O Lord, with shame and sorrow
     We open now the door:
   Dear Saviour, enter, enter,
     And leave us nevermore.

448   7.6.8.6.8.6.8.6.

1 BENEATH the cross of Jesus
     I fain would take my stand,
   The shadow of a mighty rock,
     Within a weary land;
   A home within the wilderness,
     A rest upon the way,
   From the burning of the noontide heat,
     And the burden of the day.

2 O safe and happy shelter!
     O refuge tried and sweet!
   O trysting-place where heaven's love
     And heaven's justice meet!
   As to the holy patriarch
     That wondrous dream was given,
   So seems my Saviour's cross to me,
     A ladder up to heaven.

3 There lies, beneath its shadow,
     But on the farther side,
   The darkness of an awful grave
     That gapes both deep and wide:
   And there between us stands the cross,
     Two arms outstretched to save;
   Like a watchman set to guard the way
     From that eternal grave.

4 Upon that cross of Jesus
    Mine eye at times can see
The very dying form of One
    Who suffered there for me;
And from my smitten heart, with tears,
    Two wonders I confess—
The wonders of His glorious love,
    And my own worthlessness.

5 I take, O cross, thy shadow,
    For my abiding place;
I ask no other sunshine
    Than the sunshine of His face;
Content to let the world go by,
    To know no gain nor loss—
My sinful self my only shame,
    My glory all the cross.

449   8.7.8.7.D.

1 I'VE found a Friend, oh, such a Friend!
    He loved me ere I knew Him;
He drew me with the cords of love,
    And thus He bound me to Him:
And round my heart still closely twine
    Those ties which naught can sever,
For I am His, and He is mine
    For ever and for ever.

2 I've found a Friend, oh, such a Friend!
    He bled, He died to save me;
And not alone the gift of life,
    But His own self He gave me:
Naught that I have my own I call,
    I hold it for the Giver:
My heart, my strength, my life, my all,
    Are His, and His for ever.

3 I've found a Friend, oh, such a Friend!
    All power to Him is given
To guard me on my onward course,
    And bring me safe to heaven.
Th' eternal glories gleam afar,
    To nerve my faint endeavour:
So now to watch! to work! to war!
    And then—to rest for ever!

4 I've found a Friend, oh, such a Friend!
    So kind and true and tender,
So wise a Counsellor and Guide,
    So mighty a Defender:
From Him, who loves me now so well,
    What power my soul can sever?
Shall life, or death, or earth, or hell?
    No; I am His for ever!

450   6.4.6.4.10.10

1 I LIFT my heart to Thee,
        Saviour Divine!
    For Thou art all to me,
        And I am Thine.
Is there on earth a closer bond than
    this,
That "my Belovèd's mine, and I am
    His"?

2   Thine am I by all ties;
        But chiefly Thine,
    That through Thy sacrifice
        Thou, Lord, art mine.
By Thine own cords of love, so sweetly
    wound
Around me, I to Thee am closely
    bound.

3   How can I, Lord, withhold
        Life's brightest hour
    From Thee; or gathered gold
        Or any power?
Why should I keep one precious thing
    from Thee,
When Thou hast given Thine own dear
    Self for me?

4   I pray Thee, Saviour, keep
        Me in Thy love,
    Until death's holy sleep
        Shall me remove
To that fair realm where, sin and
    sorrow o'er,
Thou and Thine own are one for ever-
    more.

451   P.M.

1 Is there a heart that is willing to lay
    Burdens on Jesus' breast?
He is so loving, and gentle, and true—
    Come unto Him and rest.

        Lord, it is I who need Thy love,
            Need Thy strength, and need
                Thy power;
        Oh, keep me, use me, and hold me
            fast,
            Each moment, each day, each
                hour.

148

2 Is there a heart that is lonely today,
    Needing a faithful friend?
Jesus will always keep close by your side,
    Loving you to the end.

3 Is there a heart that has failed to o'ercome
    Sin with its mighty power?
Jesus is stronger than Satan and sin,
    Trust Him this very hour.

4 Is there a heart that is longing to bring
    Blessing to some lost soul?
Jesus is willing the weakest to use,
    Let Him thy life control.

452   C.M.

1 IN truth and grace I want to grow
    Like Jesus, day by day;
And scatter sunshine where I go
    Along my pilgrim way.

    Like Jesus, like Jesus,
      I want to be like Jesus;
    I love Him so, I want to grow
      Like Jesus, day by day.

2 I want to live a life of love
    Like Jesus, day by day;
And point some soul to heaven above
    Along my pilgrim way.

3 I want to do some kindly deed
    Like Jesus, day by day;
And for His kingdom sow the seed
    Along my pilgrim way.

453   6.4.6.4.6.6.6.4.

1 SAVIOUR! Thy dying love
    Thou gavest me,
Nor should I aught withhold,
    My Lord, from Thee;
In love my soul would bow,
My heart fulfil its vow,
Some offering bring Thee now,
    Something for Thee.

2 At the blest mercy-seat,
    Pleading for me,
My feeble faith looks up,
    Jesus, to Thee:

Help me the cross to bear,
Thy wondrous love declare,
Some song to raise, or prayer—
    Something for Thee.

3 Give me a faithful heart—
    Likeness to Thee—
That each departing day
    Henceforth may see
Some work of love begun,
Some deed of kindness done,
Some wanderer sought and won,
    Something for Thee.

4 All that I am and have—
    Thy gifts so free—
In joy, in grief, through life,
    O Lord, for Thee!
And when Thy face I see,
My ransomed soul shall be,
Through all eternity,
    Something for Thee.

454   P.M.

1 DOWN in the valley with my Saviour I would go,
Where the flowers are blooming and the sweet waters flow;
Everywhere He leads me I would follow, follow on;
Walking in His footsteps till the crown be won.

    Follow! follow! I would follow Jesus;
    Anywhere, everywhere, I would follow on!
    Follow! follow! I would follow Jesus!
    Everywhere He leads me I would follow on!

2 Down in the valley with my Saviour I would go,
Where the storms are sweeping and the dark waters flow;
With His hand to lead me I will never, never fear;
Danger cannot harm me if my Lord is near.

3 Down in the valley or upon the mountain steep,
Close beside my Saviour would my soul ever keep;

He will lead me safely in the path that
    He has trod,
Up to where they gather on the hills of
    God.

455   7.6.7.6.D.

1 SHINE on me, O Lord Jesus,
    And let me ever know
The grace that shone from Calvary,
    Where Thou didst love me so.
"My child, I am thy Saviour,
    'Tis not what thou dost feel,
But Mine own gracious promise
    Which does thy pardon seal."

2 Shine in me, O Lord Jesus,
    And let Thy searching light
Reveal each hidden purpose,
    Each thought as in Thy sight.
"My child, I am thy Searcher,
    I try each loving heart,
For I would have most holy
    All who in Me have part."

3 Shine through me, then, Lord Jesus,
    That all the world may see
The life I live is Thy life,
    And thus be drawn to Thee.
"My child, I am thy Power;
    With those who hear My voice
I ever dwell, and use them,
    Thus making them rejoice."

4 Shine out, shine out, Lord Jesus,
    Thou Light of all the world;
Oh, let Thy Gospel banner
    Be everywhere unfurled!
"My child, hast thou forgotten
    That name is also thine?
My fruit is borne on branches,
    Not by the parent Vine."

5 Arise and shine, Lord Jesus,
    Thou Bright and Morning Star;
I long for Thine appearing,
    When peace shall follow war.
"My child, before I gather
    My family in one,
Its number needs completing;
    T'wards this, what hast thou done?"

456   P.M.

1 MORE holiness give me,
    More strivings within;
More patience in suffering,
    More sorrow for sin;
More faith in my Saviour,
    More sense of His care;
More joy in His service,
    More purpose in prayer.

2 More gratitude give me,
    More trust in the Lord;
More zeal for His glory,
    More hope in His Word;
More tears for His sorrows,
    More pain at His grief;
More meekness in trial,
    More praise for relief.

3 More purity give me,
    More strength to o'ercome;
More freedom from earth-stains,
    More longings for home;
More fit for the kingdom,
    More used would I be,
More blessed and holy,
    More, Saviour, like Thee!

457   8.7.8.7.7.7.

1 ONE there is above all others
    Well deserves the name of Friend;
His is love beyond a brother's—
    Costly, free, and knows no end:
        They who once His kindness prove
        Find it everlasting love.

2 Which of all our friends, to save us,
    Could, or would, have shed his blood?
Christ, the Saviour, died to have us
    Reconciled in Him to God:
        This was boundless love indeed!
        Jesus is a Friend in need.

3 When He lived on earth abased,
    "Friend of sinners" was His Name;
Now above all glory raised,
    He rejoices in the same:
        Still He calls them brethren,
        friends,
        And to all their wants attends.

4 Oh, for grace our hearts to soften!
   Teach us, Lord, at length to love;
We, alas! forget too often
   What a Friend we have above;
      But when home our souls are
         brought,
      We will love Thee as we ought.

458　　　　　　　　8.8.8.8.8.8.

1 JESUS, my Lord, my God, my All,
Hear me, blest Saviour, when I call;
Hear me, and from Thy dwelling-
   place
Pour down the riches of Thy grace;
   Jesus, my Lord, I Thee adore,
   Oh, make me love Thee more and
      more.

2 Jesus, too late I Thee have sought,
How can I love Thee as I ought?
And how extol Thy matchless fame,
The glorious beauty of Thy Name?
   Jesus, my Lord, I Thee adore,
   Oh, make me love Thee more and
      more.

3 Jesus, what didst Thou find in me,
That Thou hast dealt so lovingly?
How great the joy that Thou hast
   brought,
So far exceeding hope or thought!
   Jesus, my Lord, I Thee adore,
   Oh, make me love Thee more and
      more.

4 Jesus, of Thee shall be my song,
To Thee my heart and soul belong;
All that I have or am is Thine,
And Thou, blest Saviour, Thou art
   mine.
   Jesus, my Lord, I Thee adore,
   Oh, make me love Thee more and
      more.

459　　　　　　　　7.6.7.6.

1 IN full and glad surrender
   I give myself to Thee,
Thine utterly and only
   And evermore to be.

2 O Son of God, who lov'st me,
   I will be Thine alone;
And all I have and am, Lord,
   Shall henceforth be Thine own!

3 Reign over me, Lord Jesus;
   Oh, make my heart Thy throne:
It shall be Thine, dear Saviour,
   It shall be Thine alone.

4 Oh, come and reign, Lord Jesus;
   Rule over everything!
And keep me always loyal
   And true to Thee, my King.

460　　　　　　　　P.M.

1 NEARER, still nearer, close to Thy
      heart,
   Draw me, my Saviour, so precious
      Thou art;
Fold me, oh, fold me close to Thy
      breast,
   Shelter me safe in that "Haven of
      Rest."

2 Nearer, still nearer, nothing I bring,
   Naught as an offering to Jesus my
      King;
Only my sinful, now contrite heart,
   Grant me the cleansing Thy blood
      doth impart.

3 Nearer, still nearer; Lord, to be Thine,
   Sin, with its follies, I gladly resign;
All of its pleasures, pomp and its pride,
   Give me but Jesus, my Lord cruci-
      fied.

4 Nearer, still nearer, while life shall last,
   Till all its struggles and trials are
      past;
Then through eternity, ever I'll be
   Nearer, my Saviour, still nearer to
      Thee.

461　　　　　　　　11.11.11.11.

1 MY Saviour, I love Thee, I know Thou
      art mine;
For Thee all the pleasures of sin I
      resign;

151

My gracious Redeemer, my Saviour, art
  Thou;
If ever I loved Thee, my Saviour, 'tis
  now.

2 I love Thee because Thou hast first
    lovèd me,
And purchased my pardon on Calvary's
  tree;
I love Thee for wearing the thorns on
  Thy brow;
If ever I loved Thee, my Saviour, 'tis
  now.

3 In mansions of glory and endless
    delight,
I'll ever adore Thee in heaven so
  bright;
I'll sing, with the glittering crown on
  my brow,
"If ever I loved Thee, my Saviour, 'tis
  now."

462   P.M.

1 I HAVE such a wonderful Saviour,
    Who helps me wherever I go;
That I must be telling His goodness,
  That everybody should know.

    Everybody should know,
    Everybody should know;
  I have such a wonderful Saviour,
    That everybody should know.

2 His mercy and love are unbounded,
    He makes me with gladness o'er-
    flow;
Oh, He is "the Chief of ten thousand":
  That everybody should know!

3 He helps me when trials surround me,
    His grace and His goodness to show;
Oh, how can I help but adore Him,
  That everybody should know!

4 My life and my love I will give Him,
    And faithfully serve Him below,
Who brought me His wondrous salva-
  tion
That everybody should know.

463   P.M

1   WHEN we walk with the Lord,
      In the light of His Word,
What a glory He sheds on our way!
    While we do His good will
      He abides with us still,
And with all who will trust and obey!

      Trust and obey!
      For there's no other way
      To be happy in Jesus—
      But to trust and obey.

2   Not a shadow can rise,
      Not a cloud in the skies,
But His smile quickly drives it away;
    Not a doubt nor a fear,
      Not a sigh nor a tear,
Can abide while we trust and obey!

3   Not a burden we bear,
      Not a sorrow we share,
But our toil He doth richly repay:
    Not a grief nor a loss,
      Not a frown nor a cross,
But is blest if we trust and obey.

4   But we never can prove
      The delights of His love
Until all on the altar we lay;
    For the favour He shows,
      And the joy He bestows,
Are for them who will trust and obey.

5   Then in fellowship sweet
      We will sit at His feet,
Or we'll walk by His side in the way;
    What He says we will do,
      Where He sends we will go—
Never fear, only trust and obey!

464   P.M.

1 "BURIED with Christ," and raised with
    Him too;
What is there left for me to do?
Simply to cease from struggling and
  strife,
Simply to "walk in newness of life."
    Glory be to God!

2 "Risen with Christ," my glorious Head,
   Holiness, now, the pathway I tread;
Beautiful thought, while walking there-
   in:
"He that is dead is freed from sin."
     Glory be to God!

3 "Living with Christ," who "dieth no
   more,"
Following Christ, who goeth before,
I am from bondage utterly freed,
Reckoning self as "dead indeed."
     Glory be to God!

4 Living for Christ, my members I yield,
Servants to God, for evermore sealed;
"Not under law," I'm now "under
   grace,"
Sin is dethroned, and Christ takes its
   place.
     Glory be to God!

5 Growing in Christ; no more shall be
   named
Things of which now I'm truly
   ashamed;
"Fruit unto holiness" will I bear,
Life evermore the end I shall share.
     Glory be to God!

465   7.7.7.7.7.7.

1 JESUS, Master, whose I am,
   Purchased Thine alone to be,
By Thy blood, O spotless Lamb,
   Shed so willingly for me,
Let my heart be all Thine own,
Let me live to Thee alone.

2 Other lords have long held sway;
   Now, Thy Name alone to bear,
Thy dear voice alone obey,
   Is my daily, hourly prayer:
Whom have I in heaven but Thee?
Nothing else my joy can be.

3 Jesus, Master, whom I serve,
   Though so feebly and so ill,
Strengthen hand and heart and nerve
   All Thy bidding to fulfil;
Open Thou mine eyes to see
All the work Thou hast for me.

4 Jesus, Master, wilt Thou use
   One who owes Thee more than all?
As Thou wilt! I would not choose;
   Only let me hear Thy call.
Jesus, let me always be,
In Thy service, glad and free.

466   6.6.6.6.8.8.

1 I BRING my sins to Thee,
   The sins I cannot count,
That all may cleansèd be
   In Thy once-opened fount.
I bring them, Saviour, all to Thee:
The burden is too great for me.

2 My heart to Thee I bring,
   The heart I cannot read,
A faithless, wandering thing,
   An evil heart indeed.
I bring it, Saviour, now to Thee,
That fixed and faithful it may be.

3 My joys to Thee I bring—
   The joys Thy love has given,
That each may be a wing
   To lift me nearer heaven.
I bring them, Saviour, all to Thee,
For Thou hast purchased all for me.

4 My life I bring to Thee,
   I would not be my own;
O Saviour, let me be
   Thine ever, Thine alone!
My heart, my life, my all, I bring
To Thee, my Saviour and my King.

467   8.7.8.7.

1 JESUS calls us; o'er the tumult
Of our life's wild, restless sea,
Day by day His sweet voice soundeth,
Saying, "Christian, follow Me."

2 As of old apostles heard it
By the Galilean lake,
Turned from home and toil and kindred,
Leaving all for His dear sake.

3 Jesus calls us from the worship
Of the vain world's golden store:
From each idol that would keep us,
Saying, "Christian, love Me more."

4 In our joys, and in our sorrows,
  Days of toil, and hours of ease,
Still He calls, in cares and pleasures,
  "Christian, love Me more than these."

5 Jesus calls us—by Thy mercies,
  Saviour, may we hear Thy call;
Give our hearts to Thy obedience,
  Serve and love Thee best of all.

468   6.6.6.6.6.6.

1 I GAVE My life for thee,
  My precious blood I shed,
That thou might'st ransomed be,
  And quickened from the dead:
I gave My life for thee;
What hast thou given for Me?

2 I spent long years for thee
  In weariness and woe,
That an eternity
  Of joy thou mightest know:
I spent long years for thee;
Hast thou spent *one* for Me?

3 My Father's home of light,
  My rainbow-circled throne,
I left for earthly night,
  For wanderings sad and lone:
I left it all for thee;
Hast thou left aught for Me?

4 I suffered much for thee,
  More than thy tongue can tell
Of bitter agony
  To rescue thee from hell:
I suffered much for thee;
What canst thou bear for Me?

5 Lord, let my life be given,
  And every moment spent,
For God, for souls, for heaven,
  And all earth's ties be rent.
Thou gav'st Thyself for me,
Now I give all for Thee.

469   L.M.

1 WHEN I survey the wondrous cross
  On which the Prince of glory died,
My richest gain I count but loss,
  And pour contempt on all my pride.

2 Forbid it, Lord, that I should boast,
  Save in the cross of Christ my God:
All the vain things that charm me
    most,
  I sacrifice them to His blood.

3 See from His head, His hands, His feet,
  Sorrow and love flow mingled down:
Did e'er such love and sorrow meet,
  Or thorns compose so rich a crown?

4 Were the whole realm of nature mine,
  That were an offering far too small;
Love so amazing, so divine,
  Demands my soul, my life, my all!

470   8.7.8.7.

1 COME, Thou Fount of every blessing,
  Tune my heart to sing Thy grace;
Streams of mercy, never ceasing,
  Call for songs of loudest praise.

2 Jesus sought me when a stranger,
  Wandering from the fold of God;
He, to rescue me from danger,
  Interposed His precious blood.

3 Oh, to grace how great a debtor
  Daily I'm constrained to be!
Let that grace, Lord, like a fetter,
  Bind my wandering heart to Thee.

4 Prone to wander, Lord, I feel it,
  Prone to leave the God I love:
Here's my heart; Lord, take and seal it,
  Seal it from Thy courts above.

471   8.8.8.7.

1 I AM not skilled to understand
  What God hath willed, what God hath
    planned;
I only know at His right hand
  Stands One who is my Saviour!

2 I take Him at His word indeed:
  "Christ died for sinners," this I read;
And in my heart I find a need
  Of Him to be my Saviour!

3 That He should leave His place on
   high,
  And come for sinful man to die,
  You count it strange?—so once did I,
   Before I knew my Saviour!

4 And oh, that He fulfilled may see
  The travail of His soul in me,
  And with His work contented be,
   As I with my dear Saviour!

5 Yea, living, dying, let me bring
  My strength, my solace from this
   spring,
  That He who lives to be my King
   Once died to be my Saviour.

472   C.M.

1 O JESUS, King most wonderful,
  Thou Conqueror renowned;
  Thou Sweetness most ineffable,
   In whom all joys are found:

2 When once Thou visitest the heart,
  Then truth begins to shine;
  Then earthly vanities depart,
   Then kindles love divine.

3 Jesus! Thy mercies are untold
  Through each returning day;
  Thy love exceeds a thousand-fold
   Whatever we can say.

4 May every heart confess Thy Name,
  And ever Thee adore;
  And, seeking Thee, itself inflame
   To seek Thee more and more.

5 Thee may our tongues for ever bless;
  Thee may we love alone;
  And ever in our lives express
   The image of Thine own.

6 Grant us, while here on earth we stay,
  Thy love to feel and know;
  And when from hence we pass away,
   To us Thy glory show.

473   6.5.6.5.

1 O MY Saviour, lifted
   From the earth for me,
  Draw me, in Thy mercy,
   Nearer unto Thee.

2 Lift my earth-bound longings,
   Fix them, Lord, above;
  Draw me with the magnet
   Of Thy mighty love.

3 And I come, Lord Jesus;
   Dare I turn away?
  No! Thy love hath conquered,
   And I come today.

4 Bringing all my burdens,
   Sorrow, sin and care;
  At Thy feet I lay them,
   And I leave them there.

474   11.11.11.11.

1 TAKE time to be holy, speak oft with
   thy Lord,
  Abide in Him always, and feed on His
   Word.
  Make friends of God's children, help
   those who are weak;
  Forgetting in nothing His blessing to
   seek.

2 Take time to be holy, the world rushes
   on;
  Spend much time in secret with Jesus
   alone.
  By looking to Jesus like Him thou
   shalt be;
  Thy friends, in thy conduct, His likeness shall see.

3 Take time to be holy, let Him be thy
   Guide;
  And run not before Him whatever
   betide:
  In joy or in sorrow still follow thy
   Lord,
  And, looking to Jesus, still trust in His
   Word.

4 Take time to be holy, be calm in thy
   soul;
  Each thought and each temper beneath
   His control.
  Thus led by His Spirit to fountains of
   love
  Thou soon shalt be fitted for service
   above.

475 P.M.

1 HAST Thou not a blessing for me,
  For me, Thy sinful child?
Although I've wandered far from Thee
  O'er deserts waste and wild.

    Hast Thou not a blessing for me,
    A blessing for me, a blessing for
      me?
    Hast Thou not a blessing for
      me?
    A blessing even for me!

2 My heart is all defiled with sin,
  But Jesus, He has died:
Oh! cleanse me in the precious blood
  That flowed from His dear side.

3 My Saviour intercedes for me
  Before Thy throne on high:
Oh, look upon His precious blood,
  And save me, or I die.

4 My Father, bless Thy feeble child,
  And fill me with Thy love:
And may Thy Holy Spirit fit
  Me for Thy fold above.
    Oh, yes! Thou hast a blessing
      for me!
    A blessing even for me.

476 P.M.

1 PRAISE the Saviour, ye who know
    Him:
Who can tell how much we owe Him?
Gladly let us render to Him
  All we have and are!

2 Jesus is the Name that charms us,
He for conflict fits and arms us;
Nothing moves and nothing harms us
  When we trust in Him.

3 Trust in Him, ye saints, for ever;
He is faithful, changing never;
Neither force nor guile can sever
  Those He loves from Him.

4 Keep us, Lord, oh, keep us cleaving
To Thyself, and still believing,
Till the hour of our receiving
  Promised joys in heaven!

5 Then we shall be where we would be,
Then we shall be what we should be,
Things which are not now, nor could be
  Then shall be our own.

477 6.5.6.5.D

1 IN the heart of Jesus
    There is love for you,
Love most pure and tender,
    Love most deep and true;
Why should you be lonely,
    Why for friendship sigh,
When the heart of Jesus
    Has a full supply?

2 In the mind of Jesus
    There is thought for you,
Warm as summer sunshine,
    Sweet as morning dew;
Why should you be fearful,
    Why take anxious thought,
Since the mind of Jesus
    Cares for those He bought?

3 In the field of Jesus
    There is work for you;
Such as even angels
    Might rejoice to do:
Why stand idly sighing
    For some life-work grand,
While the field of Jesus
    Seeks your reaping hand?

4 In the home of Jesus
    There's a place for you;
Glorious, bright, and joyous,
    Calm and peaceful too:
Why then, like a wanderer,
    Roam with weary pace,
If the home of Jesus
    Holds for you a place?

478 10.10.10.10.

1 GOD made me for Himself, to serve Him
    here,
With love's pure service and in filial
    fear;
To show His praise, for Him to labour
    now;
Then see His glory where the angels
    bow.

2 All needful grace was mine through His
    dear Son,
Whose life and death my full salvation
    won;
The grace that would have strengthened
    me, and taught;
Grace that would crown me when my
    work was wrought.

3 And I, poor sinner, cast it all away;
Lived for the toil or pleasure of each
    day;
As if no Christ had shed His precious
    blood,
As if I owed no homage to my God.

4 O Holy Spirit, with Thy fire divine,
Melt into tears this thankless heart of
    mine;
Teach me to love what once I seemed to
    hate,
And live to God, before it be too late.

479   10.10.10.10.

1 I WILL love Jesus and serve Him; for
    see
How the dear Saviour has watched
    over me!
How He has guarded and guided my
    way!
How He has kept me by night and by
    day!

    Him will I love, and His will I be,
    All because He has first lovèd me.
    Him will I love, and His will I be,
    All because He loves me.

2 I will love Jesus and learn of His will,
Trusting Him ever, through good and
    through ill;
Seeking His blessing, where'er I may be,
Knowing He loveth and careth for me.

3 I will love Jesus! and, sure of His love,
I shall be safe as the blessed above;
Oh, when He calls to the glory on
    high,
How we will praise Him—the angels
    and I!

480   8.8.6.8.8.6.

1 O LOVE Divine, how sweet Thou art!
When shall I find my willing heart
    All taken up by Thee?
I thirst, I faint, I die to prove
The greatness of redeeming love,
    The love of Christ to me.

2 Stronger His love than death or hell;
Its riches are unsearchable:
    The first-born sons of light
Desire in vain its depths to see;
They cannot reach the mystery,
    The length, and breadth, and height.

3 God only knows the love of God:
Oh, that it now were shed abroad
    In this poor stony heart!
For love I sigh, for love I pine:
This only portion, Lord, be mine—
    Be mine this better part!

4 Oh, that I could for ever sit
With Mary at the Master's feet!
    Be this my happy choice:
My only care, delight, and bliss,
My joy, my heaven on earth, be this,
    To hear the Bridegroom's voice.

481   7.7.7.7.

1 HEAVENLY Father, bless me now;
At the cross of Christ I bow;
Take my guilt and grief away,
Hear and heal me now, I pray.

2 Now, O Lord, this very hour
Send Thy grace and show Thy power;
While I rest upon Thy Word,
Come and bless me now, O Lord.

3 Now, just now, for Jesus' sake,
Lift the clouds, the fetters break:
While I look, and as I cry,
Touch and cleanse me, or I die.

4 Never did I so adore
Jesus Christ, Thy Son, before;
Now the time! and this the place!
Gracious Father, show Thy grace.

The Christian Life

482 7.7.7.7.

1 TAKE my life, and let it be
Consecrated, Lord, to Thee;
Take my moments and my days,
Let them flow in ceaseless praise.

2 Take my hands, and let them move
At the impulse of Thy love;
Take my feet, and let them be
Swift and beautiful for Thee.

3 Take my voice, and let me sing
Always, only, for my King;
Take my lips, and let them be
Filled with messages from Thee.

4 Take my silver and my gold,
Not a mite would I withhold;
Take my intellect, and use
Every power as Thou shalt choose.

5 Take my will, and make it Thine;
It shall be no longer mine:
Take my heart, it is Thine own;
It shall be Thy royal throne.

6 Take my love; my Lord, I pour
At Thy feet its treasure store:
Take myself, and I will be
Ever, only, all, for Thee.

483 10.7.10.7.

1 I AM Thine, O Lord; I have heard Thy voice,
As it told Thy love to me;
But I long to rise in the arms of faith,
And be closer drawn to Thee.

Draw me near- . . . er, nearer,
blessèd Lord,
To the cross where Thou hast died;
Draw me nearer, nearer, nearer,
blessèd Lord,
To Thy precious wounded side.

2 Consecrate me now to Thy service, Lord,
By the power of grace divine;
Let my soul look up with a steadfast hope,
And my will be lost in Thine.

3 Oh, the pure delight of a single hour
That before Thy throne I spend,
When I kneel in prayer, and with Thee, my God,
I commune as friend with friend.

4 There are depths of love that I cannot know
Till I cross the narrow sea;
There are heights of joy that I may not reach
Till I rest in peace with Thee.

484 7.6.7.6.D.

1 I LOVE, I love my Master,
I will not go out free!
For He is my Redeemer;
He paid the price for me.
I would not leave His service,
It is so sweet and blest;
And in the weariest moments
He gives the truest rest.

2 My Master shed His life-blood
My vassal life to win,
And save me from the bondage
Of tyrant self and sin.
He chose me for His service,
And gave me power to choose
That blessèd, perfect freedom,
Which I shall never lose.

3 I would not halve my service,
His only it must be!
His *only*—Who so loved me,
And gave Himself for me.
Rejoicing and adoring,
Henceforth my song shall be—
"I love, I love my Master,
I will not go out free!"

485 8.7.8.8.7.

1 OH, the bitter shame and sorrow
That a time could ever be,
When I let the Saviour's pity
Plead in vain, and proudly answered,
"All of self, and none of Thee!"

2 Yet He found me; I beheld Him
Bleeding on the accursèd tree,
Heard Him pray, "Forgive them, Father!"
And my wistful heart said faintly—
"Some of self, and some of Thee."

158

3 Day by day His tender mercy,
    Healing, helping, full, and free,
Sweet and strong, and, ah! so patient,
Brought me lower, while I whispered,
    "Less of self, and more of Thee."

4 Higher than the highest heavens,
    Deeper than the deepest sea,
Lord, Thy love at last has conquered;
Grant me now my supplication—
    "None of self, and all of Thee."

486   7.7.7.7.7.7.

1 WHEN this passing world is done,
When has sunk yon radiant sun,
When I stand with Christ on high,
Looking o'er life's history:
Then, Lord, shall I fully know,
Not till then, how much I owe.

2 When I stand before the throne,
Dressed in beauty not my own;
When I see Thee as Thou art,
Love Thee with unsinning heart:
Then, Lord, shall I fully know,
Not till then, how much I owe.

3 When the praise of heaven I hear,
Loud as thunder to the ear,
Loud as many waters' noise,
Sweet as harp's melodious voice:
Then, Lord, shall I fully know,
Not till then, how much I owe.

4 E'en on earth, as through a glass,
Darkly let Thy glory pass:
Make forgiveness feel so sweet,
Make Thy Spirit's help so meet;
E'en on earth, Lord, let me know
Something of the debt I owe.

5 Chosen not for good in me,
Wakened up from wrath to flee:
Hidden in the Saviour's side,
By the Spirit sanctified;
Teach me, Lord, on earth to show,
By my love, how much I owe.

487   6.6.6.6.8.8.

1 JOIN all the glorious names
    Of wisdom, love, and power,
That ever mortals knew,
    That angels ever bore:
All are too mean to speak His worth,
Too mean to set my Saviour forth.

2 Great Prophet of my God,
    My tongue would bless Thy Name:
By Thee the joyful news
    Of our salvation came,
The joyful news of sins forgiven,
Of hell subdued and peace with heaven.

3 Jesus, my great High Priest,
    Offered His blood, and died;
My guilty conscience seeks
    No sacrifice beside:
His powerful blood did once atone,
And now it pleads before the throne.

4 I love my Shepherd's voice;
    His watchful eye shall keep
My wandering soul among
    The thousands of His sheep:
He feeds His flock, He calls their
    names,
His bosom bears the tender lambs.

5 My Saviour and my Lord,
    My Conqueror and my King,
Thy sceptre and Thy sword,
    Thy reigning grace I sing:
Thine is the power; behold, I sit
In willing bonds beneath Thy feet.

488   10.10.10.10.

1 JESUS   has   loved   me—wonderful
    Saviour!
Jesus has loved me, I cannot tell
    why;
Came He to rescue sinners all worthless,
My heart He conquered—for Him I
    would die.

        Glory   to   Jesus—wonderful
            Saviour!
        Glory to Jesus, the One I
            adore;
        Glory   to   Jesus—wonderful
            Saviour!
        Glory to Jesus, and praise
            evermore.

2 Jesus has saved me—wonderful
    Saviour!
  Jesus has saved me, I cannot tell
    how;
  All that I know is, He was my ransom,
    Dying on Calvary with thorns on
      His brow.

3 Jesus will lead me—wonderful
    Saviour!
  Jesus will lead me, I cannot tell
    where;
  But I will follow, through joy or
    sorrow,
    Sunshine or tempest, sweet peace or
      despair.

4 Jesus will crown me—wonderful
    Saviour!
  Jesus will crown me, I cannot tell
    when;
  White throne of splendour hail I with
    gladness,
    Crowned in the presence of angels
      and men.

489   8.8.8.6.

1 JUST as I am, Thine own to be,
  Friend of the young, who lovest me,
  To consecrate myself to Thee,
    O Jesus Christ—I come.

2 In the glad morning of my day,
  My life to give, my vows to pay,
  With no reserve, and no delay—
    With all my heart, I come.

3 I would live ever in the light,
  I would work ever for the right,
  I would serve Thee with all my might—
    Therefore to Thee I come.

4 Just as I am, young, strong, and free,
  To be the best that I can be,
  For truth, and righteousness, and Thee,
    Lord of my life—I come.

5 And for Thy sake to win renown,
  And then to take the victor's crown,
  And at Thy feet to lay it down,
    O Master, Lord—I come.

490   8.8.8.3.

1 SEEK ye first, not earthly pleasure,
  Fading joy and failing treasure;
  But the love that knows no measure
    Seek ye first.

2 Seek ye first, not earth's aspirings,
  Ceaseless longings, vain desirings;
  But your precious soul's requirings
    Seek ye first.

3 Seek ye first God's peace and blessing—
  Ye have all if this possessing;
  Come, your need and sin confessing:
    Seek Him first.

4 Seek Him first; then, when forgiven,
  Pardoned, made an heir of heaven,
  Let your life to Him be given:
    Seek this first.

5 Seek this first: be pure and holy;
  Like the Master, meek and lowly;
  Yielded to His service wholly:
    Seek this first.

6 Seek the coming of His kingdom;
  Seek the souls around to win them;
  Seek to Jesus Christ to bring them:
    Seek this first.

7 Seek this first. His promise trying—
  It is sure, all need supplying.
  Heavenly things—on Him relying—
    Seek ye first.

491   11.11.11.11.

1 How loving is Jesus who came from the
    sky,
  In tenderest pity for sinners to die!
  His hands and His feet, they were
    nailed to the tree,
  And all this He suffered for sinners like
    me!

2 How gladly does Jesus free pardon
    impart
  To all who receive Him by faith in their
    heart!
  No evil befalls them, their home is
    above,
  And Jesus throws round them the arms
    of His love.

3 How precious is Jesus to all who
believe!
And out of His fulness what grace they
receive!
When weak He supports them, when
erring He guides,
And everything needful He kindly
provides.

4 Oh, give then to Jesus your earliest
days:
They only are blessed who walk in His
ways:
In life and in death He will still be
your Friend,
For those whom He loves He will love
to the end.

492   C.M.

1 O GOD, I thank Thee for Thy Word,
Which bids me choose the right;
And now I kneel before Thee, Lord,
To make my choice tonight.

2 Although of very little worth,
And stained by sin beside,
I place my life at Thy command,
For ever on Thy side.

3 Not blindly, with unthinking haste,
Or mere emotion stirred;
I choose the life with Christ in God,
And rest upon Thy Word.

4 Gladly with heart and hand and soul
Accept Thy service free,
And find my joy and strength in this,
That Thou hast chosen me.

The Christian Life: (6) Pilgrimage and Conflict

493   8.7.8.7.8.8.7.

1 WE come unto our fathers' God:
Their Rock is our salvation:
The Eternal Arms, their dear abode,
We make our habitation:
We bring Thee, Lord, the praise they
brought;
We seek Thee as Thy saints have
sought
In every generation.

2 The fire divine, their steps that led,
Still goeth bright before us;
The heavenly shield, around them
spread,
Is still high holden o'er us:
The grace those sinners that subdued,
The strength those weaklings that re-
newed,
Doth vanquish, doth restore us.

3 The cleaving sins that brought them
low
Are still our souls oppressing;
The tears that from their eyes did
flow
Fall fast, our shame confessing;
As with Thee, Lord, prevailed their
cry,
So our strong prayer ascends on high,
And bringeth down Thy blessing.

4 Their joy unto their Lord we bring;
Their song to us descendeth:
The Spirit who in them did sing
To us His music lendeth.
His song in them, in us, is one;
We raise it high, we send it on—
The song that never endeth!

5 Ye saints to come, take up the strain,
The same sweet theme endeavour!
Unbroken be the golden chain!
Keep on the song for ever!
Safe in the same dear dwelling-place,
Rich with the same eternal grace,
Bless the same boundless Giver!

494   8.7.8.7.

1 Lo! the day of God is breaking;
See the gleaming from afar!
Sons of earth, from slumber waking,
Hail the Bright and Morning Star!

 Hear the call! Oh, gird your
armour on,
  Grasp the Spirit's mighty sword,
 Take the helmet of salvation,
  Pressing on to battle for the
Lord!

2 Trust in Him who is your Captain,
   Let no heart in terror quail;
Jesus leads the gathering legions;
   In His Name we shall prevail.

3 Onward marching, firm and steady,
   Faint not, fear not Satan's frown,
For the Lord is with you alway,
   Till you wear the victor's crown.

4 Conquering hosts with banners waving,
   Sweeping on o'er hill and plain,
Ne'er shall halt till swells the anthem,
   "Christ o'er all the world doth
      reign!"

495
6.6.6.6.

1 LORD, we have come to Thee
   In answer to Thy call,
And now, from sin set free,
   We gladly yield Thee all.

2 Lord, keep us strong for Thee,
   Uphold us by Thy might,
Lest we should ever grow
   Discouraged in the fight.

3 Lord, keep us unashamed
   In standing up for Thee,
Help us to bear the cross,
   And witness manfully.

4 Lord, may we serve Thee well,
   And help some other soul
To run the heavenly race,
   And with us reach the goal.

5 Lord, teach us how to pray,
   And show us what we need;
We know that Thou dost hear
   When Jesus' Name we plead.

6 Lord, may we love Thy Word,
   And read it every day;
Teach us Thy holy will,
   Then help us to obey.

7 Lord, teach us how to praise.
   May life with tongue unite
To sing Thy praise with joy,
   And serve Thee with delight.

496
P.M·

1 CONQUERING now and still to conquer,
   Rideth a King in His might,
Leading the host of all the faithful
   Into the midst of the fight:
See them with courage advancing!
   Clad in their brilliant array,
Shouting the Name of their Leader,
   Hear them exultingly say:

   "Not to the strong is the battle,
      Not to the swift is the race;
   Yet to the true and the faithful
      Victory is promised through
         grace."

2 Conquering now and still to conquer:
   Who is this wonderful King?
Whence all the armies which He
      leadeth,
   While of His glory they sing?
He is our Lord and Redeemer,
   Saviour and Monarch divine;
They are the stars that for ever
   Bright in His kingdom will shine.

3 Conquering now and still to conquer:
   Jesus, Thou Ruler of all,
Thrones and their sceptres all shall
      perish,
   Crowns and their splendour shall
      fall;
Yet shall the armies Thou leadest,
   Faithful and true to the last,
Find in Thy mansions eternal
   Rest, when their warfare is past.

497
11.10.11.10.

1 HARK, hark! my soul; angelic songs are
      swelling
   O'er earth's green fields and ocean's
      wave-beat shore:
How sweet the truth those blessèd
      strains are telling
   Of that new life when sin shall be no
      more!

   Angels of Jesus, angels of light,
Singing to welcome the pilgrims of the
   night.

162

2 Onward we go, for still we hear them
singing,
"Come, weary souls, for Jesus bids
you come."
And through the dark, its echoes
sweetly ringing,
The music of the Gospel leads us
home.

3 Far, far away, like bells at evening
pealing,
The voice of Jesus sounds o'er land
and sea;
And laden souls, by thousands meekly
stealing,
Kind Shepherd, turn their weary
steps to Thee.

4 Rest comes at length, though life be
long and dreary,
The day must dawn, and darksome
night be past;
Faith's journey ends in welcome to the
weary,
And Heaven, the heart's true home,
will come at last.

5 Angels! sing on: your faithful watches
keeping,
Sing us sweet fragments of the songs
above;
Till morning's joy shall end the night of
weeping,
And life's long shadows break in
cloudless love.

498   11.11.11.11.

1 YIELD not to temptation, for yielding
is sin;
Each victory will help you some other
to win;
Fight manfully onward, dark passions
subdue,
Look ever to Jesus, He'll carry you
through.

Ask the Saviour to help you,
Comfort, strengthen, and keep you;
He is willing to aid you,
He will carry you through.

2 Shun evil companions, bad language
disdain,
God's Name hold in reverence, nor take
it in vain;

Be thoughtful and earnest, kind-
hearted and true,
Look ever to Jesus, He'll carry you
through.

3 To him that o'ercometh God giveth a
crown,
Through faith we shall conquer,
though often cast down;
He, who is our Saviour, our strength
will renew;
Look ever to Jesus, He'll carry you
through.

499   7.7.7.3.

1 "CHRISTIAN, seek not yet repose,"
Hear thy gracious Saviour say;
"Thou art in the midst of foes:
Watch and pray."

2 Principalities and powers,
Mustering their unseen array,
Wait for thy unguarded hours:
"Watch and pray."

3 Gird thy heavenly armour on,
Wear it ever night and day;
Ambushed lies the evil one:
"Watch and pray."

4 Hear the victors who o'ercame,
Still they mark each warrior's way;
All with one sweet voice exclaim,
"Watch and pray."

5 Hear, above all, hear thy Lord,
Him thou lovest to obey;
Hide within thy heart His word:
"Watch and pray."

6 Watch, as if on that alone
Hung the issue of the day;
Pray, that help may be sent down:
"Watch and pray."

500   S.M.

1   ARM, soldiers of the Lord!
The fight is set with wrong;
Take shield and breastplate, helm and
sword,
And sing your battle-song.

2   Stand fast for Love, your Lord;
   Faith be your mighty shield;
And let the Spirit's burning sword
   Flash foremost in the field.

3   Truth be your girdle strong;
   And hope your helmet shine,
Whene'er the battle seemeth long
   And wearied hearts repine.

4   With news of gospel peace
   Let your swift feet be shod;
Your breastplate be the righteousness
   That keeps the soul for God.

5   And for the weary day,
   And for the slothful arm,
For wounds, defeat, distress, dismay,
   Take prayer, the heavenly charm.

6   "From strength to strength" your cry,
   Your battlefield the world;
Strike home, and press where Christ on high
   His banner hath unfurled.

501
6.5.6.5.D.

1 WHO is on the Lord's side?
   Who will serve the King?
Who will be His helper
   Other lives to bring?
Who will leave the world's side?
   Who will face the foe?
Who is on the Lord's side?
   Who for Him will go?
     By Thy grand redemption,
      By Thy grace divine,
     We are on the Lord's side:
      Saviour, we are Thine!

2 Not for weight of glory,
   Not for crown and palm,
Enter we the army,
   Raise the warrior-psalm;
But for love that claimeth
   Lives for whom He died:
He whom Jesus nameth
   Must be on His side!
     By Thy love constraining,
      By Thy grace divine,
     We are on the Lord's side:
      Saviour, we are Thine!

3 Jesus, Thou hast bought us,
   Not with gold or gem,
But with Thine own life-blood,
   For Thy diadem.
With Thy blessing filling
   All who come to Thee,
Thou hast made us willing,
   Thou hast made us free.
     By Thy grand redemption,
      By Thy grace divine,
     We are on the Lord's side:
      Saviour, we are Thine!

4 Fierce may be the conflict,
   Strong may be the foe;
But the King's own army
   None can overthrow;
Round His standard ranging,
   Victory is secure,
For His truth unchanging
   Makes the triumph sure.
     Joyfully enlisting,
      By Thy grace divine,
     We are on the Lord's side:
      Saviour, we are Thine!

5 Chosen to be soldiers
   In an alien land,
"Chosen, called, and faithful,"
   For our Captain's band.
In His service royal,
   Let us not grow cold;
Let us be right loyal,
   Noble, true, and bold.
     Master, Thou wilt keep us,
      By Thy grace divine,
     Always on the Lord's side,
      Saviour, always Thine!

502
P.M.

1 HARK to the call that resounds from heaven,
     Be prepared!
Rise in the strength that in Christ is given,
     Be prepared!
   Laying every weight aside,
   Looking only to our Guide,
   Sure of the path, though all untried,

While we watch and we pray and trust
in Him.
    Be prepared,
    "Watch and pray
That ye enter not into temptation."

When our Captain bids us follow,
    Be prepared!
Should He lead to joy or sorrow,
    Be prepared!
    Forward march with footsteps
      sure,
    Or if He shall say, "Endure,"
    Under His command secure,
We are sure of a glorious victory.

When the tempter seeks to harm us,
    Be prepared!
Wiles of his need not alarm us
    If prepared.
    Christ our strength, and Christ
      our shield,
    Taught by Him the sword to
      wield,
    Satan cannot hold the field,
While we're strong in the might of
    Christ our Lord.

And for the last great heavenly roll-
    call
    Be prepared!
When thy King shall take His king-
    dom,
    Be prepared!
    Having His salvation claimed,
    And the Name of Jesus named,
    At His coming not ashamed,
We receive at His hand the crown of
    life.

503   7.6.7.6.D.

THE Church's one foundation
    Is Jesus Christ her Lord;
She is His new creation
    By water and the Word:
From heaven He came and sought her
    To be His holy Bride,
With His own blood He bought her,
    And for her life He died.

Elect from every nation,
    Yet one o'er all the earth,
Her charter of salvation
    One Lord, one faith, one birth;

One holy Name she blesses,
    Partakes one holy food,
And to one hope she presses,
    With every grace endued.

3 Though with a scornful wonder
    Men see her sore oppressed,
By schisms rent asunder,
    By heresies distressed:
Yet saints their watch are keeping,
    Their cry goes up, "How long?"
And soon the night of weeping
    Shall be the morn of song.

4 'Mid toil and tribulation,
    And tumult of her war,
She waits the consummation
    Of peace for evermore;
Till with the vision glorious
    Her longing eyes are blest,
And the great Church victorious
    Shall be the Church at rest.

5 Yet she on earth hath union
    With God the Three in One,
And mystic sweet communion
    With those whose rest is won.
Oh, happy ones and holy!
    Lord, give us grace that we
Like them, the meek and lowly,
    On high may dwell with Thee!

504   P.M.

1 SOLDIER, soldier, fighting in the world's
    great strife,
On thyself relying, battling for thy
    life;
    Trust thyself no longer,
    Trust to Christ—He's stronger:
"I can all things, all things do
Through Christ, which strengtheneth
    me."

2 In your daily duty, standing up for
    right,
Are you sometimes weary—heart not
    always light?
    Doubt your Saviour never,
    This your motto ever:
"I can all things, all things do
Through Christ, which strengtheneth
    me."

3 If your way be weary He will help you
    through—
Help you in your troubles and your
    pleasures too;
Say, when Satan's by you;
Say, when all things try you:
"I can all things, all things do
Through Christ, which strengtheneth
    me."

4 In a world of trouble, tempted oft to
    stray,
You need never stumble; Satan cannot
    stay—
Will but tempt you vainly,
If you tell him plainly
"I can all things, all things do
Through Christ, which strengtheneth
    me."

5 Jesus' power is boundless—boundless
    as the sea;
He is always able, able to keep me—
Power bring from my weakness,
Glory from my meekness:
"I can all things, all things do
Through Christ, which strengtheneth
    me."

505   11.11.11.5.

1 LORD of our life, and God of our
    salvation,
Star of our night, and Hope of every
    nation,
Hear and receive Thy Church's sup-
    plication,
    Lord God Almighty!

2 Lord, Thou canst help when earthly
    armour faileth,
Lord, Thou canst save when sin itself
    assaileth;
Lord, o'er Thy Church nor death nor
    hell prevaileth:
    Grant us Thy peace, Lord.

3 Peace in our hearts our evil thoughts
    assuaging,
Peace in Thy Church where brothers are
    engaging,
Peace when the world its busy war is
    waging:
    Calm Thy foes' raging.

4 Grant us Thy help till backward th
    are driven,
Grant them Thy truth, that they m
    be forgiven;
Grant peace on earth, and after
    have striven,
    Peace in Thy heaven.

506   7.6.7.6.

1 STAND up! stand up for Jesus!
    Ye soldiers of the cross;
Lift high His royal banner,
    It must not suffer loss:
From victory unto victory
    His army shall He lead,
Till every foe is vanquished,
    And Christ is Lord indeed.

2 Stand up! stand up for Jesus!
    The trumpet call obey;
Forth to the mighty conflict
    In this His glorious day!
Ye that are men, now serve Him
    Against unnumbered foes;
Let courage rise with danger,
    And strength to strength oppose

3 Stand up! stand up for Jesus!
    Stand in His strength alone;
The arm of flesh will fail you;
    Ye dare not trust your own.
Put on the Gospel armour,
    And, watching unto prayer,
Where duty calls, or danger,
    Be never wanting there.

4 Stand up! stand up for Jesus!
    The strife will not be long;
This day the noise of battle—
    The next the victor's song.
To him that overcometh
    A crown of life shall be;
He, with the King of glory,
    Shall reign eternally.

507   P.

1 ONLY an armour-bearer, firmly
    stand,
Waiting to follow at the King's com
    mand;
Marching if "onward" shall the orde
    be;

Standing by my Captain, serving faithfully.

Hear ye the battle cry, "Forward!" the call,
See, see the faltering ones, backward they fall:
Surely my Captain may depend on
me,
Though but an armour-bearer I
may be.

Only an armour-bearer, now in the
field,
Guarding a shining helmet, sword, and
shield;
Waiting to hear the thrilling battle-
cry,
Ready then to answer, "Master, here
am I."

Only an armour-bearer, yet may I
share
Glory immortal, and a bright crown
wear;
If in the battle to my trust I'm true,
Mine shall be the honours in the Grand
Review.

508   P.M.

WE are soldiers every one,
And the fight is just begun;
And the Captain ever stands hard by,
For He sees our every need,
And our inmost thoughts doth read,
As we Satan's host defy.

Then forward all, for the Captain's
nigh:
Then fight full well, for He stands
hard by
With a victor's crown.

When the foes are thick around,
And we try to stand our ground,
And each heart is ever beating high;
Then the soldiers of the Lord
Use the Spirit's mighty sword,
And assure the victory.

When our sins about us lower,
And we feel their mighty power,

When our hearts are nearly faint with
fear,
Then we look to Him above,
Whom we honour and we love,
And He says, "Be of good
cheer."

4   When the battle-clouds are past
And we find our home at last,
Then the joy of every heart shall be:
The song of living praise
To the Father of all days,
That shall sound from sea to sea.

509   L.M.

1 STAND up for Jesus, Christian, stand!
Firm as a rock on ocean's strand!
Beat back the waves of sin that roll
Like raging floods around thy soul!

Stand up for Jesus, nobly stand!
Firm as a rock on ocean's strand!
Stand up, His righteous cause
defend;
Stand up for Jesus, your best Friend.

2 Stand up for Jesus, Christian, stand!
Sound forth His Name o'er sea and
land!
Spread ye His glorious Word abroad,
Till all the world shall own Him Lord!

3 Stand up for Jesus, Christian, stand!
Lift high the cross with steadfast
hand!
Till heathen lands, with wondering eye,
Its rising glory shall descry.

4 Stand up for Jesus, Christian, stand!
Soon with the blest, immortal band
We'll dwell for aye, life's journey o'er,
In realms of light on heaven's bright
shore.

510   P.M.

1 STANDING by a purpose true,
Heeding God's command,
Honour them, the faithful few!
All hail to Daniel's band!

Dare to be a Daniel!
Dare to stand alone!
Dare to have a purpose firm!
Dare to make it known!

2 Many mighty men are lost,
　　Daring not to stand,
Who for God had been a host
　　By joining Daniel's band.

3 Many giants, great and tall,
　　Stalking through the land,
Headlong to the earth would fall,
　　If met by Daniel's band.

4 Hold the Gospel banner high!
　　On to victory grand!
Satan and his host defy,
　　And shout for Daniel's band!

511   P.M.

1 BE strong in the Lord, ye soldiers,
　　Be strong in His power and might;
Gird on you His perfect armour,
　　And stand up for truth and right.
His armour will never fail you,
　　Victorious you shall be
'Gainst all the wiles of Satan,
　　From sin's dominion free.

　　Be strong in the Lord, ye soldiers,
　　　　Be strong in His power and
　　　　might;
　　Gird on you His perfect armour—
　　　　Be strong, be strong, and fight!

2 The hosts of Satan's army
　　Are ranged against the Lord,
And, while we're standing idle,
　　Make havoc with the sword.
Come, join the King's own army,
　　And fight for all that's true,
The voice of sin resisting,
　　Through Christ, who strengtheneth
　　you.

3 Not human foes we're fighting,
　　But evil powers of sin,
'Gainst rulers of this world's darkness,
　　Around us and within.
Then take Salvation's helmet,
　　Hold fast the shield of Faith,
And, trusting Him who gave it,
　　Be faithful unto death.

4 The Captain of our salvation
　　Is standing ever near;
Take courage, then, ye soldiers,
　　What cause have ye to fear?

Though Satan's host should number
　　A thousand 'gainst a score,
Count Christ, your heavenly Captain,
　　For thrice ten thousand more.

512   P.M.

1 HARK, 'tis the watchman's cry,
　　"Wake, brethren, wake!"
Jesus, our Lord, is nigh,
　　Wake, brethren, wake!
Sleep is for sons of night,
Ye are children of the light,
Yours is the glory bright:
　　Wake, brethren, wake!

2 Call to each waking band,
　　"Watch, brethren, watch!"
Clear is our Lord's command,
　　Watch, brethren, watch!
Be ye as men that wait
Ready at their Master's gate,
E'en though He tarry late:
　　Watch, brethren, watch!

3 Heed we the steward's call,
　　"Work, brethren, work!"
There's room enough for all,
　　Work, brethren, work!
This vineyard of our Lord
Constant labour will afford;
Yours is a sure reward:
　　Work, brethren, work!

4 Hear we the Shepherd's voice,
　　"Pray, brethren, pray!"
Would ye His heart rejoice,
　　Pray, brethren, pray!
Sin calls for constant fear,
Weakness needs the strong One near:
Long as ye tarry here,
　　Pray, brethren, pray!

5 Now sound the final chord,
　　"Praise, brethren, praise!"
Thrice holy is the Lord,
　　Praise, brethren, praise!
What more befits the tongues,
Soon to lead the angels' songs,
While heaven the note prolongs?
　　Praise, brethren, praise!

513   7.6.7.6.D.

WE'RE marching to the conflict
  In heavenly armour clad,
We're singing as we're marching,
  For Jesus makes us glad:
We know we shall be victors
  When ends this mortal strife,
For Jesus leads His army,
  The "Children of the Light."

    Marching to the conflict
      In heavenly armour clad,
    We're singing as we're marching,
      For Jesus makes us glad.

We're marching to the conflict,
  And guarding every part:
The shield of Faith is turned to stay
  And quench each fiery dart;
Stronger than bands of iron,
  Truth girds us for the strife;
King Jesus is the Way, the Truth,
  And our eternal Life.

We're marching to the conflict,
  And, till the tumult cease,
Our feet are always carrying
  Sweet messages of Peace
To those who, faint and weary,
  Steel their proud hearts no more,
But wide to Christ, their Saviour-
    King,
  Open the long-closed door.

Bright on each head there glitters
  Salvation for a crest,
Earnest to every warrior child
  Of God's eternal rest:
Each heart is safely sheltered
  'Neath Christ's own Righteousness,
More lasting covering by far
  Than our poor soiled dress.

We're marching to the conflict,
  Grasping our two-edged sword,
Which never yet returned void,
  For 'tis God's holy Word:
Its point is sharp for ever,
  Both hilt and blade are proof,
For forged it was by God's own hand,
  His blessèd Word of truth.

We're marching on to conquest,
  And soon we all shall stand,
Waving the palm of victory,
  On heaven's golden strand;

Blessing the day when Jesus' voice
  Called us from shades of night
To join His victor army,
  The "Children of the Light."

514   P.M.

1 WHERE the flag is flying, where the
    fight is keen,
  Where the trumpet-call is ringing,
There you find the soldiers, steady and
    serene,
  There you hear the sound of singing:
Servants of the Master, scorning fear or
    flight,
  Fighting for the Truth, the Life, the
    Light!

    Soldiers of the Master, onward
      tread,
    Telling out the grand old story!
    Ready day by day Jesus to obey,
    Soldiers of the King of Glory.

2 Where the darkness reigneth, where the
    power of sin
  Binds the heart of man in sadness,
There you find the soldiers, waiting
    souls to win,
  Bringing them to light and gladness,
Servants of the Master, strong in love
    and might,
  Fighting for the Truth, the Life, the
    Light!

3 Where the doubts are thickest, where
    the strength of youth
  Falls beneath the chains of error,
There you find the soldiers, with the
    lamp of truth,
  Freeing men from thoughts of terror.
Servants of the Master, strong in faith
    and sight,
  Fighting for the Truth, the Life, the
    Light!

4 Where from angel chorus through the
    heavenly dome
  Rings a song of triumph splendid,
There you find the soldiers entering
    their home,
  By the heavenly hosts attended.

Servants of the Master, clad in spotless
white,
One with Him in Truth, in Life, in
Light!

Colin Sterne.
*Copyright. By permission of the National Sunday
School Union.*

515 6.5.6.5.D.

1 JESUS, Prince and Saviour,
As we look to Thee,
Thou of faith the Author,
Finisher wilt be.
Every weight and hindrance,
Each besetting sin,
Lay we gladly from us,
In the race to win.

Looking unto Jesus,
Patiently we run,
Trusting Thee to finish
What Thou hast begun.

2 Thou, with joy before Thee,
Didst endure the cross,
All the shame despising,
Counting not the loss.
From the grave triumphant
Victor Thou didst stand;
Now in grace art seated,
At Thy God's right hand.

3 Give us grace, dear Saviour
To consider Thee,
Lest we faint in battle,
Lest we weary be.
So that, sin resisting,
Striving unto blood,
We, too, may be victors,
Through Thy dying love.

516 P.M.

1 PATIENT to bear;
Ready to dare,
Ever against the wrong;
Trusting the Lord;
Waiting His word;
Serving with joyful song.

Deep in the heart let Jesus abide,
Lifting the soul to song;
Safe in His love whatever betide,
Quit you like men—be strong!

2 Fearing no foe,
Forward still go,
Bearing His banner high;
Through praise or blame,
Strong in His Name,
Daring to do, or die!

3 Dark though the day,
Rough though the way,
Trust, and be ever brave;
Light He will send,
Ways He will mend—
Mighty His arm to save.

517 7.6.7.6.D.

1 ASHAMED to be a Christian!
Afraid the world should know
I'm on the way to Zion,
Where joys eternal flow!
Afraid to wear Thy colours,
Or blush to follow Thee!
Forbid it, O my Saviour,
That I should ever be.

2 Ashamed to be a Christian!
To love my God and King!
The fire of zeal is burning,
My soul is on the wing:
I want a faith made perfect,
That all the world may see
I stand a living witness
Of mercy rich and free.

3 Ashamed to be a Christian!
My guilty fear, depart!
I will not heed the tempter
That whispers to my heart.
Dear Saviour, though unworthy,
Yet this my only plea—
Thy all-atoning merit:
For Thou hast died for me.

518 P.M

1 WHEN upon life's billows you ar
tempest-tossed,
When you are discouraged, thinking a
is lost,

170

Count your many blessings, name them
one by one,
And it will surprise you what the Lord
hath done.

> Count . . . your blessings, name
> them one by one,
> Count . . . your blessings, see
> what God hath done;
> Count . . . your blessings, name
> them one by one,
> And it will surprise you what the
> Lord hath done.

Are you ever burdened with a load of
care?
Does the cross seem heavy you are
called to bear?
Count your many blessings, every
doubt will fly,
And you will be singing as the days go
by.

When you look at others with their
lands and gold,
Think that Christ has promised you
His wealth untold;
Count your many blessings; wealth can
never buy
Your reward in heaven, nor your home
on high.

So, amid the conflict, whether great or
small,
Do not be discouraged, God is over all;
Count your many blessings, angels will
attend,
Help and comfort give you to your
journey's end.

519　　　　　　　　　　P.M.

Oh, we are volunteers in the army of
the Lord,
Forming into line at our Captain's
word;
We are under marching orders to take
the battle-field,
And we'll ne'er give o'er the fight till
the foe shall yield.

> Come and join the army, the
> army of the Lord;
> Jesus is our Captain; we rally at
> His word;

Sharp will be the conflict with
the powers of sin,
But with such a Leader we are
sure to win.

2 The glory of our flag is the emblem of
the dove,
Gleaming are our swords from the forge
of love;
We go forth, but not to battle for
earthly honours vain;
'Tis a bright immortal crown that we
seek to gain.

3 Our foes are in the field, pressing hard
on every side:
Envy, anger, hatred, with self and
pride;
They are cruel, fierce, and strong, ever
ready to attack:
We must watch, and fight, and pray, if
we'd drive them back.

4 Oh, glorious is the struggle in which we
draw the sword!
Glorious is the kingdom of Christ our
Lord!
It shall spread from sea to sea, it shall
reach from shore to shore,
And His people shall be blessed for
evermore.

520　　　　　　　11.11.11.11.

1 MARCH onward, march onward! our
banner of light
Is waving before us majestic and
bright;
March onward through trial, temptation, and strife,
No rest from the conflict—the battle of
life.

> Press forward, look upward, be
> strong in the Lord,
> Our hope in His mercy, our trust in
> His Word;
> Press forward, look upward, march
> homeward and sing,
> "All glory to Jesus, to Jesus our
> King."

The Christian Life

2 March onward, undaunted, whate'er
    may oppose;
  The sword of the Spirit will vanquish
    our foes;
  Though legions of darkness our path-
    way assail,
  If prayer be our watchword, they can-
    not prevail.

3 The shaft of the tempter will strike, but
    in vain,
  Our buckler of faith in Immanuel's
    Name;
  The storm-cloud may gather, the
    thunder may roll,
  Yet God is the Refuge and Rock of the
    soul.

4 March onward, oh, vision of rapture
    untold!
  The victors for Jesus ere long shall
    behold
  The land of our promise, the home of
    our rest,
  And dwell with our Captain eternally
    blest.

521
P.M.

1 O GOD, by whose almighty grace
  Unworthy sinners have a place
    In Christ, our Saviour-King,
  Whose life hath brought us from the
    dead,
  Whose power hath safely kept and led,
    Thy praise we sing!
  Oh, guard our hearts and tune our
    song,
  And give us victory all along!

    Through Jesus Christ, the same
    yesterday, and today, and for ever
    and ever.

2 To Thy great Word, the Word of truth,
  Oh, help us to take heed in youth,
    And by it cleanse our way!
  And as we walk this sin-stained shore,
  Oh, let our path shine more and more
    To perfect day!
  Oh, light the way and guide our feet
  Until the journey be complete!

3 From selfishness our hearts defend;
  And, since we know Thee as our Friend
    Some others may we bring.
  Our work and witness richly bless,
  And help us boldly to confess
    Our Lord and King!
  Teach us Thy great salvation's plan,
  And guard us from the fear of man:

4 Teach us to look to Christ alone,
  To trust His strength, and not our own
    And thus to conquer sin;
  To live the life that God hath planned
  And take the victory from His hand,
    And so to win!
  Our hearts, our all, we yield to Thee,
  That more than conquerors we may be

522
6.5.6.5.6.6.6.5

1 HE who would valiant be
    'Gainst all disaster,
  Let him in constancy
    Follow the Master.
  There's no discouragement
  Shall make him once relent
  His first avowed intent
    To be a pilgrim.

2 Who so beset him round
    With dismal stories
  Do but themselves confound—
    His strength the more is.
  No foes shall stay his might,
  Though he with giants fight:
  He will make good his right
    To be a pilgrim.

3 Since, Lord, Thou dost defend
    Us with Thy Spirit,
  We know we at the end
    Shall life inherit.
  Then fancies flee away!
  I'll fear not what men say,
  I'll labour night and day
    To be a pilgrim.

523
P.M.

1 O GOD and Saviour of the sons of men,
  We, Thy crusaders, would Thy love
    acclaim;
  In our fresh manhood make us, through
    Thy Name,
    More than conquerors, more than
    conquerors.

172

2 The battle rages cruel, fierce, and long;
  We hold no parley with the powers of wrong;
  In Christ, our Saviour, stronger than the strong,
    More than conquerors, more than conquerors.

3 Help us, Lord Jesus, in the hour of strife;
  Cover our heads in battle, guard our life;
  Lest we should lose our crown, the victor's prize—
    More than conquerors, more than conquerors.

4 Bright in the east behold the Morning Star,
  The Saviour coming in the clouds afar;
  Soon is the triumph, soon the end of war,
    More than conquerors, more than conquerors.

5 Jesus, we hail Thee, Lord of earth and heaven,
  For Thou wast slain, and from the grave art risen;
  To Thee the glory and the power be given,
    Thou, more than Conqueror, more than Conqueror.

524   S.M.

1 SOLDIERS of Christ, arise,
  And put your armour on,
  Strong in the strength which God supplies
  Through His eternal Son:

2 Strong in the Lord of hosts,
  And in His mighty power;
  Who in the strength of Jesus trusts
  Is more than conqueror.

3 Stand then in His great might,
  With all His strength endued;
  And take, to arm you for the fight,
  The panoply of God.

4 From strength to strength go on,
  Wrestle, and fight, and pray;
  Tread all the powers of darkness down,
  And win the well-fought day:

5 That, having all things done,
  And all your conflicts past,
  Ye may o'ercome through Christ alone,
  And stand complete at last.

525   6.5.6.5.D.

1 ONWARD, Christian soldiers,
  Marching as to war,
  Looking unto Jesus,
    Who is gone before:
  Christ, the royal Master,
  Leads against the foe;
  Forward into battle,
    See, His banners go.

      Onward, Christian soldiers,
        Marching as to war,
      Looking unto Jesus,
        Who is gone before.

2 At the Name of Jesus
    Satan's host doth flee;
  On then, Christian soldiers,
    On to victory!
  Hell's foundations quiver
    At the shout of praise:
  Brothers, lift your voices:
    Loud your anthems raise.

3 Like a mighty army,
    Moves the Church of God:
  Brothers, we are treading
    Where the saints have trod;
  We are not divided,
    All one body we,
  One in hope and doctrine,
    One in charity.

4 Crowns and thrones may perish,
    Kingdoms rise and wane;
  But the Church of Jesus
    Constant will remain:
  Gates of hell can never
    'Gainst that Church prevail;
  We have Christ's own promise,
    And that cannot fail.

5 Onward, then, ye people,
　Join our happy throng;
Blend with ours your voices
　In the triumph-song;
Glory, praise, and honour,
　Unto Christ the King;
This through countless ages
　Men and angels sing.

526　　　　　　　　　P.M.

1 Do you fear the foe will in the conflict
　win?
Is it dark without you—darker still
　within?
Clear the darkened windows, open wide
　the door,
　Let the blessèd sunshine in.

　　Let the blessèd sunshine in,
　　Let the blessèd sunshine in:
　Clear the darkened windows, open
　　wide the door,
　　Let the blessèd sunshine in.

2 Does your faith grow fainter in the
　cause you love?
Are your prayers unanswered from the
　throne above?
Clear the darkened windows, open wide
　the door,
　Let the blessèd sunshine in.

8 Would you go rejoicing on the upward
　way,
Knowing naught of darkness—dwelling
　in the day?
Clear the darkened windows, open wide
　the door,
　Let the blessèd sunshine in.

527　　　　　　　　　P.M.

1 SOUND the battle cry,
See! the foe is nigh;
Raise the standard high
　For the Lord!
Gird your armour on,
Stand firm every one,
Rest your cause upon
　His holy Word!

　　Rouse, then, soldiers!
　　Rally round the banner!
　　Ready, steady,
　　Pass the word along.

Onward! forward!
Shout aloud Hosanna!
　Christ is Captain
　Of the mighty throng!

2 Strong to meet the foe,
Marching on we go,
While our cause we know
　Must prevail;
Shield and banner bright
Gleaming in the light,
Battling for the right,
　We ne'er can fail!

3 O Thou God of all,
Hear us when we call!
Help us, one and all,
　By Thy grace:
When the battle's done,
And the victory won,
May we wear the crown
　Before Thy face!

528　　　　　　　6.5.6.5.D.

1 GLEAMING in the sunshine,
　Floating in the air,
See the banner waving,
　Beautiful and fair:
In the Saviour's army
　It shall lead us on,
Till the battle's over,
　Till the victory's won.

　　Gleaming in the sunshine,
　　Floating in the air,
　　See the banner waving,
　　Beautiful and fair.

2 Jesus is our Captain,
　Jesus is our King;
Joyfully for Jesus
　We will fight and sing:
He supplies our armour—
　Truth and faith and love;
He will bring us safely
　To our home above.

3 In the Saviour's army,
　Ripe for heaven, are seen
Those who bore the banner
　When the strife was keen:
Men and maidens gather,
　In the flush of youth,
Round the blessed standard,
　Round the flag of truth.

4 And the smiling faces,
　And the beaming eyes,
Of the little children
　He will not despise;
Thousands in His army
　Mighty deeds have done:
With the love of Jesus
　They have fought and won.

5 "Come, ye heavy-laden,"—
　'Tis the Saviour's voice:
Hear His invitation,
　Make Him now your choice!
Join His glorious army,
　Join without delay;
'List beneath His banner
　While it is today.

529 P.M.

1 WE praise Thee, Lord, whose wondrous grace
Has turned our wandering feet,
And led us into heavenly ways
　That we Thy Son should meet.
And now we tread the narrow road;
　We long to do the right, Lord;
And pray for strength, as men of God,
　To *Flee* and *Follow* and *Fight*, Lord.

2 We'll *flee* from each unholy thing,
　From every evil thought,
From passion's snare, from worldly care,
　From pride, with folly fraught;
And as, awakened by Thy call,
　We fled from wrath to Thee, Lord;
So help us still, from all things ill,
　As men of God, to *flee*, Lord.

3 We'll *follow* on to know the Lord,
　We'll keep along His track;
Forgetting all that lies behind,
　We'll never once look back!
The way grows brighter on before,
　We hope Thy Day to see, Lord;
So let us gird our loins the more,
　And gladly *follow* Thee, Lord.

4 We'll *fight*! for there is many a foe
　From whom we may not run;
As Israel fought with Amalek,
　So fighting must be done!
The fight of Faith our fight shall be,
　Till faith shall end in sight, Lord;
As men of God we'll live for Thee,
　And *Flee* and *Follow* and *Fight*, Lord!

530 11.10.11.10.

1 TRUE-HEARTED, whole-hearted! faithful and loyal,
　King of our lives, by Thy grace we will be!
Under Thy standard, exalted and royal,
　Strong in Thy strength we will battle for Thee!
　　Peal out the watchword, and silence it never,
　　　Song of our spirits, rejoicing and free:
　　"True-hearted, whole-hearted, now and for ever,
　　　King of our lives, by Thy grace we will be!"

2 True-hearted, whole-hearted! fullest allegiance
　Yielding henceforth to our glorious King!
Valiant endeavour and loving obedience
　Freely and joyously now would we bring.

3 True-hearted! Saviour, Thou knowest our story,
　Weak are the hearts that we lay at Thy feet;
Sinful and treacherous! yet, for Thy glory,
　Heal them and cleanse them from sin and deceit.

4 True-hearted, whole-hearted! Saviour, all-glorious,
　Take Thy great power and reign Thou alone
Over our wills and affections victorious—
　Freely surrendered and wholly Thine own.

175

531
6.5.6.5.D.

1 FORWARD be our watchword,
    Steps and voices joined;
Seek the things before us,
    Not a look behind:
Burns the fiery pillar
    At our army's head;
Who shall dream of shrinking,
    By our Captain led?

    Forward through the desert,
        Through the toil and fight;
    Canaan lies before us,
        Zion beams with light.

2 Forward, when in childhood
    Buds the infant mind;
All through youth and manhood,
    Not a thought behind:
Speed through realms of nature,
    Climb the steps of grace,
Faint not, till in glory
    Gleams our Father's face.

    Forward, all the lifetime,
        Climb from height to height,
    Till the head be hoary,
        Till the eve be light.

3 Glories upon glories
    Hath our God prepared,
By the souls that love Him
    One day to be shared;
Eye hath not beheld them,
    Ear hath never heard,
Nor of these hath uttered
    Thought or speech a word.

    Forward, ever forward,
        Clad in armour bright,
    Till the veil be lifted,
        Till our faith be sight.

4 Far o'er yon horizon
    Rise the city towers,
Where our God abideth,
    That fair home is ours:
Flash the streets with jasper,
    Shine the gates with gold,
Flows the gladdening river,
    Shedding joys untold.

    Thither, onward thither,
        In the Spirit's might;
    Pilgrims, to your country,
        Forward into light!

532
P.M.

1 THE walls of Jericho were strong;
    But stronger was the mighty Lord:
And He—the Captain of God's host—
    Had given them His faithful word,
That if they would the walls surround,
    And would the trumpets blow;
He then would give them victory,
    And overthrow their foe.

2 The gates of Jericho were strong—
    They could not any stronger be:
But there was One who them defied—
    And with the host of God was He.
No work for Him would be too great,
    Too hard to undertake;
For He could burst the gates of brass,
    The bars of iron break.

3 And we, O Lord, are waging war
    Against the mighty hosts of sin;
And neither skill nor strength have we,
    So oft have we defeated been.
But if Thou wilt our Captain be,
    Our weakened ranks command,
Then led by Thee we'll face the foe,
    His fierce assaults withstand.

4 Strong Son of God! we need more faith
    In Thine almighty power to save:
Oh, hear the prayer of contrite hearts,
    As we Thy keeping grace would
        crave;
Help us to trust in Thee alone,
    To save us every day;
Oh, make us, in the rest of faith,
    Triumphant all the way!

533
P.M.

1 THERE'S a royal banner given for dis-
        play
    To the soldiers of the King;
As an ensign fair we lift it up today,
    While as ransomed ones we sing.

        Marching   on! . . . Marching
            on! . . .
        For Christ count everything
            but loss;
        And to crown Him King, . . .
            toil and sing,
        'Neath the banner of the
            cross!

2 Though the foe may rage and gather as
    the flood,
  Let the standard be displayed!
And beneath its folds, as soldiers of the
    Lord,
  For the truth be not dismayed!

3 Over land and sea, wherever man may
    dwell,
  Make the glorious tidings known;
Of the crimson banner now the story
    tell,
  While the Lord shall claim His own!

4 When the glory dawns—'tis drawing
    very near;
  It is hastening day by day—
Then before our King the foe shall dis-
    appear,
  And the cross the world shall sway!

534   S.M.D.

1 A FEW more years shall roll,
  A few more seasons come,
And we shall be with those that rest
  Asleep within the tomb.
Then, O my Lord, prepare
  My soul for that great day;
Oh, wash me in Thy precious blood,
  And take my sins away.

2 A few more suns shall set
  O'er these dark hills of time,
And we shall be where suns are not—
  A far serener clime.
Then, O my Lord, prepare
  My soul for that bright day;
Oh, wash me in Thy precious blood,
  And take my sins away.

3 A few more storms shall beat
  On this wild rocky shore,
And we shall be where tempests cease,
  And surges swell no more.
Then, O my Lord, prepare
  My soul for that calm day;
Oh, wash me in Thy precious blood,
  And take my sins away.

4 A few more struggles here,
  A few more partings o'er,
A few more toils, a few more tears,
  And we shall weep no more.

Then, O my Lord, prepare
  My soul for that blest day;
Oh, wash me in Thy precious blood,
  And take my sins away.

5 'Tis but a little while
  And He shall come again,
Who died that we might live—who
    lives
  That we with Him may reign:
Then, O my Lord, prepare
  My soul for that glad day;
Oh, wash me in Thy precious blood,
  And take my sins away.

535   7.6.7.6.

1 O HAPPY band of pilgrims,
  If onward ye will tread
With Jesus as your Fellow,
  To Jesus as your Head!

2 Oh, happy, if ye labour
  As Jesus did for men:
Oh, happy, if ye hunger
  As Jesus hungered then!

3 The faith by which ye see Him,
  The hope in which ye yearn,
The love that through all troubles
  To Him alone will turn:

4 What are they but His heralds
  To lead you to His sight?
What are they save the effluence
  Of uncreated light?

5 The trials that beset you,
  The sorrows ye endure,
The manifold temptations
  That death alone can cure:

6 What are they but His jewels
  Of right celestial worth?
What are they but the ladder
  Set up to heaven on earth?

7 The cross that Jesus carried,
  He carried as your due;
The crown that Jesus weareth,
  He weareth it for you.

8 O happy band of pilgrims,
  Look upward to the skies,
Where such a light affliction
  Shall win you such a prize!

536
8.7.8.7.D.

1 THROUGH the night of doubt and sorrow
Onward goes the pilgrim band,
Singing songs of expectation,
Marching to the promised land.
Clear before us through the darkness
Gleams and burns the guiding light;
Brother clasps the hand of brother,
Stepping fearless through the night.

2 One the light of God's own presence
O'er His ransomed people shed,
Chasing far the gloom and terror,
Brightening all the path we tread.
One the object of our journey,
One the faith which never tires,
One the earnest looking forward,
One the hope our God inspires.

3 One the strain the lips of thousands
Lift as from the heart of one;
One the conflict, one the peril,
One the march in God begun.
One the gladness of rejoicing
On the far eternal shore,
Where the One Almighty Father
Reigns in love for evermore.

4 Onward, therefore, pilgrim brothers,
Onward with the cross our aid:
Bear its shame, and fight its battle,
Till we rest beneath its shade.
Soon shall come the great awaking;
Soon the rending of the tomb;
Then the scattering of all shadows,
And the end of toil and gloom.

537
P.M.

1 DARE to do right! dare to be true!
You have a work that no other can do;
Do it so bravely, so kindly, so well,
Angels will hasten the story to tell.

    Dare, dare, dare to do right!
    Dare, dare, dare to be true!
    Dare to be true! dare to be true!

2 Dare to do right! dare to be true!
God, who created you, cares for you too;
Treasures the tears that His striving ones shed,
Counts and protects every hair of your head.

3 Dare to do right! dare to be true!
Keep the great judgment-seat always in view;
Look at your work as you'll look at it then,
Scanned by Jehovah, and angels, and men.

4 Dare to do right! dare to be true!
Jesus, your Saviour, will carry you through;
City and mansion, and throne all in sight,
Can you not dare to be true and do right?

538
L.M.

1 FIGHT the good fight with all thy might,
Christ is thy strength, and Christ thy right;
Lay hold on life, and it shall be
Thy joy and crown eternally.

2 Run the straight race through God's good grace,
Lift up thine eyes, and seek His face;
Life with its way before us lies,
Christ is the path, and Christ the prize.

3 Cast care aside, lean on thy Guide;
His boundless mercy will provide;
Lean, and the trusting soul shall prove
Christ is its life, and Christ its love.

4 Faint not, nor fear, His arms are near,
He changeth not, and thou art dear;
Only believe, and thou shalt see
That Christ is all in all to thee.

539
P.M.

1 THERE'S a fight to be fought, and a race to be run,
There are dangers to meet by the way,
But the Lord is my light and the Lord is my life,
And the Lord is my strength and stay.
On His word I depend, He's my Saviour and Friend;
And He tells me to trust and obey;

For the Lord is my light and the Lord
  is my life,
    And the Lord is my strength and
    stay.

2 In His wonderful love, He came down
    from above
    To suffer and die on the tree,
  Now He's reigning up there, where
    He's gone to prepare
    A place in His kingdom for me.
  Let us sing as we go, for He loveth us
    so,
  We can never be lost by the way;
  For the Lord is our light and the Lord
    is our life,
    And the Lord is our strength and
    stay.

3 Then He'll bring us at length, by His
    infinite strength,
    To the land that is fairer than day;
  For the Lord is my light and the Lord
    is my life,
    And the Lord is my strength and
    stay.
  So we'll sing to His praise, to the end of
    our days,
    As we travel each dangerous way;
  For the Lord is my light and the Lord
    is my life,
    And the Lord is my strength and
    stay.

540   6.10.10.6.

1   BLESSED be God, our God!
  Who gave for us His well-belovèd Son,
  The gift of gifts, all other gifts in one—
    Blessed be God, our God!

2   What will He not bestow,
  Who freely gave this mighty gift un-
    bought,
  Unmerited, unheeded, and unsought—
    What will He not bestow?

3   He spared not His Son!
  'Tis this that silences each rising fear;
  'Tis this that bids the hard thought dis-
    appear—
    He spared not His Son!

4   Who shall condemn us now?
  Since Christ has died, and risen, and
    gone above
  For us to plead at the right hand of
    Love,
    Who shall condemn us now?

5   'Tis God that justifies!
  Who shall recall the pardon or the
    grace,
  Or who the broken chain of guilt re-
    place?
    'Tis God that justifies!

6   The victory is ours!
  For us in might came forth the Mighty
    One;
  For us He fought the fight, the triumph
    won—
    The victory is ours!

541   7.7.7.7.

1 OFT in danger, oft in woe,
Onward, Christians, onward go;
Fight the fight, maintain the strife,
Strengthened with the Bread of life.

2 Onward, Christians, onward go!
Join the war, and face the foe:
Will ye flee in danger's hour?
Know ye not your Captain's power?

3 Let your drooping hearts be glad:
March, in heavenly armour clad;
Fight, nor think the battle long,
Soon shall victory tune your song.

4 Let not sorrow dim your eye,
Soon shall every tear be dry;
Let not fears your course impede,
Great your strength, if great your need.

5 Onward, then, to battle move,
More than conquerors ye shall prove;
Though opposed by many a foe,
Christian soldiers, onward go!

542   8.7.8.7.D.

1 LORD, our meeting now is ended,
    Homeward must our steps be turned;
So we gather here to thank Thee
    For the lessons we have learned,

Of the Father's love almighty,
　Of the Holy Spirit's power,
Of the Christ who died to save us,
　And will keep us every hour.

2 Let us never, never waver,
　　Never compromise nor yield,
　Never let our light be hidden,
　　Nor our love to Thee concealed;
　Never be ashamed to own Thee,
　　Though the world may scoff and jeer;
　Fill us with the love of Jesus,
　　Perfect love that casts out fear.

3 May we find our all in Jesus,
　　In our risen, living King,
　Strength to suffer, power to conquer,
　　Tongue to speak and voice to sing.
　Love to win and joy to brighten,
　　Grace to keep from every fall—
　Yesterday, today, for ever,
　　Christ Himself our All in all.

4 So with mingled joy and sadness,
　　From each other we must part,
　Yet in Jesus still united,
　　Bound together heart to heart;
　Shining by His light reflected,
　　Growing daily in His grace,
　Till His glory burst upon us,
　　And we "see Him face to face."

543　　　　　　　　6.5.6.5.

1 LIFT your voices, soldiers,
　　Raise your hearts on high,
　Jesus is our Captain,
　　We to Him draw nigh.

　　　Jesus is our Captain,
　　　　Jesus is our Friend;
　　　Jesus gives us victory,
　　　　Victory to the end.

2 When you're tempted, soldiers,
　　When your hearts are sad,
　Jesus is your safeguard,
　　Christ can make you glad.

3 When sin's heavy burden
　　Hangs upon your soul,
　Jesus' blood can cleanse you,
　　Christ can make you whole.

4 Trust your Captain, soldiers,
　　Trust Him all the way—
　Marching, fighting, dying,
　　May we always say:

544　　　　　　　　6.5.6.5.D.

1 CHRISTIAN, dost thou see them
　　On the holy ground,
　How the hosts of darkness
　　Compass thee around?
　Christian, up and smite them,
　　Counting gain but loss;
　Smite them, Christ is with thee,
　　Soldier of the cross.

2 Christian, dost thou feel them,
　　How they work within,
　Striving, tempting, luring,
　　Goading into sin?
　Christian, never tremble;
　　Never be downcast;
　Gird thee for the conflict,
　　Watch, and pray, and fast.

3 Christian, dost thou hear them,
　　How they speak thee fair?
　"Quit thy weary vigil,
　　Cease from watch and prayer;"
　Christian, answer boldly,
　　"While I breathe I pray:"
　Peace shall follow battle,
　　Night shall end in day.

4 "Well I know thy trouble,
　　O My servant true;
　Thou art very weary—
　　I was weary too:
　But that toil shall make thee
　　Some day all Mine own,
　And the end of sorrow
　　Shall be near My throne."

545　　　　　　　　C.M.D.

1 THE Son of God goes forth to war,
　　A kingly crown to gain;
　His blood-red banner streams afar!
　　Who follows in His train?
　Who best can drink his cup of woe,
　　Triumphant over pain,
　Who patient bears his cross below,
　　He follows in His train.

The martyr first, whose eagle eye
  Could pierce beyond the grave;
Who saw his Master in the sky,
  And called on Him to save.
Like Him, with pardon on his tongue,
  In midst of mortal pain,
He prayed for them that did the wrong:
  Who follows in his train?

A glorious band, the chosen few
  On whom the Spirit came,
Twelve valiant saints, their hope they knew,
  And mocked the cross and flame.
They met the tyrant's brandished steel,
  The lion's gory mane;
They bowed their necks the death to feel:
  Who follows in their train?

A noble army, men and boys,
  The matron and the maid,
Around the Saviour's throne rejoice,
  In robes of light arrayed.
They climbed the steep ascent of heaven
  Through peril, toil, and pain;
O God, to us may grace be given
  To follow in their train.

546　　　　　　　　7.7.7.7.

1 SOLDIERS of the Cross, arise!
  Gird you with your armour bright;
Mighty are your enemies,
  Hard the battle you must fight.

2 O'er a faithless, fallen world
  Raise your banner in the sky;
Let it float there wide unfurled;
  Bear it onward, lift it high.

3 'Mid the homes of want and woe,
  Strangers to the living Word,
Let the Saviour's heralds go,
  Let the voice of hope be heard.

4 Where the shadows deepest lie,
  Carry truth's unsullied ray;
Where are crimes of blackest dye,
  There the saving sign display.

5 To the weary and the worn
  Tell of realms where sorrows cease;
To the outcast and forlorn
  Speak of mercy and of peace.

6 Guard the helpless, seek the strayed;
  Comfort troubles, banish grief;
In the might of God arrayed,
  Scatter sin and unbelief.

7 Be the banner still unfurled,
  Still unsheathed the Spirit's sword,
Till the kingdoms of the world
  Are the kingdom of the Lord.

547　　　　　　　11.10.11.10.

1 "WE rest on Thee"—our Shield and our Defender!
  We go not forth alone against the foe;
Strong in Thy strength, safe in Thy keeping tender,
  "We rest on Thee, and in Thy Name we go."

2 Yea, "in Thy Name," O Captain of salvation!
  In Thy dear Name, all other names above;
Jesus our Righteousness, our sure Foundation,
  Our Prince of glory and our King of love.

3 "We go" in faith, our own great weakness feeling,
  And needing more each day Thy grace to know:
Yet from our hearts a song of triumph pealing;
  "We rest on Thee, and in Thy Name we go."

4 "We rest on Thee"—our Shield and our Defender!
  Thine is the battle, Thine shall be the praise,
When passing through the gates of pearly splendour,
  Victors—we rest *with* Thee, through endless days.

181

548
7.6.8.6.D.

1 STAND fast for Christ thy Saviour!
    Stand fast whate'er betide!
Keep thou the Faith, unstained, un-
        shamed,
    By keeping at His side;
    Be faithful, ever faithful,
    Where'er thy lot be cast,
Stand fast for Christ! Stand fast for
        Christ!
    Stand faithful to the last.

2 Strong-founded like a lighthouse,
    That stands the storm and shock,
So be thy soul as if it shared
    The granite of the rock:
    Then far beyond the breakers,
    Let thy calm light be cast,
Stand fast for Christ! Stand fast for
        Christ!
    Stand faithful to the last.

3 Stout-hearted like a soldier
    Who never leaves the fight,
But meets the foeman face to face
    And meets him with his might:
    So bear thee in thy battles
    Until the war be past—
Stand fast for Christ! Stand fast for
        Christ!
    Stand faithful to the last.

4 Against each fair temptation
    Be swift upon thy guard,
Resist the devil, and his flight
    Shall be thy rich reward;
    And God's consoling angels
    Shall come when he has passed—
Stand fast like Christ! Stand fast like
        Christ!
    Stand faithful to the last.

5 Stand fast for Christ thy Saviour!
    He once stood fast for thee,
And standeth still, and still shall stand
    For all eternity—
    Be faithful, oh, be faithful,
    To love so true, so vast—
Stand fast for Christ! Stand fast for
        Christ!
    Stand faithful to the last.

549
P.M.

1 BE our joyful song today,
        Jesus! only Jesus!
He who takes our sins away,
        Jesus! only Jesus!
Name with every blessing rife,
Be our joy and hope through life,
Be our strength in every strife,
        Jesus! only Jesus!

2 Once we wandered far from God,
        Knowing not of Jesus;
Treading still the downward road
        Leading far from Jesus;
Till the Spirit taught us how
'Neath the Saviour's yoke to bow,
And we fain would follow now,
        Jesus! only Jesus!

3 Be our trust through years to come,
        Jesus! only Jesus!
Password to our heavenly home,
        Jesus! only Jesus!
When from sin and sorrow free,
On through all eternity,
This our theme and song shall be,
        Jesus! only Jesus!

550
8.7.8.7

1 FATHER, hear the prayer we offer!
    Not for ease that prayer shall be,
But for strength that we may ever
    Live our lives courageously.

2 Not for ever in green pastures
    Do we ask our way to be:
But by steep and rugged pathways
    Would we strive to climb to Thee.

3 Not for ever by still waters
    Would we idly, quietly stay;
But would smite the living fountains
    From the rocks along our way.

4 Be our strength in hours of weakness,
    In our wanderings be our Guide;
Through endeavour, failure, danger,
    Father, be Thou at our side.

5 Let our path be bright or dreary,
    Storm or sunshine be our share;
May our souls, in hope unweary,
    Make Thy work our ceaseless prayer.

551
P.M.

MAY the mind of Christ our Saviour
Live in me from day to day,
By His love and power controlling
All I do and say.

May the Word of God dwell richly
In my heart from hour to hour,
So that all may see I triumph
Only through His power.

May the peace of God my Father
Rule my life in everything,
That I may be calm to comfort
Sick and sorrowing.

May the love of Jesus fill me,
As the waters fill the sea.
Him exalting, self abasing;
This is victory.

May I run the race before me,
Strong and brave to face the foe,
Looking only unto Jesus
As I onward go.

May His beauty rest upon me
As I seek the lost to win,
And may they forget the channel,
Seeing only Him.

552
L.M.

1 "TAKE up thy cross," the Saviour said,
"If thou would'st My disciple be;
Deny thyself, the world forsake,
And humbly follow after Me."

2 Take up thy cross; let not its weight
Fill thy weak soul with vain alarm:
His strength shall bear thy spirit up,
And brace thy heart and nerve thine
arm.

3 Take up thy cross, nor heed the shame,
Nor let thy foolish pride rebel;
Thy Lord for thee the cross endured
To save thy soul from death and
hell.

4 Take up thy cross then in His strength,
And calmly every danger brave;
'Twill guide thee to a better home,
And lead to victory o'er the grave.

5 Take up thy cross and follow Him,
Nor think till death to lay it down;
For only he who bears the cross
May hope to wear the glorious
crown.

553
11.10.11.10.

1 "QUIT you like men!" Life's battle lies
before you;
Will ye prove traitors to your Prince
above?
Will ye desert His standard floating o'er
you,
The bannered cross of Jesus' dying
love?

Faithful and loyal, Lord, may
we be:
Living or dying, still faithful
unto Thee:
Serving the Christ, and in serving Him made free.

2 "Quit you like men!" Heaven's victor-
voices call you;
Oh, be ashamed of all your coward
shame!
Let not the fear of man or fiend appal
you,
They always win who fight in Jesus'
Name.

3 "Quit you like men!" No longer slaves
of passion,
Led by your lusts or mammon's
selfish greed;
No more enthralled by some unholy
fashion—
Freed by God's Son, then are ye free
indeed!

4 "Quit you like men!" Be true to your
true nature:
Are not our bodies temples of our
God?
Grow up in Christ to manhood's fullest
stature;
Tread in the steps the Perfect Man
hath trod.

5 "Quit you like men!" Behold the Man
  that liveth
    And once was slain, that ye may live
    to God;
  Take to your hearts the eternal life He
    giveth—
    Peace, power, and pardon, purchased
    with His blood.

554
6.5.6.5.D.

1 BRIGHTLY gleams our banner,
    Pointing to the sky,
  Waving wanderers onward
    To their home on high.
  Journeying o'er the desert
    Gladly thus we pray,
  And with hearts united
    Take our heavenward way.

    Brightly gleams our banner,
      Pointing to the sky,
    Waving wanderers onward
      To their home on high.

2 Jesus, Lord and Master,
    At Thy sacred feet,
  Here with hearts rejoicing
    See Thy children meet.
  Often have we left Thee,
    Often gone astray;
  Keep us, mighty Saviour,
    In the narrow way.

3 Pattern of our childhood,
    Once Thyself a child,
  Make our childhood holy,
    Pure, and meek, and mild.
  In the hour of danger
    Whither can we flee,
  Save to Thee, dear Saviour,
    Only unto Thee?

4 All our days direct us
    In the way we go;
  Lead us on victorious
    Over every foe;
  Bid Thine angels shield us
    When the storm-clouds lower;
  Pardon Thou and save us
    In the last dread hour.

5 Then with saints and angels
    May we join above,
  Offering prayers and praises
    At Thy throne of love.
  When the march is over,
    Then come rest and peace,
  Jesus in His beauty,
    Songs that never cease.

555
P.M

1 WHITHER, pilgrims, are you going,
    Going each with staff in hand?
  We are going on a journey,
    Going at our King's command,
  Over hills and plains and valleys,
  We are going to His palace, (Repeat)
    Going to the better land.

2 Tell us, pilgrims, what you hope for
    In that far-off, better land?
  Spotless robes, and crowns of glory,
    From a Saviour's loving hand.
  We shall drink of life's clear river,
  We shall dwell with God for ever, (Rep.
    In that bright, that better land.

3 Pilgrims, may we travel with you
    To that bright and better land?
  Come and welcome, come and welcome
    Welcome to our pilgrim band.
  Come, oh, come! and do not leave us;
  Christ is waiting to receive us, (Rep.)
    In that bright, that better land.

556
P.M

1   HARK to the sound of voices!
      Hark to the tramp of feet!
    Is it a mighty army
      Treading the busy street?
    Nearer it comes and nearer,
      Singing a glad refrain:
  List what they say as they haste away
    To the sound of a martial strain:

    "Marching beneath the banner,
      Fighting beneath the cross,
    Trusting in Him who saves us,
      Ne'er shall we suffer loss!
    Singing the songs of homeland,
      Loudly the chorus rings,
  We march to the fight in our armour
    bright
    At the call of the King of kings."

2
  Out of the mist of error,
    Out of the realms of night,
  Out of the pride of learning,
    Seeking the home of light;
  Out of the strife for power,
    Out of the greed of gold,
Onward they roam to their heavenly
    home,
  And the treasure that grows not old.

3
  Out of the bonds of evil,
    Out of the chains of sin,
  Ever they're pressing onward,
    Fighting the fight within;
  Holding the passions under,
    Ruling the sense with soul,
Wielding the sword in the Name of the
    Lord,
  As they march to their heavenly goal.

4
  On, then, ye gallant soldiers,
    On to your home above!
  Yours is the truth and glory,
    Yours is the power and love.
  Here are ye trained for heroes,
    Yonder ye serve the King;
March to the light 'neath the banner
    white,
  With the song that ye love to sing:

557   8.7.8.7.D.

1 GIRD thy loins up, Christian soldier,
  Lo! thy Captain calls thee out:
Let the danger make thee bolder,
  War in weakness, dare in doubt.
Buckle on thy heavenly armour;
  Patch up no inglorious peace;
Let thy courage wax the warmer
  As thy foes and fears increase.

2 Bind thy golden girdle round thee,
  Truth to keep thee firm and right:
Never shall the foe confound thee
  While the truth maintains thy fight.
Righteousness within thee rooted
  May appear to take thy part;
But let righteousness imputed
  Be the breastplate of thy heart.

3 Shod with gospel preparation,
  In the paths of promise tread;
Let the hope of free salvation
  As a helmet guard thy head.
When beset with various evils
  Wield the Spirit's two-edged sword;
Cut thy way through hosts of devils,
  While they fall before the Word.

4 But, when dangers closer threaten,
  And thy soul draws near to death,
When assaulted sore by Satan,
  Then upraise the shield of faith;
Fiery darts of fierce temptations,
  Intercepted by thy God,
There shall lose their force in patience,
  Sheathed in love, and quenched in
    blood.

5 Though to speak thou art not able,
  Always pray and never rest;
Prayer's a weapon for the feeble,
  Weakest souls can wield it best.
Ever on thy Captain calling,
  Make thy worst condition known;
He shall hold thee up when falling,
  Or shall lift thee up when down.

Heaven

558   7.6.8.6.D.

1 TEN thousand times ten thousand,
  In sparkling raiment bright;
The armies of the ransomed saints
  Throng up the steeps of light:
'Tis finished, all is finished,
  Their fight with death and sin;
Fling open wide the golden gates,
  And let the victors in.

2 What rush of Hallelujahs
  Fills all the earth and sky!
What ringing of a thousand harps
  Bespeaks the triumph nigh!
Oh, day for which creation
  And all its tribes were made!
Oh, joy, for all its former woes
  A thousandfold repaid!

3 Oh, then what raptured greetings
   On Canaan's happy shore!
What knitting severed friendships up,
   Where partings are no more!
Then eyes with joy shall sparkle
   That brimmed with tears of late;
Orphans no longer fatherless,
   Nor widows desolate.

4 Bring near Thy great salvation,
   Thou Lamb for sinners slain;
Fill up the roll of Thine elect,
   Then take Thy power and reign!
Appear, Desire of nations,
   Thine exiles long for home;
Show in the heavens Thy promised
   sign;
   Thou Prince and Saviour, come!

559   7.6.7.6.7.6.7.5.

1 THE sands of time are sinking,
   The dawn of heaven breaks;
The summer morn I've sighed for,
   The fair sweet morn awakes;
Dark, dark hath been the midnight,
   But day-spring is at hand,
And glory, glory dwelleth
   In Immanuel's land.

2 O Christ, He is the fountain,
   The deep, sweet well of love.
The streams on earth I've tasted;
   More deep I'll drink above;
There, to an ocean fulness,
   His mercy doth expand,
And glory, glory dwelleth
   In Immanuel's land.

3 With mercy and with judgment
   My web of time He wove,
And aye the dews of sorrow
   Were lustred by His love:
I'll bless the hand that guided,
   I'll bless the heart that planned,
When throned where glory dwelleth
   In Immanuel's land.

4 Oh, I am my Beloved's,
   And my Belovèd's mine;
He brings a poor vile sinner
   Into His house of wine.

I stand upon His merit;
   I know no other stand,
Not e'en where glory dwelleth
   In Immanuel's land.

5 The bride eyes not her garment,
   But her dear bridegroom's face:
I will not gaze at glory,
   But on my King of grace;
Not at the crown He giveth,
   But on His piercèd hand:
The Lamb is all the glory
   Of Immanuel's land.

6 I've wrestled on towards heaven,
   'Gainst storm and wind and tide,
Now like a weary traveller
   That leaneth on his guide,
Amid the shades of evening,
   While sinks life's lingering sand,
I hail the glory dawning
   In Immanuel's land.

560   C.M.

1 AROUND the throne of God in heaven
   Thousands of children stand,
Children whose sins are all forgiven,
   A holy, happy band:

     Singing glory, glory, glory.

2 What brought them to that world
    above,
   That heaven so bright and fair,
Where all is peace and joy and love?
   How came those children there?

3 Because the Saviour shed His blood
   To wash away their sin;
Bathed in that pure and precious flood,
   Behold them white and clean!

4 On earth they sought the Saviour's
    grace,
   On earth they loved His Name;
So now they see His blessèd face,
   And stand before the Lamb.

561   11.11.11.11.

1 BRIGHT home of our Saviour, what
    glories await
The spirits that pass through thy
   bright, pearly gate!

What anthems of rapture, unceasing
and high,
Compose the loud chorus that gladdens
the sky!

Home! home! sweet, sweet home!
Prepare me, dear Saviour, for yonder
blest home.

2 The home of the ransomed, the land of
the blest;
Where pilgrims shall enter a glorious
rest,
Shall wander in gladness through
pastures of green,
And drink the still waters of pleasures
serene.

3 The home that our Saviour has gone to
prepare—
No heart can conceive of the blessedness there;
Of raptures unending awaiting the just
When pure in His likeness they rise
from the dust.

4 We bless Thee, dear Saviour, who call'st
us to share
The beautiful home Thou hast gone to
prepare;
We trust in Thy mercy that, washed
from our sin,
Through yonder bright gates we may
all enter in.

562　　　　P.M.
1 THERE is a happy land,
Far, far away,
Where saints in glory stand,
Bright, bright as day.
Oh, how they sweetly sing,
Worthy is our Saviour King!
Loud let His praises ring—
Praise, praise for aye!

2 Come to this happy land,
Come, come away:
Why will ye doubting stand?
Why still delay?
Oh, we shall happy be,
When, from sin and sorrow free,
Lord, we shall live with Thee,
Blest, blest for aye!

3 Bright in that happy land
Beams every eye;
Kept by a Father's hand,
Love cannot die:
On then to glory run,
Be a crown, a kingdom won;
And bright above the sun
Reign, reign for aye.

563　　　　C.M.D.
1 THE roseate hues of early dawn,
The brightness of the day,
The crimson of the sunset sky,
How fast they fade away!
Oh, for the pearly gates of heaven,
Oh, for the golden floor,
Oh, for the Sun of Righteousness
That setteth nevermore!

2 O'er the dull ocean broods the night,
And all the strand is dark,
Save where a line of broken foam
Lies at low-water mark.
Oh, for the land that needs no night,
Where never night shall be;
Oh, for the quiet home in heaven,
Where there is no more sea!

3 The highest hopes we cherish here,
How fast they tire and faint!
How many a spot defiles the robe
That wraps an earthly saint!
Oh, for a heart that never sins,
Oh, for a soul washed white,
Oh, for a voice to praise our King,
Nor weary day or night!

4 Here faith is ours, and heavenly hope,
And grace to lead us higher;
But there are perfectness and peace
Beyond our best desire.
Oh, by Thy love and anguish, Lord,
Oh, by Thy life laid down,
Grant that we fall not from Thy grace,
Nor cast away our crown!

564　　　　P.M.
1 THERE is a city bright,
Closed are its gates to sin;
Naught that defileth,
Naught that defileth,
Can ever enter in.

Heaven

2 Saviour, I come to Thee!
O Lamb of God, I pray,
Cleanse me and save me,
Cleanse me and save me,
Wash all my sins away.

3 Lord, make me, from this hour,
Thy loving child to be;
Kept by Thy power,
Kept by Thy power,
From all that grieveth Thee:

4 Till in the snowy dress
Of Thy redeemed I stand,
Faultless and stainless,
Faultless and stainless,
Safe in that happy land!

565 P.M.

1 I HAVE read of a beautiful city,
Far away in the kingdom of God;
I have read how its walls are of jasper,
How its streets are all golden and broad:
In the midst of the street is life's river,
Clear as crystal, and pure to behold;
But not half of that city's bright glory
To mortals has ever been told.

Not half has ever been told,
Not half has ever been told,
Not half of that city's bright glory
To mortals has ever been told.

2 I have read of bright mansions in heaven,
Which the Saviour has gone to prepare;
And the saints who on earth have been faithful
Rest for ever with Christ over there:
There no sin ever enters, nor sorrow,
The inhabitants never grow old;
But not half of the joys that await them
To mortals has ever been told.

3 I have read of white robes for the righteous,
Of bright crowns which the glorified wear,
When our Father shall bid them, "Come, enter;
And My glory eternally share":

How the righteous are evermore blessèd,
As they walk through the streets of pure gold;
But not half of the wonderful story
To mortals has ever been told.

4 I have read of a Christ so forgiving,
That vile sinners may ask and receive
Peace and pardon for every transgression,
If when asking they only believe:
I have read how He'll guide and protect us,
If for safety we enter His fold;
But not half of His goodness and mercy
To mortals has ever been told.

566 6.4.6.4.6.6.6.4.

1 I'M but a stranger here,
Heaven is my home;
Only a sojourner,
Heaven is my home:
Danger and sorrow stand
Round me on every hand;
Heaven is my Fatherland,
Heaven is my home.

2 What though the tempest rage?
Heaven is my home!
Short is my pilgrimage,
Heaven is my home:
And time's wild, wintry blast
Soon will be over-past:
I shall reach home at last,
Heaven is my home.

3 There at my Saviour's side,
Heaven is my home!
I shall be glorified,
Heaven is my home:
There are the good and blest,
Those I love most and best,
And there I too shall rest,
Heaven is my home.

4 Therefore I'll murmur not,
Heaven is my home;
Whate'er my earthly lot,
Heaven is my home:
For I shall surely stand
There at my Lord's right hand;
Heaven is my Fatherland,
Heaven is my home.

188

567   7.6.7.6.D.

1 JERUSALEM the golden,
  With milk and honey blest,
Beneath thy contemplation
  Sink heart and voice oppressed:
I know not, oh, I know not,
  What joys await us there,
What radiancy of glory,
  What bliss beyond compare.

2 They stand, those halls of Zion,
  All jubilant with song;
And bright with many an angel,
  And all the martyr-throng:
The Prince is ever in them,
  The daylight is serene,
The pastures of the blessèd
  Are decked in glorious sheen.

3 There is the throne of David,
  And there, from care released,
The shout of them that triumph,
  The song of them that feast;
And they who with their Leader
  Have conquered in the fight,
For ever and for ever
  Are clothed in robes of white.

4 Oh, sweet and blessed country,
  The home of God's elect!
Oh, sweet and blessèd country
  That eager hearts expect!
Jesus, in mercy bring us
  To that dear land of rest,
Who art, with God the Father,
  And Spirit, ever blest.

568   10.10.10.4.

1 FOR all the saints, who from their
  labours rest,
Who Thee by faith before the world
  confessed,
Thy Name, O Jesus, be for ever blest.
      Hallelujah!

2 Thou wast their Rock, their Fortress,
  and their Might:
Thou, Lord, their Captain in the well-
  fought fight;
Thou, in the darkness drear, their one
  true Light.
      Hallelujah!

3 Oh, may Thy soldiers, faithful, true,
  and bold,
Fight as the saints, who nobly fought
  of old,
And win, with them, the victor's crown
  of gold.
      Hallelujah!

4 Oh, blest communion, fellowship
  divine!
We feebly struggle, they in glory shine!
Yet all are one in Thee, for all are
  Thine.
      Hallelujah!

5 And when the strife is fierce, the warfare long,
Steals on the ear the distant triumph-
  song,
And hearts are brave again, and arms
  are strong.
      Hallelujah!

6 The golden evening brightens in the
  west:
Soon, soon to faithful warriors cometh
  rest;
Sweet is the calm of Paradise the blest.
      Hallelujah!

7 But lo! there breaks a yet more
  glorious day;
The saints triumphant rise in bright
  array:
The King of Glory passes on His way.
      Hallelujah!

8 From earth's wide bounds, from
  ocean's farthest coast,
Through gates of pearl streams in the
  countless host,
Singing to Father, Son, and Holy
  Ghost—
      Hallelujah!

569   8.6.8.8.6.

1 ETERNAL Light! Eternal Light!
  How pure the soul must be
When, placed within Thy searching
  sight,
It shrinks not, but with calm delight
  Can live, and look on Thee!

2 The spirits that surround Thy throne
  May bear the burning bliss;
But that is surely theirs alone,
  Since they have never, never known
  A fallen world like this.

3 Oh, how shall I, whose native sphere
  Is dark, whose mind is dim,
Before the Ineffable appear,
  And on my naked spirit bear
  The uncreated beam?

4 There is a way for man to rise
  To that sublime abode;
An Offering and a Sacrifice,
  A Holy Spirit's energies,
  An Advocate with God:

5 These, these prepare us for the sight
  Of holiness above;
The sons of ignorance and night
  May dwell in the Eternal Light,
  Through the Eternal Love.

570 P.M.

1 LET us sing of His love once again—
  Of the love that can never decay,
Of the blood of the Lamb who was slain,
  Till we praise Him again in that day.

      In the sweet . . . "by-and-by"
        We shall meet on that beauti-
        ful shore;
      In the sweet . . . "by-and-by"
        We shall meet on that beauti-
        ful shore.

2 There is cleansing and healing for all
  Who will wash in the life-giving
  flood,
There is life everlasting and joy
  At the right hand of God through the
  blood.

3 Even now while we taste of His love,
  We are filled with delight at His
  Name;
But what will it be when above
  We shall join in the song of the
  Lamb?

571 C.M.

1 How bright these glorious spirits shine!
  Whence all their white array?
How came they to the blissful seats
  Of everlasting day?

2 Lo! these are they from suffering
  great,
  Who came to realms of light;
And in the blood of Christ have washed
  Those robes that shine so bright.

3 Now with triumphal palms they stand
  Before the throne on high,
And serve the God they love, amidst
  The glories of the sky.

4 Hunger and thirst are felt no more,
  Nor suns with scorching ray;
God is their Sun, whose cheering
  beams
  Diffuse eternal day.

5 The Lamb, who dwells amidst the
  throne,
  Shall o'er them still preside,
Feed them with nourishment divine,
  And all their footsteps guide.

6 'Midst pastures green He'll lead His
  flock,
  Where living streams appear;
And God the Lord from every eye
  Shall wipe off every tear.

7 To Father, Son, and Holy Ghost,
  The God whom we adore,
Be glory, as it was, is now,
  And shall be evermore.

The Bible

572　　6.4.6.4.D.

1 BREAK Thou the Bread of Life,
　Dear Lord, to me,
As Thou didst break the bread
　Beside the sea;
Beyond the sacred page
　I seek Thee, Lord,
My spirit longs for Thee,
　Thou Living Word.

2 Thou art the Bread of Life,
　O Lord, to me,
Thy Holy Word the truth
　That saveth me;
Give me to eat and live
　With Thee above,
Teach me to love Thy truth,
　For Thou art love.

3 Oh, send Thy Spirit, Lord,
　Now unto me,
That He may touch my eyes
　And make me see;
Show me the truth concealed
　Within Thy Word,
And in Thy Book revealed
　I see Thee, Lord.

4 Bless Thou the Bread of Life
　To me, to me,
As Thou didst bless the loaves
　By Galilee;
Then shall all bondage cease,
　All fetters fall,
And I shall find my peace,
　My All in all.

573　　7.6.7.6.D.

1 WE love the blessèd Bible,
　The glorious Word of God;
The lamp for those who travel
　O'er all life's dreary road;
The watchword in life's battle,
　The chart on life's dark sea;
The everlasting Bible.
　It shall our teacher be.

2 Who would not love the Bible,
　So beautiful and wise!
Its teachings charm the simple,
　And all point to the skies;
Its stories all so mighty
　Of men so brave to see;
Divinely-given Bible,
　It shall our teacher be.

3 But most we love the Bible,
　For there we children learn
How Christ took on our childhood,
　Our hearts to Him to turn;
And how He bowed to sorrow,
　That we His face might see;
The Bible, oh! the Bible—
　It shall our teacher be.

4 Then we will hold the Bible—
　The glorious Book of God;
We'll ne'er forsake the Bible,
　Through all life's future road.
And when we shall be dying,
　Whenever that may be,
The comfort of the Bible
　Shall still our solace be.

574　　S.M.

1 WE thank Thee, Lord, indeed,
　That Thou Thy Word hast given,
To light our path in this dark world,
　And safely guide to Heaven.

2 To warn of sinful steps,
　And point our road each day,
To keep us in the one safe path,
　The strait and narrow way.

3 Bless those who with us read
　Thy wondrous Book of Light,
That all of us with one desire
　May strive to do the right.

4 As Thy commands we seek
　Within Thy Word each day,
Teach us what Thou wilt have us do,
　Then teach us to obey.

5 Oh, give us minds to learn,
　And hearts to know Thy will,
And make us willing, cheerful, strong,
　Thy bidding to fulfil!

6 We feel our weakness, Lord,
　But knowing Thou art near,
When we are weak, then we are strong,
　We need not, will not, fear.

575
11.10.11.10.

1 CLING to the Bible, though all else be
taken;
Lose not its precepts so precious and
pure;
Souls that are sleeping its tidings
awaken:
Life from the dead in its promises
sure.
Cling to the Bible!
Cling to the Bible!
Cling to the Bible!
Our lamp and our guide!

2 Cling to the Bible!—this jewel and
treasure
Brings life eternal, and saves fallen
man;
Surely its value no mortal can measure:
Seek for its blessing, O soul, while
you can!

3 Lamp for the feet that in by-ways have
wandered,
Guide for the youth that would
otherwise fall;
Hope for the sinner whose life has been
squandered;
Staff for the aged, and best Book for
all!

576
6.6.6.6.

1 ONCE more before we part
We bless the Saviour's Name;
Let every tongue and heart
Join to extol the Lamb.

2 We on Thy holy Word
Would feed, and live, and grow;
Go on to know Thee, Lord,
And practise what we know.

3 Lord, in Thy grace we came,
Thy blessing still impart;
We met in Thine own Name,
And in Thy Name we part.

577
C.M.

1 WE seek Thee, Lord, for in Thy Word
Such tender love we see;
With beckoning hand Thou still dost
stand,
And bid us come to Thee.

2 Close to Thine arm, from care an
harm,
Once more the children press;
Oh, let Thy grace in every place
Our Scripture Union bless!

3 Thy help we plead, that as we read
True light our souls may fill,
Till every heart be taught its part
In God's own loving will.

4 One hope we claim, one steadfast aim
Though scattered far and wide—
One path to share, one cross to bear,
As brethren side by side.

5 From far around, with gladsome sound
Our pilgrim song is heard,
While through the night is gleamin
bright
The lantern of God's Word.

6 With this their guide, through path
untried
Thy children's steps have trod;
Till little feet have reached the street
Before the throne of God.

7 Grant us at last, our journey past,
To meet from every land,
Through Thy dear love in heaven to
prove
One grand united band!

578
C.M

1 THE Spirit breathes upon the Word,
And brings the truth to sight;
Precepts and promises afford
A sanctifying light.

2 A glory gilds the sacred page,
Majestic, like the sun:
It gives a light to every age;
It gives, but borrows none.

3 The hand that gave it still supplies
The gracious light and heat:
His truths upon the nations rise—
They rise, but never set.

4 Let everlasting thanks be Thine
For such a bright display
As makes a world of darkness shine
With beams of heavenly day.

5 My soul rejoices to pursue
　The steps of Him I love,
Till glory breaks upon my view
　In brighter worlds above.

579   C.M.

1 FATHER of mercies, in Thy Word
　What endless glory shines!
For ever be Thy Name adored
　For these celestial lines.

2 Here springs of consolation rise
　To cheer the fainting mind,
And thirsty souls receive supplies,
　And sweet refreshment find.

3 Here the Redeemer's welcome voice
　Spreads heavenly peace around;
And life and everlasting joys
　Attend the blissful sound.

4 Oh, may these hallowed pages be
　My ever dear delight!
And still new beauties may I see,
　And still increasing light.

5 Divine Instructor, gracious Lord,
　Be Thou for ever near;
Teach me to love Thy sacred Word,
　And view my Saviour here.

580   7.7.7.7.

1 HOLY Bible, Book divine,
Precious treasure, thou art mine;
Mine, to tell me whence I came,
Mine, to tell me what I am.

2 Mine, to chide me when I rove,
Mine, to show a Saviour's love;
Mine thou art to guide and guard,
Mine, to punish or reward;

3 Mine, to comfort in distress,
Suffering in this wilderness;
Mine, to show, by living faith,
Man can triumph over death;

4 Mine, to tell of joys to come,
And the rebel sinner's doom;
Holy Bible, Book divine,
Precious treasure, thou art mine!

581   C.M.

1 THY Word is like a garden, Lord,
　With flowers bright and fair,
And every one who seeks may pluck
　A lovely nosegay there.

2 Thy Word is like a deep, deep mine,
　And jewels rich and rare
Are hidden in its mighty depths
　For every searcher there.

3 Thy Word is like the starry host;
　A thousand rays of light
Are seen to guide the traveller,
　And make his pathway bright.

4 Thy Word is like a glorious choir,
　And loud its anthems ring;
Though many tongues and parts unite,
　It is one song they sing.

5 Thy Word is like an armoury,
　Where soldiers may repair,
And find for life's long battle-day
　All needful weapons there.

6 Oh! may I love Thy precious Word,
　May I explore its mine!
May I its fragrant flowers glean,
　May light upon me shine!

7 Oh! may I find my armour there—
　Thy Word my trusty sword;
I'll learn to fight with every foe
　The battle of the Lord.

582   P.M.

1 OH, wonderful, wonderful Word of the
　　Lord!
　True wisdom its pages unfold;
And though we may read them a
　　thousand times o'er,
　They never, no, never grow old.
Each line has a treasure, each promise
　　a pearl,
　That all if they will may secure;
And we know that when time and the
　　world pass away,
　God's Word shall for ever endure.

2 Oh, wonderful, wonderful Word of the
Lord!
The lamp that our Father above
So kindly has lighted to teach us the
way
That leads to the arms of His love;
Its warnings, its counsels, are faithful
and just;
Its judgments are perfect and pure;
And we know that when time and the
world pass away,
God's Word shall for ever endure.

3 Oh, wonderful, wonderful Word of the
Lord!
Our only salvation is there;
It carries conviction down deep in the
heart,
And shows us ourselves as we are.
It tells of a Saviour, and points to the
cross,
Where pardon we now may secure;
For we know that when time and the
world pass away,
God's Word shall for ever endure.

4 Oh, wonderful, wonderful Word of the
Lord!
The hope of our friends in the past;
Its truth, where so firmly they anchored
their trust,
Through ages eternal shall last.
Oh, wonderful, wonderful Word of the
Lord!
Unchanging, abiding, and sure;
For we know that when time and the
world pass away,
God's Word shall for ever endure.

583　　　　　　　　　　P.M.

1 GUARD the Bible well, all its foes repel,
The sweet story tell of the Lord:
Guard what God revealed, as our sun
and shield;
Never, never yield His holy Word.

Rouse, then, Christians! Rally for
the Bible!
Work on, pray on, spread the
truth abroad;
Stand, then, like men, in the cause
triumphant,
For the Bible is the Word of
God.

2 Book of love divine, precious Word of
Thine,
Let it ever shine all abroad:
In the Spirit's might we must win the
fight.
For this Gospel light, the truth of
God.

3 Shout the Bible song, swell the mighty
throng!
In the cause be strong for the right
Look to God in prayer when the foe you
dare,
And for ever wear His armour bright.

4 O ye Christian band, for this Bible
stand!
By the Lord's command, ne'er give
o'er;
Lead the army on, till the strife is
done,
And the cause is won for evermore.

584　　　　　　　　　6.6.6.6.

1 LORD, Thy Word abideth,
And our footsteps guideth;
Who its truth believeth
Light and joy receiveth.

2 When our foes are near us,
Then Thy Word doth cheer us,
Word of consolation,
Message of salvation.

3 When the storms are o'er us,
And dark clouds before us,
Then its light directeth,
And our way protecteth.

4 Who can tell the pleasure,
Who recount the treasure,
By Thy Word imparted
To the simple-hearted?

5 Word of mercy, giving
Succour to the living;
Word of life, supplying
Comfort to the dying.

6 Oh, that we discerning
Its most holy learning,
Lord, may love and fear Thee,
Evermore be near Thee!

585 8.7.8.4.

1 BOOK of grace and Book of glory!
  Gift of God to age and youth,
Wondrous is thy sacred story,
  Bright, bright with truth!

2 Book of love! in accents tender
  Speaking unto such as we;
May it lead us, Lord, to render
  All, all to Thee.

3 Book of hope! the spirit sighing,
  Sweetest comfort finds in thee,
As it hears the Saviour crying,
  "Come, come to Me!"

4 Book of peace! when nights of sorrow
  Fall upon us drearily,
Thou wilt bring a shining morrow,
  Full, full of Thee.

5 Book of life! when we, reposing,
  Bid farewell to friends we love,
Give us, for the life then closing,
  Life, life above.

586 L.M.

1 THERE is a lamp whose steady light
Guides the poor traveller in the night:
'Tis God's own Word! Its beaming ray
Can turn the midnight into day.

2 There is a storehouse of rich fare,
Supplied with plenty and to spare:
'Tis God's own Word! It spreads a feast
For every hungering, thirsty guest.

3 There is a chart whose tracings show
The onward course when tempests blow:
'Tis God's own Word! There, there are found
Directions for the homeward bound.

4 There is a tree whose leaves impart
Health to the burdened, contrite heart:
'Tis God's own Word! It cures of sin,
And makes the guilty conscience clean.

5 Give me this lamp to light my road,
This storehouse for my daily food;
Give me this chart for life's rough sea,
These healing leaves, this heavenly tree.

587 C.M.

1 LAMP of our feet, whereby we trace
  Our path when wont to stray;
Stream from the fount of heavenly grace;
  Brook by the traveller's way;

2 Bread of our souls, whereon we feed;
  True manna from on high;
Our guide and chart, wherein we read
  Of realms beyond the sky;

3 Pillar of fire, through watches dark,
  And radiant cloud by day;
When waves would whelm our tossing bark,
  Our anchor and our stay;

4 Word of the everlasting God,
  Will of His glorious Son,
Without thee how could earth be trod,
  Or heaven itself be won?

5 Yet to unfold thy hidden worth,
  Thy mysteries to reveal,
That Spirit, which first gave thee forth,
  Thy volume must unseal.

6 Lord, grant that we aright may learn
  The wisdom it imparts,
And to its heavenly teaching turn
  With simple, childlike hearts.

588 7.6.7.6.D.

1 O WORD of God Incarnate!
  O Wisdom from on high!
O Truth unchanged, unchanging,
  O Light of our dark sky;
We praise Thee for the radiance
  That from the hallowed page,
A lantern to our footsteps,
  Shines on from age to age.

2 The Church from her dear Master
  Received the gift divine,
And still that light she lifteth
  O'er all the earth to shine;
It is the golden casket
  Where gems of truth are stored;
It is the heaven-drawn picture
  Of Christ, the living Word.

3 It floateth like a banner
  Before God's host unfurled;
It shineth like a beacon
  Above the darkling world;
It is the chart and compass
  That o'er life's surging sea,
'Mid mists and rocks and quicksands,
  Still guide, O Christ, to Thee.

589   P.M.
1 THANK God for the Bible! 'tis there
    that we find
  The story of Christ and His love:
How He came down to earth from His
    beautiful home
  In the mansions of glory above:
    Thanks to Him we will bring,
    Praise to Him we will sing,
For He came down to earth from His
    beautiful home
  In the mansions of glory above.

2 While He lived on this earth to the sick
    and the blind,
  And to mourners, His blessings were
    given;
And He said, "Let the little ones come
    unto Me,
  For of such is the kingdom of
    heaven."

Jesus calls us to come,
  He's prepared us a home,
For He said, "Let the little ones come
    unto Me,
  For of such is the kingdom of
    heaven."

3 In the Bible we read of a beautiful
    land,
  Where sorrow and pain never come;
For Jesus is there with a heavenly
    band,
  And 'tis there He's prepared us a
    home.
    Jesus calls—shall we stay?
    No! we'll gladly obey;
For Jesus is there with a heavenly
    band,
  And 'tis there He's prepared us a
    home.

4 Thank God for the Bible! its truth o'er
    the earth
  We'll scatter with bountiful hand;
But we never can tell what the Bible
    is worth
  Till we go to that beautiful land.
    There our thanks we will bring,
    There with angels we'll sing,
And its worth we can tell, when with
    Jesus we dwell,
  In heaven, that beautiful land.

Morning Hymns

590   7.5.7.5.7.7.
1 EVERY morning the red sun
    Rises warm and bright;
But the evening cometh on,
    And the dark cold night:
There's a bright land far away,
Where 'tis never-ending day.

2 Every spring the sweet young flowers
    Open bright and gay,
Till the chilly autumn hours
    Wither them away:
There's a land we have not seen,
Where the trees are always green.

3 Little birds sing songs of praise
    All the summer long;
But in colder, shorter days
    They forget their song:
There's a place where angels sing
Ceaseless praises to their King.

4 Christ our Lord is ever near
    Those who follow Him;
But we cannot see Him here,
    For our eyes are dim:
There's a happy, glorious place,
Where men always see His face.

196

Who shall go to that fair land?
  All who love the right;
Holy children there shall stand
  In their robes of white:
For that heaven, so bright and blest,
Is our everlasting rest.

591   C.M.

MY Father, for another night
  Of quiet sleep and rest,
For all the joy of morning light,
  Thy holy Name be blest.

Now with the new-born day I give
  Myself anew to Thee,
That as Thou willest I may live,
  And what Thou willest be.

Whate'er I do, things great or small,
  Whate'er I speak or frame,
Thy glory may I seek in all,
  Do all in Jesus' Name.

My Father, for His sake, I pray,
  Thy child accept and bless,
And lead me by Thy grace today
  In paths of righteousness.

592   L.M.

AWAKE, my soul, and with the sun
Thy daily stage of duty run;
Shake off dull sloth, and joyful rise
To pay thy morning sacrifice.

All praise to Thee, who safe hast kept,
And hast refreshed me while I slept;
Grant, Lord, when I from death shall
  wake,
I may of endless life partake.

Lord, I my vows to Thee renew:
Disperse my sins as morning dew;
Guard my first springs of thought and
  will,
And with Thyself my spirit fill.

Direct, control, suggest this day
All I design, or do, or say;
That all my powers with all their
  might
In Thy sole glory may unite.

5 Praise God, from whom all blessings
    flow;
Praise Him, all creatures here below;
Praise Him above, ye heavenly host;
Praise Father, Son, and Holy Ghost.

593   C.M.

1 THIS is the day the Lord hath made,
  He calls the hours His own;
Let heaven rejoice, let earth be glad,
  And praise surround the throne.

2 Today He rose and left the dead,
  And Satan's empire fell;
Today the saints His triumphs spread,
  And all His wonders tell.

3 Hosanna to the anointed King,
  To David's holy Son!
Make haste to help us, Lord, and bring
  Salvation from Thy throne.

4 Blest be the Lord, who comes to men
  With messages of grace;
Who comes, in God His Father's
    Name,
  To save our sinful race.

5 Hosanna in the highest strains
  The Church on earth can raise;
The highest heavens in which He
    reigns
Shall give Him nobler praise.

594   7.6.7.6.D.

1 O DAY of rest and gladness,
  O day of joy and light,
O balm of care and sadness,
  Most beautiful, most bright;
On thee the high and lowly,
  Before the eternal throne,
Sing Holy, Holy, Holy,
  To the great Three in One.

2 On thee, at the creation,
  The light first had its birth;
On thee, for our salvation,
  Christ rose from depths of earth;
On thee our Lord victorious
  The Spirit sent from heaven;
And thus on thee most glorious
  A triple light was given.

3 Thou art a cooling fountain
    In life's dry, dreary sand,
From thee, like Pisgah's mountain,
    We view our promised land;
A day of sweet refection,
    A day of holy love,
A day of resurrection
    From earth to things above.

4 Today on weary nations
    The heavenly manna falls,
To holy convocations
    The silver trumpet calls,
Where Gospel-light is glowing
    With pure and radiant beams,
And living water flowing
    With soul-refreshing streams.

5 New graces ever gaining
    From this our day of rest,
We reach the rest remaining
    To spirits of the blest.
To Holy Ghost be praises,
    To Father and to Son;
The Church her voice upraises
    To Thee, blest Three in One.

595   6.6.8.6.6.8

1 How pleased and blest was I
    To hear the people cry,
"Come, let us seek our God today!"
    Yes, with a cheerful zeal
    We haste to Zion's hill,
And there our vows and homage pay.

2 Zion, thrice happy place,
    Adorned with wondrous grace,
And walls of strength embrace thee
    round;
    In thee our tribes appear,
    To pray and praise, and hear
The sacred Gospel's joyful sound.

3 There David's greater Son
    Hath fixed His royal throne;
He sits for grace and judgment there.

He bids the saints be glad,
He makes the sinner sad,
And humble souls rejoice with fear.

4 May peace attend thy gate,
    And joy within thee wait,
To bless the soul of every guest:
    The man that seeks thy peace,
    And wishes thine increase,
A thousand blessings on him rest.

5 My tongue repeats her vows,
    Peace to this sacred house!
For there my friends and kindred dwell
    And, since my glorious God
    Makes thee His blest abode,
My soul shall ever love thee well.

596   6.6.6.6.D

1 JESUS, we love to meet
    On this Thy holy day:
We worship round Thy seat
    On this Thy holy day:
Thou tender, heavenly Friend,
To Thee our prayers ascend;
O'er our young spirits bend
    On this Thy holy day.

2 We dare not trifle now
    On this Thy holy day:
In silent awe we bow
    On this Thy holy day:
Check every wandering thought,
And let us all be taught
To serve Thee as we ought
    On this Thy holy day.

3 We listen to Thy Word
    On this Thy holy day:
Bless all that we have heard
    On this Thy holy day:
Go with us when we part,
And to each youthful heart
Thy saving grace impart
    On this Thy holy day.

Evening Hymns

597 P.M.

1 LORD, it is eventide: the light of day is
waning;
  Far o'er the golden land earth's
  voices faint and fall;
Lowly we pray to Thee for strength and
love sustaining,
  Lowly we ask of Thee Thy peace
  upon us all.
    Oh, grant unto our souls—

    Light that groweth not pale
    With day's decrease,
    Love that never can fail
    Till life shall cease;
    Joy no trial can mar,
    Hope that shineth afar,
    Faith serene as a star,
    And Christ's own peace.

2 Lord, it is eventide: we turn to Thee for
healing,
  Like those of Galilee who came at
  close of day;
Speak to our waiting souls, their
hidden founts unsealing,
  Touch us with hands divine that take
  our sin away.
    Oh, grant unto our souls—

3 Saviour, Thou knowest all, the trial and
temptation,
  Knowest the wilfulness and way-
  wardness of youth;
Help us to cling to Thee, our strength
and our salvation,
  Help us to find in Thee the one
  eternal Truth.
    Oh, grant unto our souls—

4 Lord, it is eventide: our hearts await
Thy giving,
  Wait for that peace divine that none
  can take away,
Peace that shall lift our souls to loftier
heights of living,
  Till we abide with Thee in everlasting
  day.
    Oh, grant unto our souls—

598 8.8.8.8.8.8.

1 SWEET Saviour, bless us ere we go;
  Thy Word into our minds instil,
And make our lukewarm hearts to
glow
  With lowly love and fervent will.
Through life's long day and death's
dark night,
O gentle Jesus, be our Light!

2 The day is done, its hours have run,
  And Thou hast taken count of all,
The scanty triumphs grace hath won,
  The broken vow, the frequent fall.
Through life's long day and death's
dark night,
O gentle Jesus, be our Light!

3 Grant us, dear Lord, from evil ways
  True absolution and release;
And bless us, more than in past days,
  With purity and inward peace.
Through life's long day and death's
dark night,
O gentle Jesus, be our Light!

4 Do more than pardon; give us joy,
  Sweet fear, and sober liberty,
And simple hearts without alloy
  That only long to be like Thee.
Through life's long day and death's
dark night,
O gentle Jesus, be our Light!

5 For all we love, the poor, the sad,
  The sinful, unto Thee we call;
Oh, let Thy mercy make us glad:
  Thou art our Jesus, and our All.
Through life's long day and death's
dark night,
O gentle Jesus, be our Light!

599 L.M.

1 SUN of my soul, Thou Saviour dear,
It is not night if Thou be near;
Oh, may no earth-born cloud arise
To hide Thee from Thy servant's eyes!

Evening Hymns

2 When the soft dews of kindly sleep
  My wearied eyelids gently steep,
Be my last thought, how sweet to rest
For ever on my Saviour's breast!

3 Abide with me from morn till eve,
  For without Thee I cannot live;
Abide with me when night is nigh,
For without Thee I dare not die.

4 If some poor wandering child of Thine
  Have spurned today the voice divine,
Now, Lord, the gracious work begin;
Let him no more lie down in sin.

5 Watch by the sick; enrich the poor
  With blessings from Thy boundless
    store:
Be every mourner's sleep tonight
Like infant's slumbers, pure and light.

6 Come near and bless us when we wake,
  Ere through the world our way we
    take;
Till, in the ocean of Thy love,
We lose ourselves in heaven above.

600   7.6.7.6.8.8.

1 THE day is past and over;
  All thanks, O Lord, to Thee;
  I pray Thee now that sinless
  The hours of dark may be:
O Jesus, keep me in Thy sight,
And guard me through the coming
  night.

2 The joys of day are over;
  I lift my heart to Thee,
  And ask Thee that offenceless
  The hours of dark may be:
O Jesus, keep me in Thy sight,
And guard me through the coming
  night.

3 The toils of day are over;
  I raise the hymn to Thee,
  And ask that free from peril
  The hours of dark may be:
O Jesus, keep me in Thy sight,
And guard me through the coming
  night.

4 Be Thou my soul's preserver,
  For Thou alone dost know
  How many are the perils
  Through which I have to go:
O loving Jesus, hear my call,
And guard and save me from them all.

601   10.10.10.10

1 ABIDE with me, fast falls the eventide:
The darkness deepens: Lord, with me
  abide;
When other helpers fail, and comforts
  flee,
Help of the helpless, oh, abide with
  me.

2 Swift to its close ebbs out life's little
  day;
Earth's joys grow dim, its glories pass
  away;
Change and decay in all around I see;
O Thou, who changest not, abide with
  me.

3 I need Thy presence every passing
  hour:
What but Thy grace can foil the
  tempter's power?
Who like Thyself my guide and stay
  can be?
Through cloud and sunshine, Lord,
  abide with me.

4 I fear no foe, with Thee at hand to
  bless,
Ills have no weight, and tears no
  bitterness.
Where is death's sting? where, grave,
  thy victory?
I triumph still, if Thou abide with me.

5 Reveal Thyself before my closing eyes,
Shine through the gloom, and point me
  to the skies:
Heaven's morning breaks, and earth's
  vain shadows flee:
In life, in death, O Lord, abide with
  me.

602   L.M.

1 AT even, ere the sun was set,
  The sick, O Lord, around Thee lay;
Oh, in what divers pains they met!
  Oh, with what joy they went away!

Once more 'tis eventide, and we
  Oppressed with various ills draw
    near.
What if Thy form we cannot see?
  We know and feel that Thou art
    here.

O Saviour Christ, our woes dispel:
  For some are sick; and some are sad;
And some have never loved Thee well;
  And some have lost the love they
    had;

And some have found the world is
    vain,
  Yet from the world they break not
    free;
And some have friends who give them
    pain,
  Yet have not sought a Friend in
    Thee.

And none, O Lord, have perfect rest,
  For none are wholly free from sin;
And they who fain would serve Thee
    best
  Are conscious most of wrong within.

O Saviour Christ, Thou too art Man;
  Thou hast been troubled, tempted,
    tried;
Thy kind but searching glance can
    scan
  The very wounds that shame would
    hide.

Thy touch has still its ancient power;
  No word from Thee can fruitless
    fall;
Hear, in this solemn evening hour,
  And in Thy mercy heal us all.

603
    10.10.10.10.

SAVIOUR, again to Thy dear Name we
    raise
With one accord our parting hymn of
    praise;
We stand to bless Thee ere our worship
    cease,
Then, lowly kneeling, wait Thy word
    of peace.

2 Grant us Thy peace upon our home-
    ward way;
  With Thee begun, with Thee shall end
    the day:
  Guard Thou the lips from sin, the
    hearts from shame,
  That in this house have called upon
    Thy Name.

3 Grant us Thy peace, Lord, through the
    coming night,
  Turn Thou for us its darkness into
    light;
  From harm and danger keep Thy
    children free,
  For dark and light are both alike to
    Thee.

4 Grant us Thy peace throughout our
    earthly life,
  Our balm in sorrow, and our stay in
    strife;
  Then, when Thy voice shall bid our
    conflict cease,
  Call us, O Lord, to Thine eternal
    peace.

604
    L.M.

1 GLORY to Thee, my God, this night,
  For all the blessings of the light;
  Keep me, oh, keep me, King of kings,
  Beneath Thine own almighty wings.

2 Forgive me, Lord, for Thy dear Son,
  The ill that I this day have done;
  That with the world, myself, and Thee,
  I, ere I sleep, at peace may be.

3 Teach me to live, that I may dread
  The grave as little as my bed;
  Teach me to die, that so I may
  Rise glorious at the last great day.

4 Oh, may my soul on Thee repose,
  And may sweet sleep mine eyelids
    close—
  Sleep that may me more vigorous
    make
  To serve my God when I awake.

5 Praise God, from whom all blessings
    flow;
Praise Him, all creatures here below;
Praise Him above, ye heavenly host;
Praise Father, Son, and Holy Ghost!

605   6.5.6.5.

1 Now the day is over,
    Night is drawing nigh,
Shadows of the evening
    Steal across the sky.

2 Now the darkness gathers,
    Stars their watches keep,
Birds and beasts and flowers
    Soon will be asleep.

3 Jesus, give the weary
    Calm and sweet repose;
With Thy tenderest blessing
    May mine eyelids close.

4 Grant to little children
    Visions bright of Thee;
Guard the sailors tossing
    On the deep blue sea.

5 Comfort every sufferer
    Watching late in pain;
Those who plan some evil
    From their sin restrain.

6 Through the long night watches
    May Thine angels spread
Their white wings above me,
    Watching round my bed.

7 When the morning wakens,
    Then may I arise
Pure and fresh and sinless
    In Thy holy eyes.

8 Glory to the Father,
    Glory to the Son,
And to Thee, blest Spirit,
    Whilst all ages run.

606   9.8.9.8.

1 THE day Thou gavest, Lord, is ended,
    The darkness falls at Thy behest;
To Thee our morning hymns ascended,
    Thy praise shall sanctify our rest.

2 We thank Thee that Thy Church un
    sleeping,
    While earth rolls onward into light
Through all the world her watch i
    keeping,
    And rests not now by day or night

3 As o'er each continent and island
    The dawn leads on another day,
The voice of prayer is never silent,
    Nor dies the strain of praise away.

4 The sun that bids us rest is waking
    Our brethren 'neath the western sky
And hour by hour fresh lips ar
    making
    Thy wondrous doings heard on high

5 So be it, Lord; Thy throne shall never
    Like earth's proud empires, pas
    away;
Thy kingdom stands, and grows fo
    ever,
    Till all Thy creatures own Thy sway

607   8.7.8.7

1 SAVIOUR, breathe an evening blessing,
    Ere repose our spirits seal;
Sin and want we come confessing;
    Thou canst save, and Thou canst
    heal.

2 Though destruction walk around us,
    Though the arrows past us fly,
Angel-guards from Thee surround us;
    We are safe if Thou art nigh.

3 Though the night be dark and dreary,
    Darkness cannot hide from Thee;
Thou art He who, never weary,
    Watchest where Thy people be.

4 Should swift death this night o'ertake
    us,
    And our couch become our tomb,
May the morn in heaven awake us,
    Clad in light and deathless bloom.

608   8.7.8.7.4.7.

1 LORD, dismiss us with Thy blessing,
  Fill our hearts with joy and peace;
Let us each, Thy love possessing,
  Triumph in redeeming grace:
      Oh, refresh us!
  Travelling through this wilderness.

2 Thanks we give, and adoration,
  For Thy Gospel's joyful sound;
May the fruits of Thy salvation
  In our hearts and lives abound:
      May Thy presence
  With us evermore be found!

3 So, whene'er the signal's given
  Us from earth to call away,
Borne on angels' wings to heaven,
  Glad the summons to obey,
      May we ever
  Reign with Christ in endless day!

609   7.7.7.7.4.

1 DAY is dying in the west,
Heaven is touching earth with rest:
Wait and worship while the night
Sets her evening lamps alight
      Through all the sky.

    Holy, Holy, Holy, Lord God of
      hosts!
    Heaven and earth are full of Thee;
    Heaven and earth are praising
      Thee,
      O Lord most high.

2 Lord of life, beneath the dome
Of the universe, Thy home,
Gather us, who seek Thy face,
To the fold of Thy embrace,
      For Thou art nigh.

3 While the deepening shadows fall,
Heart of love enfolding all,
Through the glory and the grace
Of the stars that veil Thy face,
      Our hearts ascend.

4 When for ever from our sight
Pass the stars, the day, the night,
Lord of angels, on our eyes
Let eternal morning rise,
      And shadows end.

610   8.8.7.8.8.7.

1 FATHER, in high heaven dwelling,
May our evening song be telling
  Of Thy mercy large and free:
Through the day Thy love hath fed us,
Through the day Thy care hath led us,
  With divinest charity.

2 This day's sins, oh, pardon, Saviour,
Evil thoughts, perverse behaviour,
  Envy, pride, and vanity:
From the world, the flesh, deliver,
Save us now, and save us ever,
  O Thou Lamb of Calvary!

3 From enticements of the devil,
From the might of spirits evil,
  Be our shield and panoply:
Let Thy power this night defend us,
And a heavenly peace attend us,
  And angelic company.

4 Whilst the night-dews are distilling,
Holy Ghost, each heart be filling
  With Thine own serenity:
Softly let the eyes be closing,
Loving souls on Thee reposing,
  Ever-blessèd Trinity!

Overseas Missions

611   P.M.

1 GOD is working His purpose out, as
    year succeeds to year;
God is working His purpose out, and
    the time is drawing near—
Nearer and nearer draws the time, the
    time that shall surely be,
When the earth shall be filled with the
    glory of God, as the waters cover
    the sea.

2 From utmost East to utmost West,
    where'er man's foot has trod,
By the mouth of many messengers goes
    forth the voice of God;
Give ear to Me, ye continents—ye isles,
    give ear to Me,
That the earth may be filled with the
    glory of God, as the waters cover
    the sea.

3 What can we do to work God's work,
    to prosper and increase
  The brotherhood of all mankind—the
    reign of the Prince of Peace?
  What can we do to hasten the time—
    the time that shall surely be,
  When the earth shall be filled with the
    glory of God, as the waters cover
    the sea?

4 March we forth in the strength of God
    with the banner of Christ un-
    furled,
  That the light of the glorious Gospel
    of truth may shine throughout the
    world:
  Fight we the fight with sorrow and sin,
    to set their captives free,
  That the earth may be filled with the
    glory of God, as the waters cover
    the sea.

5 All we can do is nothing worth, unless
    God blesses the deed;
  Vainly we hope for the harvest, till God
    gives life to the seed;
  Yet nearer and nearer draws the time—
    the time that shall surely be—
  When the earth shall be filled with the
    glory of God, as the waters cover
    the sea.

612　　　　　　　　　8.7.8.7.D.

1 "For My sake and the Gospel's, go
    And tell redemption's story";
  His heralds answer, "Be it so,
    And Thine, Lord, all the glory!"
  They preach His birth, His life, His
    cross,
    The love of His atonement,
  For whom they count the world but
    loss,
    His Easter, His enthronement.

2 Hark, hark, the trump of jubilee
    Proclaims to every nation,
  From pole to pole, by land and sea,
    Glad tidings of salvation.
  As nearer draws the day of doom,
    While still the battle rages,
  The heavenly Day-spring, through the
    gloom,
    Breaks on the night of ages.

3 Still on and on the anthems spread
    Of hallelujah voices,
  In concert with the holy dead,
    The warrior-Church rejoices:
  Their snow-white robes are washed in
    blood,
    Their golden harps are ringing;
  Earth and the Paradise of God
    One triumph-song are singing.

4 He comes, whose Advent trumpet
    drowns
    The last of time's evangels—
  Emmanuel crowned with many crowns
    The Lord of saints and angels:
  O Life, Light, Love, the great I AM,
    Triune, who changest never;
  The throne of God and of the Lamb
    Is Thine, and Thine for ever!

613　　　　　　　　　7.5.7.5.7.7.

1 Let the song go round the earth,
    Jesus Christ is Lord!
  Sound His praises, tell His worth,
    Be His Name adored;
  Every clime and every tongue
  Join the grand, the glorious song!

2 Let the song go round the earth!
    From the eastern sea,
  Where the daylight has its birth,
    Glad, and bright, and free:
  China's millions join the strains,
  Waft them on to India's plains.

3 Let the song go round the earth!
    Lands where Islam's sway
  Darkly broods o'er home and hearth
    Cast their bonds away!
  Let His praise from Afric's shore
  Rise and swell her wide lands o'er!

4 Let the song go round the earth!
    Where the summer smiles;
  Let the notes of holy mirth
    Break from distant isles!
  Inland forests dark and dim,
  Snow-bound coasts give back the
    hymn.

5 Let the song go round the earth!
　Jesus Christ is King!
With the story of His worth
　Let the whole world ring!
Him creation all adore
Evermore and evermore!

614   8.7.8.7.D.

1 JESUS is calling the children
　　Into His loving embrace,
Calling by words sweet and gentle,
　　And by the love in His face:
From every land 'neath the sunrise,
　Homes full of sadness or joy,
Jesus is calling the children,
　Calling to each girl and boy.

2 See how in Africa's sunshine
　　Quickly "Black Brother" has heard,
And how the children of China
　　Eagerly wait for His Word;
Trustfully venture the children
　　From the far isles of the sea,
While the brown maiden of India
　　Lovingly rests on His knee.

3 No one can count all the children,
　　Yet Jesus' love is the same,
Seeking to bless those who love Him,
　　And those who know not His Name:
Joyful the day, and so happy
　　When the wide circle complete,
From all the world little children
　　Nestle in love at His feet.

615   C.M.

1 OUR Saviour's voice is soft and sweet
　　When, bending from above,
He bids us gather round His feet
　　And calls us by His love.

2 But while our youthful hearts rejoice
　　That thus He bids us come,
"Jesus!" we cry with pleading voice,
　　"Bring heathen wanderers home."

3 They never heard the Saviour's name,
　　They have not learned His way:
They do not know His grace, who came
　　To take their sins away.

4 Dear Saviour, let the joyful sound
　　In distant lands be heard;
And, oh, wherever sin is found,
　　Send forth Thy pardoning word!

5 And if our lips may breathe a prayer,
　　Though raised in trembling fear,
Oh, let Thy grace our hearts prepare
　　And choose some heralds here!

616   P.M.

1 COMING, coming, yes, they are,
Coming, coming, from afar;
From the wild and scorching desert,
　Afric's sons of colour deep;
Jesus' love has drawn and won them,
　At His cross they bow and weep.

2 Coming, coming, yes, they are,
Coming, coming, from afar;
From the fields and crowded cities,
　China gathers to His feet;
In His love Shem's gentle children
　Now have found a safe retreat.

3 Coming, coming, yes, they are,
Coming, coming, from afar;
From the Indies and the Ganges,
　Steady flows the living stream,
To love's ocean, to His bosom,
　Calvary their wondering theme.

4 Coming, coming, yes, they are,
Coming, coming, from afar;
From the steppes of Russia dreary,
　From Slavonia's scattered lands,
They are yielding soul and spirit
　Into Jesus' loving hands.

5 Coming, coming, yes, they are,
Coming, coming, from afar;
From the frozen realms of midnight
　Over many a weary mile,
To exchange their soul's long winter
　For the summer of His smile.

6 Coming, coming, yes, they are,
Coming, coming, from afar;
All to meet in plains of glory,
　All to sing His praises sweet;
What a chorus, what a meeting,
　With the family complete!

617   8.7.8.7.D.

1 HARK! the voice of Jesus crying:
  "Who will go and work today?
Fields are white and harvest waiting;
  Who will bear the sheaves away?"
Loud and strong the Master calleth,
  Rich reward He offers thee;
Who will answer, gladly saying,
  "Here am I: send me, send me"?

2 If you cannot speak like angels,
    If you cannot preach like Paul,
You can tell the love of Jesus,
    You can say He died for all.
If you cannot rouse the wicked
    With the Judgment's dread alarms,
You can lead the little children
    To the Saviour's waiting arms.

3 If, among the older people,
    You may not be apt to teach,
"Feed My lambs," said Christ our
    Shepherd,
"Place the food within their reach."
And it may be that the children
    You have led with trembling hand
Will be found among your jewels
    When you reach the better land.

4 Let none hear you idly saying,
    "There is nothing I can do,"
While the souls of men are dying,
    And the Master calls for you.
Take the task He gives you gladly,
    Let His work your pleasure be;
Answer quickly when He calleth,
    "Here am I: send me, send me!"

618   6.6.4.6.6.6.4.

1 THOU whose almighty Word
Chaos and darkness heard,
    And took their flight,
Hear us, we humbly pray,
And where the Gospel day
Sheds not its glorious ray,
    Let there be light!

2 Thou who didst come to bring
On Thy redeeming wing
    Healing and sight,
Health to the sick in mind,
Sight to the inly blind,
Oh, now to all mankind,
    Let there be light!

3 Spirit of truth and love,
Life-giving, holy Dove,
    Speed forth Thy flight;
Move on the waters' face,
Bearing the lamp of grace,
And in earth's darkest place
    Let there be light!

4 Holy and blessed Three,
Glorious Trinity,
    Wisdom, Love, Might;
Boundless as ocean's tide,
Rolling in fullest pride,
Through the world, far and wide,
    Let there be light!

619   P.M

1 WE'VE a story to tell to the nations,
    That shall turn their hearts to the
      right:
A story of truth and sweetness,
    A story of peace and light:

        For the darkness shall turn to
          dawning,
          And the dawning to noonday
            bright,
        And Christ's great kingdom shall
          come on earth,
          The kingdom of Love and Light.

2 We've a song to be sung to the nations
    That shall lift their hearts to the
      Lord:
A song that shall conquer evil,
    And shatter the spear and sword:

3 We've a message to give to the nations
    That the Lord who reigneth above
Hath sent us His Son to save us,
    And show us that God is love:

4 We've a Saviour to show to the nations
    Who the path of sorrow has trod,
That all of the world's great peoples
    Might come to the truth of God:

620   P.M.

1 WE have heard the joyful sound:
    Jesus saves! Jesus saves!
Tell the message all around:
    Jesus saves! Jesus saves!

Bear the news to every land,
  Climb the steeps and cross the
    waves;
Onward!—'tis our Lord's command:
  Jesus saves! Jesus saves!

2 Waft it on the rolling tide:
  Jesus saves! Jesus saves!
Say to sinners far and wide,
  Jesus saves! Jesus saves!
Sing, ye islands of the sea;
  Echo back, ye ocean caves;
Earth shall keep her jubilee:
  Jesus saves! Jesus saves!

3 Sing above the toil and strife,
  Jesus saves! Jesus saves!
By His death and endless life
  Jesus saves! Jesus saves!
Sing it softly through the gloom,
  When the heart for mercy craves;
Sing in triumph o'er the tomb,
  Jesus saves! Jesus saves!

4 Give the winds a mighty voice:
  Jesus saves! Jesus saves!
Let the nations now rejoice:
  Jesus saves! Jesus saves!
Shout salvation full and free
  To every strand that ocean laves;
This our song of victory,
  Jesus saves! Jesus saves!

621   7.6.7.6.D.

1 THE whole wide world for Jesus—
  This shall our watchword be,
Upon the highest mountain,
  Down by the widest sea—
The whole wide world for Jesus!
  To Him all men shall bow,
In city or in prairie—
  The world for Jesus now!

    The whole wide world, the whole
      wide world—
    Proclaim the Gospel tidings
      through the whole wide world;
    Lift up the cross for Jesus, His
      banner be unfurled—
    Till every tongue confess Him
      through the whole wide world!

2 The whole wide world for Jesus,
  Inspires us with the thought
That every son of Adam
  Has by His blood been bought;
The whole wide world for Jesus!
  Oh, faint not by the way!
The cross shall surely conquer
  In this our glorious day.

3 The whole wide world for Jesus—
  The marching order sound—
Go ye, and preach the Gospel
  Wherever man is found;
The whole wide world for Jesus!
  Our banner is unfurled—
We battle now for Jesus,
  And faith demands the world!

4 The whole wide world for Jesus:
  In the Father's house above
Are many wondrous mansions—
  Mansions of light and love;
The whole wide world for Jesus!
  Ride forth, O conquering King,
Through all the mighty nations
  The world to glory bring!

622   7.6.7.6.D.

1 FROM Greenland's icy mountains,
  From India's coral strand;
Where Afric's sunny fountains
  Roll down their golden sand;
From many an ancient river,
  From many a palmy plain,
They call us to deliver
  Their land from error's chain.

2 What though the spicy breezes
  Blow soft o'er Ceylon's isle;
Though every prospect pleases,
  And only man is vile!
In vain with lavish kindness
  The gifts of God are strown;
The heathen in his blindness
  Bows down to wood and stone.

3 Can we, whose souls are lighted
  With wisdom from on high—
Can we, to men benighted
  The lamp of life deny?
Salvation! oh, salvation!
  The joyful sound proclaim,
Till each remotest nation
  Has learned Messiah's Name.

4 Waft, waft, ye winds, His story;
  And you, ye waters, roll,
Till like a sea of glory
  It spreads from pole to pole;
Till o'er our ransomed nature
  The Lamb for sinners slain,
Redeemer, King, Creator,
  In bliss returns to reign.

623   11.10.11.10.

1 FAR, far away in heathen darkness
    dwelling,
  Millions of souls for ever may be
    lost;
Who, who will go—Salvation's story
    telling—
  Looking to Jesus, counting not the
    cost?

      "All power is given unto Me!
  All power is given unto Me! Go
  ye into all the world and preach
  the Gospel; and lo! I am with you
  alway."

2 See, o'er the world, wide open doors
    inviting;
  Soldiers of Christ, arise and enter in!
Christians, awake! your forces all
    uniting,
  Send forth the Gospel, break the
    chains of sin!

3 "Why will ye die?" the voice of God is
    calling;
  "Why will ye die?" re-echo in His
    Name;
Jesus hath died to save from death
    appalling;
  Life and salvation therefore go pro-
    claim.

4 God speed the day when those of every
    nation,
  "Glory to God" triumphantly shall
    sing;
Ransomed, redeemed, rejoicing in
    salvation,
  Shout, "Hallelujah, for the Lord is
    King!"

624   9.8.9.8.D.

1 I HEAR ten thousand voices singing
    Their praises to the Lord on high;
Far distant shores and hills are ringing
    With anthems of their nations' joy:
"Praise ye the Lord! for He has given,
    To lands in darkness hid, His light;
As morning rays light up the heaven,
    His Word has chased away our
      night."

2 On China's shores I hear His praises,
    From lips that once kissed idol
      stones;
Soon as His banner He upraises,
    The Spirit moves the breathless
      bones—
"Speed, speed Thy Word o'er land and
    ocean;
    The Lord in triumph has gone
      forth:
The nations hear with strange emotion,
    From East to West, from South to
      North."

3 The song has sounded o'er the waters
    And India's plains re-echo joy;
Beneath the moon sit India's daughters,
    Soft singing, as the wheel they ply—
"Thanks to Thee, Lord! for hopes of
    glory,
    For peace on earth to us revealed;
Our cherished idols fell before Thee,
    Thy Spirit has our pardon sealed."

625   L.M.

1 JESUS shall reign where'er the sun
  Doth his successive journeys run:
His kingdom stretch from shore to
    shore
Till moons shall wax and wane no
    more.

2 For Him shall endless prayer be made,
  And princes throng to crown His head:
His name like sweet perfume shall rise
  With every morning sacrifice.

3 People and realms of every tongue
  Dwell on His love with sweetest song,
And infant voices shall proclaim
  Their early blessings on His Name.

4 Blessings abound where'er He reigns;
  The prisoner leaps to lose his chains,
  The weary find eternal rest,
  And all the sons of want are blest.

5 Let every creature rise and bring
  Peculiar honours to our King:
  Angels, descend with songs again,
  And, earth, repeat the loud Amen.

626   8.6.8.6.8.8.

1 LORD JESUS, Thou that lovest
    Each little child like me,
  Oh, take my life and use it,
    And let me shine for Thee;

Oh, give me little tasks to do
To show how much I love Thee too.

2 I know in distant countries,
    Beyond the deep blue sea,
  Are many little children
    Thou lovest just like me;
  But they have never heard Thy Name,
  And do not know that Jesus came.

3 Lord, let me send Thy message
    Across the deep blue sea,
  To tell those little children
    What Thou hast done for me;
  Oh, show me, Lord, what I can do,
  That they may know and love Thee
    too.

Hymns for Younger Children

627   7.6.7.6.D.

1 I LOVE to hear the story,
    Which angel voices tell,
  How once the King of glory
    Came down on earth to dwell.
  I am both weak and sinful,
    But this I surely know—
  The Lord came down to save me,
    Because He loved me so.

    I love to hear the story,
      Which angel voices tell,
    How once the King of glory
      Came down on earth to dwell.

2 I'm glad my blessed Saviour
    Was once a child like me,
  To show how pure and holy
    His little ones might be:
  And if I try to follow
    His footsteps here below,
  He never will forget me,
    Because He loves me so.

3 To sing His love and mercy
    My sweetest songs I'll raise;
  And though I cannot see Him,
    I know He hears my praise:
  For He has kindly promised
    That even I may go
  To sing among His angels,
    Because He loves me so.

628   12.11.12.11.

1 HE smiled as He stretched out His
      arms in glad welcome,
    While little ones hastened to press
      round His knee,
  While He laid His kind hand on each
      little fair forehead,
    Saying, "Suffer the children to come
      unto Me."

2 "Send not from My presence the child-
      ren: I love them,
    And they shall be merry and joyous
      and free;
  But bring them where blessings of
      heaven are dropping,
    Oh, suffer the children to come unto
      Me."

3 We come, then, dear Saviour, by words
      and by prayers,
    Oh, Thine, Thine alone may the little
      ones be;
  Still stretch out Thy kind arms, still
      give us a welcome,
    Say, "Suffer the children to come
      unto Me."

4 And when our young feet touch the
      waters of Jordan,
    Oh, then may Thy children be dear
      unto Thee;

Take our hands, lift us up to the
   palaces golden,
Say, "Suffer the children to come
   unto Me!"

629   7.6.7.6.D.

1 THE wise may bring their learning,
   The rich may bring their wealth;
And some may bring their greatness,
   And some bring strength and
     health;
We too would bring our treasures
   To offer to the King:
We have no wealth or learning—
   What shall we children bring?

2 We'll bring Him hearts that love Him,
   We'll bring Him thankful praise,
And young souls meekly striving
   To walk in holy ways:
And these shall be the treasures
   We offer to the King,
And these are gifts that even
   The poorest child may bring.

3 We'll bring the little duties
   We have to do each day,
We'll try our best to please Him
   At home, at school, at play:
And better are these treasures
   To offer to our King
Than richest gifts without them;
   Yet these a child may bring.

630   L.M.

1 JESUS, who lived above the sky,
Came down to be a Man and die;
And in the Bible we may see
How very good He used to be.

2 He went about—He was so kind—
To cure poor people who were blind;
And many who were sick and lame,
He pitied them, and did the same.

3 And more than that, He told them too
The things that God would have them
   do;
And was so gentle and so mild,
He would have listened to a child.

4 But such a cruel death He died:
He was hung up and crucified!
And those kind hands that did such
   good
They nailed them to a cross of wood!

5 And so He died: and this is why
He came to be a Man and die:
The Bible says He came from heaven
That we might have our sins forgiven.

6 He knew how wicked man had been,
And knew that God must punish sin;
So, out of pity, Jesus said
He'd bear the punishment instead.

631   8.7.8.7.

1 LITTLE children, follow Jesus,
   None so good and kind as He;
Hear His voice, for children pleading,
   "Suffer them to come to Me."

2 Like a shepherd He will tend you
   As you walk life's narrow way,
Homeward bear upon His bosom
   Those who from His sweet fold stray.

3 Yes, He knows the little children
   Are as lambs so weak and small;
And not one must be forsaken,
   Since He died to save them all.

4 Little children, follow Jesus
   Through the world so big and wide;
Let Him be your tender Shepherd,
   Follow closely at His side.

632   11.11.11.11.

1 AWAY in a manger, no crib for a bed,
The little Lord Jesus laid down His
   sweet head,
The stars in the bright sky looked down
   where He lay—
The little Lord Jesus asleep on the
   hay.

2 The cattle are lowing, the Baby awakes,
But little Lord Jesus, no crying He
   makes.
I love Thee, Lord Jesus! look down
   from the sky,
And stay by my side until morning is
   nigh.

3 Be near me, Lord Jesus; I ask Thee to
    stay
Close by me for ever, and love me, I
    pray.
Bless all the dear children in Thy
    tender care,
And fit us for heaven to live with Thee
    there.

633   7.7.7.7.

1 LAMB of God, I look to Thee,
Thou shalt my example be;
Thou art gentle, meek, and mild;
Thou wast once a little child.

2 Fain I would be as Thou art;
Give me Thy obedient heart:
Thou art pitiful and kind;
Let me have Thy loving mind.

3 Let me above all fulfil
God my heavenly Father's will;
Never His good Spirit grieve,
Only to His glory live.

4 Loving Jesus, holy Lamb,
In Thy gracious hands I am:
Make me, Saviour, what Thou art,
Live Thyself within my heart.

634   7.7.7.7.

1 GOD our Father, now we lift
    Joyful hearts in glowing praise
For Thy great and lovely gift,
    Childhood's sweet and happy days.

2 From Thy kind and loving hand
    Come the gifts of life so free,
All the beauties of the land,
    All the wonders of the sea.

3 But a fairer gift than all
    Is our gracious Saviour-Friend,
Who from heaven to manger-stall
    Did in wondrous love descend.

4 Oh, how filled with deeds of love
    Was the life of Him who died!
Dwelling now in heights above,
    Still He calls us to His side.

5 Dear Lord Jesus, brighter still
    Youth's fresh hours if Thou art near,
With Thy grace our hearts now fill,
    Driving out all doubt and fear.

6 Keep us Thine, along the years
    As life's milestones each are passed;
Through the laughter and the tears
    Lead us to Thy home at last.

635   P.M.

1 I THINK when I read that sweet story of
    old,
    When Jesus was here among men,
How He called little children, as lambs
    to His fold,
    I should like to have been with them
    then.
I wish that His hands had been placed
    on my head,
    That His arm had been thrown
    around me,
And that I might have seen His kind
    look when He said,
    "Let the little ones come unto Me."

2 Yet still to His footstool in prayer I
    may go,
    And ask for a share in His love;
And if I now earnestly seek Him
    below,
    I shall see Him and hear Him above,
In that beautiful place He has gone to
    prepare
    For all who are washed and for-
    given;
And many dear children are gathering
    there,
    "For of such is the kingdom of
    heaven."

3 But thousands and thousands, who
    wander and fall,
    Never heard of that heavenly home;
I should like them to know there is
    room for them all,
    And that Jesus has bid them to
    come.
I long for the joy of that glorious time,
    The sweetest, and brightest, and
    best;
When the dear little children of every
    clime
    Shall crowd to His arms and be blest.

636   P.M.

1 HERE'S a message of love, come down
    from above,
  To invite little children to heaven;
In God's blessed Book poor sinners
    may look,
  And see how all sin is forgiven.
For there they may read how Jesus did
    bleed,
  His life everlasting to give;
He cleanseth the soul, He maketh us
    whole,
  That with Him in heaven we may
    live.

2 And then, when they die, He takes
    them on high,
  To be with Him in heaven above;
For so kind is His heart, that He never
    will part
  From a child that has tasted His
    love.
And oh, what delight in heaven so
    bright,
  When they see the dear Saviour's
    face,
On His beauty to gaze, and sing to His
    praise,
  And rejoice in His own boundless
    grace!

637   P.M.

1 WE are marching on, with shield and
    banner bright;
We will work for God, and battle for the
    right;
We will praise His Name, rejoicing in
    His might,
  And we'll work till Jesus calls.
From the youthful ranks our army we
    prepare,
As we rally round our blessèd standard
    here;
And the Saviour's cross we early learn
    to bear,
  While we work till Jesus calls.

    Then awake, . . . then awake, . . .
      Happy song, . . . happy song, . . .
    Shout for joy, . . . shout for joy, . . .
      As we gladly march along.
    We are marching onward, singing
      as we go,

To the promised land where living
    waters flow;
Come and join our ranks as pil-
    grims here below,
  Come and work till Jesus calls.

2 We are marching on: our Captain, ever
    near,
Will protect us still, His gentle voice
    we hear:
Let the foe advance, we'll never, never
    fear,
  For we'll work till Jesus calls.
Then awake, awake, our happy, happy
    song;
We will shout for joy, and gladly
    march along;
In the Lord of hosts let every heart be
    strong,
  While we work till Jesus calls.

3 We are marching on the strait and
    narrow way
That will lead to life and everlasting
    day,
To the smiling fields that never will
    decay:
  But we'll work till Jesus calls.
We are marching on, and pressing
    towards the prize,
To a glorious crown beyond the glowing
    skies,
To the radiant fields where pleasure
    never dies,
  And we'll work till Jesus calls.

638   8.7.8.7.

1 JESUS loves the little children,
  Once He took them on His knee,
Gently put His arms around them,
  Saying, "Let them come to Me!"

2 Oh! He loves to see them kneeling,
  And, with hands together, pray;
Loves to hear them call Him Jesus,
  If they mean the words they say.

3 Once He gave His life to buy them
  Back from Satan's evil ways,
And at last to heaven take them,
  There to sing His worth and praise.

4 If they trust Him as their Saviour,
   He will wash their sins away;
He will take their hand and lead them
   All along the narrow way.

5 He would have them love each other,
   And be truthful, meek, and mild,
Doing as their parents bid them,
   As He did when once a Child.

6 Then when He shall come to call them,
   They shall see Him face to face,
And with saints and angels praise Him
   For His matchless love and grace.

639   C.M.

1 GOD is in heaven: Can He hear
   A little prayer like mine?
Yes, that He can; I need not fear;
   He'll listen unto mine.

2 God is in heaven: Can He see
   When I am doing wrong?
Yes, that He can; He looks at me
   All day and all night long.

3 God is in heaven: Would He know
   If I should tell a lie?
Yes; though I said it very low,
   He'd hear it in the sky.

4 God is in heaven: Does He care,
   And is He good to me?
Yes: all I have to eat or wear,
   'Tis God that gives it me.

5 God is in heaven: May I pray
   To go there when I die?
Yes; seek Him, trust Him, and one day
   He'll call me to the sky.

640   8.6.7.6.7.6.7.6.

1 THERE'S a Friend for little children
   Above the bright blue sky,
A Friend who never changes,
   Whose love will never die:
Unlike our friends by nature,
   Who change with changing years,
This Friend is always worthy
   The precious Name He bears.

2 There's a home for little children
   Above the bright blue sky,
Where Jesus reigns in glory—
   A home of peace and joy:
No home on earth is like it,
   Nor can with it compare,
For everyone is happy,
   Nor could be happier, there.

3 There's a crown for little children
   Above the bright blue sky,
And all who look to Jesus
   Shall wear it by and by;
A crown of brightest glory
   Which He will then bestow
On those who found His favour
   And loved Him here below.

4 There's a song for little children
   Above the bright blue sky,
A song that will not weary,
   Though sung continually;
A song which even angels
   Can never, never sing;
They know not Christ as Saviour,
   But worship Him as King.

5 There's a robe for little children
   Above the bright blue sky;
A harp of sweetest music
   And palms of victory;
And all above is treasured,
   And found in Christ alone:
Oh, come, dear little children,
   That all may be your own.

641   8.7.8.7.

1 SAVIOUR, while my heart is tender,
   I would yield that heart to Thee,
All my powers to Thee surrender,
   Thine and only Thine to be.

2 Take me now, Lord Jesus, take me;
   Let my youthful heart be Thine:
Thy devoted servant make me,
   Fill my soul with love divine.

3 Send me, Lord, where Thou wilt send
   me,
   Only do Thou guide my way;
May Thy grace through life attend me,
   Gladly then will I obey.

4 Let me do Thy will, or bear it,
   I would know no will but Thine;
Should'st Thou take my life, or spare it,
   I that life to Thee resign.

5 Thine I am, O Lord, for ever,
   To Thy service set apart;
Suffer me to leave Thee never,
   Seal Thine image on my heart.

642   6.5.6.5.

1 LET me learn of Jesus:
   He is kind to me;
Once He died to save me,
   Nailed upon the tree.

2 If I go to Jesus,
   He will hear me pray,
Make me good and holy,
   Take my sins away.

3 Let me think of Jesus:
   He is full of love,
Looking down upon me
   From His throne above.

4 If I trust in Jesus,
   If I do His will,
Then I shall be happy,
   Safe from every ill.

5 Oh, how good is Jesus!
   May He hold my hand,
And at last receive me
   To a better land!

643   6.5.6.5.

1 IF I come to Jesus,
   He will make me glad:
He will give me pleasure
   When my heart is sad.

      If I come to Jesus,
         Happy I shall be;
      He is gently calling
         Little ones like me.

2 If I come to Jesus,
   He will hear my prayer;
For He loves me dearly,
   And my sins did bear.

3 If I come to Jesus,
   He will take my hand;
He will kindly lead me
   To a better land.

4 There, with happy children,
   Robed in snowy white,
I shall see my Saviour,
   In that world so bright.

644   6.5.6.5.

1 IN our dear Lord's garden
   Planted here below,
Many tiny flowerets
   In sweet beauty grow.

2 Christ, the loving Gardener,
   Tends these blossoms small,
Loves the little lilies
   And the cedars tall.

3 Nothing is too little
   For His gentle care,
Nothing is too lowly
   In His love to share.

4 Jesus loves the children,
   Children such as we,
Blessed them when their mothers
   Brought them to His knee.

5 Jesus calls the children,
   Bids them come and stand
In His pleasant garden,
   Watered by His hand.

6 Lord, Thy call we answer:
   Take us in Thy care,
Train us in Thy garden
   In Thy work to share.

645   P.M.

1   "LITTLE child, I call thee to Me,
      I will take thee for My own;
   Sin forsaking, Me embracing,
      Choose Me for thy King alone."

         Yes, Lord Jesus; yes, Lord Jesus;
            yes, Lord Jesus.

2   "Little child, I bid thee listen
    Every time I speak to thee;
Do My pleasure, then the treasure
  Of My love I'll give to thee.

3   "Little child, I bid thee follow
    Everywhere that I may lead;
Always cheerful, never fearful,
  Trusting Me in every need.

4   "Little child, remember always
    That the Lord hates every sin;
Then be careful and be prayerful,
  Watch and pray lest wrong begin."

646   8.3.8.3.D.

1 LISTEN to the voice of Jesus,
    Oh, so sweet!
As the little children gather
    Round His feet;
Young ones to His knees are climbing,
    There to rest,
Older ones stand round Him waiting
    To be blest.

2 When the mothers who had brought
    them
    Heard men say,
" 'Tis no place for little children;
    Go away!"
They were sorry—but their sorrow
    Soon was gone,
For He raised His hands and blessed
    them
    Every one.

3 And He said to His disciples,
    "These are Mine;
In the kingdom of My Father
    They shall shine;
Send them not away, but rather
    Bring them near;
Even little ones may love their
    Saviour dear."

4 Still He loves the little children,
    You and me;
And He wants us all to love Him
    Faithfully.
Let us, then, with hearts and voices
    Gladly say:
"I am Thine, O blessèd Jesus,
    Thine for aye!"

647   P.M.

1 THE fields are all white,
    And the reapers are few;
We children are willing,
    But what can we do
To work for our Lord in His harvest?

2 Our hands are so small,
    And our words are so weak,
We cannot teach others;
    How then shall we seek
To work for our Lord in His harvest?

3 We'll work by our prayers,
    By the gifts we can bring,
By small self-denials;
    The least little thing
May work for our Lord in His harvest.

4 Until, by and by,
    As the years pass, at length,
We too may be reapers,
    And go forth in strength
To work for our Lord in His harvest.

648   7.7.7.7.7.7.

1 LITTLE children, join to sing
Glory, glory to our King;
Christ is risen from the dead,
Crowns unfading wreathe His head.
He is Conqueror o'er the grave!
Mighty to redeem and save!

2 Now behold Him high enthroned,
Mercy beaming from His face:
By adoring angels owned,
God of holiness and grace;
Little children, join to sing
Glory, glory to our King.

3 Jesus, on us deign to shine,
Warm our hearts and tune our tongues;
May we with the blest combine,
Share their joy and swell their songs;
And with hearts and voices sing
Glory, glory to our King.

649   7.7.7.7.7.7.

1 CHILDREN, you have gone astray,
  Far from God and peace and heaven!
Would you leave that dangerous way?
  Would you have your sins forgiven?
Christ can all your sins forgive:
Look to Jesus, look and live!

2 Children, you have sinful hearts!
    Jesus Christ can make you whole;
He can inward grace impart,
    Sanctify and save your soul.
Jesus a new heart can give;
Look to Jesus, look and live!

3 Children, you may shortly die!
    Jesus died your souls to save:
If you to the Saviour fly,
    You shall live beyond the grave.
Life eternal He will give;
Look to Jesus, look and live!

650   S.M.

1 I OFTEN say my prayers,
    But do I ever pray?
And do the wishes of my heart
    Go with the words I say?

2 I may as well kneel down
    And worship gods of stone,
As offer to the living God
    A prayer of words alone.

3 For words without the heart
    The Lord will never hear;
Nor will He to those lips attend
    Whose prayers are not sincere.

4 Lord, teach me what I need,
    And teach me how to pray;
Nor let me ask Thee for Thy grace
    Not feeling what I say.

651   8.5.8.3.

1 JESUS, Friend of little children,
    Be a Friend to me;
Take my hand and ever keep me
    Close to Thee.

2 Show me what my love should cherish,
    What, too, it should shun;
Lest my feet for poison-flowers
    Swift should run.

3 Teach me how to grow in goodness,
    Daily as I grow;
Thou hast been a Child, and surely
    Thou dost know.

4 Fill me with Thy gentle meekness,
    Make my heart like Thine;
Like an altar-lamp then let me
    Burn and shine.

5 Step by step, oh, lead me onward,
    Upward into youth,
Wiser, stronger still becoming
    In Thy truth.

6 Never leave me, nor forsake me,
    Ever be my Friend;
For I need Thee from life's dawning
    To its end.

652   6.5.6.5.

1 WE are little children,
    Very young indeed,
But the Saviour's promise
    Each of us may plead.

    If we seek Him early,
      If we come today,
    We can be His little friends,
    He has said we may.

2 Little friends of Jesus—
    What a happy thought!
What a precious promise
    In the Bible taught!

3 Little friends of Jesus,
    Walking by His side,
With His arm around us,
    Every step to guide.

4 We must love Him dearly,
    With a constant love,
Then we'll go and see Him
    In our home above.

653   6.5.6.5.D.

1 JESUS is our Shepherd,
    Wiping every tear;
Folded in His bosom
    What have we to fear?
Only let us follow
    Whither He doth lead,
To the thirsty desert
    Or the dewy mead.

2 Jesus is our Shepherd—
   Well we know His voice!
How its gentle whisper
   Makes our heart rejoice!
Even when He chideth,
   Tender is His tone;
None but He shall guide us,
   We are His alone.

3 Jesus is our Shepherd:
   For the sheep He bled;
Every lamb is sprinkled
   With the blood He shed;
Then on each He setteth
   His own secret sign—
"They that have My Spirit,
   These," saith He, "are Mine."

4 Jesus is our Shepherd:
   Guarded by His arm,
Though the wolves may raven,
   None can do us harm;
When we tread death's valley,
   Dark with fearful gloom,
We will fear no evil,
   Victors o'er the tomb.

654   P.M.

1 THE world looks very beautiful,
   And full of joy to me;
The sun shines out in glory
   On everything I see;
I know I shall be happy
   While in the world I stay,
For I will follow Jesus
   All the way.

   For I will follow Jesus,
   For I will follow Jesus,
   For I will follow Jesus
   All the way.

2 I'm but a youthful pilgrim;
   My journey's just begun;
They say I'll meet with sorrow
   Before my journey's done.
The world is full of trouble,
   And trials too, they say;
But I will follow Jesus
   All the way.

3 Then, like a little pilgrim,
   Whatever I may meet,
I'll take it—joy or sorrow—
   And lay at Jesus' feet.
He'll comfort me in trouble,
   He'll wipe my tears away;
With joy I'll follow Jesus
   All the way.

4 Then trials cannot vex me,
   And pain I need not fear,
For when I'm close by Jesus,
   Grief cannot come too near.
Not even death can harm me,
   When death I meet one day;
To heaven I'll follow Jesus
   All the way.

655   P.M.

1 WHEN He cometh, when He cometh,
   To make up His jewels,
All His jewels, precious jewels,
   His loved and His own.

      Like the stars of the morning,
         His bright crown adorning,
      They shall shine in their beauty,
         Bright gems for His crown.

2 He will gather, He will gather,
   The gems for His kingdom:
All the pure ones, all the bright ones,
   His loved and His own.

3 Little children, little children
   Who love their Redeemer,
Are the jewels, precious jewels,
   His loved and His own.

656   P.M.

1 TELL me the stories of Jesus
   I love to hear;
Things I would ask Him to tell me
   If He were here;
Scenes by the wayside,
   Tales of the sea;
Stories of Jesus,
   Tell them to me.

Hymns for Younger Children

(Girls.)

2 First let me hear how the children
Stood round His knee;
And I shall fancy His blessing
Resting on me;
Words full of kindness,
Deeds full of grace,
All in the lovelight
Of Jesus' face.

(Boys.)

3 Into the city I'd follow
The children's band,
Waving a branch of the palm-tree
High in my hand;
One of His heralds,
Yes, I would sing
Loudest hosannas!
Jesus is King!

(All.)

4 Tell me, in accents of wonder,
How rolled the sea,
Tossing the boat in a tempest
On Galilee!
And how the Master,
Ready and kind,
Chided the billows
And hushed the wind.

(Girls.)

5 Tell how the sparrow that twitters
On yonder tree,
And the sweet meadow-side lily
May speak to me—
Give me their message,
For I would hear
How Jesus taught us
Our Father's care.

(All.)

6 Show me that scene in the garden,
Of bitter pain;
And of the cross where my Saviour
For me was slain—
Sad ones or bright ones,
So that they be
Stories of Jesus,
Tell them to me.

657   7.7.7.7.7.7.

1 SAVIOUR, bless a little child,
Teach my heart the way to Thee;
Make it gentle, good, and mild;
Loving Saviour, care for me.

Jesus, hear Thy child today;
Hear, oh, hear me when I pray!

2 I am young, but Thou hast said
All who will may come to Thee;
Feed my soul with living bread;
Loving Saviour, care for me.

3 Jesus, help me, I am weak;
Let me put my trust in Thee;
Teach me how and what to speak;
Loving Saviour, care for me.

4 I would never go astray,
Never turn aside from Thee;
Keep me in the heavenly way;
Loving Saviour, care for me.

658   8.6.8.6.8.6.

1 I CANNOT do great things for Him
Who did so much for me;
But I would like to show my love,
Lord Jesus, unto Thee:
Faithful in very little things,
O Saviour, may I be.

2 There are small things in daily life
In which I may obey,
And thus may show my love to Thee;
And always—every day—
There are some little loving words
Which I for Thee may say.

3 There are small crosses I may take,
Small burdens I may bear,
Small acts of faith and deeds of love,
Small sorrows I may share;
And little bits of work for Thee
I may do everywhere.

4 I ask Thee, Lord, to give me grace
My little place to fill,
That I may ever walk with Thee
And ever do Thy will;
And in each duty, great or small,
I may be faithful still.

659
7.7.7.7.

1 FATHER, lead me day by day,
Ever in Thine own sweet way,
Teach me to be pure and true,
Show me what I ought to do.

2 When in danger, make me brave;
Make me know that Thou canst save:
Keep me safe by Thy dear side;
Let me in Thy love abide.

3 When I'm tempted to do wrong,
Make me steadfast, wise and strong;
And when all alone I stand,
Shield me with Thy mighty hand.

4 When my heart is full of glee,
Help me to remember Thee—
Happy most of all to know
That my Father loves me so.

5 When my work seems hard and dry,
May I press on cheerily;
Help me patiently to bear
Pain and hardship, toil and care.

6 May I do the good I know,
Be Thy loving child below,
Then at last go home to Thee,
Evermore Thy child to be.

660
7.7.7.7.

1 BLESSÈD Jesus, meek and mild,
Stoop to hear a little child;
At Thy feet I come to pray;
Saviour, turn me not away.

2 Take away my load of sin,
Make me clean and pure within;
Teach me all I need to know;
Be my Shepherd here below.

3 In my childhood may I be
Gentle, meek, and pure, like Thee;
Help me every sin to leave,
Lest Thy loving heart I grieve.

4 Tender Jesus, Thou didst call
To Thine arms the children small;
I o! I come, and humbly pray,
Saviour, cast me not away.

661
7.7.7.7.

1 JESUS loves me! this I know,
For the Bible tells me so;
Little ones to Him belong,
They are weak, but He is strong.

Yes, Jesus loves me,
Yes, Jesus loves me,
Yes, Jesus loves me,
The Bible tells me so.

2 Jesus loves me! He who died
Heaven's gate to open wide;
He will wash away my sin,
Let His little child come in.

3 Jesus loves me! loves me still,
When I'm very weak and ill;
From His shining throne on high
Comes to watch me where I lie.

4 Jesus loves me! He will stay
Close beside me all the way;
If I love Him, when I die
He will take me home on high.

662
6.5.6.5.

1 I'M a little pilgrim,
And a stranger here;
Though this world is pleasant,
Sin is always near.

Jesus loves our pilgrim band,
He will lead us by the hand,
Lead us to the better land,
Happy home on high.

2 Mine's a better country,
Where there is no sin;
Where the tones of sorrow
Never enter in.

3 But a little pilgrim
Must have garments clean,
If he'd wear the white robes
And with Christ be seen.

4 Jesus, cleanse and save me,
Teach me to obey:
Holy Spirit, guide me
On my heavenly way.

5 I'm a little pilgrim,
And a stranger here;
But my home in heaven
Cometh ever near.

663   7.7.7.3.

1 COME, ye children, sweetly sing
  Praises to your Saviour-King;
  Hearts and voices gladly bring:
      Praise His Name!

2 Jesus is the children's Friend,
  Loving, faithful, to the end;
  Richest gifts from Him descend,
      Joy and peace.

3 Once from heaven to earth He came,
  Suffered death, contempt, and blame,
  Died upon a cross of shame,
      Crowned with thorns.

4 'Twas our sinful souls to save
  Thus His precious blood He gave.
  Ransomed now from sin's dark grave,
      We may sing.

5 Blessed Jesus, loving, kind,
  We would early seek and find;
  And our souls in covenant bind,
      Thine to be.

6 For our sins we deeply grieve,
  But Thy promise we believe—
  "Him that cometh I receive:"
      Lord, we come.

7 Help us love Thee more and more,
  Serve Thee truly evermore,
  Till Thy mercy we adore
      In heaven above.

664   8.7.8.7.

1 JESUS, tender Shepherd, hear me,
      Bless Thy little lamb tonight;
  Through the darkness be Thou near me,
      Keep me safe till morning light.

2 All this day Thy hand has led me,
      And I thank Thee for Thy care;
  Thou hast clothed me, warmed, and fed me,
      Listen to my evening prayer.

3 Let my sins be all forgiven,
      Bless the friends I love so well;
  Take me, when I die, to heaven,
      Happy there with Thee to dwell.

665   8.4.8.4.

1 JESUS is calling the children
      Unto His side;
  Stretching His arms to receive them,
      Op'ning them wide.

          Gently to lead them,
              Guard them and feed them,
          Jesus is calling, is calling, the
              lambs to His fold.

2 Jesus is calling the children;
      Why do they stay
  Out in the wilderness wandering,
      Going astray?

3 Jesus is calling the children:
      Echo the call;
  Tell them He waits for their coming,
      Wanting them all.

4 Jesus is calling the children,
      Calling today;
  Hasten, each one, for the blessing,
      Do not delay!

5 Jesus is calling the children:
      Here, Lord, are we;
  Safe in the Good Shepherd's keeping
      Ever to be.

666   P.M.

1   WHEN mothers of Salem
      Their children brought to Jesus,
  The stern disciples drove them back,
      And bade them depart:
  But Jesus saw them ere they fled,
  And sweetly smiled and kindly said,
  "Suffer little children to come unto Me.

2   "For I will receive them,
      And fold them in My bosom;
  I'll be a Shepherd to those lambs,
      Oh, drive them not away!
  For if their hearts to Me they give,
  They shall with Me in glory live:
  Suffer little children to come unto Me."

3   How kind was our Saviour
      To bid those children welcome!
  But there are many thousands who
      Have never heard His Name;
  The Bible they have never read,
  They know not that the Saviour said,
  "Suffer little children to come unto
      Me."

4   Oh, soon may the heathen
    Of every tribe and nation
Fulfil Thy blessed word, and cast
    Their idols all away;
  Oh, shine upon them from above,
  And show Thyself a God of love;
Teach the little children to come unto
    Thee.

667   8.7.8.7.

1 Do you know what makes us happy,
    When so many hearts are sad?
We are little friends of Jesus,
    That is why we are so glad.

      We are little friends, we are loving
        friends,
        We are happy, happy little
        friends of Jesus;
      We are little friends, we are loving
        friends;
        We are happy all day long.

2 Jesus loves the children dearly,
    In His Word He tells them so;
Once He took them up and blessed
    them,
    Many, many years ago.

3 We are little lambs of Jesus;
    He, our Shepherd kind and dear,
Speaks, and though we do not see Him,
    In our hearts His voice we hear.

668   6.5.6.5.D.

1 I BELONG to Jesus—
    'Twas a happy day
When His blood most precious
    Washed my sins away;
When His Holy Spirit
    Changed my heart of stone,
Set His mark upon me,
    Sealed me for His own.

2 I belong to Jesus—
    So I'll try to spend
All my life in pleasing
    My almighty·Friend.
Since He is so holy,
    I must watch and pray
That I may grow like Him
    More and more each day.

3 I belong to Jesus—
    Therefore I can sing,
For I'm safe and happy
    Underneath His wing;
But so many round me
    Are all dark and cold:
I must try to bring them
    Into Jesus' fold.

4 I belong to Jesus—
    Soon He will be here;
If I love and trust Him,
    What have I to fear?
Round about Him gathered
    Will His people be;
And I'm sure that Jesus
    Will remember me.

669   C.M.

1 I LOVE to think, though I am young,
    My Saviour was a child;
That Jesus walked this earth along
    With feet all undefiled.

2 He kept His Father's word of truth,
    As I am taught to do;
And while He walked the paths of
    youth,
    He walked in wisdom too.

3 I love to think that He who spake
    And made the blind to see,
And called the sleeping dead to wake,
    Was once a child like me:

4 That He who wore the thorny crown,
    And tasted death's despair,
Had a kind mother like my own,
    And knew her love and care.

5 I know 'twas all for love of me
    That He became a child,
And left the heavens, so fair to see,
    And trod earth's pathway wild.

6 Then, Saviour, who wast once a Child,
    A child may come to Thee;
And, oh! in all Thy mercy mild,
    Dear Saviour, come to me.

670
C.M.

1 GOD make my life a little light
  Within the world to glow;
A little flame that burneth bright,
  Wherever I may go.

2 God make my life a little flower
  That giveth joy to all,
Content to bloom in native bower,
  Although the place be small.

3 God make my life a little song
  That comforteth the sad;
That helpeth others to be strong,
  And makes the singer glad.

4 God make my life a little staff
  Whereon the weak may rest,
That so what health and strength I
  have
  May serve my neighbours best.

5 God make my life a little hymn
  Of tenderness and praise;
Of faith—that never waxeth dim,
  In all His wondrous ways.

671
6.5.6.5.

1 JESUS, high in glory,
  Lend a list'ning ear;
When we bow before Thee,
  Children's praises hear.

2 Though Thou art so holy,
  Heaven's almighty King,
Thou wilt stoop to listen
  While Thy praise we sing.

3 We are little children,
  Weak and apt to stray;
Saviour, guide and keep us
  In the heavenly way.

4 Save us, Lord, from sinning,
  Watch us day by day;
Help us now to love Thee,
  Take our sins away.

5 Then when Thou shalt call us
  To our heavenly home,
We will gladly answer,
  "Saviour, Lord, we come."

6 In the many mansions,
  From all sin set free,
Loud shall be our praises
  When Thy face we see.

672
6.5.6.5

1 JESUS, meek and gentle,
  Son of God most High,
Pitying, loving Saviour,
  Hear Thy children's cry!

2 Pardon our offences,
  Loose our captive chains,
Break down every idol
  Which our soul detains.

3 Give us holy freedom,
  Fill our hearts with love,
Draw us, Holy Jesus,
  To the realms above.

4 Lead us on our journey,
  Be Thyself the Way
Through this earthly darkness
  To eternal day.

5 Jesus, meek and gentle,
  Son of God most High,
Pitying, loving Saviour,
  Hear Thy children's cry!

673
8.3.8.3.

1 JESUS, the children are calling;
  Oh, draw near!
Fold the young lambs in Thy bosom,
  Shepherd dear.

2 Slow are our footsteps and failing,
  Oft we fall:
Jesus, the children are calling;
  Hear their call!

3 Cold is our love, Lord, and narrow;
  Large is Thine,
Faithful, and strong, and tender:
  So be mine!

4 Gently, Lord, lead Thou our mothers;
  Weary they:
Bless all our sisters and brothers
  Night and day.

5 Fathers themselves are God's children;
    Teach them still:
Let the good Spirit show all men
    God's wise will.

6 Now to the Father, Son, Spirit,
    Three in one,
Bountiful God of our fathers,
    Praise be done!

674   7.7.7.7.

1 GENTLE Jesus, meek and mild,
Look upon a little child;
Pity my simplicity,
Suffer me to come to Thee.

2 Fain I would to Thee be brought;
Blessèd Lord, forbid it not;
In the kingdom of Thy grace
Give a little child a place.

3 Lamb of God, I look to Thee;
Thou shalt my example be;
Thou art gentle, meek, and mild;
Thou wast once a little child.

4 Fain I would be as Thou art;
Give me Thy obedient heart;
Thou art pitiful and kind,
Let me have Thy loving mind.

5 Loving Jesus, gentle Lamb,
In Thy gracious hands I am;
Make me, Saviour, what Thou art,
Live Thyself within my heart.

675   7.6.7.6.

1 LOOKING upward every day,
    Sunshine on our faces;
Pressing onward every day
    Toward the heavenly places.

2 Growing every day in awe,
    For Thy Name is holy;
Learning every day to love
    With a love more lowly.

3 Walking every day more close
    To our Elder Brother;
Growing every day more true
    Unto one another.

4 Every day more gratefully
    Kindnesses receiving,
Every day more readily
    Injuries forgiving.

5 Leaving every day behind
    Something which might hinder;
Running swifter every day,
    Growing purer, kinder.

6 Lord, so pray we every day,
    Hear us in Thy pity,
That we enter in at last
    To the Holy City.

676   7.7.7.5.

1 GENTLE Saviour, ever nigh,
Though adored by hosts on high
Thou wilt listen to the cry
    Of a little child.

2 Cleanse my heart from every sin,
Make me pure and good within;
Ere the cares of life begin
    Save a little child.

3 Give me strength to do the right
Day by day from morn till night;
Make my life sincere and bright;
    Bless a little child.

4 When my feet are prone to stray
From the strait and narrow way,
In that dark and evil day
    Keep a little child.

5 Bless me all life's journey through;
Let Thy grace my heart renew;
Make me holy, wise, and true,
    Thine obedient child.

677
C.M.

1 THE still small voice that speaks within,
   I hear it when at play
   I speak the loud and angry word
   That drives my friend away.

         The voice within, the voice
            within,
         Oh, may I have a care;
         It speaks to warn from every
            sin,
         And God has placed it there.

2 If falsehood whispers to my heart
   To tell a coward lie,
   To hide some careless thing I've done,
   I hear the sad voice nigh.

3 If selfishness would bid me keep
   What I should gladly share,
   I hear again the inner voice,
   And then with shame forbear.

4 I thank Thee, Father, for this friend,
   Whom I would always heed;
   Oh, may I hear the slightest tone
   In every time of need!

678
7.6.8.6.

1 I WANT to be like Jesus,
   So lowly and so meek,
   For no one marked an angry word
   That ever heard Him speak:
   I want to be like Jesus,
   So frequently in prayer;
   Alone upon the mountain top
   He met His Father there.

2 I want to be like Jesus:
   I never, never find
   That He, though persecuted, was
   To anyone unkind:
   I want to be like Jesus,
   Engaged in doing good,
   So that of me it may be said,
   "She hath done what she could."

3 I want to be like Jesus,
   Who kindly said to all,
   "Let little children come to Me;"
   I would obey the call:
   But oh! I'm not like Jesus,
   As anyone may see;
   O gentle Saviour, send Thy grace,
   And make me like to Thee!

679
P.M

1 JESUS wants me for a sunbeam,
   To shine for Him each day;
   In every way try to please Him,
   At home, at school, at play.

         A sunbeam, a sunbeam,
         Jesus wants me for a sunbeam,
         A sunbeam, a sunbeam,
            I'll be a sunbeam for Him.

2 Jesus wants me to be loving,
   And kind to all I see;
   Showing how pleasant and happy
   His little one can be.

3 I will ask Jesus to help me,
   To keep my heart from sin;
   Ever reflecting His goodness,
   And always shine for Him.

4 I'll be a sunbeam for Jesus,
   I can, if I but try,
   Serving Him moment by moment,
   Then live with Him on high.

680
7.6.8.8.6.

1 OH, what can little hands do
   To please the King of heaven?
   The little hands some work may try
   To help the poor in misery:
   Such grace to mine be given.

2 Oh, what can little lips do
   To please the King of heaven?
   The little lips can praise and pray,
   And gentle words of kindness say:
   Such grace to mine be given.

3 Oh, what can little eyes do
   To please the King of heaven?
   The little eyes can upward look,
   And learn to read God's holy Book:
   Such grace to mine be given.

4 Oh, what can little hearts do
   To please the King of heaven?
   Our hearts, if God His Spirit send,
   Can love and trust their Saviour
      Friend:
   Such grace to mine be given.

5   Though small is all that we can do
To please the King of heaven;
When hearts and hands and lips unite
To serve the Saviour with delight,
They're precious in His sight.

681

6.5.6.5.

1 JESUS, tender Saviour,
    Hast Thou died for me?
Make me very thankful
    In my heart to Thee.

2 When the sad, sad story
    Of Thy grief I read,
Make me very sorry
    For my sins indeed.

3 Now I know Thou livest,
    And dost plead for me:
Make me very thankful
    In my prayers to Thee.

4 Soon I hope in glory
    At Thy side to stand;
Make me fit to meet Thee
    In that happy land.

682

L.M.

1 WE are but little children weak,
    Nor born in any high estate;
What can we do for Jesus' sake,
    Who is so high, and good, and great?

2 When deep within our swelling hearts
    The thoughts of pride and anger rise;
When bitter words are on our tongues,
    And tears of passion in our eyes:

3 Then we may stay the angry blow,
    Then we may check the hasty word;
Give gentle answers back again,
    And fight a battle for our Lord.

4 With smiles of peace, and looks of love,
    Light in our dwellings we may make;
Bid kind good humour brighten there—
    And still do all for Jesus' sake.

There's not a child so small and weak
    But has his little cross to take,
His little work of love and praise
    That he may do for Jesus' sake.

683

S.M.

1 I'M not too young to sin,
    I'm not too young to die,
I'm not too little to begin
    A life of faith and joy.

2 I'm not too young to know
    The Saviour's love to me
In coming down to earth below
    To die upon the tree.

3 I'm not too young to love,
    I'm not too young to pray,
To look to Jesus up above,
    And all His Word obey.

4 Jesus, I love Thy Name;
    From evil set me free,
And ever keep Thy little lamb
    Who puts his trust in Thee.

684

P.M.

1 JESUS bids us shine
    With a pure, clear light;
Like a little candle
    Burning in the night.
In this world of darkness,
    So we must shine—
You in your small corner,
    And I in mine.

2 Jesus bids us shine,
    First of all for Him;
Well He sees and knows it
    If our light grows dim.
He looks down from heaven
    To see us shine—
You in your small corner,
    And I in mine.

3 Jesus bids us shine,
    Then, for all around;
Many kinds of darkness
    In this world abound—
Sin and want and sorrow;
    So we must shine—
You in your small corner
    And I in mine.

685   10.10.10.10. (Dactylic.)

1 I AM so glad that our Father in heaven
  Tells of His love in the Book He has
    given;
  Wonderful things in the Bible I see;
  This is the dearest, that Jesus loves
    me.

    I am so glad that Jesus loves me,
    Jesus loves me, Jesus loves me;
    I am so glad that Jesus loves me,
    Jesus loves even me.

2 Though I forget Him, and wander
    away,
  Still He doth love me wherever I
    stray;
  Back to His dear, loving arms would I
    flee,
  When I remember that Jesus loves me.

3 Oh, if there's only one song I can sing
  When in His beauty I see the great
    King!
  This shall my song in eternity be,
  "Oh, what a wonder that Jesus loves
    me!"

4 Jesus loves me, and I know I love Him;
  Love brought Him down my poor soul
    to redeem;
  Yes, it was love made Him die on the
    tree:
  Oh, I am certain that Jesus loves me!

5 If one should ask of me, how can I
    tell?
  Glory to Jesus, I know very well!
  God's Holy Spirit with mine doth
    agree,
  Constantly witnessing—Jesus loves
    me.

6 In this assurance I find sweetest rest,
  Trusting in Jesus, I know I am blest;
  Satan, dismayed, from my soul now
    doth flee,
  When I just tell him that Jesus loves
    me.

686   P.M.

1 LEAD me to Jesus, lead me to Jesus;
    Help me to love Him, help me to
      pray;
  He is my Saviour: I would believe
    Him;
    I would be like Him—show me the
      way.

      Quickly haste and come where
        happy children meet;
      Hither come and sing the
        Saviour's praises sweet:
      Rest from thy pleasures, rest
        from thy play,
      Come to our meeting, come
        away.

2 Lead me to Jesus; He will receive me;
    He is so loving, gentle, and mild—
  Calling the children, bidding them
    welcome;
    Surely He calls me—I am a child.

3 Tell me of Jesus, tell of His mercy:
    Is there a fountain flowing so free?
  All who are willing drink of its waters—
    Say, is that fountain flowing for me?

4 Lord, I am coming: Jesus, my Saviour,
    Pity my weakness; make me Thy
      child:
  I would receive Thee, trust and believe
    Thee;
    I would be like Thee—gentle and
      mild.

687   7.7.7.7.

1 LOVING Shepherd of Thy sheep,
  Keep Thy lamb, in safety keep;
  Nothing can Thy power withstand,
  None can pluck me from Thy hand.

2 Loving Saviour, Thou didst give
  Thine own life that we might live,
  And the hands outstretched to bless
  Bear the cruel nails' impress.

3 I would praise Thee every day,
  Gladly all Thy will obey,
  Like Thy blessed ones above,
  Happy in Thy precious love.

4 Loving Shepherd, ever near,
Teach Thy lamb Thy voice to hear;
Suffer not my steps to stray
From the strait and narrow way.

5 Where Thou leadest I would go,
Walking in Thy steps below,
Till before my Father's throne
I shall know as I am known.

688   7.7.7.5.

1 JESUS, when He left the sky,
And for sinners came to die,
In His mercy passed not by
Little ones like me.

2 Mothers then the Saviour sought
In the places where He taught,
And to Him their children brought—
Little ones like me.

3 Did the Saviour say them nay?
No! He kindly bade them stay,
Suffered none to turn away
Little ones like me.

4 'Twas for them His life He gave,
To redeem them from the grave;
Jesus able is to save
Little ones like me.

5 Children, then, should love Him now,
Strive His holy will to do:
Pray to Him and praise Him too—
Little ones like me.

Special Occasions

689   8.8.8.8.8.8.

1 ETERNAL Father, strong to save,
Whose arm hath bound the restless
    wave,
Who bidd'st the mighty ocean deep
Its own appointed limits keep:
    Oh, hear us when we cry to Thee
    For those in peril on the sea!

2 O Christ, whose voice the waters heard,
And hushed their raging at Thy word,
Who walkedst on the foaming deep,
And calm amid the storm didst sleep:
    Oh, hear us when we cry to Thee
    For those in peril on the sea!

3 O Holy Spirit, who didst brood
Upon the waters dark and rude,
And bid their angry tumult cease,
And give, for wild confusion, peace:
    Oh, hear us when we cry to Thee
    For those in peril on the sea!

4 O Trinity of love and power,
Our brethren shield in danger's hour;
From rock and tempest, fire and foe,
Protect them wheresoe'er they go:
    Thus evermore shall rise to Thee
    Glad hymns of praise from land and
        sea.

690   6.5.6.5.D.

1 JESUS, blessèd Saviour,
    Help us now to raise
Songs of glad thanksgiving,
    Songs of holy praise.
Oh, how kind and gracious
    Thou hast always been!
Oh, how many blessings
    Every day has seen!
    Jesus, blessèd Saviour,
        Now our praises hear,
    For Thy grace and favour
        Crowning all the year.

2 Jesus, holy Saviour,
    Only Thou canst tell
How we often stumbled,
    How we often fell!
All our sins (so many!),
    Saviour, Thou dost know:
In Thy blood most precious
    Wash us white as snow.
    Jesus, blessèd Saviour,
        Keep us in Thy fear,
    Let Thy grace and favour
        Pardon all the year.

3 Jesus, loving Saviour,
    Only Thou dost know
All that may befall us
    As we onward go;

So we humbly pray Thee,
 Take us by the hand,
Lead us ever upward
 To the better land.
  Jesus, blessèd Saviour,
  Keep us ever near,
  Let Thy grace and favour
  Shield us all the year.

4 Jesus, precious Saviour,
 Make us all Thine own,
Make us Thine for ever,
 Make us Thine alone.
Let each day, each moment
 Of this glad new year
Be for Jesus only,
 Jesus, Saviour dear.
  Then, O blessèd Saviour,
  Never need we fear:
  For Thy grace and favour
  Crown our bright New Year.

691   6.5.6.5.D.

1 STANDING at the portal
 Of the opening year,
Words of comfort meet us,
 Hushing every fear:
Spoken through the silence
 By our Father's voice,
Tender, strong, and faithful,
 Making us rejoice.

  Onward, then, and fear not,
  Children of the day!
  For His Word shall never,
  Never pass away!

2 I, the Lord, am with thee,
 Be thou not afraid,
I will help and strengthen,
 Be thou not dismayed!
Yea, I will uphold thee
 With My own right hand;
Thou art called and chosen
 In My sight to stand.

3 For the year before us,
 Oh, what rich supplies!
For the poor and needy
 Living streams shall rise;
For the sad and sinful
 Shall His grace abound;
For the faint and feeble
 Perfect strength be found.

4 He will never fail us,
 He will not forsake;
His eternal covenant
 He will never break.
Resting on His promise,
 What have we to fear?
God is all-sufficient
 For the coming year.

692   7.5.7.5.D.

1 FATHER, let me dedicate
 All this year to Thee,
In whatever worldly state
 Thou wilt have me be:
Not from sorrow, pain, or care,
 Freedom dare I claim;
This alone shall be my prayer,
 "Glorify Thy Name."

2 Can a child presume to choose
 Where or how to live?
Can a Father's love refuse
 All the best to give?
More Thou givest every day
 Than the best can claim,
Nor withholdest aught that may
 Glorify Thy Name.

3 If in mercy Thou wilt spare
 Joys that yet are mine;
If on life, serene and fair,
 Brighter rays may shine:
Let my glad heart, while it sings,
 Thee in all proclaim,
And, whate'er the future brings,
 "Glorify Thy Name."

4 If Thou callest to the cross,
 And its shadow come,
Turning all my gain to loss,
 Shrouding heart and home;
Let me think how Thy dear Son
 To His glory came,
And in deepest woe pray on,
 "Glorify Thy Name."

693   7.7.7.7.D.

1 COME, ye thankful people, come,
Raise the song of harvest-home:
All is safely gathered in
Ere the winter storms begin;

God our Maker doth provide
For our wants to be supplied;
Come to God's own temple, come,
Raise the song of harvest-home!

2 All the world is God's own field,
Fruit unto His praise to yield;
Wheat and tares together sown,
Unto joy or sorrow grown;
First the blade, and then the ear,
Then the full corn shall appear;
Lord of harvest, grant that we
Wholesome grain and pure may be.

3 For the Lord our God shall come,
And shall take His harvest home;
From His field shall in that day
All offences purge away;
Give His angels charge at last
In the fire the tares to cast;
But the fruitful ears to store
In His garner evermore.

4 Even so, Lord, quickly come
To Thy final harvest-home,
Gather Thou Thy people in,
Free from sorrow, free from sin;
There for ever purified,
In Thy presence to abide:
Come, with all Thine angels, come;
Raise the glorious harvest-home.

694 P.M.

1 WE plough the fields, and scatter
The good seed on the land,
But it is fed and watered
By God's almighty hand;
He sends the snow in winter,
The warmth to swell the grain,
The breezes, and the sunshine,
The soft refreshing rain.

All good gifts around us
Are sent from heaven above:
Then thank the Lord, oh, thank the Lord,
For all His love.

2 He only is the Maker
Of all things near and far;
He paints the wayside flower,
He lights the evening star.

The winds and waves obey Him,
By Him the birds are fed;
Much more to us, His children,
He gives our daily bread.

3 We thank Thee, then, O Father,
For all things bright and good,
The seed-time and the harvest,
Our life, our health, our food.
Accept the gifts we offer
For all Thy love imparts,
And, what Thou most desirest,
Our humble, thankful hearts.

695 11.10.11.10.

1 HERE, Lord, we offer Thee all that is
fairest,
Bloom from the garden, and flowers
from the field;
Gifts for the stricken ones, knowing
Thou carest
More for the love than the wealth
that we yield.

2 Send, Lord, by these to the sick and the
dying;
Speak to their hearts with a message
of peace;
Comfort the sad, who in weakness are
lying;
Grant the departing a gentle release.

3 Raise, Lord, to health again those who
have sickened,
Fair be their lives as the roses in
bloom;
Give of Thy grace to the souls Thou
hast quickened,
Gladness for sorrow, and brightness
for gloom.

4 We, Lord, like flowers, must bloom and
must wither,
We, like these blossoms, must fade
and must die;
Gather us, Lord, to Thy bosom for
ever,
Grant us a place in Thy house in the
sky.

696
6.6.6.6.8.8.

1   To Thee, our God, we fly
      For mercy and for grace:
    Oh, hear our lowly cry,
      And hide not Thou Thy face.
O Lord, stretch forth Thy mighty hand,
And guard and bless our Fatherland.

2   Arise, O Lord of hosts;
      Be jealous for Thy Name;
    And drive from out our coasts
      The sins that put to shame.
O Lord, stretch forth Thy mighty hand,
And guard and bless our Fatherland.

3   The powers ordained by Thee
      With heavenly wisdom bless;
    May they Thy servants be,
      And rule in righteousness.
O Lord, stretch forth Thy mighty hand,
And guard and bless our Fatherland.

4   Give peace, Lord, in our time,
      Oh, let no foe draw nigh,
    Nor lawless deed of crime
      Insult Thy majesty.
O Lord, stretch forth Thy mighty hand,
And guard and bless our Fatherland.

697
6.6.4.6.6.6.4.

1 GOD save our gracious Queen,
Long live our noble Queen,
    God save the Queen:
Send her victorious,
Happy and glorious,
Long to reign over us;
    God save the Queen!

2 Thy choicest gifts in store
On her be pleased to pour:
    Long may she reign:
May she defend our laws,
And ever give us cause
To sing with heart and voice,
    God save the Queen!

698
6.6.4.6.6.6.4.

1 GOD bless our native land,
May heaven's protecting hand
    Still guard her shore;

May peace her sway extend,
Foe be transformed to friend,
And Britain's power depend
    On war no more.

2 Through changes time shall bring,
O Lord, preserve the Queen;
    Long may she reign.
Her heart inspire and move
With wisdom from above;
And in a nation's love
    Her throne maintain.

3 May just and righteous laws
Uphold the public cause
    And bless our isle.
Home of the brave and free,
The land of liberty,
We pray that still on thee
    Kind heaven may smile!

4 And not this land alone,
But be Thy mercies known
    From shore to shore;
Lord, make the nations see
That men should brothers be,
And form one family
    The wide world o'er.

699
P.M.

1 GOD be with you till we meet again!
By His counsels guide, uphold you;
With His sheep securely fold you;
God be with you till we meet again!

    Till we meet . . . Till we meet . . .
    Till we meet at Jesus' feet; . . .
    Till we meet . . . Till we meet . . .
    God be with you till we meet again!

2 God be with you till we meet again!
'Neath His wings securely hide you,
Daily manna still provide you;
God be with you till we meet again!

3 God be with you till we meet again!
When life's perils thick confound you,
Put His loving arms around you;
God be with you till we meet again!

4 God be with you till we meet again!
Keep love's banner floating o'er you,
Smite death's threatening wave before
    you,
God be with you till we meet again!

Vespers, Doxology and Benediction

700   S.M.

LORD, keep us safe this night,
  Secure from all our fears;
May angels guard us while we sleep,
  Till morning light appears.

701   8.7.8.7.7.7.

THROUGH the day Thy love has spared
    us,
  Now we lay us down to rest;
Through the silent watches guard us;
  Let no foe our peace molest:
    Jesus, Thou our Guardian be;
    Sweet it is to trust in Thee!

702   L.M.

PRAISE God, from whom all blessings
    flow;
Praise Him, all creatures here below;
Praise Him above, ye heavenly host;
Praise Father, Son, and Holy Ghost.

703   P.M.

THE Lord bless and keep thee,
  Make His face shine;
Unto thee gracious be,
  Both thee and thine.
Lift up His countenance,
  Send thee release
From sin besetting thee,
  And give thee peace.   Amen.

Praise and Worship

See also Hymns 1–63

704

1 IMMORTAL, invisible, God only wise,
  In light inaccessible hid from our eyes,
  Most blessèd, most glorious, the
      Ancient of Days,
  Almighty, victorious, Thy great Name
      we praise.

2 Unresting, unhasting, and silent as
      light,
  Nor wanting, nor wasting, Thou rulest
      in might;
  Thy justice like mountains high soaring
      above,
  Thy clouds which are fountains of
      goodness and love.

3 To all life Thou givest, to both great
      and small;
  In all life Thou livest, the true life of
      all;
  We blossom and flourish as leaves on
      the tree,
  And wither and perish, but naught
      changeth Thee.

4 Great Father of Glory, pure Father of
      Light,
  Thine angels adore Thee, all veiling
      their sight;
  All laud we would render, oh, help us
      to see
  'Tis only the splendour of light hideth
      Thee.

5 Immortal, invisible, God only wise,
  In light inaccessible hid from our
      eyes,
  Most blessed, most glorious, the
      Ancient of Days,
  Almighty, victorious, Thy great Name
      we praise.

705

1 AND can it be that I should gain
    An int'rest in the Saviour's blood?
  Died He for me, who caused His pain?
    For me, who Him to death pursued?
  Amazing love! how can it be
  That Thou, my God, should'st die for
      me?

2 'Tis mystery all! The immortal dies!
   Who can explore His strange design?
In vain the first-born seraph tries
   To sound the depths of love Divine!
'Tis mercy all! let earth adore,
Let angel minds inquire no more.

3 He left His Father's throne above,
   So free, so infinite His grace;
Emptied Himself of all but love,
   And bled for Adam's helpless race;
'Tis mercy all, immense and free;
For, O my God, it found out me.

4 Long my imprisoned spirit lay
   Fast bound in sin and nature's night;
Thine eye diffused a quickening ray,
   I woke, the dungeon flamed with
      light;
My chains fell off, my heart was free;
I rose, went forth, and followed Thee.

5 No condemnation now I dread;
   Jesus, and all in Him, is mine!
Alive in Him, my living Head,
   And clothed in righteousness divine,
Bold I approach the eternal throne,
And claim the crown, through Christ
   my own.

706

1 FILL Thou my life, O Lord my God,
   In every part with praise,
That my whole being may proclaim
   Thy being and Thy ways.

2 Not for the lip of praise alone,
   Nor e'en the praising heart,
I ask, but for a life made up
   Of praise in every part:

3 Praise in the common things of life,
   Its goings out and in;
Praise in each duty and each deed,
   However small and mean.

4 Fill every part of me with praise:
   Let all my being speak
Of Thee and of Thy love, O Lord,
   Poor though I be and weak.

5 So shalt Thou, Lord, from me, e'en me,
   Receive the glory due;
And so shall I begin on earth
   The song for ever new.

6 So shall each fear, each fret, each care,
   Be turned into a song;
And ev'ry winding of the way
   The echo shall prolong.

7 So shall no part of day or night
   From sacredness be free;
But all my life, in every step,
   Be fellowship with Thee.

707

1 To Thee, and to Thy Christ, O God,
   We sing, we ever sing;
For He the lonely wine-press trod,
   Our cup of joy to bring.
His glorious arm the strife maintained,
   He marched in might from far;
His robes were with the vintage
      stained,
   Red with the wine of war.

2 To Thee, and to Thy Christ, O God,
   We sing, we ever sing;
For He invaded death's abode
   And robbed him of his sting.
The house of dust enthralls no more,
   For He, the strong to save,
Himself doth guard that silent door,
   Great Keeper of the grave.

3 To Thee, and to Thy Christ, O God,
   We sing, we ever sing;
For He hath crushed beneath His rod
   The world's proud rebel king.
He plunged in His imperial strength
   To gulfs of darkness down,
He brought His trophy up at length,
   The foiled usurper's crown.

4 To Thee, and to Thy Christ, O God,
   We sing, we ever sing;
For He redeemed us with His blood
   From every evil thing.
Thy saving strength His arm upbore,
   The arm that set us free;
Glory, O God, for evermore
   Be to Thy Christ and Thee.

708

1 THOU hidden source of calm repose,
Thou all-sufficient love divine;
My help and refuge from my foes,
Secure I am, if Thou art mine:
From sin and grief, from guilt and shame,
I hide me, Jesus, in Thy Name.

2 Thy mighty Name salvation is,
And keeps my happy soul above;
Comfort it brings, and power and peace,
And joy and everlasting love:
To me, with Thy dear Name, are given
Pardon and holiness and Heaven.

3 Jesus, my All in all Thou art,
My rest in toil, mine ease in pain;
The med'cine of my broken heart;
In war, my peace; in loss, my gain;
My smile beneath the tyrant's frown;
In shame, my glory and my crown:

4 In want, my plentiful supply;
In weakness, mine almighty power;
In bonds, my perfect liberty;
My light in Satan's darkest hour;
In grief, my joy unspeakable;
My life in death; my heaven, my all.

709

1 MY song is love unknown,
My Saviour's love to me;
Love to the loveless shown,
That they might lovely be.
Oh, who am I,
That for my sake
My Lord should take
Frail flesh, and die?

2 He came from His blest throne
Salvation to bestow;
But men made strange, and none
The longed-for Christ would know:
But oh, my Friend,
My Friend indeed,
Who at my need
His life did spend.

3 Sometimes they strew His way,
And His sweet praises sing;
Resounding all the day
Hosannas to their King:
Then "Crucify!"
Is all their breath,
And for His death
They thirst and cry.

4 They rise and needs will have
My dear Lord made away;
A murderer they save,
The Prince of life they slay.
Yet cheerful He
To suff'ring goes,
That He His foes
From thence might free.

5 In life, no house, no home
My Lord on earth might have;
In death, no friendly tomb,
But what a stranger gave.
What may I say?
Heaven was His home;
But mine the tomb
Wherein He lay.

6 Here might I stay and sing,
No story so divine;
Never was love, dear King,
Never was grief like Thine.
This is my Friend,
In whose sweet praise
I all my days
Could gladly spend.

710

1 PRAISE to the Lord, the Almighty, the King of creation;
O my soul, praise Him, for He is thy health and salvation;
All ye who hear,
Brothers and sisters, draw near,
Praise Him in glad adoration.

2 Praise to the Lord, Who doth prosper thy work and defend thee;
Surely His goodness and mercy here daily attend thee:
Ponder anew
What the Almighty can do,
If with His love He befriend thee.

3 Praise to the Lord, Who, when tem-
    pests their warfare are waging,
Who, when the elements madly around
    thee are raging,
      Biddeth them cease,
      Turneth their fury to peace,
Whirlwinds and waters assuaging.

4 Praise to the Lord, Who, when dark-
    ness and sin are abounding,
Who, when the godless do triumph, all
    virtue confounding,
      Sheddeth His light,
      Chaseth the horrors of night,
Saints with His mercy surrounding.

5 Praise to the Lord! Oh, let all that is in
    me adore Him!
All that hath life and breath, come now
    with praises before Him!
      Let the Amen
      Sound from His people again:
Gladly for aye we adore Him.

711

1 OH, praise ye the Lord!
    Praise Him in the height;
Rejoice in His Word,
    Ye Angels of light;
Ye heavens, adore Him
    By Whom ye were made,
And worship before Him,
    In brightness arrayed.

2 Oh, praise ye the Lord!
    Praise Him upon earth,
In tuneful accord,
    Ye sons of new birth;
Praise Him Who hath brought you
    His grace from above,
Praise Him Who hath taught you
    To sing of His love.

3 Oh, praise ye the Lord,
    All things that give sound,
Each jubilant chord,
    Re-echo around;
Loud organs, His glory
    Forth tell in deep tone,
And sweet harp the story
    Of what He hath done.

4 Oh, praise ye the Lord!
    Thanksgiving and song
To Him be outpoured
    All ages along:
For love in creation,
    For Heaven restored,
For grace of salvation,
    Oh, praise ye the Lord!

712

1 THOU art the Everlasting Word,
    The Father's only Son;
God manifestly seen and heard,
    And Heaven's belovèd One;
Worthy, O Lamb of God, art Thou
That every knee to Thee should
    bow.

2 In Thee most perfectly expressed
    The Father's glories shine;
Of the full Deity possessed,
    Eternally Divine:
Worthy, O Lamb of God, art Thou
That every knee to Thee should
    bow.

3 True image of the Infinite,
    Whose essence is concealed;
Brightness of uncreated light;
    The heart of God revealed:
Worthy, O Lamb of God, art Thou
That every knee to Thee should
    bow.

4 But the high mysteries of Thy Name
    An angel's grasp transcend;
The Father only—glorious claim!—
    The Son can comprehend:
Worthy, O Lamb of God, art Thou
That every knee to Thee should
    bow.

5 Throughout the universe of bliss,
    The centre Thou, and sun;
The eternal theme of praise is this,
    To Heaven's belovèd One:
Worthy, O Lamb of God, art Thou
That every knee to Thee should
    bow.

713

1 STAND up, and bless the Lord,
   Ye people of His choice;
   Stand up, and bless the Lord your God
   With heart, and soul, and voice.

2 Though high above all praise,
   Above all blessing high,
   Who would not fear His holy Name,
   And laud and magnify?

3 Oh, for the living flame
   From His own altar brought,
   To touch our lips, our minds inspire,
   And wing to Heav'n our thought.

4 God is our strength and song,
   And His salvation ours;
   Then be His love in Christ proclaimed
   With all our ransomed powers.

5 Stand up, and bless the Lord,
   The Lord your God adore;
   Stand up, and bless His glorious Name
   Henceforth for evermore.

714

1 GREAT God of wonders! all Thy ways
   Display the attributes divine;
   But countless acts of pardoning grace
   Beyond Thine other wonders shine:
   Who is a pardoning God like Thee?
   Or who has grace so rich and free?

2 In wonder lost, with trembling joy
   We take the pardon of our God;
   Pardon for crimes of deepest dye,
   A pardon bought with Jesus' blood:

3 Pardon—from an offended God!
   Pardon—for sins of deepest dye!
   Pardon—bestowed through Jesus'
       blood!
   Pardon—that brings the rebel nigh!

4 Oh, may this strange, this matchless
       grace,
   This God-like miracle of love,
   Fill the wide earth with grateful praise,
   As now it fills the choirs above!

This hymn may be sung to tune 'Credo' (124).

715

1 O GOD of Bethel, by Whose hand
   Thy people still are fed,
   Who through this weary pilgrimage
   Hast all our fathers led;

2 Our vows, our prayers, we now present
   Before Thy throne of grace;
   God of our fathers, be the God
   Of their succeeding race.

3 Through each perplexing path of life
   Our wandering footsteps guide;
   Give us each day our daily bread,
   And raiment fit provide.

4 Oh, spread Thy covering wings around,
   Till all our wanderings cease,
   And at our Father's loved abode
   Our souls arrive in peace.

This hymn may be sung to tune 'Martyrdom' (404).

716

1 WHAT was it, O our God,
   Led Thee to give Thy Son,
   To yield Thy Well-beloved
   For us by sin undone?
   'Twas love unbounded led Thee thus
   To give Thy Well-beloved for us.

2 What led the Son of God
   To leave His throne on high,
   To shed His precious blood,
   To suffer and to die?
   'Twas love, unbounded love to us,
   Led Him to die and suffer thus.

3 What moved Thee to impart
   Thy Spirit from above,
   That He might fill our heart
   With heavenly peace and love?
   'Twas love, unbounded love to us,
   Moved Thee to give Thy Spirit thus.

4 What love to Thee we owe,
   Our God, for all Thy grace!
   Our hearts may well o'erflow
   In everlasting praise;
   Help us, O Lord, to praise Thee thus
   For all thy boundless love to us.

This hymn may be sung to tunes 'St. John' (696) or 'Samuel' (400).

717

1 JESUS, the Name high over all,
    In hell, or earth, or sky;
Angels and men before it fall,
    And devils fear and fly.

2 Jesus, the Name to sinners dear,
    The Name to sinners given;
It scatters all their guilty fear,
    It turns their hell to heaven.

3 Jesus the prisoner's fetters breaks,
    And bruises Satan's head;
Power into strengthless souls He
    speaks,
    And life into the dead.

4 Oh, that the world might taste and see
    The riches of His grace!
The arms of love that compass me
    Would all mankind embrace.

5 His only righteousness I show,
    His saving truth proclaim:
'Tis all my business here below
    To cry, "Behold the Lamb!"

6 Happy, if with my latest breath
    I may but gasp His Name:
Preach Him to all, and cry in death,
    "Behold, behold the Lamb!"

This hymn may be sung to tune 'Richmond (706).

General

718

1 O MASTER, let me walk with Thee
In lowly paths of service free;
Tell me Thy secret; help me bear
The strain of toil, the fret of care.

2 Help me the slow of heart to move
By some clear, winning word of love;
Teach me the wayward feet to stay,
And guide them in the homeward way.

3 Teach me Thy patience; still with Thee
In closer, dearer company,
In work that keeps faith sweet and
    strong,
In trust that triumphs over wrong.

4 In hope that sends a shining ray
Far down the future's broadening way;
In peace that only Thou canst give,
With Thee, O Master, let me live.

719

1 MASTER, speak! Thy servant heareth,
    Longing for Thy gracious word,
Longing for Thy voice that cheereth:
    Master, let it now be heard.
I am listening, Lord. for Thee;
What hast Thou to say to me?

2 Often through my heart is pealing
    Many another voice than Thine,
Many an unwilled echo stealing
    From the walls of this Thy shrine.
Let Thy longed-for accents fall;
Master, speak! and silence all.

3 Master, speak! though least and lowest,
    Let me not unheard depart;
Master, speak! for oh, Thou knowest
    All the yearning of my heart,
Knowest all its truest need;
Speak! and make me blest indeed.

4 Master, speak! and make me ready,
    When Thy voice is truly heard,
With obedience glad and steady,
    Still to follow every word.
I am listening, Lord, for Thee:
Master, speak, oh, speak to me!

5 Speak to me by name, O Master,
    Let me know it is to me;
Speak, that I may follow faster,
    With a step more firm and free,
Where the Shepherd leads the flock
In the shadow of the Rock!

General

720

1 COME, let us sing of a wonderful love,
    Tender and true;
Out of the heart of the Father above,
    Streaming to me and to you;
        Wonderful love
Dwells in the heart of the Father
    above.

2 Jesus, the Saviour, this gospel to tell,
    Joyfully came;
Came with the helpless and hopeless to
    dwell,
    Sharing their sorrow and shame;
        Seeking the lost,
Saving, redeeming at measureless cost.

3 Jesus is seeking the wanderers yet;
    Why do they roam?
Love only waits to forgive and forget;
    Home! weary wanderer, home!
        Wonderful love
Dwells in the heart of the Father
    above.

4 Come to my heart, O Thou wonderful
    love,
    Come and abide,
Lifting my life till it rises above
    Envy and falsehood and pride;
        Seeking to be
Lowly and humble, a learner of Thee.

721

1 MY Saviour, Thou hast offered rest:
    Oh, give it, then, to me;
The rest of ceasing from myself,
    To find my all in Thee.

2 This cruel self, oh, how it strives
    And works within my breast
To come between Thee and my soul,
    And keep me back from rest.

3 How many subtle forms it takes
    Of seeming verity,
As if it were not safe to rest
    And venture all on Thee.

4 O Lord, I seek a holy rest,
    A victory over sin;
I seek that Thou alone should'st reign
    O'er all without, within.

5 In Thy strong hand I lay me down,
    So shall the work be done:
For who can work so wondrously
    As the Almighty One?

6 Work on, then, Lord, till on my soul
    Eternal light shall break,
And, in Thy likeness perfected,
    I "satisfied" shall wake.

722

1 MAKE me a captive, Lord,
    And then I shall be free;
Force me to render up my sword,
    And I shall conq'ror be.
I sink in life's alarms
    When by myself I stand;
Imprison me within Thine arms,
    And strong shall be my hand.

2 My heart is weak and poor
    Until it master find:
It has no spring of action sure,
    It varies with the wind:
It cannot freely move
    Till Thou hast wrought its chain,
Enslave it with Thy matchless love
    And deathless it shall reign.

3 My power is faint and low
    Till I have learned to serve:
It wants the needed fire to glow,
    It wants the breeze to nerve;
It cannot drive the world
    Until itself be driven;
Its flag can only be unfurled
    When Thou shalt breathe from
        Heaven.

4 My will is not my own
    Till Thou hast made it Thine;
If it would reach the monarch's throne
    It must its crown resign:
It only stands unbent
    Amid the clashing strife
When on Thy bosom it has leant,
    And found in Thee its life.

This hymn may be sung to tune 'Leominster'
(534).

237

723

1 THINE arm, O Lord, in days of old,
    Was strong to heal and save;
It triumphed o'er disease and death,
    O'er darkness and the grave.
To Thee they went—the blind, the dumb,
    The palsied and the lame,
The leper with his tainted life,
    The sick with fevered frame.

2 And, lo! Thy touch brought life and health,
    Gave speech, and strength, and sight;
And youth renewed and frenzy calmed
    Owned Thee, the Lord of light:
And now, O Lord, be near to bless,
    Almighty as of yore,
In crowded street, by restless couch,
    As by Gennesaret's shore.

3 Be Thou our great Deliverer still,
    Thou Lord of life and death;
Restore and quicken, soothe and bless,
    With Thine almighty breath;
To hands that work and eyes that see
    Give wisdom's heavenly lore,
That whole and sick, and weak and strong,
    May praise Thee evermore.

724

1 I AM waiting for the dawning
    Of the bright and blessèd day,
When the darksome night of sorrow
    Shall have vanished far away:
When, for ever with the Saviour,
    Far beyond this vale of tears,
I shall swell the song of worship
    Through the everlasting years.

2 I am looking at the brightness—
    See, it shineth from afar—
Of the clear and joyous beaming
    Of the bright and morning Star.
Through the dark grey mist of morning
    Do I see its glorious light;
Then away with every shadow
    Of this sad and weary night.

3 I am waiting for the coming
    Of the Lord Who died for me;
Oh, His words have thrilled my spirit,
    "I will come again for thee."
I can almost hear His footfall
    On the threshold of the door,
And my heart, my heart is longing
    To be with Him evermore.

725

1 LORD, in the fulness of my might
    I would for Thee be strong;
While runneth o'er each dear delight
    To Thee should soar my song.

2 I would not give the world my heart,
    And then profess Thy love;
I would not feel my strength depart
    And then Thy service prove.

3 I would not with swift-winged zeal
    On the world's errands go,
And labour up the heavenly hill
    With weary feet and slow.

4 Oh, not for Thee my weak desires,
    My poorer, baser part!
Oh, not for Thee my fading fires,
    The ashes of my heart!

5 Oh, choose me in my golden time,
    In my dear joys have part;
For Thee the glory of my prime,
    The fulness of my heart!

6 I cannot, Lord, too early take
    The covenant divine:
Oh, ne'er the happy heart may break
    Whose earliest love was Thine.

726

1 CHRIST, Whose glory fills the skies,
    Christ, the true, the only Light,
Sun of Righteousness, arise,
    Triumph o'er the shades of night;
Dayspring from on high, be near;
Day-star, in my heart appear.

2 Dark and cheerless is the morn
    Unaccompanied by Thee;
Joyless is the day's return,
    Till Thy mercy's beams I see,
Till Thou inward light impart,
Glad my eyes, and warm my heart.

3 Visit, then, this soul of mine,
    Pierce the gloom of sin and grief;
Fill me, Radiancy divine,
    Scatter all my unbelief;
More and more Thyself display,
Shining to the perfect day.
This hymn may be sung to tune 'Heathlands'
(465).

727

1 O LITTLE town of Bethlehem,
    How still we see thee lie!
Above thy deep and dreamless sleep
    The silent stars go by.
Yet in thy dark streets shineth
    The everlasting light;
The hopes and fears of all the years
    Are met in thee tonight.

2 O morning stars, together
    Proclaim the holy birth,
And praises sing to God the King,
    And peace to men on earth;
For Christ is born of Mary,
    And, gathered all above,
While mortals sleep, the angels keep
    Their watch of wondering love.

3 How silently, how silently,
    The wondrous gift is given!
So God imparts to human hearts
    The blessings of His Heaven.
No ear may hear His coming;
    But in this world of sin,
Where meek souls will receive Him,
    still
    The dear Christ enters in.

4 O holy Child of Bethlehem,
    Descend to us, we pray;
Cast out our sin, and enter in,
    Be born in us today.
We hear the Christmas angels
    The great glad tidings tell:
Oh, come to us, abide with us,
    Our Lord Emmanuel.

728

1 PRAISE Him, praise Him, all ye little
    children,
    He is love, He is love;
Praise Him, praise Him, all ye little
    children,
    He is love, He is love.

2 Thank Him, thank Him, all ye little
    children,
    He is love, He is love;
Thank Him, thank Him, all ye little
    children,
    He is love, He is love.

3 Love Him, love Him, all ye little
    children,
    He is love, He is love;
Love Him, love Him, all ye little
    children,
    He is love, He is love.

4 Crown Him, crown Him, all ye little
    children,
    He is love, He is love;
Crown Him, crown Him, all ye little
    children,
    He is love, He is love.

729

1 OVER the sea there are little brown
    children,
    Fathers and mothers and babies
    dear;
They have not heard of the Father in
    Heaven,
    No one has told them that God is
    near.
    Swift let the message go over the
    water,
    Telling the children God is near.

2 Sometimes at night when the darkness
    gathers,
    Little brown children begin to fear;
They have not heard of the dear Lord
    Jesus,
    No one has told them that He is near.
    Swift let the message go over the
    water, etc.

3 Little brown children, the teachers are
     coming,
   Speeding to love you, and help, and
     cheer;
 Soon you shall hear of the dear Lord
     Jesus,
     Soon they will tell you that God is
       near.
     Swift let the message go over the
       water, etc.

This hymn may be sung to tune 575 with slight
modifications.

730

WE bring to Thee our off'rings;
   Receive them, Lord, we pray,
 To bless Thy little children,
   In countries far away.
 Lord, grant that soon Thy light may
   shine
 Wide over all this world of Thine.

This verse may be sung to tunes 600 and 626.

731

1 DEAR Jesus, ever at my side,
     How loving Thou must be
  To leave Thy home in Heaven, to guide
     A little child like me.

2 Thy beautiful, Thy shining face,
     I see not, though so near,
  The sweetness of Thy soft, low voice
     I am too deaf to hear.

3 I cannot feel Thee touch my hand
     With pressure light and mild,
  To check me, as my mother does
     Her erring little child.

4 But I have felt Thee in my thoughts
     Fighting with sin for me;
  And when my heart loves God, I
     know
  The sweetness comes from Thee.

5 And when, dear Saviour, I kneel down,
     Morning and night, to prayer,
  Something there is within my heart
     That tells me Thou art there.

6 Yes, when I pray Thou prayest, too,
     Thy prayer is all for me;
  But when I sleep Thou sleepest
     not
     But watchest patiently.

(The first verse may be repeated at the end.)

Communion

See also No. 407

732

1 By Christ redeemed, in Christ restored,
   We keep the memory adored,
   And show the death of our dear Lord
     Until He come.

2 His body broken in our stead
   Is seen in this memorial bread,
   And so our feeble love is fed
     Until He come.

3 The drops of His dread agony,
   His life-blood shed for us, we see;
   The wine shall tell the mystery
     Until He come.

4 And thus that dark betrayal-night
   With the last advent we unite,
   By one blest chain of loving rite,
     Until He come.

5 Until the trump of God be heard,
   Until the ancient graves be stirred,
   And with the great commanding word
     The Lord shall come.

6 Oh, blessed hope! with this elate,
   Let not our hearts be desolate,
   But, strong in faith, in patience wait
     Until He come.

733

1 ACCORDING to Thy gracious word,
  In meek humility,
This will I do, my dying Lord,
  I will remember Thee.

2 Thy body, broken for my sake,
  My bread from heaven shall be;
Thy cup of blessing I will take
  And thus remember Thee.

3 Can I Gethsemane forget?
  Or there Thy conflict see,
Thine agony and bloody sweat
  And not remember Thee?

4 When to the cross I turn mine eyes,
  And rest on Calvary,
O Lamb of God, my sacrifice,
  I must remember Thee.

5 Remember Thee, and all Thy pains,
  And all Thy love to me;
Yea, while a breath, a pulse remains,
  Will I remember Thee.

6 And when these failing lips grow
    dumb,
  And mind and memory flee,
When Thou shalt in Thy kingdom
    come,
  Jesus, remember me.

734

1 I HUNGER and I thirst;
  Jesus, my manna be;
Ye living waters, burst
  Out of the rock for me.

2 Thou bruised and broken Bread,
  My lifelong wants supply;
As living souls are fed,
  Oh, feed me, or I die.

3 Thou true life-giving Vine,
  Let me Thy sweetness prove;
Renew my life with Thine,
  Refresh my soul with love.

4 For still the desert lies
  My thirsting soul before;
O living waters, rise
  Within me evermore.

735

1 SWEET feast of love divine!
  'Tis grace that makes us free
To feed upon this bread and wine
  In memory, Lord, of Thee.

2 Here every welcome guest
  Waits, Lord, from Thee to learn
The secrets of Thy Father's breast,
  And all Thy grace discern.

3 Here conscience ends its strife,
  And faith delights to prove
The sweetness of the Bread of life,
  The fulness of Thy love.

4 Thy blood that flowed for sin
  In symbol here we see,
And feel the blessèd pledge within,
  That we are loved of Thee.

5 But if this glimpse of love
  Is so divinely sweet,
What will it be, O Lord, above,
  Thy gladdening smile to meet—

6 To see Thee face to face,
  Thy perfect likeness wear,
And all Thy ways of wondrous grace
  Through endless years declare!

736

1 AMIDST us our Beloved stands,
And bids us view His pierced hands,
Points to His wounded feet and side—
Blest emblems of the Crucified.

2 What food luxurious loads the board,
When at His table sits the Lord!
The wine how rich, the bread how
    sweet,
When Jesus deigns the guests to meet!

3 If now, with eyes defiled and dim,
  We see the signs, but see not Him,
  Oh, may His love the scales displace,
  And bid us see Him face to face!

4 Thou glorious Bridegroom of our hearts,
  Thy present smile a heaven imparts.
  Oh, lift the veil, if veil there be,
  Let every saint Thy beauties see!

737

1 OH, come, Thou stricken Lamb of God!
  Who shedd'st for us Thine own life-
    blood,
  And teach us all Thy love; then pain
  Were light, and life or death were gain.

2 Take Thou our hearts, and let them be
  For ever closed to all but Thee;
  Thy willing servants, may we wear
  The seal of love for ever there.

3 How blest are they who still abide
  Close sheltered by Thy watchful side;
  Who life and strength from Thee
    receive,
  And with Thee move, and in Thee
    live!

4 O Lord, enlarge our scanty thought
  To know the wonders Thou hast
    wrought;
  Unloose our stammering tongues to tell
  Thy love, immense, unsearchable.

5 First-born of many brethren Thou,
  To Whom both Heaven and earth
    must bow—
  Heirs of Thy shame, and of Thy throne
  We bear the cross, and seek the crown.

738

1 SIT down beneath His shadow,
  And rest with great delight;
  The faith that now beholds Him
  Is pledge of future sight.

2 Our Master's love remember,
  Exceeding great and free;
  Lift up thy heart in gladness,
  For He remembers thee.

3 Bring every weary burden,
  Thy sin, thy fear, thy grief;
  He calls the heavy laden,
  And gives them kind relief.

4 A little while, though parted,
  Remember, wait, and love;
  Until He comes in glory,
  Until we meet above;

5 Till in the Father's Kingdom
  The heavenly feast is spread;
  And we behold His beauty,
  Whose blood for us was shed.

Index of First Lines

243

Index of First Lines

Index of First Lines

NOTE.—To facilitate reference, Hymns commencing " Oh " are placed under vocative "O".

Index of First Lines

248

Index of First Lines

Index of First Lines